REPRODUCING
RACE

REPRODUCING RACE

The Paradox of Generation Mix

Rainier Spencer

LYNNE
RIENNER
PUBLISHERS

BOULDER
LONDON

Published in the United States of America in 2011 by
Lynne Rienner Publishers, Inc.
1800 30th Street, Boulder, Colorado 80301
www.rienner.com

and in the United Kingdom by
Lynne Rienner Publishers, Inc.
3 Henrietta Street, Covent Garden, London WC2E 8LU

Library of Congress Cataloging-in-Publication Data
Spencer, Rainier.
Reproducing race : the paradox of generation mix / Rainier Spencer.
      p. cm.
  Includes bibliographical references and index.
  ISBN 978-1-58826-751-1 (hardcover : alk. paper)
  ISBN 978-1-58826-776-4 (pbk. : alk. paper)
  1. Racially mixed people—Race identity—United States.
2. Post-racialism—United States. 3. United States—Race relations.
4. Racism—United States. 5. Marginality, Social—United States. I. Title.
  E184.A1S725 2011
  305.800973—dc22

                        2010026517

British Cataloguing in Publication Data
A Cataloguing in Publication record for this book
is available from the British Library.

Printed and bound in the United States of America

∞   The paper used in this publication meets the requirements
    of the American National Standard for Permanence of
    Paper for Printed Library Materials Z39.48-1992.

5 4 3 2 1

To Nicole and GiGi
Daughter, Granddaughter
Joys of Life

Contents

Part 3 The Mulatto Future

Acknowledgments

In celebrating publication of this book, I would like to first of all acknowledge two women who have had profoundly positive effects on my life. The first is my wife, Jackie, whose companionship, warmth, and forbearance I surely do not deserve. The second is my former adviser but eternal mentor, Patricia Penn Hilden, who quite literally made me possible as a scholar. If I were to write a thousand books, each one would contain an acknowledgment of her impact upon my scholarly life.

In regard to this book in particular, I want to thank three people who, while they may not have realized it, were tremendous sources of support and comfort during the eighteen or so months I was writing it. My colleagues Alan Simmons and Liam Frink were always available to listen with great tolerance to my progress updates. Also in this group is my dean, Chris Hudgins, not for granting sabbaticals or other time off, which I neither requested nor used, but for simply listening charitably to my occasional progress reports, often given as a means of keeping myself going. Several colleagues, Bill Jankowiak, Jiemin Bao, and again Alan Simmons, responded to a request for comment on a particular question, and I thank them for the feedback they provided so generously.

Moving outside my own institution, very special thanks are due to Heather Dalmage and Kerry Ann Rockquemore. A number of scholars whom I did not know previously were gracious enough to respond to my out-of-the-blue e-mails asking questions about their work, otherwise soliciting comment, or simply complimenting them on something of theirs I had read. I count among these Jenifer Bratter, Michele Elam, Nancy Leong, Minkah Makalani, Rachel Moran, Eve Raimon, Tommie Shelby, Catherine Squires, and Michael Thornton. I am so very pleased to have renewed my relationship with Lynne Rienner Publishers, and I thank Lynne for her vision and for her confidence in my work. An unexpected pleasure was once again working with Lesli Athanasoulis, whose capable editorial hands inspire the greatest trust. My gratitude is due as well to Lynne Rienner staff members Claire Vlcek, Karen Maye, and especially to Debra Topping for her outstanding cover design. I give heartfelt thanks also for the very fine copyediting efforts of Rosemary Carstens, and to Heather Jones for her excellent indexing work. Finally, while his name does not appear in the text or the bibliography, I want to acknowledge the deep debt I owe to Steven Riley, who maintains the mixed-race scholarly website, "Mixed Race Studies: Scholarly Perspectives on the Mixed Race Experience" (http://www.mixedracestudies.org/wordpress/), which is the most comprehensive and objective clearinghouse for scholarly publications related to critical mixed-race theory of which I am aware. It is through this very robust resource that I came across a goodly number of the scholarly references I cite in this book.

I saw myself, the stain of the black blood swelling through my veins—yes, I actually saw some such picture in my head, a flood darkening through all the arteries and veins of my body—no, a stain spreading in a glass of clear water.

—Robert Penn Warren,
Band of Angels

She is not one who can't be white and won't be black.

—Frances E. W. Harper,
Iola Leroy, or Shadows Uplifted

Introduction

This is a book about mulattoes—past, present, and future, as well as known, unknown, and denied.[1] The mulatto is the subject of my discussion, the basis of my argument, the voice I aim to empower. I am intending in this book to quite self-consciously and quite freely use the term *mulatto*, to bring it out of the state of historical suspended animation it has been in. Some will no doubt view this as something of a retrograde maneuver, but I would counter that it is instead a progressive move. I mean to speak the unspeakable in this book; not that mulatto is in fact an offensive word in any sense, but its current acceptable usage is limited very tightly to the past tense. For a variety of reasons, one does not speak of mulattoes today. To call a living person a mulatto would certainly be considered an insult. Indeed, to refer even to a nonliving person as a mulatto might be considered insulting depending on the time period in which the person lived. For instance, making reference as a mulatto to someone who died in the late twentieth century would be much more likely to be considered insulting than the same reference made to a person who died in the late nineteenth or early twentieth century. The reasons for this are related to the same kinds of euphemistic games that have taken place with other descriptive terms. For example, Negroes became colored people, who became Afro-American, who became black or African American. But unlike this example, *mulatto* was never replaced by a supposedly more progressive term; it simply faded from use.

Another kind of fading is taking place today, and it is one of the primary reasons I chose to write this book. I am referring to the purposeful fading of the mulatto—not just as a referent but as a concept altogether—from the American consciousness for the purpose of substituting what is seemingly another thing—but as I shall demonstrate, is in fact not at all another thing—in its place. This other thing that is not an other thing goes by a variety of names: "Generation Mix," "Generation M," "Generation M(ultiracial)," "Generation E. A.," "Remix Generation," and certainly several other just as authentically hip names that I have not as yet come across.[2] Rather than inject yet more "hipness" into this already crowded field, I shall utilize the existing term *Generation Mix*, by which I will mean people (typically, but not necessarily, young people) who consider themselves to be the immediately mixed or first-generation offspring of parents who are members of different biological racial groups.[3] Generation Mix will generally be included when I discuss the membership, although not the leadership, of the American Multiracial Identity Movement, the amorphous entity that advocates on a variety of levels for acceptance of multiracial identity as a new variety of biological race. In this book, I will also make reference to the black/white members of Generation Mix as a subset of that group and of the American Multiracial Identity Movement.

Popular wisdom suggests that we are in the midst of a transformation in the way race is constructed in the United States. According to this view, individuals of mixed race, particularly first-generation multiracial people, are confounding the US racial order with their ambiguous phenotypes and purported ability to serve as living bridges between races. From his generally well-received March 18, 2008, speech on race, in which he positioned himself as having a direct and personal understanding of both black and white anger, and to his reference to himself as a "mutt," President Barack Obama and his historic election have bolstered this view significantly.[4] Indeed, many Americans hail Obama's mixed-race background as portending quite literally our postracial future. It is a seductive promise. Will, as we are assured, the (multi)racial ambiguity of Generation Mix represent the vanguard of a new US racial order? Will it undermine centuries of racial hierarchy and veneration of whiteness? These are important questions that demand far more serious attention and discussion than they are typically allotted. They are questions that demand much deeper analysis than our glossy newsmagazine society is motivated to provide.

All too often we are told that the (multi)racial ambiguity of Generation Mix will shatter the old racial order in the United States. We are told that this ambiguity will destabilize the current racial hierarchy, and, indeed, will eventually topple it as race itself becomes impossible to determine. And, apparently, we owe all of this to the legions of mixed-race teenagers who are proclaiming their racial newness while celebrating what they declare is their absolute difference from the members of existing racial groups. This is a claim, however, that hardly ever receives even the minimal sort of analysis one might expect for so important a topic. To put it colloquially, so pronounced and so affected is the celebration of Generation Mix that it is difficult for dissenters from this viewpoint to get a word in edgewise. As Catherine Squires points out, scholars whose analyses present challenges to this claim are "not the ones normally consulted by the mainstream press."[5]

From academic supporters of multiraciality who assume too readily roles as scholarly cheerleaders as opposed to serving as the intellectual referees they should be, to popular media writers who are more interested in the production of hip storylines than in responsible journalism, we are witnessing nothing less than a self-inflicted and self-authorized societal hoodwinking of the first order.

That may seem a rather harsh indictment, undercutting the progressive role that has been assigned to multiracialism of late. But it would be every bit as unwise to underestimate the degree to which we Americans allow ourselves to be influenced by the manipulations of the popular media as it would be to underestimate the ferocious tenacity of those who are invested heavily in maintaining the current racial order—most especially the status of whiteness—even if it means making concessions in the form of minor adjustments to the US racial template that appear to privilege this newfound multiracial ambiguity. The vital point that seems always to be missed in the ubiquitous celebration of Generation Mix is that racial ambiguity, in and of itself, is no guarantee of political progressiveness, racial destabilization, or, indeed, of anything in particular.

Thankfully, though, not all scholars are allowing themselves to be swept up in the unreflective emotionalism of the ambiguity avalanche. A small group of critical multiracial identity theorists (among whom I include myself)—a group distinct from the more fashionable academic multiracial identity advocates—is attempting to bring the requisite scholarly rigor to what has otherwise been a generally mindless celebration of biological race and biological racial ambiguity. As Squires informs us, "this 'ambiguity,' however, is not part of the 'fluidity' of race lauded by scholars of passing, for example. This ambiguity is about exoticism and intrigue, providing opportunities for consumers to fantasize and speculate about the Other with no expectations of critical consideration of power and racial categories."[6] Squires makes an important point, for it is crucial to be able to separate racial ambiguity that is utilized to work consciously against racial hierarchies in the United States from racial ambiguity that is simply a form of self-interested celebration and faddishness that ends up reinforcing those very hierarchies. Pointing out this essential difference is a goal that shall remain in the forefront throughout this book as I reflect upon and interrogate racial ambiguity, multiracial identity, and mulattoes from a variety of perspectives that attend to the future of the US racial order.

When we consider mulattoes, we must of course consider hypodescent, the longstanding mechanism by which mulattoes are said to be produced. Although hypodescent developed in various ways throughout the Americas as a result of European colonization and slavery, it achieved its most extreme formulation in British North America, where (aside from notable exceptions in locales such as New Orleans, LA, and Charleston, SC) the particular evolution of slavery relegated all degrees of black-white mixture to the black category. We must recognize as well that biological race, hypodescent, mulattoes, monoracial people, and multiracial people today are all figments of the American imaginary, as they have been for centuries. As I have argued elsewhere and will reiterate and expand upon in this book, the multiracial idea is the key to dissolving the hold that biological race maintains on us, but not in the way propounded by the American Multiracial Identity Movement.[7] As I shall describe in Part 3, in an effort in which the multiracial idea will be fundamental, rather than the addition of another nonwhite group to the US racial order, what is needed to accomplish this task is what I term *racial suicide*.

The connecting factor in all of this is hypodescent and the mulattoes it is believed to produce. Though hypodescent applies de facto only to blacks, it is the basis for the entire structuring of the US racial paradigm. This is so because the category at the top of the racial hierarchy, *white*, has no way to constitute itself absent its relation to blackness, a phenomenon that has been well established by the related fields we now call critical race theory and whiteness studies, and exemplified by the work of scholars such as Cheryl Harris and David Roediger. For example, Abby Ferber makes the point in her argument that whiteness requires an *other*, specifically blackness, in order to establish itself as an identity.[8] One might reasonably inquire whether something other than blackness could serve the function of the constitutive other, but I do not, at this point, believe so. Certainly, there are deep historical reasons why blackness serves this purpose, and I do not think that the Hispanic, Asian, or Native American categories possess the historical and still current level of revulsion that continues to mark blackness.

For several centuries, the primary racial dynamic in the United States has been the black/white one, with Native Americans being too few in number and also too somatically close to whiteness to stand as the kind of *other* that Afro-Americans were and still are. This is reflected easily in the unsuccessful late nineteenth-century attempt to assimilate Native Americans fully into US (white) society, a horrifyingly destructive mission that included removing children forcibly from their parents and sending them to boarding schools where their language and religion were punished out of them.[9] Certainly, no such effort has ever been mounted to "assimilate the blacks!" And until the relatively recent wave of Asian and Hispanic immigration over the past forty or so years, those two categories were not only too limited geographically but also too small in number to represent the kind of *othering* fear that blackness did and still does. Moreover, despite a current rise in anti-immigrant feeling that is largely anti-Hispanic, there is also a countermovement, what Eduardo Bonilla-Silva calls "the Latin-Americanization of whiteness in the United States."[10] As in the case of some Asians, many Hispanics are taking advantage of multiracialism to transition to a state of *hon-*

orary whiteness, a phenomenon whose corollary is that, once again, Afro-Americans are seen as the group to avoid.

As we know, Hispanic ancestry is assimilable to whiteness based on the fact that the paradigm recognizes both white and nonwhite Hispanic categories. We also know that Native American ancestry has long been assimilable to whiteness, from the much more open rules and laws governing Native American/white marriage throughout the nation's history to the aforementioned program to assimilate Native Americans. Finally, it is becoming clear that Asian ancestry can be assimilable to whiteness as well. From the desirability of Asian women to white males, and the resulting children, to the significant differences in wealth, education, and status that many Asian Americans (though certainly far from all) enjoy, it has become clear that over the course of several generations, a person of Asian/white descent can indeed become white in a way that a person of black/white descent in the identical generational status cannot, as long as the latter person's sub-Saharan African ancestry is known.[11]

A key failure of opponents of the US racial paradigm has been an inability to articulate correctly the most critical aspect of the paradigm's nature. We like to think that we understand the paradigm, that in fact it is really a very simple idea consisting of four or five races with whites at the top of the hierarchy, followed in order by Asians, Hispanics (if conceived of racially), Native Americans, and then blacks.[12] It is true that this conception of the paradigm is certainly accurate, but it does not go far enough. Without further analysis, the key element of its being—its essentiality, one might say—is left unrevealed and, as a consequence, unproblematized. That essentiality is whiteness. This is why, despite all the various arguments they might deploy in attempting to de-emphasize the black/white binary, approaches such as Ronald Sundstrom's labored but inert critique invariably miss the mark, for they tend to disregard or even ignore the power of whiteness and white supremacy.[13] What Sundstrom and others fail to account for is that without the blackness that is produced and reproduced by whiteness, there is no white supremacy.

The fact is that whiteness, while it has been forced by recent population trends to expand its boundaries by accepting specific and limited amounts of Asian, Hispanic, or Native American ancestry, cannot admit the public entry of blackness and still remain white. In the simplest sense, the entire paradigm reduces to the centuries-old dichotomy of black and white. This is surely not to say that members of the other groups live trouble-free lives untouched by racism, but rather that there simply is no US racial paradigm without blackness serving as the antipode of whiteness. Everything else flows from this primary, primordial relationship. Long before it became possible to even offer an academic description of the US racial paradigm there was the de facto reality that the offspring of a black/white heterosexual encounter could be black or mixed-race, but not white. Lost in the media and academic frenzy over Generation Mix is the crucial reality that the ideology of the American Multiracial Identity Movement does absolutely nothing to challenge or subvert this age-old racial equation and, as we shall see in the pages that follow, actually does much to rejuvenate and endorse it. Unless something arrives to deconstruct in a radical way the status of whiteness at the top of the hierarchy, there is no hope for any real change to the racial order.

What must be understood and not allowed to become lost amidst the contemporary celebration of supposed racial ambiguity is that none of the claims to progressiveness made by Generation Mix have even the slightest impact upon the maintenance and administration of the US racial order because they have no impact upon the status of whiteness. As Heather Dalmage reminds us, "the myth of white racial purity, based on a biological notion of race, is indeed the foundation upon which the U.S. racist system was constructed. Yet a multiracial category will not challenge purity as the basis for whiteness. . . . Naming another category does not detract from white privilege; it may simply help individual whites fine-tune identities grounded in notions of superiority."[14] We may shuffle the intermediate categories, we may add nonwhite categories, and we may even see whiteness expand a bit to include some previously excluded people, but as long as black remains both at the bottom of the hierarchy and unassimilable to whiteness (while whiteness is easily assimilable to blackness), and as long as it remains impossible for a black woman to be seen as giving naturally conceived birth to a white child (while the reverse case continues its unproblematic acceptance), nothing has changed.[15] Acknowledging this lack of change, Steve Garner points out that "the guys in the middle might be playing musical chairs, but it is not in any substantial way that the category 'White' seems to be diminishing through the mixed category."[16]

The evil that is biological race in the US context begins and ends with the hard fact of hypodescent and the resulting exclusion of blackness from any participation in whiteness. Hypodescent allows for whiteness to participate in blackness, but not for blackness to participate in whiteness owing to the fact that whiteness cannot remain white when mixed with blackness. This, again, simply is the US racial paradigm in its most basic form. The solution does not lie in altering the paradigm so that it is somehow more equal or so that it includes more groups; the solution lies in rejecting both the paradigm and the hypodescent that forms its primary building block. Both the US racial paradigm and hypodescent are corruptions that should not be accommodated by any thinking person or by any coherent ideology, for they are primary vehicles of continued antiblackness and white supremacy in this country.

Recognizing this, if it were demonstrated that multiracial ideology depends in any way upon the very same hypodescent that undergirds the US racial paradigm, or indeed if it supports that paradigm in any way, such a revelation would represent a serious and very damaging problem for the American Multiracial Identity Movement, at least in terms of any question of its philosophical or intellectual validity, as well as any claims attributing to it the promise of a racially transcendent disruption of the paradigm. That the multiracial movement and its ideology are indeed entangled thoroughly with hypodescent will be a central and driving claim of this book. I will be making this point in a variety of ways throughout the book, arguing that those who proclaim that multiracial identity will destroy race are in fact living a lie. Some people who are nonwhite, including the black/white members of Generation Mix, may well be able to distance themselves from blackness, but such movement has no ultimate effect on the US racial order; it merely adds an additional category. For how can multiracial identity deconstruct race when it requires the system of racial categorization to even announce itself?

In relation to this, it is one of the primary contentions of this book that there is an important but suppressed relationship between American mulattoes and Generation Mix, a relationship that I shall endeavor to elaborate in the following chapters. That relationship revolves around the concept of biological racial mixture and whether that mixture is used to support or challenge the idea of biological race. My contention is that there is nothing particularly new or avant-garde about Generation Mix and, moreover, that its black/white members cannot with any consistency or philosophical validity distinguish themselves from the American mulattoes they claim to be both newer than and different from. The problem, though, goes beyond the mundane and perhaps neutral fact that Generation Mix is simply wrong about this. I argue that such claims of newness and difference, far from transcending race, serve instead to support contemporary antiblackness and white supremacy. This realization, therefore, moves these claims from the mere contemplation of accuracy and inaccuracy to the realm of moral consideration.

I have purposely, and I hope wisely, chosen a tripartite structure of past, present, and future for this book because, in addition to a certain aesthetic value, such a structure serves to highlight in an especially strong way the connections I am going to make in regard to mulattoes and the black/white members of Generation Mix today. Part 1, "The Mulatto Past," seeks to provide a brief and limited history of white American thought regarding mulattoes. Chapters 2 and 3 concern the representation of mulattoes from the late nineteenth through the early twentieth centuries by white men who were invested in and operating from commonsense and "obvious" (to them) notions of white superiority and Negro (and therefore mulatto) inferiority. Various long-lasting and deprecatory mulatto myths resulted from these representations. In Chapter 2, "The Mixed-Race Background," we shall see that from the late nineteenth century to the beginning of the early twentieth century, these myths were mainly physical or biological in nature. Chapter 3, "Of Tragic Mulattoes and Marginal Men," concerns the more emotional and psychological myth of the marginal man that began to arise at the dawn of the twentieth century, and that will figure so prominently throughout the remainder of the book. The myth of the marginal man developed out of the tragic mulatto characterization represented in the plantation literature of white, often abolitionist, writers but that was given important scholarly substance in the early twentieth century by the emergent discipline of sociology. The notion of the marginal man—the inherently conflicted mulatto who rejects blackness and desires desperately to be white—while a fantasy stirred by the racist projection of white men's own inner insecurities, nonetheless gained an authoritative currency in academic literature.

The racist myth of the marginal man was powerful, but as I will show via a review of contemporaneous literature by American mulatto writers in Chapter 4, "Mulatto Writers on Marginality," it was rejected soundly by the very people it was intended to represent in so objectifying a way. Through an examination of their novels concerning racial passing, these formidable American writers—Charles Chesnutt, James Weldon Johnson, Walter White, Nella Larsen, and Jessie Fauset—relate to us their views concerning the motivations, attitudes, and racial identity choices of American mulattoes. What they have to tell us about supposed mulatto marginality flies in the face of white male sociologists' psychological projection onto mulatto bodies of an insatiable desire for whiteness. Following an analysis of these mulatto writers' works as regards the question of marginality, I undertake in Chapter 5, "Imitations of Life," an extensive review of the *Imitation of Life* trilogy, the 1933 novel, and 1934 and 1959 films of that name, a review that seeks to illustrate the staying power through the years of the marginal man idea in the US popular consciousness, despite its utter falseness.

Chapter 6, "Rejecting a Shared Past," addresses the question of just who is a mulatto today; the way the answer to that question impacts the relationship between Afro-Americans, mulattoes, and the black/white members of Generation Mix. This will lay the foundation for ensuing discussions in Parts 2 and 3 regarding the purported specialness of Generation Mix and the likelihood that recognition of multiracial identity will lead to the dismantling of race in the United States. In all, the aim of Part 1 is first and foremost to demonstrate that the black/white members of today's Generation Mix are mulattoes, and that the narcissistic celebration of Generation Mix as new and different is an affront and an insult to the untold generations of American mulattoes who have come before.

In Part 2, "The Mulatto Present," I endeavor to refute the increasingly popular notion that Generation Mix represents a progressive step toward deconstructing the US racial order. Acknowledging the important work of Jared Sexton, in Chapter 7, "Postraciality, Multiraciality, and Antiblackness," I situate Generation Mix and the American Multiracial Identity Movement firmly in the orbit of contemporary antiblackness and white supremacy.[17] Refuting the notion of Generation Mix as a racially transcendent phenomenon, in Chapters 8 and 9 I examine in a critical way several never-questioned claims about multiracial identity that are presented typically as authoritative reasons for supporting multiracial ideology. Chapter 8, "Resurrecting Old Myths of Mulatto Marginality," draws a critical link between the psycho-emotional myths of Chapter 3 and today's claims of Generation Mix superiority, demonstrating that modern-day assertions of multiracial superiority represent a resurrection and a dubious recasting of long-discredited myths of mulatto marginality. I devote Chapter 9, "The False Promise of Racial Bridging," to an extended deconstruction of the claim that black/white multiracials partake of white culture, and are thereby more cosmopolitan racially than "regular" Afro-Americans, thus making them better able—indeed situating them uniquely—to serve as bridges for racial reconciliation. Rather than performing as racial bridges, I argue instead that Generation Mix provides cover for activist white mothers of black/white children to continue distancing their children from blackness.[18]

In Chapter 10, "Assessing the New Millennium Marginal Man," I question notions of identity that serve as bases for multiracial ideology and demonstrate that many of the claims made by multiracial activists and by scholars who support multiracial identity are—when held up to intellectual scrutiny—simply insupportable. Most importantly, I demonstrate that today's Generation Mix, especially its black/white component, has resurrected the dead myth of the marginal man with its racist, antiblack foundation, and has breathed new life into that specious legend. The result is the fact that the American Multiracial Identity Movement and Generation Mix have associated themselves, sometimes quite openly, with a theory so racist and so demeaning to Afro-Americans that it belies the disarmingly fulsome message of harmony and reconciliation recited so often by the multiracial movement.

Part 3, "The Mulatto Future," advances beyond the necessary criticisms of the US racial order and of the American Multiracial Identity Movement, and reaches for theoretical and practical strategies that can finally free us from our half-a-millennium of enthrallment to the false consciousness of biological race, and most especially whiteness. Despite the fact that multiracial advocates and the popular media all too frequently advance the notion that multiracial identity will lead to the demise of race in the United States, no one ever offers a remotely adequate argument for or demonstration of precisely how this is to be accomplished. Addressing this yawning vacuum, I assess the notion of presumed (multi)racial transcendence and show that there is absolutely no reason to suspect that it is accurate. In support of this analysis, the idea of multiracialism as representing a militant stance to assume vis-à-vis the US racial paradigm is evaluated in Chapter 11, "Whither Multiracial Militancy?," and is found wanting.

Chapter 12, "Conserving the Racial Order," is concerned with power, with understanding the purpose of the ubiquitous racial check boxes so often railed against by multiracial advocates, and with questions about the sustainability of a multiracial category through time. In Chapter 13, "Mulatto (and White) Writers on Deconstructing Race," I call on three of our early twentieth-century American mulatto authors from Chapter 4 (Chesnutt, Johnson, and Larsen) along with several slightly earlier white authors of a similar mind to assist in demonstrating the fallaciousness of race in the hope that this time we will heed the ways that their cogent analyses serve to deconstruct race. After these analyses, I suggest that it may be necessary to speak the mulatto into existence, albeit contingently and only temporarily, in order to speak race out of existence.

Finally, in Chaper 14, "Beyond Generation Mix," I reiterate that the pervasive and tenacious persistence of whiteness must be the target of all successful antiracist efforts, that mass celebration of Generation Mix contributes nothing to that important cause and in fact hampers it to a significant degree. I acknowledge the difficulty of the work that will have to be undertaken in order to undo whiteness, and I certainly agree with David Roediger that "with whites today having on average more than nine times the household wealth of African Americans and Latinos, and with white male incarceration rates at less than one-seventh those of African American males, desires to claim white identity and to defend the relative advantages attached to it will persist unless dramatic changes occur, even in the wake of post–civil rights gains for sections of communities of color."[19] This crucial task must not be underestimated.

Notes

1. Race terms in this book are always a reference to people's misguided belief in biological race and the US racial paradigm. Given that my topic concerns the notion of racially mixed people in the United States, my use of such terms is necessary as I endeavor to engage the debate using the linguistic tools currently at our disposal. Race terms in this book, therefore, should always be read as if preceded by the words *so-called*. The only alternatives would have been to utilize far too many italicizations or to deploy cumbersome phraseology such as "persons who are perceived as, or who consider themselves to be, black" (or "white," "black/white," "mulatto," or "multiracial," etc.), which would have distracted unacceptably from the text itself.

2. Kimberly M. DaCosta, "Mixing It Up," *Contexts* (Fall 2005): 15; DaCosta,

Making Multiracials: State, Family, and Market in the Redrawing of the Color Line (Stanford, CA: Stanford University Press, 2007), 21; Elliott Lewis, *Fade: My Journeys in Multiracial America* (New York: Carroll & Graf, 2006), 259–268; Catherine R. Squires, *Dispatches from the Color Line: The Press and Multiracial America* (Albany: State University of New York Press, 2007), 161; Ruth La Ferla, "Generation E. A.: Ethnically Ambiguous," *New York Times*, December 28, 2003, ST1, ST9; Sushi Das, "They've Got the Look," *The Age*, April 20, 2004, http://www .theage.com.au/articles/2004/04/19/1082357106748.html." I include "Remix Generation" while acknowledging its primarily international usage; the other terms are all well in use in the United States.

3. "First-generation" multiracial individuals are taken to be those whose parents are presumed to be unmixed members of two distinct racial groups (i.e., black/white, Asian/Native American, etc.). The fact that this is scientific nonsense appears to have no impact on the thinking of those who advocate this particular identity.

4. In Obama's own words, discussing the acquisition of a White House dog for his two daughters: "Obviously, a lot of shelter dogs are mutts like me." Jeff Zeleny, "Obama, in His New Role as President-Elect, Calls for Stimulus Package," *New York Times*, November 8, 2008, A10.

5. Squires, *Dispatches from the Color Line*, 51.

6. Ibid., 169.

7. Rainier Spencer, *Spurious Issues: Race and Multiracial Identity Politics in the United States* (Boulder: Westview, 1999), 196–197; Spencer, "Beyond Pathology and Cheerleading: Insurgency, Dissolution, and Complicity in the Multiracial Idea," in *The Politics of Multiracialism: Challenging Racial Thinking*, ed. Heather M. Dalmage, 108–119 (Albany: State University of New York Press, 2004).

8. Abby Ferber, *White Man Falling: Race, Gender, and White Supremacy* (Lanham, MD: Rowman & Littlefield, 1998).

9. Patricia P. Hilden, *When Nickels Were Indians: An Urban, Mixed-Blood Story* (Washington, DC: Smithsonian Institution Press, 1995), 151–153.

10. Eduardo Bonilla-Silva, "'New Racism,' Color-Blind Racism, and the Future of Whiteness in America," in *White Out: The Continuing Significance of Racism*, ed. Ashley W. Doane and Eduardo Bonilla-Silva, 277 (New York: Routledge, 2003).

11. As Rebecca King-O'Riain explains, "images of Asian American women (and men) as feminine may also be a key factor in the gender dynamics of Asian/white interracial couplings where the woman tends to be Asian and the man white." Rebecca C. King-O'Riain, "Model Majority? The Struggle for Identity Among Multiracial Japanese Americans," in *The Politics of Multiracialism: Challenging Racial Thinking*, ed. Heather M. Dalmage, 183 (Albany: State University of New York Press, 2004).

12. While commentators might debate the relative placement of each of the middle groups within the paradigm, the endpoints—white and black—are fixed absolutely.

13. Ronald R. Sundstrom, *The Browning of America and the Evasion of Social Justice* (Albany: State University of New York Press, 2008), chap 3.

14. Heather M. Dalmage, *Tripping on the Color Line: Black-White Multiracial Families in a Racially Divided World* (New Brunswick, NJ: Rutgers University Press, 2000), 150.

15. I want to make clear that I see no intrinsic value in being assimilable to whiteness. I am here making a specific point about the exclusivity of whiteness in that it will extend the possibility of assimilation to some members of other groups

but not to blacks. This exclusivity of whiteness vis-à-vis blackness is, as I shall demonstrate in the chapters to follow, mirrored by a similar exclusivity exercised against blackness by the ideology of the American Multiracial Identity Movement.

16. Steve Garner, *Racisms: An Introduction* (Thousand Oaks, CA: Sage, 2010), 101.

17. Jared Sexton, *Amalgamation Schemes: Antiblackness and the Critique of Multiracialism* (Minneapolis: University of Minnesota Press, 2008).

18. When I use the term *white mothers of black/white children* throughout this book I am referring specifically to those white mothers who have or who do indoctrinate their black/white children to a multiracial identity. It is not a reference to all white mothers of black/white children either now or in the past, but is rather a reference to a very specific subset of them.

19. David R. Roediger, *How Race Survived U.S. History: From Settlement and Slavery to the Obama Phenomenon* (New York: Verso, 2008), 212.

Part 1
The Mulatto Past

2

The Mixed-Race Background

Pity the poor mulatto, to whom history has not been at all kind. It has been an extended and hard fall from grace for this formerly somewhat more fashionable figure. But that notoriety, such as it might have been, was long ago. Very much as in the case of the word *Negro*, *mulatto* is a term very few people today would assent to being called. Its origins have been obscured (it does not derive from "little mule," regardless of how many people—some quite desperately—might want it to), and its content mangled (mulatto house slaves did not enjoy privileged lives under slavery vis-à-vis presumably darker field slaves).[1] What remains is a despised caricature of what formerly was a perfectly good word, albeit in the troublesome context of biological race understandings.

My aim in Part 1, beginning with this chapter, is to bring the mulatto of US history (and, as we shall see, of today) to the table of discussion concerning contemporary multiracial identity. I intend to accomplish this through a general accounting of racist thought about the mulatto and then a refutation of that thought, so that we are left with a correct impression as to who—and if one prefers, what—the mulatto both was and is. It is not my intention to offer anything approaching a complete and comprehensive history of the mulatto. Others have already done this much more admirably that I could have—John Mencke, Werner Sollors, and Joel Williamson being three names that come immediately to mind.[2] Rather, my purpose here is to utilize the excellent work done by these and other scholars as a framework for assessing past, present, and future conceptions of mixed race and mixed-race identity in the United States.

While there have been looser definitions over the centuries, a mulatto in the British North American and United States framework referred to a person of sub-Saharan African and European intermixture—whether the immediate offspring of one presumably unmixed white parent and one presumably unmixed black parent or a descendant of such a person. Other combinations and gradations in North America and elsewhere have been accorded different terminologies, such as mestize, mustee, octoroon, quadroon, sambo, and so on, but these are not my focus at present. While acknowledging the possibility of greater or lesser overlap with some of these other descriptors, I am in this book concerned very specifically with the standard idea of the American mulatto.[3] It is an idea with a rich history to be sure, but one whose popular understandings have been overdetermined in a negative way both by pure empirical incompetence on the one hand and by a particularly nauseating brand of maudlin sentimentality on the other. What is especially fascinating and instructive, however, is the specific way the figure of the mulatto—avoided overtly by those in the American Multiracial Identity Movement—is nonetheless being revived and appropriated *by* that same movement, albeit in a more covert manner. And it is precisely such nonexplicit appropriation, which I shall explore in detail in Part 2, that makes this phenomenon all the more intriguing.

Of those Americans who profess to know something about the mulatto, the majority are doubtless informed by the late nineteenth- to early twentieth-century view that presented this figure as (with a few notable exceptions) an emotionally, psychologically, and physically marginal being. With this popular but incorrect historical view serving as a kind of vulgar reference point, it is therefore not surprising that the mulatto has been so very much wrapped up in layer upon layer of dysfunction and weakness. It was a view based quite distinctly on an underlying presumption held by whites that the interracial sex involved in producing the mulatto was both monumental and abysmal. Indeed, this sex was an abomination, most forcefully and most especially when the female partner was white, somewhat less so when the male partner was white. But it was this abominable status that gave rise to the specific qualities of the mulatto figure that resulted in its condition of presumptive marginality.

These qualities are as well known as they are fallacious: that mulattoes are sterile, that they are prone to certain diseases and debilities, that they are unstable emotionally, that they reject blackness and desire desperately to be white, that they are unable to find satisfaction and social acceptance and are thus doomed to eternal disaffection and alienation, and so on. According to Ashley Montagu, "claims have been made in the past, and continue to be implicit in racist thought, that 'miscegenation' . . . leads to physical disharmonies of various sorts. There is no truth whatever in such claims."[4] Yet by making these claims and projecting these qualities onto the mulatto, white men of the late nineteenth and early twentieth centuries assured themselves that beyond interracial sex itself constituting an abominable act, it also produced a negative result in the form of tainted children who were themselves abominations, thereby providing even further proof that interracial sex was against nature. "Indeed, polygenist ideas of mulatto inferiority and sterility, the unnaturalness of racial mixing, and the need to maintain racial purity subsequently did much to determine how white America in the late nineteenth and early twentieth centuries perceived mixed-bloods and reacted to the idea of racial amalgamation."[5]

The seeds of these pseudoscientific and racist notions can be found in the white male psyche as far back as the very beginnings of sub-Saharan African/European contact in British North America. Analyzing the motivations and actions of British colonists in North America, Winthrop Jordan captures the irrational and inconsistent attitude of the white man in this regard: "Interracial propagation was a constant reproach that he was failing to be true to himself. Sexual intimacy strikingly symbolized a union he wished to avoid. If he could not restrain his sexual nature, he could at least reject its fruits and thus solace himself that he had done no harm."[6] The determining effect of white men in these matters, their early and continuing dominance on these shores, their power to project their own inner psychoses away from themselves, their ability to transform those psychoses into problems for nonwhite and nonmale others, should not be underestimated. Discussing the phenomenon of racially mixed marriages in the early twentieth century—indeed, seeking to explain it—a prominent sociologist advised that it is "perhaps not generally understood to what extent sexually satiated prostitutes seek Negro men in their search for new stimulation, [*sic*] The same thing is true of many debauched white men," as if no normal white woman would have a genuine interest in a Negro man, and no normal white man would have a genuine interest in a Negro woman.[7] Rather, the reality is that the psychological projections of white men have been a consistent motif throughout US history.

Noting a similar process of psychological rationalization still extant hundreds of years after the colonial period, Gunnar Myrdal identifies a "sort of collective guilt on the part of white people for the large-scale miscegenation, which has so apparently changed the racial character of the Negro people," as enforcing an interest among whites to "discount the proportion of mulattoes and believe that a greater part of the Negro people is pure bred than is warranted by the facts."[8] Because white Americans wanted to "keep biological distance from the [Negro] out-race," they engaged in these types of racial self-delusions, which included systematic census undercounts of mulattoes as well as the general fantasy that white men were not procreating with Negroes.[9] These contradictory impulses to maintain biological distance from Negroes, on the one hand, and the consistent contribution of white men in particular to miscegenation on the other, resulted in this guilty refusal to face the facts regarding the mixed status of Afro-Americans.[10]

That interracial sex involving black men and white women was policed far more judiciously than interracial sex involving white men and black women hardly requires mentioning.[11] When Jordan notes of the white male colonist that "by classifying the mulatto as a Negro he was in effect denying that intermixture had occurred at all," not only is this a statement about the politics of hypodescent, but it is also an important statement about the crucial difference between whether a white man or a white woman was involved in miscegenation. For the white man it was relatively easy to walk away from a mulatto child he had fathered, perhaps as soon as immediately upon conception. For the white woman, however, the physical facts of pregnancy and childbirth provided the script of a far different narrative, making it much easier to charge and convict a white woman of miscegenation than a white man. Writing about the law in British North America, Sollors offers that "whereas white women were generally punished for bearing children by black or Mulatto men, white men were typically not penalized for impregnating black or Mulatto women."[12] As Abby Ferber puts it, "a mulatto child born to a white woman . . . was a threat to the entire system of slavery and white supremacy" because such a birth "directly usurped white male power and control over both white women and black men. Mulatto children born to black women, on the other hand, were signs of white male power over the rights and access to all women."[13]

Hence white men could very easily, although quite contradictorily, rail against miscegenation in public while nonetheless being avid and secure practitioners of it in private from the early days of colonial America through the Jim Crow South, as evidenced by a comment made by a white man to John Howard Griffin as he was passing for black while conducting research in the Deep South in 1959: "We figure we're doing you people a favor to get some white blood in your kids."[14] Griffin's silent response is compellingly on target: "The grotesque hypocrisy slapped me as it does all Negroes. It is worth remembering when the white man talks of the Negro's lack of sexual morality, or when he speaks with horror about mongrelization and with fervor about racial purity. Mongrelization is already a widespread reality in the South—it has been exclusively the white man's contribution to the Southern Way of Life."[15]

As Myrdal, writing in the mid-twentieth century, reports, "the belief that practically all Negro women lack virtue and sexual morals bolsters up a collective bad conscience for the many generations of miscegenation. At the same time, it is, occasionally, a wishful expression of sexual appetite on the part of white men. The belief in the strong sexual urge and the superior sexual skill and capacity of Negro women (the 'tigress' myth) has more obviously this latter function. The belief that Negro males have extraordinarily large genitalia is to be taken as an expression of a similar sexual envy and, at the same time, as part of the social control devices to aid in preventing intercourse between Negro males and white females."[16] The sexual tension surrounding black men and white women—a tension amplified many times over by the seemingly collective psychosis of white men—is both an old and a continuing story, whether one utilizes as a reference Jordan, Myrdal, Eldridge Cleaver, or the most recent white supremacist publication of one's choice.[17]

Indeed, white supremacist literature, both past and present, is fairly rife with references to "mulatto zombies" and "half-White mongrels," attesting to both the unease as well as the fascination of its adherents with the products of racial mixture.[18] As far back as *The Leopard's Spots*, Thomas Dixon's mythological 1902 novel of post–Civil War Reconstruction and Redemption, his heroic white supremacist characters are driven by one essential problem throughout the book. That problem is: "Shall the future American be an Anglo-Saxon or a Mulatto?"[19] In line with Ferber's excellent analysis of white supremacy, white supremacist absorption with the threat of a "mongrel breed of mulattoes" is considered incorrectly by most Americans to be "extremist," but instead represents merely a difference in terms of volume when placed in the context of general white attitudes in America.[20] Beneath whatever emotionally placid and politically correct veneers we may wish to apply for our own comfort, black male/white female sexual contact most especially still excites tremendous curiosity, revulsion, and hostility in this society.

This is exemplified famously in William Faulkner's 1936 novel, *Absalom, Absalom!*, with its interwoven themes of bigamy, incest, and miscegenation swirling around the reader's investigation into the mystery surrounding the motive for why one young man has killed another young man.[21] It would be useful to make a chart in order to keep track of the sexual forays of the novel's central figure, Thomas Sutpen, and the resulting but often unacknowledged sibling ties he thereby creates. To be brief, Sutpen has sex with a black female slave, producing a daughter; then with a lawful white second wife (the slave is not the first wife, as I shall soon explain), producing in turn a white brother and sister of that slave daughter; and then with an arguably mentally challenged fifteen-year-old white girl who is his handyman's granddaughter, producing a daughter who along with her young mother is killed on the day of her birth by that grandfather. In the search for a male heir to replace his own son who has repudiated his birthright, Sutpen also suggests engaging in unmarried copulation with the niece of his now-deceased second wife, who is outraged and rejects his offer to marry her on the condition that the resulting child is a boy. From Sutpen's perspective all this perversity is seen as simply representing logical and necessary steps in his own grand design and not as immoral in any way.

But the most important sexual act of Thomas Sutpen takes place prior to any of these already mentioned. Years before in the West Indies, he marries a woman whom he believes to be white, but who actually has Negro blood, and has a son with her. After discovering the truth of this first wife's ancestry, Sutpen divorces her, provides materially for both her and the son, and returns to the United States in order to continue his plan for building a large estate. Decades afterward, however, a plan of revenge hatched by Sutpen's discarded first wife results in the inevitable fall of the House of Sutpen when she arranges for Sutpen's white daughter, Julia, to fall in love with the disowned son whom she has placed so as to become friends with Sutpen's recognized son, Henry. Since the disowned son, Charles Bon, has had a marriage ceremony with an octoroon woman in New Orleans, the reader is thereby presented in turn with three different reasons for why Sutpen's recognized son, Henry, murders Charles. These reasons are revealed in turn as the novel progresses, and are: bigamy (Charles is already married to the octoroon), incest (Charles is Julia's half brother), and miscegenation (Charles has Negro ancestry).

From Henry's perspective the first two reasons are argued away, as the marriage to the octoroon can be seen reasonably as not being a real marriage, and even the incest can be justified on the grounds that European royalty have done the same thing: "Henry said suddenly, cried suddenly: 'But kings have done it! Even dukes!'"[22] But it is the miscegenation that cannot be overcome once Henry learns of Charles's Negro ancestry. In one of the novel's most famous lines, Charles says as much to his half brother Henry: "'So it's the miscegenation, not the incest, which you can't bear.'"[23] As Henry struggles to come to grips with this shocking revelation, he says to Charles: "'You are my brother,'" to which Charles replies: "'No I'm not. I'm the nigger that's going to sleep with your sister. Unless you stop me, Henry.'"[24]

In presenting this admittedly scanty analysis of Faulkner's *Absalom, Absalom!* (there is so much of the novel that is relevant in an indirect way to my arguments, but which must of necessity be bypassed), I would point out that we are given unproblematic miscegenation in the form of Sutpen's having a daughter by a black female slave, and of Sutpen's engaging in unknowing miscegenation with his first wife. Even his repudiation and divorce of that first wife is seen as unproblematic to him personally, but merely as being incompatible with his grand design: "'I found that she was not and could never be, through no fault of her own, adjunctive or incremental to the design which I had in mind, so I provided for her and I put her aside.'"[25] In other words, having sex with his first wife (white man/black woman) did not taint him personally in any way. But the intention of the part-Negro son of that union to marry Sutpen's own white daughter—the bigamy and the incest notwithstanding—is too much for the novel to contain, resulting in the fratricidal killing of Charles by Henry. I would argue that Faulkner captures in *Absalom, Absalom!* the interracial sexual dynamic that is still most prominent in US society even today—that sexual contact between black men and white women is seen often as an abomination far beyond other abominations.

A similar illustration may be drawn from the nest of incest animating Richard Hildreth's 1852 abolitionist novel, *The White Slave* (published originally under a different title in 1836 and not including the later-added chapters 37–59), in which the half siblings Archy and Cassy Moore share the same father, Colonel Charles Moore, who is also their mutual owner.[26] Cassy is aware that Colonel Moore is her father, but not that he is Archy's as well, while Archy is aware of all the twisted relationships they have been entangled in due to slavery. Despite knowing that Cassy is his sister, Archy falls in love with and marries her informally before God, but the lovers are soon parted by Colonel Moore, who despite being Cassy's father, desires her sexually for himself just as he did both her and Archy's slave mothers respectively. Hildreth here argues against slavery on the ground that it produces this sort of immorality through the nonrecognition of paternity and the inevitable violence thereby done to familial relations.

The specific point for my argument here, though, is that Hildreth's Colonel Moore has fathered numerous children on his plantation by engaging in temporary sexual relationships with several of his female slaves, a fact that Archy notes will bring to Colonel Moore no public condemnation as long as the colonel does not acknowledge them as his children. Indeed, it is only Cassy's impassioned plea, "'Master,—Father! . . . what is it you would have of your own daughter?'" that halts his attempted rape of her.[27] Doubtless Colonel Moore, despite desiring to have sex with his mulatto daughter, would not stand to hear of his eldest white daughter Caroline so much as receiving the honorable attentions of the most highly refined man imaginable who nonetheless possesses sub-Saharan African ancestry. Hildreth, in the chapters added in the later edition of his book, gives great attention to anti-abolitionist fervor in both the North and the South, a fervor centering in part on the fear of emancipated black slaves "taking possession of the wives and daughters of their masters."[28]

Although she does not make an overt comment on the social unacceptability of black male/while female sexual contact, Pauline Hopkins, in her serialized novel of 1902–1903, *Of One Blood*, goes even further in demonstrating the reach and impunity of white male desire under slavery by showing us the evil of multigenerational incest made possible by the peculiar institution.[29] In this novel, a Southern white man has sex with the daughter begotten by his father and that father's slave.[30] But this is not all, for, in addition to this man fathering two sons and a daughter by his half sister, these children later come together as adult acquaintances in Boston after the Civil War, not realizing that they are siblings. A bevy of plot twists, including treachery, murder, and long-ago baby switching, results in first one brother and then the other marrying his sister, causing their grandmother, while relating the sordid story to the shocked daughter, to remark that "dese things jes' got to happen in slavery, but I isn't gwine to wink at de debbil's work wif both eyes open."[31] Most significant for my argument here, the white father of these three siblings decides to sell their mother (his half sister) and two of them (the third being retained as his false newborn son through the unbeknownst baby switching) when he marries a white woman who will not allow him to continue his miscegenist ways. The important point is that, absent his new wife's objections, he had seen no problem with his participation in white male/black female sexual contact. The difference between the dynamic highlighted by Faulkner, Hildreth, and Hopkins, and the general disposition of US society today, if there is indeed any difference, is one of degree only.

Some readers might object that I am exaggerating the case here, dredging up long-lost racist attitudes that are no longer in existence in the modern era. However, one need look only as far as the very close Tennessee Senate race of 2006 between white Republican Bob Corker and Afro-American Democrat Harold Ford to see that I am not overstating the facts. In that campaign, a controversial late October television political advertisement loomed very large: "The commercial, financed by the Republican National Committee, was aimed at Representative Harold E. Ford Jr., the black Democrat from Memphis whose campaign for the Senate this year has kept the Republicans on the defensive in a state where they never expected to have trouble holding the seat. The spot, which was first broadcast last week and was disappearing from the air on Wednesday, featured a series of people in mock man-on-the-street interviews talking sarcastically about Mr. Ford and his stands on issues including the estate tax and national security. The controversy erupted over one of the people featured: an attractive white woman, bare-shouldered, who declares that she met Mr. Ford at a 'Playboy party,' and closes the commercial by looking into the camera and saying, with a wink, 'Harold, call me.'"[32]

Ford eventually lost this very close Senate race, and while commentators may debate whether the advertisement did or did not play a decisive role in giving the Senate seat to Corker, a different issue than the advertisement's ultimate effectiveness is more significant for my purposes here. The major point, in my view, is that the Republican National Committee felt that this advertisement would prove effective with its targeted group.[33] If the intended point was merely some suggestion of an inappropriately hedonistic lifestyle on the part of Ford, why not use a nonwhite woman, especially when in a Southern state the particular race/sex combination highlighted in the advertisement would obviously carry such negative and emotional historical baggage? The answer is that the black man/white woman nexus is precisely what the producers of this advertisement wanted to exploit at this very late stage of a very close political contest.

One might also cite as a modern example of discomfort with the black male/white female pairing the very strong public reaction to the October

1990 cover of *The Cable Guide*, featuring white actor Jamie Lee Curtis draped seductively over the shirtless back of Afro-American professional football player Willie Gault. The cover shows Curtis and Gault, their heads touching, with Curtis's left arm alongside Gault's head and the fingers of her left hand in Gault's hair, while her right leg is lifted and cradled by Gault's right arm and held close to his side. According to Curtis, the cover inspired a "deluge of hate mail, mostly from Whites who were offended by a White woman posing with a Black man. . . . And the letters they (the magazine) got about this were unbelievably scary that in 1990 people still feel this way. It was so frightening! And all of a sudden this brouhaha that it's sinful to have this Black man and a White woman on a magazine cover together."[34]

Contrast the public's raw reaction to that photograph with the relatively minor controversy that ensued when during the nationally televised halftime show of the 2004 National Football League Super Bowl, white entertainer Justin Timberlake revealed the uncovered breast of Afro-American entertainer Janet Jackson immediately after informing her in front of 90 million viewers that he was "gonna have you naked by the end of this song."[35] There were motions of executive-level handwringing from the network and the league, there were sounds of displeasure from the Federal Communications Commission, and there were fines levied and later rescinded, but the incident itself never resulted in a dynamic revolving in any way around the races and sexes of the principals as in the cases of Harold Ford and the woman in the political advertisement or Willie Gault and Jamie Lee Curtis's cover photograph.[36] I find myself in agreement with Catherine Squires's analysis of the Super Bowl incident when she muses that "'African American Nelly,' for example, probably would not have been exempt from harsh criticism had he exposed the breast of, say, Britney Spears on CBS," and the same, I daresay, would undoubtedly be true of Willie Gault and Jamie Lee Curtis.[37] Finally, moving beyond sports, one need only review the number of romantic pairings featuring Afro-American men and white women in major Hollywood motion pictures and compare them to other pairings—including the pairings of white men and Afro-American women—to perceive what is still considered least acceptable in US society today. These manifestations of contemporary unease are related directly to the historical tensions I have been describing.

Prior to proceeding, there is something in relation to this that must be addressed. I am aware of certain contemporary so-called reality television shows that feature what I have no problem describing as preposterously offensive modern-day minstrels in the form of Afro-American males who are presented as the objects of desire of a variety of women, including white women. While these television shows do air and while they do have an audience, I would argue that they are still not white mainstream fare in the sense of universal acceptance and are, in fact, viewed as ridiculous farces with the participating white women being seen by other whites not as true white women but instead as skanks who are by their very participation already lost to the race. Indeed, my reference to minstrels also includes my feeling that white US audiences today who *do* view and enjoy these shows are deriving the same sort of gratuitous pleasure and personal reassurance of white superiority in viewing them that their ancestors derived viewing actual minstrel shows in the nineteenth century. For Afro-American audiences who support such degrading nonsense, however, there simply is no excuse.

The monumental and abysmal act of interracial heterosexual relations between whites and blacks—or, at least, as so categorized publicly by white males in the nineteenth century—left those white males with a self-imposed need to mark the resulting children as naturally damaged and less whole than the children of either white/white or black/black unions. This was required whether because of the white man's guilt over his enduring participation in miscegenation or because of the perceived threat to his psychic manhood in the case of black male/white female unions. In either case, as Ferber describes, "interracial sexuality threatens the borders of white identity, and mixed-race people become the living embodiment of the threat. White supremacist publications are filled with images of 'mongrels'— feared and despised because they straddle and destabilize those racial boundaries essential to securing white identity and power."[38] The continuing self-delusion of the false worldview that white males had constructed in North America necessitated that there be something very wrong with the offspring of these abysmal sexual unions.

One important line of thought in this regard was transplanted to North America from the Caribbean. Sollors reports that as long ago as 1774, in his *The History of Jamaica* "Edward Long may have been the first to suppose, against all evidence, that Mulattoes were 'defective and barren' when they 'intermarried with those of their own complexion,' which was to become a much-needed core assumption in the belief that racial differences were not distinctions of 'varieties' but really 'species' differences."[39] Long's Jamaican notion spread far and wide throughout British North America despite its obvious evidentiary emptiness. Mencke adds that "whites had long conceived of mulattoes as somehow different from both of the two parent races. Mulattoes were physically weak, notably infertile, and prone to debilitating diseases. At the same time, mulattoes were clearly intellectually superior to pure blacks, although certainly not the equal of the white man. There was also a question as to their moral character, especially since they often sprang from illegitimate interracial unions."[40]

Even so-called friends of the Negro found no difficulty in placing mulattoes on a far higher footing than unmixed blacks, going so far as to assert occasionally that the former were the equals of whites. In the 1855 abolitionist novel, *The Planter's Victim*, Samuel Smucker distinguishes mulattoes from Negroes in just this way via his description of the quadroon slave George Sanford, whose "features exhibited nothing of the distinctive characteristics of the negro; his eye was large, dark and *expressive*; his forehead was high, *prominent* and *expansive*; displaying a *dome of thought*, indicative of *mental superiority*."[41] Nor does Smucker intend for this very favorable description of George to apply to one individual alone, for he assures his readers that "there is a class of negroes in the South, generally the children of white men and mulatto women, who possess and display a degree of *natural intelligence*, refinement and delicacy of feeling, fully equal to any thing exhibited by the white race. They, of course, want the finishing touch, which education alone can give, to *natural qualities* of that kind."[42] In terms of degree, Smucker's movement of mulattoes upward and away from Negroes is not unusual—indeed, we will have occasion to observe the identical impulse when in Part 2 we assess the American Multiracial Identity Movement of today—but his elevation of mulattoes to equal footing with whites is at the extreme end for the period in which he writes. More common during this era is the assumption that mulattoes do not reach equality with whites because there is something wrong, and inherently so, with mixed-race individuals.

With the presumption in mind that the products of race mixture must somehow be problematic, the slowly maturing field of science was utilized in the late nineteenth century as a vehicle to engage in a physical deprecation of the resulting children, while in the early twentieth century the developing field of sociology served the purpose of a similar emotional/psychological deprecation. This is not to say that there was any organized conspiracy among white males to carry out this assault on mulatto physical and mental integrity. Rather, it was the quite natural outcome of racist beliefs in the superiority of one's own group. If biological race is real, and if whites are superior to blacks, then there must be something distasteful and unnatural about the sexual union of the two. Given this unnaturalness, one would expect there to be something wrong with the offspring. With this as a presumption, white males then sought ways to confirm what seemed to them an obvious truth. Edward Reuter, endeavoring in the first quarter of the twentieth century to demonstrate that the American mulatto group is always superior to the American black group, provides an example of operating with this sort of obviousness serving as a cultural and professional grammar when he writes that the "lower culture of the Negro people is of course a simple observational fact and is to be accepted as such. To question it is to deny the obvious."[43] Pointing to a similar case, Montagu remarks upon a distinguished scientist's inability to acknowledge his own racist blinders in writing about racial hybridization and the supposed resulting physical disharmonies by categorizing it as "a cautionary example of how a respected scientist's prejudices could affect his mind!"[44]

While concerning race, although not specifically mulattoes, an excellent example of this process can be seen at work in the craniometry studies of Samuel Morton. Duplicating Morton's mid-nineteenth-century experiments in assessing the cranial capacity (and, therefore, it was supposed, innate intelligence) of different racial groups, Stephen Jay Gould was unable to replicate Morton's published results placing whites at the top, followed by Asians, Amerindians, and blacks.[45] As Gould describes it, "during the summer of 1977 I spent several weeks reanalyzing Morton's data. . . . In short, and to put it bluntly, Morton's summaries are a patchwork of fudging and finagling in the clear interest of controlling a priori convictions. Yet— and this is the most intriguing aspect of the case—I find no evidence of conscious fraud; indeed, had Morton been a conscious fudger, he would not have published his data so openly."[46] "All I can discern is an a priori conviction about racial ranking so powerful that it directed his tabulations along preestablished lines. Yet Morton was widely hailed as the objectivist of his age, the man who would rescue American science from the mire of unsupported speculation."[47]

The example of Morton's susceptibility to racist a priori convictions may be seen as an echo of Long's Jamaican thesis, particularly in Sollors's observation of Long that his "story reveals the extent to which ideological desire overwhelms possible empirical counterevidence; he was an observer who knew West Indian life—and yet he could make a claim that ran against any experience."[48] Indeed, Long goes so far as to imply that although he has never heard personally of a case in which a mulatto couple actually had children together who then grew to adulthood, if there were such instances then "may we not suspect the lady, in those cases, to have privately intrigued with another man, a White perhaps?"[49] Looking back through the centuries at Long's words may inspire modern responses ranging from incredulousness to derision, but it remains the case that his notions concerning Jamaica became dominant throughout North America, affecting the direction of significant endeavors from science to law, and underscoring the power of racist thought—however false or ridiculous—to have lasting and damaging effects.

A somewhat humorous aspect of this emphasis on the physical is the white man's ever-stated assurance that he can always detect the telltale difference between a mulatto and a white person, no matter how remote the mulatto's Negro ancestry might be. This certainty, of course, is far more along the lines of wishful thinking than actual fact, and stems quite significantly from the absolute necessity that Negro "blood" not enter the white community's collective bloodstream, which is still the foremost paranoid nightmare of white supremacist ideology. From the size, shape, or color of the half moons (lunulae) under the fingernails to the color of the quick at the tips of the fingernails, to darkened outlines around the iris of the eyes to the coloring of the whites of the eyes, to other nonexistent physical features, whites have engaged in this psychodrama of self-deception.

In her 1842 short story, "The Quadroons" (reprinted 1846), Lydia Maria Child describes one black/white character this way: "The iris of her large, dark eye had the melting, mezzotinto outline, which remains the last vestige of African ancestry."[50] In his 1859 play, *The Octoroon*, Dion Boucicault has the title character, Zoe, say to her white lover: "George, do you see that hand you hold; look at these fingers, do you see the nails are of a blueish tinge?"[51] Upon George's affirmation that "near the quick is a faint blue mark," Zoe then says: "Look in my eyes; is not the same colour in the white?"[52] When George remarks that "it is their beauty," Zoe continues: "Could you see the roots of my hair you would see the same dark fatal mark. Do you know what it is?"[53] In answer to George's admission that he does not know, Zoe replies: "That—that is the ineffaceable curse of Cain. Of the blood that feeds my heart, one drop in eight is black—bright red as the rest may be, that one drop poisons all the flood."[54]

Afro-American writers have often lampooned such foolishness directly by having white characters make boastful pronouncements regarding their *African-detection* abilities directly in the presence of light mulattoes, even going so far as demonstrating smugly their race-perception prowess in this regard by examining those mulattoes' hands or eyes prior to making a grand pronouncement validating the "whiteness" of those mulatto characters. Nella Larsen demonstrates the former approach in her 1928 novel, *Quicksand*, through the thoughts of the mulatto character Irene Redfield, who wonders briefly whether she has been detected while passing as white in a Chicago restaurant: "Absurd! Impossible! White people were so stupid about such things for they all that they usually asserted that they were able to tell; and by the most ridiculous means, finger-nails, palms of hands, shapes of ears, teeth, and other equally silly rot. They always took her for an Italian, a Spaniard, a Mexican, or a gipsy. Never, when she was alone, had they even remotely seemed to suspect that she was a Negro."[55]

Frances Harper provides a typical example of the latter technique in her 1893 novel, *Iola Leroy, or Shadows Uplifted*, when she has a racist physician declare, in conversation with several people, one of whom is a light mulatto the physician does not recognize as such: "'Oh, there are tricks of blood which always betray them. My eyes are more practiced than yours. I can always tell them.'" Of course this physician is proven wrong, spectacularly and embarrassingly so, just a few pages later.[56] The hilarity of such scenes aside, they nonetheless provide a useful illustration of the way that whites have insisted historically on the assertion of physical difference—both of Negroes from whites and of mulattoes from Negroes—in the furtherance of a white supremacist agenda.

Not all critiques of this type were comic, however. Pauline Hopkins, in her 1900 novel, *Contending Forces*, provides an instance of the false ascription of Negro ancestry that results in horrific consequences when she has a white, North Carolina roughneck declare of a white woman: "'Strikes me, Hank, thet thet ar female's got a black streak in her somewhar. . . . Thar's too much cream color in the face and too little blud seen under the skin fer a genooine white 'ooman.'"[57] As part of a plot to kill this woman's husband and steal his property, the rumor is spread that she is part-black, which immediately after her husband's murder results in her being whipped savagely and mercilessly before being thrown into slavery, whereupon she commits suicide, leaving the futures of her two young, enslaved, and now fatherless white sons to the hands of fate.[58] While some readers may point to a suggestion by the author that this woman and her husband might have had possible black ancestry as a result of their origins in Bermuda, Hopkins forecloses that possibility by writing of one of those two sons when he marries a black woman: "Thus he was *absorbed* into that unfortunate race, of whom it is said that a man had better be born dead than to come into the world as part and parcel of it."[59] Were this son already part black, it would not make sense to speak of him having been "absorbed" in this way. In the example of the mother's misery, the importance of white purity and of being able to prove physical race purity could not have been illustrated with more clarity.

It of course makes perfect sense that the first route taken in terms of "proofs" of mulatto inferiority was the physical. The relatively meager nineteenth-century intellectual arsenal available to those interested in such questions, combined with racist ideologies and predetermined conclusions of white superiority, would have made such "proofs" seem quite natural in an age of budding scientism. Mencke writes of this time that "the mulatto was generally perceived to be more intelligent than the black, as well as physically more attractive because of the predominance of white rather than black physical characteristics. In these terms, the mulatto was clearly superior to blacks. At the same time, it was widely believed that the mulatto was constitutionally weak, prone to debilitating diseases, and like all hybrids— basically infertile—facts which indicated certain basic inferiorities to both of the parent races."[60] As an example of this thinking, premier anthropologist Louis Agassiz "gave expression to his belief in the Mulattoes' 'sickly physique and their impaired fecundity.'"[61] Hopkins captures this sentiment in the form of a clergyman who had, during a sermon, "'thanked God that the mulatto race was dying out, because it was a mongrel mixture which combined the worst elements of the two races. Lo, the poor mulatto! Despised by the blacks of his own race, scorned by the whites! Let him go out and hang himself!'"[62]

Audrey Smedley relates the popular mid-nineteenth-century view that the "mulatto was a degenerate and abnormal hybrid. This hybrid might be slightly superior intellectually to the full-blooded Negro but still remained much inferior to the true white. Physically and morally, hybrids lacked the vigor of the pure types and, if left to themselves, would soon become extinct."[63] The belief that mulattoes were inferior physically to both blacks and whites was also "confirmed" by two US government groups' Civil War measurements of soldiers: "Through a variety of measurements of body dimensions, head size, vision, teeth, strength, respiration, and pulmonary capacity, the researchers in both groups found, as might be expected, that Negroes were distinctly inferior to whites. More important for the present study, they established that, as earlier racialists had argued, the mulatto was physiologically inferior to both of the original stocks."[64] These two issues (Negro physical inferiority to whites, and mulatto physical inferiority to both Negroes and whites) are related in an even more direct way than might at first be obvious, for if there was a hereditary difference—a species difference—between Negroes and whites, with whites being superior, then "Mulattoes who had to serve as the proof of the difference were argued out of existence. Suggesting at least a 'weakening' of the offspring of amalgamation thus became crucial to racial theory."[65]

While we now see these racist theories as ridiculously false and based very clearly on white men's own deep racial insecurities, occasionally they produced conclusions that seem to go even beyond the pale if for no other reason than that just as in the case of Long's Jamaica, simple observation in the available laboratory of the slave South should have proved them quite readily to be wildly false. For instance, one line of argument declared that "the union of a Negro man and a white woman was frequently sterile, but that of a Negro woman and a white man was quite as productive as a marriage within either race. Mulatto children, although prolific when backcrossed with either of the parent races, were not fully fertile among themselves. Thus there could be no stable mulatto race; without the continuous replenishment of its numbers by further intercourse between white men and Negro women, the mulatto group, physically weak and short-lived, would either die out or 'revert' to the dominant type."[66] That the most productive combination mentioned involved the sexual contribution of white men should come as no surprise. Beyond the seemingly obligatory infertility, other examples of mulatto disability were also noted in this particular argument: "Not only were the hybrids of widely disparate races partially infertile, they were likely to be mentally, morally, and physically inferior to either parent group."[67]

In the midst of this nonsense, a pair of simple and devastating critiques of the mulatto debility thesis comes by way of Frederick Law Olmsted, writing of his travels in the slave South during the early 1850s. On one of his journeys Olmsted took the time to inquire as to the physical differences between pure blacks and mulattoes. Asking two plantation overseers and a plantation manager whether mulattoes were "more subject to illness" or whether they appeared "to be of weaker constitutions," he received a general consensus from these white men that apart from questions of working in extreme heat, mulattoes were no weaker than pure blacks.[68] The plantation manager went so far as to state his beliefs that mulattoes "were equally strong and no more liable to illness," that he had "never had reason to think them of weaker constitution," and that he "had not noticed that their children were weaker or more subject to disease than others."[69] The voices of these and other close observers of mulattoes and pure blacks did not make their way into the pseudoscientific treatises of the day, however.

Equally decisive, Olmsted later asked a slave nurse who was caring for some twenty to thirty infants, some of whom "were evidently the offspring of white fathers," to point out the healthiest and the sickliest of the children.[70] While she tended to mostly point out "pure" black children as being the healthiest, when Olmsted asked her to point out the sickliest, she nonetheless did not point to any mulatto children.[71] Upon having Olmsted ask her directly "if she noticed any difference in this respect between the black and the yellow children," she replied most tellingly, "'Well, dey do say, master, dat de yellow ones is de sickliest, but I can't tell for true dat I ever see as dey was.'"[72] I would submit that this slave nurse has far more accurate information to pass on to us regarding whether or not mulattoes have defective constitutions than the sum total of pamphlets, journal articles, and books published by legions of racist white men attempting desperately to rationalize the effects of the double standard they accepted regarding miscegenation.[73] Yet, it was those legions of white men who for so very long carried the day on this matter.

And they would not very easily be denied, as can be seen though Kim Williams's report on the lengths to which white men would go to prove mulatto physical debility. Writing about decennial censuses, Williams asks us to "consider the circumstances of the introduction of the mulatto category in 1850. Added initially as a means by which to test Josiah C. Nott's theory that blacks and whites were separate species, he believed the progeny of interracial unions to be frailer and, thus, to live shorter lives. . . . 'Mulatto' appeared on all subsequent censuses through 1890—at which point 'Quadroon' and 'Octoroon' made one-time appearances—after which it was dropped in 1900 and reappeared in 1910. After a final census appearance in 1920, the decades-long search for evidence that mulattos were susceptible to early death was finally abandoned."[74] But whether in regard to early death in particular, or to mulatto debility in general, white men hardly required "evidence" to further their racist mythologies.

Writing in the early 1940s, Gunnar Myrdal provides examples of beliefs regarding mulatto physical inferiority that survived well into the twentieth century in the popular sphere even after science had jettisoned them:

"There are many popular beliefs deprecating the mulatto: that they are more criminally disposed even than Negroes in general; that they tend to be sterile; that they—having parents of two distinct races—are not harmoniously proportioned, but have a trait of one parent side by side with a trait of the other parent, paired in such a way that the two cannot function together properly; that they are more susceptible to tuberculosis; that, because Negroes have relatively long, narrow heads, Negro women, with narrow pelvises, and their mulatto offspring are endangered when they bear children of white men whose heads are rounder, and so on. These beliefs are all of a nature to discourage miscegenation and to keep up biological distance even in regard to cross-breeds."[75] But these mythological beliefs, though they would continue to survive in some respects, nonetheless gave way eventually to a different mode of analysis, one that was rooted not so much in the body proper as in the mind and in the emotions. The idea of an ill-fitting union, a misalliance, remained the driving force, but it was displaced to a less physical arena. It is to this perhaps more sophisticated view that we now turn.

Notes

1. See Jack D. Forbes, *Africans and Native Americans: The Language of Race and the Evolution of Red-Black Peoples* (Urbana and Chicago: University of Illinois Press, 1993), 145, for an explication of the "little mule" misperception; and any respectable history of American slavery for a refutation of the false distinction between house slaves and field slaves. While it is convenient to give credence to a sharp and simple dichotomy between house slaves and field slaves—especially when accompanied by the unjustified presumption that house slaves were light skinned and field slaves were dark skinned—there is no historical evidence for it. Generally speaking, except for the larger plantation operations, many house slaves resided in the slave quarters with their compatriots; and far from being privileged, while working in their owners' residences were much more easily within reach of continual and hidden abuse by those slave owners and their family members than were field slaves. Nor is there anything beyond anecdotal evidence for the notion that mulattoes were preferred as house servants. For instance, writing of the British colonial period in North America, Winthrop Jordan reports that "mulattoes seem generally to have been treated no better than unmixed Africans. The diaries, letters, travel accounts, and newspapers of the period do not indicate any pronounced tendency to distinguish mulattoes from Negroes, any feeling that their status was higher and demanded different treatment. These sources give no indication, for instance, that mulattoes were preferred as house servants or concubines." Winthrop D. Jordan, *White over Black: American Attitudes Toward the Negro, 1550–1812* (New York: W. W. Norton, 1977), 169. Moreover, Eugene Genovese finds that "blacks and mulattoes worked side by side in the plantation Big House and in the fields. Those mulattoes who received special treatment were usually kin to their white folks, and the special treatment was not always favorable. . . . Typically, the mulatto, especially the mulatto slave, was 'just another nigger' to the whites." Eugene D. Genovese, *Roll,*

Jordan, Roll: The World the Slaves Made (New York: Vintage, 1976), 429. Finally, Minkah Maklani observes that "contrary to popular belief, plantation work patterns did not reflect a mulatto-black divide with mulattos dominating house work and skilled labor. . . . Nothing indicates that mulattos were restricted primarily to non-field work." Minkah Makalani, "A Biracial Identity or a New Race? The Historical Limitations and Political Implications of a Biracial Identity," *Souls* (Fall 2001): 80.

2. John G. Mencke. *Mulattoes and Race Mixture: American Attitudes and Images, 1865–1918* (Ann Arbor: UMI Research Press, 1979); Werner Sollors, *Neither Black Nor White Yet Both: Thematic Explorations of Interracial Literature* (New York: Oxford University Press, 1997); Joel Williamson, *New People: Miscegenation and Mulattoes in the United States* (New York: Free Press, 1980). Properly speaking, Williamson provides a history of the mulatto, Mencke a history of reaction to the mulatto, and Sollors a history of mulatto-themed literature, although the three certainly overlap in numerous ways.

3. In other words, I am viewing quadroons and octoroons as varieties of mulatto. I am not here interested in them specifically as quadroons and octoroons, but rather—unless noted specifically—simply as mulattoes.

4. Ashley Montagu, *Man's Most Dangerous Myth: The Fallacy of Race*, 6th ed. (Walnut Creek, CA: AltaMira, 1997), 269.

5. Mencke, *Mulattoes and Race Mixture*, 44.

6. Jordan, *White over Black*, 177–178.

7. Edward Reuter, *The Mulatto in the United States: Including a Study of the Rôle of Mixed-Blood Races Throughout the World* (Boston: Richard G. Badger, 1918; repr. New York: Negro Universities Press, 1969), 137n38.

8. Gunnar Myrdal, *An American Dilemma: The Negro Problem and Modern Democracy* (New York: Harper & Brothers, 1944), 105.

9. Ibid. Myrdal writes in reference to white people in these passages. The specific focus on white males in the last clause of this sentence is mine.

10. I will argue in Part 2 that just as in the case of Myrdal's guilty whites, advocates of multiracial identity today also insist against logic that the Afro-American population is far less mixed than it actually is; and that also, as it was with those whites, the notion of generating biological distance from Afro-Americans is a primary impulse of the contemporary American Multiracial Identity Movement. The underlying motivation today may be different, but the result in terms of relating to Afro-Americans is the same.

11. For a comprehensive analysis of this phenomenon, see Abby Ferber, *White Man Falling: Race, Gender, and White Supremacy* (Lanham, MD: Rowman & Littlefield, 1998).

12. Sollors, *Neither Black Nor White Yet Both*, 45.

13. Ferber, *White Man Falling*, 35–36.

14. John H. Griffin, *Black Like Me* (New York: Signet, 1996), 103.

15. Ibid.

16. Myrdal, *An American Dilemma*, 108.

17. Eldridge Cleaver, *Soul on Ice* (New York: Delta, 1968). This theme of sexual tension runs throughout *Soul on Ice*, but in particular see Part Four, "White Woman, Black Man."

18. Andrew Macdonald, *The Turner Diaries* (New York: Barricade Books, 1996), 34, 207.

19. Thomas Dixon Jr., *The Leopard's Spots* (1902; repr. Gretna, LA: Firebird Press, 2001), 159, 198, 333, 383, 433, 438. This problem is phrased sometimes in reference to the future American and sometimes in reference to the future North Carolinian; it is also phrased sometimes as a question and sometimes as a proposition.

Nonetheless, the primary point Dixon raises is the impossibility of both whites and blacks living in America under terms of social equality due to the fear that such equality would lead inevitably to interracial sex and mulatto children.

20. Ibid., 198.

21. William Faulkner, *Absalom, Absalom!* (1936; repr. New York: Viking International, 1990).

22. Ibid., 273.

23. Ibid., 285.

24. Ibid., 286.

25. Ibid., 194.

26. Richard Hildreth, *The White Slave. Another Picture of Slave Life in America* (London: George Routledge, 1852; repr. Rye Brook, NY: Adamant Media, 2006).

27. Ibid., 75.

28. Ibid., 155.

29. Pauline E. Hopkins, *Of One Blood; Or, The Hidden Self* (1902–1903; repr. New York: Washington Square Press, 2004).

30. Although we are told that "Ol' marse had only one chil', a son," it is clear from the text that this reference is to his children by his legal wife only, not by his slave mistress. Hopkins, *Of One Blood*, 175–176.

31. Hopkins, *Of One Blood*, 176.

32. Robin Toner, "In Tight Senate Race, Attack Ad on Black Candidate Stirs Furor," *New York Times*, October 26, 2006, A1.

33. Despite financing the advertisement, which was produced by an external organization, the chair of the Republican National Committee claimed not to have seen it beforehand. However, even if this is true we are still left with the fact that persons very high up in Tennessee Republican political circles believed that an advertisement featuring the suggestion of sexual contact between an Afro-American man and a white woman would be effective against the prospects of that Afro-American man's campaign.

34. *Jet*, "Jamie Lee Curtis Expresses Shock About Uproar over Magazine Cover with Gault," March 4, 1991, 35.

35. Elizabeth Jensen, "Indecency Penalty Against CBS Is Rejected," *New York Times*, July 22, 2008, C1.

36. Ibid.

37. Catherine R. Squires, *Dispatches from the Color Line: The Press and Multiracial America* (Albany: State University of New York Press, 2007), 171.

38. Ferber, *White Man Falling*, 111.

39. Sollors, *Neither Black Nor White Yet Both*, 61.

40. Mencke, *Mulattoes and Race Mixture*, 85.

41. [Samuel M. Smucker], *The Planter's Victim; or, Incidents of American Slavery* (Philadelphia: Wm. White Smith, 1855), 14–15. Italics added.

42. Ibid., 21. Italics added.

43. Edward B. Reuter, "The Superiority of the Mulatto," *American Journal of Sociology* 23, no. 1 (July 1917): 87–88.

44. Montagu, *Man's Most Dangerous Myth*, 270.

45. Stephen J. Gould, *The Mismeasure of Man* (New York: W. W. Norton, 1981), 55.

46. Ibid., 54.

47. Ibid., 69. Gould's analysis of Samuel Morton is contained in Chapter 2 of his book; see also Chapter 3 of his book for a similarly revealing discussion of the roughly contemporary work of Paul Broca.

48. Sollors, *Neither Black Nor White Yet Both*, 130.

49. Edward Long, *History of Jamaica, Volume II: Reflections on Its Situation, Settlements, Inhabitants, Climate, Products, Commerce, Laws and Government* (London: T. Lowndes, 1774; repr. Montreal: McGill-Queen's University Press, 2003), 336.

50. Lydia M. Child, "The Quadroons," in *Fact and Fiction: A Collection of Stories* (New York: C. S. Francis, 1846), 63.

51. Dion Boucicault, *The Octoroon* (1859; reprinted in *Plays by Dion Boucicault*, ed. Peter Thomson, London: Cambridge University Press, 1984), 147.

52. Ibid.

53. Ibid.

54. Ibid.

55. Nella Larsen, *Quicksand*, 1928, in *Quicksand* and *Passing* (New Brunswick: Rutgers University Press, 1995).

56. Frances E. W. Harper, *Iola Leroy, or Shadows Uplifted*, 2nd ed. (Philadelphia: Garrigues, 1893; repr. Oxford: Oxford University Press, 1988), 229, 238–239.

57. Pauline E. Hopkins, *Contending Forces: A Romance Illustrative of Negro Life North and South* (Boston: The Colored Co-operative Publishing Co., 1900; repr. New York: Oxford University Press, 1988), 41.

58. Ibid., 68–71.

59. Ibid., 23, 79. Italics added.

60. Mencke, *Mulattoes and Race Mixture*, 38.

61. Sollors, *Neither Black Nor White Yet Both*, 132.

62. Hopkins, *Contending Forces*, 150.

63. Audrey Smedley, *Race in North America: Origin and Evolution of a Worldview*, 2nd ed. (Boulder: Westview, 1999), 240.

64. Mencke, *Mulattoes and Race Mixture*, 39. See also Smedley, *Race in North America*, 241.

65. Sollors, *Neither Black Nor White Yet Both*, 131.

66. George W. Stocking Jr., *Race, Culture, and Evolution: Essays in the History of Anthropology* (Chicago: University of Chicago Press, 1982), 48–49.

67. Ibid., 49.

68. Frederick L. Olmsted, *The Cotton Kingdom: A Traveller's Observations on Cotton and Slavery in the American Slave States* (1861; repr. New York: Modern Library, 1984), 459.

69. Ibid.

70. Ibid., 460.

71. Ibid.

72. Ibid.

73. Ironically, or perhaps instead quite expectedly, we shall see in the next chapter that this very same point may be made when we consider the contributions of sociology to the twentieth-century study of the mulatto.

74. Kim M. Williams, *Mark One or More: Civil Rights in Multiracial America* (Ann Arbor: University of Michigan Press, 2006), 23.

75. Myrdal, *An American Dilemma*, 107–108.

3

Of Tragic Mulattoes and Marginal Men

With the dawning of the twentieth century, and the accompanying realization that biology was not as solely determinative of human behavior as people had thought previously, the new field of sociology was well placed to take race and racial infirmity beyond the purely physical domain to one that was informed more by social and psychological pressures. According to John Mencke, "the generation between 1890 and 1950 was . . . the period during which the social sciences became established as distinct academic disciplines and the major professional journals and organizations were founded."[1] It is here as well that we begin to detect a shift from the rather more fully negative traits that were associated with the mulatto's purely physical nature to a view that, while still unfavorable, tended to place the mulatto midway between blacks and whites in terms of physical beauty and mental capability. It is here that we find what would come to be known as the *marginal man*.

It was this very placement that would be the occasion for the tragic mulatto's scholarly birth, since given the already existing psychological projections that white male sociologists chose to carry on and adopt for themselves it was quite "obvious" to them that mulattoes would of course bemoan their association with blackness while wishing pathetically and quite hopelessly for the full whiteness that could never be theirs. By this time, the tragic mulatto characterization had an existence in literary fiction. I am here discussing specifically its birth in the realm of academia but, prior to proceeding, it is important to point out that my use of "tragic mulatto" is circumscribed quite tightly, and refers specifically to a black/white literary character who desires desperately to be white or who otherwise rejects or laments her or his blackness, and whose *internal* racial struggle (as opposed to the stress of external pressures) is the chief source of intense personal tension. Such a characterization might also include an intense desire for a white lover in order to validate or otherwise solidify the desirer's own claim to whiteness. In either case, it is the character's mixed ancestry that is the primary cause of conflict and, ultimately, a tragic ending. One must therefore distinguish mulatto literary figures who merely live tragic lives or undergo tragic experiences from the more specialized psycho-emotional understanding embodied in the tragic mulatto as the specific literary trope I am invoking. Not all mulatto figures, including those female mulatto characters who were hypersexualized so as to be made the objects of lascivious white men, were necessarily tragic in this more specific sense.

For instance, some scholars point to Lydia Maria Child's "The Quadroons," as an early or even the first use of the tragic mulatto characterization, but this is a mistake.[2] Child may perhaps have developed what we might call the standard phenotype or description of the female tragic mulatto (white or near-white in appearance, compellingly beautiful, naïve socially, and fragile emotionally), but the description alone is not enough. Without the explicit psycho-emotional trauma caused specifically by racial mixture, such a mulatto character is not tragic. Neither of Child's female mulattoes in "The Quadroons," Rosalie and her daughter Xarifa, are tragic mulattoes. There is no indication in the story that either of them desires whiteness and, while both are in love with white men, they do not love them specifically *because* they are white men. And even though both characters die—one of a broken heart and one from madness—neither of these deaths is attributable to any internal racial conflict or desire for whiteness on their parts. Therefore, even though they die tragic deaths, and even though their status as mulattoes is very much integral to the story, it is not accurate to label either Rosalie or Xarifa a tragic mulatto.[3] As Werner Sollors writes of these two: "the descriptions of mother and daughter racial features are included, perhaps even stressed. However, neither is, as of yet, a victim of racially conflicting bloodstreams, and again, it is primarily the issue of enslavement and that of 'belonging' to a crude owner rather than to a chosen lover that matter."[4]

Additionally, any accurate assignation of tragic mulatto status must extend beyond the *moment of revelation* (if any, and however long in duration) and also must not be associated with any overriding crisis, such as in Pauline Hopkins's serialized novel *Hagar's Daughter* (1901–1902), in which the mulatto Hagar leaps to her intended death from a bridge over the Potomac River during an unsuccessful escape from the slavery into which she had so recently been remanded. Hagar fails to rank as a tragic mulatto for both reasons: (1) she has still not had time to adjust to life upon learning that she is part black, and (2) she is about to be recaptured, and decides to kill both herself and her infant rather than allow that capture to take place. What Hagar believes will be her final words to her child are: "'Alas, poor innocent, there is one gift for thee yet left for your unfortunate mother to bestow,—it is death. Better so than the fate reserved for us both.'"[5] Regardless of how tragic this scene is, Hagar's words here concerning "fate" are about the life of slavery that awaits them and are not in reference to any mixed-blood psychotrauma that she has in any case not yet had time to develop. Nor does the eventual death of Hagar's daughter, Jewel, to "Roman fever," a form of malaria, render the latter a tragic mulatto.[6]

The key lies in discerning the distinction between a mulatto figure who happens to undergo tragic circumstances and a true *tragic mulatto*. An interesting example of the former case that might on a surface examination be mistaken for the latter is the character of the quadroon Honoré Grandissime, f. m. c. (free man of color), in George Washington Cable's 1880 novel, *The Grandissimes*. Honoré embodies many traits that we might associate usefully with one version of the male mulatto figure—among them his being tall, slender, handsome, and refined culturally, but also his being somewhat effeminate and languorous. Throughout the novel he pines fruitlessly for the love of his life (and also wanes ever weaker and weaker physically), a love who will never consent to be his, leading ultimately to his apparent suicide by drowning in the novel's penultimate chapter.[7]

Upon this description, one might well feel tempted to grant tragic mulatto status to Honoré until one realizes that the object of his unrequited love is another mulatto, the quadroon Palmyre Philosophe, who is herself hopelessly and also fruitlessly in love with Honoré's white half brother, also named Honoré Grandissime. But just as Honoré f. m. c. fails to merit a tragic mulatto label, so too does Palmyre, for she is in no sense conflicted racially or desirous of whiteness herself. Indeed, upon her realization that the white Honoré's heart belongs irretrievably to another woman, Palmyre engages not in psycho-emotional self-destruction but instead her entire orientation shifts single-mindedly to exacting vengeance upon the blood uncle of the white Honoré, Agricola Fusilier, for wrongs done to her in previous years. Far from the emotional weakness inherent in a true tragic mulatto, Palmyre comes rather closer to embodying the spirit of energetic hostility exemplified by the quadroon Cassy in Harriet Beecher Stowe's *Uncle Tom's Cabin*.[8]

One might also consider Samuel Smucker's quadroon character, Caroline Dudley, in *The Planter's Victim* (1855), who is whipped horribly, has her days-old infant murdered while it is in her arms, dies finally during an excruciating deathbed scene lasting a full eight pages, and is even slapped in the face by her ruthless tormentor after she is dead.[9] However, Caroline's troubles stem not from any divided-blood psychotrauma on her part, but rather from her firm rejection of the incestuous sexual advances suggested by her white half brother and owner, Richard Dudley, and from her decision instead to marry her quadroon lover and fellow slave, George Sanford. Caroline's mixed-race status is therefore relevant only in terms of the physical beauty that inflames her lecherous half brother; it does not work to make her a tragic mulatto—a very specific term that unfortunately is used far too loosely and far more frequently than it should be in assessments of mixed-race literature.[10]

We find another nontragic mulatto in the person of Aurore Besançon, the narrator-hero's love interest in Mayne Reid's 1856 novel, *The Quadroon*.[11] Despite the fact that the desire on the parts of various white men to own and debauch Aurore is owing to her fantastic beauty as a quadroon, it is nonetheless the case that the tension and anxiety surrounding her in the novel is based on the legal right of men to own her as a slave, not on her mixed ancestry. Indeed, this is evident in her most plaintive and melodramatic utterance of the novel, made to her white lover, Edouard: "'I—I—oh Heavens! what am I? A slave—a slave—whom men love only to *ruin*. O God!—why is my destiny so hard? O God!'"[12] It is her specific destiny as a slave, not her destiny as a quadroon, that Aurore here laments. In no instance does Aurore herself make any reference, either negative or positive, to her mixed-race status.

We come closer to approaching a legitimate tragic mulatto characterization with Dion Boucicault's Zoe, who in that playwright's 1859 *The Octoroon*, an adaptation of Reid's novel, is based on Aurore. Significantly, as far as the internalization of mixed-race angst is concerned, Aurore and Zoe are as far apart as might be suggested by the letters of their respective first names. In contradistinction to Aurore's very clear nontragic characterization, Zoe avers that: "I'm an unclean thing—forbidden by the laws—I'm an Octoroon!"[13] When her white lover George insists that he nevertheless "can overcome the obstacle," Zoe responds, significantly: "But *I* cannot."[14] It is critical to understand that Zoe's despair is not merely a manifestation of her unhappiness in relation to the illegality of mixed-race marriage. Rather, her anguish is far more internalized, as she compares George's love for her to his having "caught the fever," his being "stung by a snake," or his being "possessed of any other poisonous or unclean thing," and then concludes by asking rhetorically if he is "not thus afflicted now."[15]

Indeed, in the two lovers' penultimate meeting (in their final meeting Zoe commits suicide by manipulating an unsuspecting George into giving her a fatal dose of poison) she says to him: "Do not weep, George—dear George, you now see what a miserable thing I am."[16] By way of comparison to the mounting unhappiness as Boucicault's play draws to its end, the final words of Reid's novel gesture instead toward the long-term marital bliss of Aurore and Edouard via the latter's reference to "the tranquil afterlife of myself and my beautiful QUADROON," a striking contrast to Zoe's ultimate fate of suicide.[17] In Sollors's view, "Zoe is precisely the figure who has internalized her racial condition as a central problem for herself, so that she invokes, as has been variously cited, the curse of Ham, the calculus of her blood drops, and her fingernails as a racial sign in order to define herself as 'unclean.'"[18] Although there are external factors, such as Zoe's sudden and unforeseen reduction to slave status, it is her internal conflict over her racial mixture that renders her a tragic mulatto.

The same is true of the mixed-race title character in Gustave de Beaumont's 1835 novel, *Marie*, who is a "gentle angel of kindness" placed "here on earth to suffer," and whose initial response to the white man who expresses his unqualified love for her is that "'the thought of happiness is too cruel for one who can never be happy.'" [19] Unlike her brother George, who accepts his blackness with pride and dies fighting against white oppression, Marie spends most of the novel languishing in despair while apologizing continuously for the long-ago act of miscegenation in her family history that makes her black. As George puts it: "'My sister blushes at her African origin—as for me, I am proud of it.'"[20] The source of George and Marie Nelson's blackness is the revelation that their mother, Theresa, "'was, through her great-grandmother, a mulatto.'"[21] The two siblings are, then, far beyond even being octoroons in terms of the remoteness of their black ancestry.

As in the case of Zoe, Marie's unhappiness does not stem merely from the practical effects of racial prejudice; rather, she also internalizes her mixed-race anxiety by lamenting the figurative drop of blood that renders her black despite all outward appearance of whiteness. Note how, in speaking to her white lover Ludovic, she makes this internalization and her guilt over it more than plain: "'My friend,' she added in a solemn tone, 'you understand nothing of my fate on earth; because my heart can love, you believe that I am worthy of love; because my brow is white, you think that I am pure. But no; my blood contains a stain which renders me unworthy of esteem or affection. Yes! My birth condemned me to the contempt of men. Without doubt this decree of destiny is deserved. The decrees of God, though sometimes cruel, are always just.'"[22] Rejecting Ludovic's entreaties of love at first, Marie assures him that "'to join your life with that of a poor creature like me is to embrace a condition worse than death!'"[23]

Citing the prevailing race prejudice of the time—which de Beaumont excoriates throughout the novel, particularly as practiced in the North— Marie justifies anti-miscegenation and racial segregation: "'Doubt not,' she added in an inspired tone, 'that God himself separated the white from the black. This separation is found everywhere: in hospitals where humans suffer, in the churches where they pray, in the prisons where they repent, in the cemeteries where they sleep the eternal sleep. . . . Alas, my friend, our mortal remains cannot mingle in the earth; is that not a sign that our souls cannot be united in Heaven?'"[24] My interest here is not the racial segregation that Marie points out, but rather her belief that this segregation is justified by divine decree, and that, by extension, she herself bears a transgenerational guilt for the miscegenation decades and decades ago that resulted in her being brought into existence. In other words, God not only despises any future union of her and Ludovic but also the past union that marks her as still black today, this latter point being expressed in Marie's describing herself as "'cursed in my mother's womb,'" and as a "'wretched girl accursed by man and God.'"[25]

Despite these feelings, Ludovic's insistent earnestness eventually wins over Marie and her father, who consents to their marriage, which, through an unfortunate omen, is interrupted by a racist New York mob before the ceremony can be completed. The two lovers then escape to the wilderness of Saginaw, Michigan, where they hope quite fruitlessly to live in isolation and peace. But the combination of the exhausting journey and a fever brought on by the environs of Saginaw lead to Marie's demise before they can be married there. Asserting that the "'unworthiness'" of her birth would follow her to the grave, she begs Ludovic for forgiveness while on her deathbed.[26] In the midst of a fever-induced delirium during a violent thunderstorm, Marie says: "'My God, I must indeed be guilty, for now you see the wrath of the Heavens!'"[27] Following this statement, Ludovic narrates Marie's final words: "This passing gleam of reason was succeeded by a crisis yet more violent than the first; an extreme agitation overcame her senses; she uttered incoherent words, phrases broken by sighs—these words left her lips: 'Accursed race, base blood, inexorable destiny'; finally she repeated my name twice, and, though delirious, she wept. She said no more."[28] There can be no doubt that Marie Nelson, lamenting unto death her fraction of blackness and internalizing tremendous guilt because of it, is a legitimate tragic mulatto in the clearest sense of the term.

As I have been arguing, it is key to distinguish a true tragic mulatto as exemplified by Zoe or Marie from what we might call an "unhappy or unlucky mulatto," regardless of the fact that literary cases of the latter are more numerous than those of the former. Sollors is surely correct to observe that in "reading the literature on the Tragic Mulatto it is also striking to find that the text in front of us only rarely seems to fit the stereotype that it supposedly so rigidly and unchangingly and ineluctably embodies," and that "some of the literary conventions that have been labeled 'Tragic Mulatto' would seem to be more appropriately called melodramatic."[29] One might certainly argue, and there is indeed a tradition of this in literary analyses of nineteenth-century works, that the tragic mulatto trope should be expanded to include what I would instead categorize as nontragic mulattoes who happen to lead unhappy or unlucky lives. For instance, the case might be advanced that the noble whiteness inherited from his father causes the male mulatto slave to be unable to accept his bondage and to therefore rebel, leading to his ultimate demise. In the opposite case, the argument might be made that the female mulatto's racial mixture leads inevitably to her misery at the hands of lascivious white men.

Yet, while I would concede that there surely are merits to these positions, I nonetheless do not believe that such characterizations deserve inclusion under the tragic mulatto idea, principally because the aforementioned situations are not exclusive to mulattoes. One need not venture far in order to find nonmulatto blacks who refuse to accept their inferiority and their bondage, resulting ultimately in their undoing. Such characters may be seen in Richard Hildreth's Thomas, who is burned alive; in Reid's Gabriel, who is destined to lose an arm; and in Cable's Bras-Coupé, who is whipped, hamstrung, and has his ears cut off before dying—each of the aforementioned punishments having been levied for various acts of resistance to slave-owner authority.[30] These nonmulatto black literary figures resisted slavery in the absence of having white ancestry, deflating the notion that similar resistance by mulattoes is attributable in some exclusive way to their partial whiteness. Sterling Brown makes this very point in noting that "Cable, in the *Grandissimes*, shows a Creole mulatto educated beyond his means, and suffering ignominy, but he likewise shows in the character of Bras-Coupè that he does not consider intrepidity and vindictiveness the monopoly of mixed-bloods."[31]

Nor is sexual pursuit and oppression by lecherous white men exclusive to female mulattoes, as one has only to consider that these mulattoes themselves are quite possibly the daughters or granddaughters of female blacks and white men at some point. Notwithstanding the fact that many mulattoes were brought into existence in the Colonial Chesapeake through consensual relations between black men and white women, and that the rather unreflective mantra that practically all mulattoes were the result of black women being raped by white men is surely overdone, it must still be acknowledged that sexual coercion of black women by white men did occur and resulted in its share of mulatto births. None of this is to suggest that female mulatto characters were not hypersexualized specifically because of their racial mixture; but rather, that such hypersexualization and even the abuse that might stem from it does not by itself confer tragic status. My point is that one cannot make the claim that being a victim of sexual oppression is somehow exclusive to mulatto females when many of those females were themselves the result of the sexual oppression of their own black mothers and grandmothers. To be sure, I would certainly agree with Eve Raimon that there is a clear literary tradition that may be described as the "paradigmatic tale of the mixed-race female slave who falls from early innocence and privilege to sexual degradation and despair," but I would disagree with referring to that tradition by the name "tragic mulatta."[32] I would instead, for the reasons I have been elaborating, see it as a variety of mulatto characterization requiring a specific name distinct from "tragic mulatto" or "tragic mulatta" proper.

So, even though refusal to accept one's inferior status might be attributed to partial-white ancestry and even though being a victim of sexual oppression might be attributed to partial-white ancestry, they cannot be said to be exclusive to that cause. It is only divided-blood psychotrauma that can be the exclusive province of the tragic mulatto. Mulatto figures may be crafted and characterized in as many ways as black or white figures; however, any hint of drama or misfortune in the life of a mulatto character results typically, and wrongly, in the ascription of tragic mulatto status to that figure when the same would not occur with black or white characters. For example, a black figure who undergoes misfortune is not labeled automatically a "tragic black" any more than a white character who dies is labeled automatically a "tragic white." Yet the idea of the tragic mulatto is so strong that it attracts to it nontragic elements that, as I have been arguing, do not belong properly to it. I therefore insist on the more restrictive understanding of the tragic mulatto trope as having to do with internal racial conflict because on the one hand it quite frankly is simply a more accurate understanding, and on the other because of the explicit connection I am about to draw between that literary trope and sociology's marginal man myth.[33]

As we shall see presently, the transition from literature's tragic mulatto to sociology's marginal man was quite effortless conceptually, for those sociologists were inclined strongly to accept the self-serving idea that mulattoes were conflicted emotionally by a hopeless desire for whiteness. As one of these early sociologists put it, "the position of the half-caste is usually an unfortunate one. The consciousness of his superiority to the more primitive stock raises a barrier against sympathetic co-operation on that side, while on the side of the dominant race he finds no willingness to grant social equality. If he is not more depraved in morals than either of the parent races he at least has acquired the reputation of being so."[34] It is not difficult to see that these early twentieth-century, white male social scientists were operating with the same kinds of "obvious" and racist cultural grammars that had animated the "professional" work of the previous century's natural scientists.

These rising social scientists merely transferred the debility of the mulatto's supposed mismatched racial condition from the physical to the emotional, from the body to the mind. "Because the Negro was not a white man with black skin but an inherently different being driven by a distinct set of instincts and traits, a union of black and white would produce a discordant individual, an impossible individual, at war within himself and ultimately self-destructive."[35] Yet we see that this movement away from the physical was less revolutionary than it might have seemed, for "while many social scientists were gradually breaking with the traditional ideas and perceptions about race, at the same time they were often merely rephrasing or recasting them in new, more sophisticated forms," for at base—whether or not acknowledged openly by social scientists—remained the determining notion that "mulattoes were possessed by an 'innate savagery' as a result of their conception in the sinful union of the white man and Negro. How could any sort of moral sense develop in a creature born out of a 'lustful debauch'?"[36]

Whereas infertility was the overriding mulatto debility for the natural scientists of the late nineteenth century, emotional instability served that function for the social scientists of the early twentieth century. Writing in 1918 about the mulatto worldwide, Edward Reuter—one of the most important of these early sociologists, particularly in regard to race and race mixture—offered his analysis that "psychologically, the mulatto is an unstable type."[37] In Reuter's view, mulattoes "despise the lower race with a bitterness born of their degrading association with it, and which is all the more galling because it needs must be concealed. They everywhere endeavor to escape it and to conceal and forget their relationship to it. They are uncertain of their own worth; conscious of their superiority to the native, they are nowhere sure of their equality with the superior group. They envy the white, aspire to equality with them, and are embittered when the realization of such ambition is denied them. They are a dissatisfied and an unhappy group."[38]

Writing specifically about mulattoes in the US North, Reuter goes on to state that "the mulattoes are the superior men and form, or tend to form, a separate and exclusive class above the race. They assume the rôle of spokesman for the race but they are not an integral part of it as are the mulatto leaders of the South. . . . The mulattoes are rather outside the race, above it. They have not given up the hope of equality with the whites; they are not satisfied to be Negroes and to find their life and their work among the members of the race. They are contemptuous of the blacks who are socially below them and envious of the whites who are socially above them."[39]

Reuter's thinly veiled goal is for mulattoes to become the leaders of a permanent Negro underclass, which he saw as already taking place in the US South but not in the North. Reuter's analysis suggests that Northern mulattoes would be happier if they would forgo the battle for social and political equality with whites and content themselves with leading their darker Negro brethren. This is the reason Reuter lavishes what praise he does upon them, proclaiming that "the mulattoes, at all times in the history of the Negro in America, have been the superior individuals of the race."[40] These twin analyses are two sides of the same coin that would become a staple of sociology: (1) mulattoes are dissatisfied because they yearn quite "obviously" and quite naturally to be white, and (2) their only happiness lies in aligning themselves with Negroes, in relation to whom they stand as superior beings.

Finally, in a discursive maneuver that conflicts significantly with the way hybridization is viewed usually in a racist context (i.e., that the superior group is always degraded by mixture with the inferior group), Reuter argues that as a racial stock, mulattoes can be improved further by the addition of Negro blood, on the condition that it is the best Negro blood possible: "Furthermore, the mulatto group continually is being improved by the addition to it of the best blood of the Negro race. The black man of ability, in almost every case, marries into the mulatto caste; and his children, with whatever of their father's superior mentality they inherit, are mulattoes. So far as his superiority is inherited, it becomes an asset to the mulatto group. . . . The mulatto group thus, on the assumption of the transmission of superior mental capacity, tends to become not only a culturally but a biologically superior group."[41]

This radical and hypocritical departure from the normal hybridization framework—for Reuter would surely not argue that the white race is improved similarly by the addition to it of the best of the mulatto stock—illustrates the degree to which he is not at all conducting research from an objective standpoint, but rather is being driven to insupportable and predetermined conclusions by the same overarching presumptions of "obviousness" that plagued his natural scientist predecessors in the study of race and race mixture. Reuter leaves no doubt regarding his double standard here, as earlier in the very same book he warns quite specifically that to "admit the ambition of the mulattoes to be white and to accept them into the white race on terms of individual merit, means ultimately a mongrelization of the population and a cultural level somewhere between that represented by the standards of the two groups."[42]

As sociology became more sophisticated, in part through the work of scholars such as Edward Reuter, it nonetheless remained no less racist and no less overdetermined by the white man's worldviews, cultural grammars, and presumptions of obviousness. In a 1928 article analyzing the varied effects of migration on immigrants and marginal people (persons living on the margins of two distinct cultures) premier sociologist Robert Park, mentor of Edward Reuter and founder of what came to be known as the Chicago School of Sociology, notes that periods of transitional crisis may differ between the two, that in fact in the case of immigrants those periods are similar to temporary phases in the lives of most people, "but in the case of the marginal man the period of crisis is relatively permanent. The result is that he tends to become a personality type. Ordinarily the marginal man is a mixed blood, like the Mulatto in the United States or the Eurasian in Asia, but that is apparently because the man of mixed blood is one who lives in two worlds, in both of which he is more or less a stranger."[43] What I find most instructive for the present context, however, is the specific way Park chooses to define the marginal man further, listing as his characteristics "spiritual instability, intensified self-consciousness, restlessness, and *malaise*."[44] The attribute of malaise meshes with Reuter's views and will be reinforced repeatedly by Park and the sociologists who follow him, and later still by psychologists as well.

Writing just a few years later, Park is moved to continue in this vein by comparing Negroes and mulattoes, concluding essentially that unlike Negroes, mulattoes are cursed by being intelligent enough and self-aware enough to realize their hopeless predicament: "The mulatto and the mixed blood are often sensitive and self-conscious to an extraordinary degree. They do not have, on the other hand, the *insouciance* and *naïveté* which makes the Negro invariably so ingratiating and agreeable a companion. Mulattoes, also, are keenly aware of the defects of the Negro, but because their status is so intimately bound up with his, they are not able to view these defects with the same objectivity and tolerance as the white man does. One of the consequences of his more intense self-consciousness is that the mulatto lives at a higher tension than the Negro. He is more intelligent because, for one thing, he is more stimulated, and, for another, takes himself more seriously."[45] Clearly, from the perspective of the white male sociologist it can only be the presence of whiteness that brings to the mulatto this seriousness, intelligence, and tension that is so "obviously" lacking in the Negro.

But apparently it is not only the biological presence of whiteness that grants this superiority to the mulatto; it is also the presumption that a questionable physical nearness to whites confers an advantage as well. Relying on myths and falsehoods that are still prevalent today regarding the mulatto in slavery (that mulattoes were preferred as house servants, that they saw themselves as superior to Negroes, etc.), Park confers on mulattoes a kind of cultural advantage as well: "The mulatto and the mixed blood are, for the reasons I have described, the product of a double inheritance, biological and cultural, that is different from that of the black man. If the mulatto displays intellectual characteristics and personality traits superior to and different from those of the black man, it is not because of his biological inheritance merely, but rather more, I am inclined to believe, because of his more intimate association with the superior cultural group."[46] This of course ignores the reality that neither mulatto slaves nor free mulattoes (excepting perhaps in very specific locales such as New Orleans) had closer interactions and relations with whites than did Negro slaves or free Negroes.[47]

Another prominent sociologist, member of the Chicago School of Sociology and student of Robert Park, Everett Stonequist, also took up the question of the mulatto during this time period. As in the cases of Park and Reuter, Stonequist extended the malaise trope through his work. As noted by Kerry Ann Rockquemore, David Brunsma, and Daniel Delgado, "Stonequist went on to more fully explain and expand upon Park's general theory by arguing that mixed-race people's awareness of the conflict between the two races created some level of identification with both groups resulting in an internalization of the group conflict as a personal problem. . . . In the case of Black/White mixed-race people in the United States, where adjustment toward the dominant group (Whites) was impossible because of White Supremacy and segregation, the marginal man was predicted to become a leader among the subordinate group (Blacks), or alternately experience withdrawal or isolation."[48]

Prior to proceeding, it will be worth stepping back and considering for a moment just how far-reaching and influential the work of scholars such as Park, Reuter, and Stonequist was during this formative period in the development of sociology. Similar to the generations of harmful effects wrought by the racist work of Louis Agassiz in the discipline of anthropology, these leading scholars of the Chicago School of Sociology would go on either directly or indirectly to train future generations of sociologists. While these men undoubtedly were outstanding scholars in numerous ways, one cannot with any legitimacy evade the fact that their theories on mulatto mentality were an extension of essentially the same racist, white male psychoses and insecurities that have plagued black women, white women, black men, and countless others here for the past four hundred years.

So it is not at all surprising that Stonequist reprises the notion that mulattoes are naturally unstable and doomed to emotional turmoil, since from his position as a white man Stonequist cannot conceive of mulattoes as not being motivated by an "obvious" need to feel superior to Negroes: "The person of mixed blood, by his dual biological and cultural origin, is identified with each group. His awareness of the conflict situation, mild or acute, signifies that in looking at himself from the standpoint of each group he experiences the conflict as a personal problem. His ambitions run counter to his feelings of self-respect: he would prefer recognition by the dominant race, but he resents its arrogance. A sense of superiority to one race is counterbalanced by a sense of inferiority to the other race. Pride and shame, love and hate, and other contradictory sentiments, mingle uneasily in his nature. The two cultures produce a dual pattern of identification and a divided loyalty, and the attempt to maintain self-respect transforms these feelings into an ambivalent attitude."[49]

Guided by the "obvious" presumption (note the word "naturally" in the following quotation) that someone who is part white desires desperately to be all white, Stonequist says of the mulatto that "naturally his attention is turned upon himself to an excessive degree: thus increased sensitiveness, self-consciousness, and race-consciousness, and indefinable *malaise*, inferiority and various compensatory mechanisms, are common traits in the marginal person."[50] It seems clear to me that rather than belonging to the mulatto, the traits listed by Stonequist are far more appropriately applied to those white men who have been and still are so obsessed with race and with defining others they see as being different racially from themselves. Approaching the matter from this perspective places the following excerpt from Stonequist's most famous book, *The Marginal Man*, in a decidedly different light:

He is not the dejected, spiritless outcast; neither is he the inhibited conformist. He is more likely to be restless and race-conscious, aggressive and radical, ambitious and creative. The lower status to which he is assigned naturally creates discontented and rebellious feelings. From an earlier, spontaneous identification with the white man, he has, under the rebuffs of a categorical race prejudice, turned about and identified himself with the Negro race. In the process of so doing, he suffers a profound inner conflict. *After all, does not the blood of the white man flow in his veins?* Does he not share the higher culture in common with the white American? Is he not legally and morally an American citizen? And yet he finds himself condemned to a lower caste in the American system! *So the mulatto is likely to think to himself.* Living in two such social worlds, between which there is antagonism and prejudice, he experiences in himself the same conflict. In his own consciousness the play and the strife of the two group attitudes take place, and the manner in which he responds forms one of the most interesting chapters in the history of the Negro.[51]

I have suggested throughout this chapter that the assertions of Park, Reuter, and Stonequist in regard to American mulattoes do not represent the reality of the time in which they wrote, that these assertions instead are the effluvial projections of a particular class of researchers being swept along in the cascading current of their own racialist and racist biases. In addition to the points I have thus far presented, we may also avail ourselves of voices from another direction, voices that will serve to bolster my argument that the early twentieth-century sociological view of the mulatto is not in the least bit reliable, despite its enduring prominence in sociological circles even today.

Notes

1. John G. Mencke, *Mulattoes and Race Mixture: American Attitudes and Images, 1865–1918* (Ann Arbor: UMI Research Press, 1979), 62.
2. Cassandra Jackson, *Barriers Between Us: Interracial Sex in Nineteenth-Century American Literature* (Bloomington: Indiana University Press, 2004), 53.
3. Lydia M. Child, "The Quadroons," in *Fact and Fiction: A Collection of Stories* (New York: C. S. Francis, 1846).
4. Werner Sollors, *Neither Black Nor White Yet Both: Thematic Explorations of Interracial Literature* (New York: Oxford University Press, 1997), 221.
5. Pauline E. Hopkins, *Hagar's Daughter: A Story of Southern Caste Prejudice, Colored American Magazine*, 1901–1902, reprinted in *The Magazine Novels of Pauline Hopkins* (Oxford: Oxford University Press, 1988), 75.
6. Ibid., 283.
7. George W. Cable, *The Grandissimes* (1880; repr. New York: Hill and Wang, 1957), 331.
8. Harriet B. Stowe, *Uncle Tom's Cabin* (1852; repr. New York: Pocket Books, 2004).
9. [Samuel M. Smucker], *The Planter's Victim; or, Incidents of American Slavery* (Philadelphia: Wm. White Smith, 1855), 176–186.

10. I have, in a previous book, been guilty of the same error. Rainier Spencer, *Spurious Issues: Race and Multiracial Identity Politics in the United States* (Boulder: Westview, 1999), 99–101.

11. Mayne Reid, *The Quadroon; or, Adventures in the Far West* (London: J. & C. Brown and Company, 1856; repr. Rye Brook, NY: Adamant Media, 2006).

12. Ibid., 145.

13. Dion Boucicault, *The Octoroon* (1859; reprinted in *Plays by Dion Boucicault*, ed. Peter Thomson, London: Cambridge University Press, 1984), 147.

14. Ibid.

15. Ibid., 153. Zoe's analogical reference to her lover being "stung by a snake" is interesting in that a snake also figures prominently in Reid's novel. In that earlier work, Aurore's white lover, Edouard, proposes rather fancifully to bypass the legal restriction against interracial marriage by sharing Aurore's blood and thereby becoming black himself: "'I shall take this gold pin from your hair, open this beautiful blue vein in your arm, drink from it, and take the oath.'" Later in the novel, we see a fascinating reference to blood in the form of Edouard's having been bitten by a rattlesnake. Even though Reid is clearly, indeed absolutely, sympathetic to his mixed-race title character, it is somewhat conspicuous nonetheless that subsequent to Edouard's earlier declaration, Reid should then have him reflect upon the snake in terms of "the effect of its poison already in my veins," and again to make note that "the poison was fast inoculating my blood. I fancied I already felt it crawling through my veins!" Reid, *The Quadroon*, 148–149, 184, 187.

16. Boucicault, *The Octoroon*, 154. I refer here of course to the original ending of *The Octoroon*, as opposed to the later version (or, indeed, versions), in which Boucicault yielded to audience demands that Zoe not die.

17. Reid, *The Quadroon*, 444.

18. Sollors, *Neither Black Nor White Yet Both*, 222.

19. Gustave de Beaumont, *Marie; or, Slavery in the United States: A Novel of Jacksonian America*, 1835, trans. Barbara Chapman (repr. Baltimore: Johns Hopkins University Press, 1999), 50, 52.

20. Ibid., 61.

21. Ibid., 55. Upon the revelation that Theresa has black ancestry, and the subsequent ruination it brings to her husband and their family, she blames herself before dying from anguish and despondency.

22. Ibid., 66.

23. Ibid.

24. Ibid.

25. Ibid., 120, 133.

26. Ibid., 166, 167.

27. Ibid., 168.

28. Ibid.

29. Sollors, *Neither Black Nor White Yet Both*, 238, 243.

30. Richard Hildreth, *The White Slave. Another Picture of Slave Life in America* (London: George Routledge, 1852; repr. Rye Brook, NY: Adamant Media, 2006), 178; Reid, *The Quadroon*, 423; Cable, *The Grandissimes*, 191–193.

31. Sterling A. Brown, "Negro Character as Seen by White Authors," *The Journal of Negro Education* 2, no. 2 (April 1933): 194.

32. Eve A. Raimon, *The "Tragic Mulatta" Revisited: Race and Nationalism in Nineteenth-Century Antislavery Fiction* (New Brunswick: Rutgers University Press, 2004), 108.

33. Indeed, Sollors refers to the nineteenth-century literary mulatto as "the ulti-mate marginal man." Sollors, *Neither Black Nor White Yet Both*, 241. Also, some readers may be aware that de Beaumont's *Marie* was not published in English until 1958; however, I cite that novel's title character as an example of a true tragic mu-latto, not necessarily as part of the ongoing literary conversation in the United States from the mid-nineteenth–early twentieth century. Even so, we should not dismiss out of hand the possibility that some US novelists may nonetheless have known about and drawn from *Marie* long before its translation from the French.

34. Ulysses G. Weatherly, "Race and Marriage," *American Journal of Sociology* 15, no. 4 (January 1910): 444.

35. Mencke, *Mulattoes and Race Mixture*, 70.

36. Ibid., 71, 126.

37. Edward Reuter, *The Mulatto in the United States: Including a Study of the Rôle of Mixed-Blood Races Throughout the World* (Boston: Richard G. Badger, 1918; repr. New York: Negro Universities Press, 1969), 102.

38. Ibid., 103.

39. Ibid., 371.

40. Ibid., 379.

41. Ibid., 396–397.

42. Ibid., 104.

43. Robert E. Park, "Human Migration and the Marginal Man," *American Journal of Sociology* 33, no. 6 (May 1928): 893.

44. Ibid.

45. Robert E. Park, "Mentality of Racial Hybrids," *American Journal of Sociology* 36 (1930–1931): 545.

46. Ibid., 547. Excepting the overtness of his statement regarding intelligence, Parks's conclusion essentially mirrors the ideological position of the American Mul-tiracial Identity Movement today, a point I shall return to in Part 2.

47. Park does make reference in his article to those locales (Charleston, SC; Sa-vannah, GA; Mobile, AL; and New Orleans, LA) where, due to very specific and limited circumstances, some mulattoes held a different status than in the rest of British Colonial America and the United States. However, in mentioning these cities, Park refers specifically and only to mixed-blood aristocracies and to slave owners giving their mulatto children superior educations. Most notably, though, when men-tioning mulattoes being preferred as house servants or mulattoes setting themselves up as being superior to Negroes, Park does not limit himself to these particular cities. Rather, he presents these as general facts and thereby adds to one of the strongest mythical falsehoods regarding American slavery.

48. Kerry Ann Rockquemore, David L. Brunsma, and Daniel J. Delgado, "Rac-ing to Theory or Retheorizing Race? Understanding the Struggle to Build a Multira-cial Identity Theory," *Journal of Social Issues* 65, no. 1 (2009): 16–17.

49. Everett V. Stonequist, "The Problem of the Marginal Man," *American Journal of Sociology* 41, no. 1 (July 1935): 6.

50. Ibid.

51. Everett V. Stonequist, *The Marginal Man: A Study in Personality and Cul-ture Conflict* (New York: Charles Scribner's Sons, 1937; repr. New York: Russell & Russell, 1961), 24–25. Italics added.

4

Mulatto Writers on Marginality

Something that is seldom, if ever, broached when discussing the mulatto-related work of Robert Park, Edward Reuter, and Everett Stonequist, work that might be summed-up by the term *marginal man*, is whether any American mulattoes were asked for advice or otherwise given the opportunity to provide input to these three thinkers' theorizing. In other words, did Park, Reuter, and Stonequist seek to verify their marginal man thesis with any of the people they were presuming to describe, or did they simply objectify those people by not even considering that the voices of American mulattoes might possibly have value for their research? The question may strike some readers as ridiculous, but it is a perfectly legitimate query. Well-spoken, well-read, intelligent mulattoes who had opinions about blackness, whiteness, racial identity, and racial passing were certainly in abundance during the first four decades of the twentieth century, and the most famous of them, at the very least, would have been known to our trio of sociologists, who might have ventured to either contact them or read some of their writings on the very subjects they themselves were about to turn into the sociological equivalent of religious dogma. Indeed, Stonequist's own (mis)appropriation of W. E. B. Du Bois's words in *The Marginal Man* is a perfect illustration of this ready awareness.

Citing Du Bois's famous "double consciousness" formulation from *The Souls of Black Folk*, Stonequist twists Du Bois's meaning in either one of two ways: (1) by arguing that double consciousness refers only to marginal Negroes, as opposed to Negroes in general, or (2) by arguing that mulattoes (such as Du Bois himself!) actually were plagued by a triple consciousness. In fact, since in Stonequist's marginal man theory Du Bois is both a racial hybrid *and* a cultural hybrid, we might suppose that he has a quadruple consciousness. As Stonequist explains it, "the marginal Negro" sees himself from two perspectives: "from that of the white man as well as the black man. . . . He has something of a dual-personality, a 'double consciousness,' to use the words of Du Bois."[1] But this is not what Du Bois meant by double consciousness, for Du Bois clearly says that "the *Negro* is a sort of seventh son."[2] Du Bois is referring here to the Negro in general, not to the educated Negro specifically and not to the mulatto specifically (i.e., those whom Stonequist would consider to be marginal Negroes), when he writes of one ever feeling "this two-ness—an American, a Negro."[3]

So whereas Du Bois states that the Negro has double consciousness, Stonequist misreads Du Bois (whether purposely or not) in asserting that it is specifically the marginal Negro who has double consciousness. Merging the sociological notion of the "looking-glass self" with Du Bois's double consciousness, Stonequist avers that for "the marginal man it is as if he were placed simultaneously between two looking-glasses, each presenting a sharply different image of himself."[4] But if Stonequist means that the looking-glass self is equivalent to single consciousness, and that double consciousness goes one step further in its application to the marginal Negro, then he has misread Du Bois, who is clear that double consciousness relates specifically, if not exclusively, to Negroes in general. If, on the other hand, Stonequist means that the looking-glass self is itself equivalent to double consciousness, then in writing of marginal Negroes being placed "between two looking-glasses" he has to be talking about what could only be called triple consciousness, and he would therefore be contradicting his own assertion a few lines previous that the marginal Negro has a double consciousness.

Tommie Shelby makes the case that Du Bois may have been referring to a more select subset of American Negroes than I am allowing for in what would be the "conventional interpretation" of this passage of *The Souls of Black Folk*.[5] Shelby's view, based on a close reading of the entire book as opposed to only the brief passage under consideration, as well as earlier writings by Du Bois, is that "Du Bois means it to apply to only (or at least mainly) black elites, specifically to those who are educated and have had some success in the white world."[6] At the very least, then, I should acknowledge that, as Shelby puts it, there are "several plausible interpretations possible."[7] But even so, I do not believe this possibility alters by very much my specific critique of Stonequist, who on this more focused interpretation would have essentially cherry picked Du Bois's seeming concurrence with him while ignoring other significant American mulatto authors whose work I shall review directly, authors whose collective voice literally screams out in rejection of the marginal man hypothesis.

The question of interpreting Du Bois on this point aside, however, we can nevertheless gain a very clear sense of whether the Chicago School of Sociology's stance on the American mulatto was or was not an accurate one. We can do this by listening to that era's mulattoes and what they have to tell us about race, race mixture, racial passing (the last because it would represent an immediate solution to the accursed duality of mulatto identity), and any unquenchable desire for whiteness they might have been struggling with. American mulattoes of that time period speak to us even today concerning these topics in the novels they wrote, which pre-date and coincide with the appearance on the scene of sociology's marginal man. I therefore want to consider a selected, expressly targeted slice of that mulatto literature during the time period leading up to and including the formulation of the marginal man hypothesis, and to compare that literature to the pronouncements of Park, Reuter, and Stonequist on the issue in question. Examining selected, major pieces of mulatto writing from 1900 through 1929 will provide a meaningful and essential window through which to interrogate the Chicago School's marginal man thesis. And let me be clear that I use the word *interrogate* here quite self-consciously, for we too often grant to academic fields such as sociology and psychology a kind of undeserved explanatory power that, once entrenched, becomes extremely difficult to later dislodge.

It is precisely such a dislodging that I shall attempt here by raising the radical question of whether American mulattoes might have something to tell us about themselves that perhaps does not cohere with the stereotyped portrait painted by Park, Reuter, and Stonequist. In undertaking this examination, I realize that some readers might be inclined to see it as a case of fact against fiction, since I will be using creative literature to make my case against the pronouncements of sociology. However, such a criticism would be mistaken for at least two reasons: (1) it would represent an unjustified privileging of the sociological view as fact when indeed the very point of this exercise is to interrogate that particular view's accuracy in this matter, and (2) such a criticism fails to appreciate the ways that creative literature is an extraordinarily powerful window on the world and also provides an extended and expansive telling of truth. Additionally, let there be no doubt that in terms of falling prey to whimsical flights of fancy, scholarly writing is no less prone to the tendency than is literary fiction; it merely takes place in an alternate idiomatic register.

Before beginning, I want to again acknowledge that what follows is not going to in any sense be an exhaustive review of mulatto literature, not even within the relatively narrow window of years I have specified above. Readers interested in a more comprehensive review would be well advised to attend to the prodigious work of Werner Sollors.[8] Rather, I will be looking at several major narrative works by American mulatto writers, both female and male, that focus on black/white racial identity and specifically on the possibility of passing for white during the narrow temporal frame I have indicated. These writers, covering a twenty-nine-year swath of history that is immediately prior to and contemporaneous with the marginal man of sociology, are diverse enough along a number of axes to give us confidence that if there is any particular message regarding mulatto attitudes that we can discern within their writings, it will be a message deserving of our serious consideration. Alternatively, if their collective writings fail to include any particular theme, most especially a theme of marginality, we must take that into consideration as well.

What we will be looking for specifically are indications that these writers support the marginal man thesis that mulattoes are naturally torn by a desire to be white, that they live uneasily with a black identity that is forced upon them and a white identity they long for but can never achieve, that they are especially attuned to and disturbed by association with the acknowledged inferiority of the blackness that is imposed upon them, and that these internal pressures and personal stresses are psychological and natural as opposed to being situational or related to practical concerns. In other words, American mulattoes naturally despise their connection to blackness, naturally aspire to whiteness, and this is a constant, natural reality for them unless they can be convinced to accept blackness by serving as the naturally more intelligent leaders of the Negroes.

The three strongest expressions of such intense marginality would be (1) madness or suicide on the part of mulatto characters, (2) mulatto characters struggling internally with the psycho-emotional malaise that is supposed to be inherent to their personalities, and (3) mulatto characters passing for white. Madness or suicide would represent the absolute inability of the marginal individual to reconcile the alleged blood battle raging within her or his veins. It would represent the complete failure of the mulatto mind to accept the tragic status accorded to its physical body. Interestingly, I can state even before beginning that we will find neither madness nor suicide as themes in the writings we will review presently. Nor will we discern any mulatto characters grappling with internal ambivalence related to a desire for whiteness. The remaining route, the path of racial passing, will however be in great evidence during the course of our examination. But, as we shall see, all passing is not equal; indeed, some episodes of passing may be described correctly as monumental and life altering while others may with equal accuracy be conceived of as merely trivial. Some incidences of passing may be the pathological result of intense psychological trauma while others may represent a cool-headedly rational means undertaken toward a specific end. To put it more directly, passing for white because one desires desperately to be white as an end in itself and irrespective of practical concerns might in fact be an expression of marginality, but passing for other reasons would not be. What must be kept in mind is that in many cases of passing the *why* is more important than the *what*.

It will therefore be critical to discover in our selected mulatto writers' works the kinds of themes that support the Chicago School's marginality thesis, and most importantly to not confuse other, more practical themes with marginality. For instance, as I have been suggesting, mere passing for white does not by itself provide evidence of marginality. Park, Reuter, and Stonequist's marginal man thesis is very specifically about psychology and motivation; it is about an inner rejection of blackness and an inner aspiration for whiteness that transcend immediate practicalities. The marginal man thesis is not about merely reacting to the unjustness of racism. It is very specifically about an urge and a yearning for whiteness that is not based on the accomplishment of specific objectives such as securing employment or gaining entry to a segregated dining establishment.[9] There is a figurative chasm between passing for white on the one hand because one burns with an intense desire for whiteness that will not be extinguished, and on the other passing for white during the day while at work, or even permanently in order to provide a better life for one's family in a racist society. There is an absolutely fundamental distinction between desiring whiteness in and of itself and desiring the benefits and rights that accrue to white status in America.

The issue therefore is motivation. I am interested in whether major American mulatto novelists writing about mulatto themes between 1900 and 1929 present evidence of dealing and struggling with the former type of passing or the latter. If we find that these writers grappled with the former type of passing, with internal struggles over an intense personal desire for whiteness, then they can be said to support the marginal man thesis. If, however, we find that these writers grappled with passing only in terms of practical goal accomplishment, as opposed to an overarching inner motivation for whiteness, then they can be said to refute the marginal man thesis. The issue again is motivation, not eventual result. To the extent that their mulatto characters struggle with a nearly irreconcilable inner yearning for whiteness—regardless of how the struggle is resolved ultimately—they can to that extent be said to support the marginal man thesis. To the extent, however, that their mulatto characters struggle with practical decisions over the outward expression of racial identity in relation to accomplishing specific goals—regardless of how the struggle is resolved ultimately—they can to that extent be said to refute the marginal man thesis.

The crucial issue for my purposes is the *why*, not the *what*. Although I am not considering white writers in this particular investigation, even if much mixed-race fiction by white writers resolved the racial dilemma by having the mixed-race character undergo a "renunciation scene" in which whiteness is rejected for blackness (which would provide absolutely essential relief to white readers by defusing the abysmal and unacceptable threat of hidden blackness infiltrating white society successfully), such renunciation alone would not impact the point I am pursuing, for my interest is in motivation, not end results.[10] Indeed, the same can be said to be true in the numerous cases of mulatto writers having their characters go through similar "renunciation scenes" (which in those cases would support the purpose of an emergent black unity). My interest is not in the ultimate result of the passing predicament, but rather in its driving impulse. Regardless of whether the mulatto character decides ultimately to pass as white or to remain a Negro, my concern is with the motivation for passing as white. Does this motivation cohere with the marginal man thesis or is its basis found elsewhere?

The works I shall consider in undertaking this tightly circumscribed investigation are six major novels by important American mulatto authors writing about mulatto characters and themes immediately prior to and during the time that Park, Reuter, and Stonequist were developing and finalizing their marginal man theory. The novels are Charles Chesnutt's *The House Behind the Cedars* (1900), James Weldon Johnson's *The Autobiography of an Ex-Colored Man* (1912), Walter White's *Flight* (1926), Nella Larsen's *Quicksand* (1928) and *Passing* (1929), and Jessie Fauset's *Plum Bun* (1929). Altogether this review will provide us with a sense of the degree to which the marginal man thesis should be relied upon as representing the truth in regard to American mulattoes or, instead, rejected as an illegitimate objectification of those mulattoes.

The following review is not intended as an in-depth literary analysis of any of these texts, but rather as a much more modest quest for a single thematic aspect in a select grouping of mulatto literature—that thematic aspect being the motivation for movements by mulatto characters (whether consummated and maintained ultimately or not) from blackness to whiteness. Since none of our major writers saw fit to have their mulatto characters either go insane or commit suicide due to any divided-blood psychotrauma raging within their beings and tearing them apart, nor to show them struggling with their mixedness qua mixedness, we will concentrate on the theme of passing for white as a manifest expression of mixed-race marginality. In the interest of maintaining focus I shall, where possible, eschew in-depth plot synopses in favor of concentrating on the passing theme and its motivation in these works.

The earliest of our texts, Chesnutt's *The House Behind the Cedars*, presents us with two mixed-race characters who pass for white during the course of the novel, John Walden/Warwick and his younger sister Rowena (Rena) Walden/Warwick. Warwick is the surname the brother adopts (as does the sister subsequently) upon deciding to pass for white, while Rena is the sister's nickname, which she uses with both her black and white identities. To put it most plainly, John Walden passes for white and becomes John Warwick because he yearns to be a lawyer and to escape the overwhelming race-based inequalities he observes in his native North Carolina surroundings. He decides to pass for white in South Carolina, which will take him away from coming into contact with any people who know him and which also offers a friendlier state law regarding race mixture and white status.

After achieving his career dream, John returns (carefully and somewhat surreptitiously) to North Carolina to urge his sister to join him in passing as white and thereby also escaping her racially imposed destiny.

Making the case to their mixed-race mother, John works to convince her of the benefit to Rena of crossing the color line: "'With such beauty and brains,' continued Warwick, 'she could leave this town and make a place for herself. The place is already made. She has only to step into my carriage— after perhaps a little preparation—and ride up the hill which I have had to climb so painfully. It would be a great pleasure to me to see her at the top.'"[11] In thinking over his plea, John's mother muses in terms that are practical, not psychological: "The life her son had described had been to her always the ideal but unattainable life. Circumstances, some beyond her control, others for which she was herself in a measure responsible, had put it forever and inconceivably beyond her reach. It had been conquered by her son. It beckoned to her daughter. The comparison of this free and noble life with the sordid existence of those around her broke down the last barrier of opposition."[12]

In neither the case of John nor that of his sister Rena does divided-blood psychotrauma play any role at all. For John, passing is the practical means to the desired end of a professional career and a life free from racist bias. Rena likewise views passing as a means, a chance to escape: "The girl's eyes lighted up. She would not have gone if her mother had wished her to stay, but she would always have regarded this as the *lost opportunity of her life*."[13] Consideration of these practical matters leads to their mother's assenting to John's request that Rena be allowed to accompany him back to South Carolina as his white sister. The major tension in the novel revolves around Rena and her racist white lover and fiancé, George Tryon. Rena's primary concerns about passing for white are that she misses her mother and that she is being untruthful to Tryon by keeping her Negro ancestry a secret from him. Again, at no time does she go through any internal psychological trauma because she is of mixed blood.

Chesnutt, via his narrator, makes clear that John and Rena's passing is about practical means and ends, nothing else: "The taint of black blood was the unpardonable sin, from the *unmerited penalty* of which there was no escape except by concealment. If there be a dainty reader of this tale who scorns a lie, and who writes the story of his life upon his sleeve for all the world to read, let him uncurl his scornful lip and come down from the pedestal of superior morality, to which assured position and *wide opportunity* have lifted him, and put himself in the place of Rena and her brother, upon whom God had lavished his best gifts, and *from whom society would have withheld all that made these gifts valuable*. To undertake what they tried to do required great courage."[14]

Ultimately, although Rena does die a sad death, it is not a tragic mulatto death, for it is not due to any inner psychological struggle on her part or to any continued striving by her to achieve whiteness. Indeed, by this part of the novel Rena has decided to renounce whiteness forever in order to lend her services to the goal of uplifting black people. Rather, she dies as a result of being the hapless victim of a twin pursuit by both George Tryon (who, having rejected Rena previously following the surprise disclosure of her mixed-race status, now desires her regardless of race) and the lascivious mulatto Jeff Wain (Chesnutt here being even-handed enough to present his readers both with positive and negative mulatto characters).

Significantly, Chesnutt also takes the time to explode several mulatto stereotypes, racist myths that are offered by various characters in the novel but which are meant to be seen quite clearly as fallacious. For instance, the kindly white Judge Archibald Straight, who initially assists John as a youngster in preparing for his eventual life of passing, is seen, just prior to the instant he first meets John, reading a pro-slavery pamphlet that argues, among other things, for "the physical and moral degeneration of mulattoes, who combined the worst qualities of their two ancestral races."[15] Yet during Judge Straight's meeting with the young John Walden, Straight is continually drawn to the boy's complete lack of Negro features and his resemblance to his deceased white father, whom the judge knew as a friend.[16] The incongruence between what Judge Straight reads in the pamphlet and what he sees with his own eyes shows us that Chesnutt was aware of such nonsense as the mulatto physical degeneration thesis, and that he inserted such details in order to make plain their fallaciousness.

At another point in the novel, Rena's lover Tryon is shown reading a medical journal attesting to the grave danger of racial amalgamation, that the "smallest trace of negro blood would inevitably drag down the superior race to the level of the inferior."[17] Finally, Chesnutt's narrator provides a direct challenge to the moral degeneracy thesis surrounding the mulatto by remarking of John and Rena that "had they possessed the sneaking, cringing, treacherous character *traditionally* ascribed to people of mixed blood," their lives would have been smoother as a result.[18] In these ways, Chesnutt demonstrates his knowledge of past and current myths about the mulatto— physical as well as psychological/emotional—weaving them in and out of the novel in a sophisticated rejection of those myths. In this, Chesnutt shows himself to be operating at a far higher level of analysis than the sociologists who would in the coming decades hold up the latter myths as unproblematic truth.

James Weldon Johnson's *The Autobiography of an Ex-Colored Man* is a work so sophisticated, so multidimensional, so monumental, that it is with the greatest humility that I undertake even so circumscribed an analysis of it in what shall follow. Being the most well-known of the six novels I am reviewing, most readers undoubtedly are aware of the basics of Johnson's *Autobiography*, in which the famous unnamed narrator flits back and forth between racial identities before finally settling on passing over into whiteness permanently. There are a variety of themes, all of them of intense interest, having to do with Johnson's novel, but I again shall be constrained to deal only with the passing theme—and, even there, specifically with the motivation for passing.

The narrator's first mention of passing is when he passes into the black world following the shocking discovery that he is not white as he had thought: "I did indeed pass into another world. From that time I looked out through other eyes, my thoughts were coloured, my words dictated, my actions limited by one dominating, all–pervading idea which constantly increased in force and weight until I finally realized in it a great, tangible fact."[19] That dominating idea is "the dwarfing, warping, distorting influence which operates upon each and every coloured man in the United States. He is forced to take his outlook in all things, not from the viewpoint of a citizen, or a man, or even a human being, but from the viewpoint of a *coloured* man."[20] Here in the first few pages of Johnson's novel we find two extremely significant facts. First, the narrator does not undergo any divided-blood psychotrauma even though he learns in a very abrupt way that he is not white; second, after discovering that he has Negro ancestry, Johnson's narrator sees his new condition through the lens of racism and unequal treatment, which are practical as opposed to psychological concerns.[21] The primary problem Johnson's narrator faces is the problem of unequal opportunity and racist bias, not divided heritage and longing for whiteness.

In Johnson's sophisticated and complex novel his narrator passes continually throughout the text. He passes for black (indeed he passes for black in a variety of black environments, wondering at the novel's end whether he has ever "really been a Negro," or has instead been merely a "privileged spectator of their inner life"), he passes for white, and in his relationship with his white millionaire friend he may arguably be said to pass for a homosexual.[22] In Chapter 13 I shall return to the narrator's continuous passing, as well as Nella Larsen's mulatto character Helga Crane, and mulatto characters from other works, and I will consider the rejection of biological race itself via continuous passing on the one hand and using race as a kind of clothing on the other in a broader discussion of the mulatto idea in regard to deconstruction of the notion of biological race altogether.

After witnessing firsthand the horror of a Georgia lynching, the narrator decides to pass permanently for white out of shame: "Shame that I belonged to a race that could be so dealt with; and shame for my country, that it, the great example of democracy to the world, should be the only civilized, if not the only state on earth, where a human being would be burned alive."[23] The shame referred to here is in no sense a personal shame. It is not the type of shame prescribed for mulattoes by the marginal man thesis, for the narrator is not ashamed of himself; rather, he is ashamed of how his country treats the members of his race. And it is, again, the practical considerations of blackness in a racist America that result in his decision to pass permanently for white: "I argued that to forsake one's race to better one's condition was no less worthy an action than to forsake one's country for the same purpose. I finally made up my mind that I would neither disclaim the black race nor claim the white race; but that I would change my name, raise a moustache, and let the world take me for what it would; that it was not necessary for me to go about with a label of inferiority pasted across my forehead."[24]

As in the case of Chesnutt's novel, the incidences of passing in *The Autobiography of an Ex-Colored Man* are motivated by practical concerns, efforts to better one's life in a racist society, and not because of any divided-blood psychotrauma. And even the lone time the narrator admits to regretting his dual heritage, it is still for practical reasons. Prior to proposing marriage to the white woman he loves, the narrator reveals to her the secret of his Negro ancestry. Her reaction of crying and distress causes the narrator to reflect subsequently that this "was the only time in my life that I ever felt absolute regret at being coloured, that I cursed the drops of African blood in my veins and wished that I were really white."[25] Despite such language of "cursing African blood" and "wishing for whiteness," this outburst is once again clearly about a practical matter—specifically, the narrator's great desire to marry the woman he loves, and the hindrance his Negro ancestry poses to that practical goal. The narrator does not in this lone instance wish he were white due to any desire for whiteness in and of itself; rather, he obviously makes this wish because it would solve his immediate dilemma and bring him the marital happiness he desires.

Flight, written in 1926 by Walter White, who would five years later begin a nearly quarter-century of service as Executive Secretary of the National Association for the Advancement of Colored People, is a most unusual passing novel in that the main character's passing as white is not a source of direct tension in the work itself, as it is in so many other passing novels, but rather serves primarily as the vehicle for a running commentary by the author on the differences between black and white society. Although throughout roughly the final third of the novel the reader expects at any moment the appearance of some sort of incident or emergency threatening the hidden identity of the main character, Mimi Daquin, no such incident ever occurs. Instead, Mimi decides in quiet isolation to renounce whiteness and to return to her young son Jean, whom she has had to live apart from for so long, to her "own people—and happiness!" even though it is the small-minded snobbery of Negro society, particularly in Atlanta and Harlem, that in the first place sets her on the path to passing as white for the time that she does.[26]

Early on, we learn that Mimi admires Mrs. Adams, who, until having been betrayed recently by a fellow colored person, had attended the opera in Atlanta by passing as white. Mimi "felt a deep warmth within her for this woman who, because she wanted so avidly the entertainment, the touch with the world of ideas, the stimulus that came from the plays which came to Atlanta, and which her race barred her from seeing respectably, made her run the risk of discovery."[27] Here again with White, as with our other mulatto authors, we get a clear sense of passing taking place in order to achieve goals and to accomplish tasks that are not possible without racial subterfuge. Indeed, long before Mimi decides to pass, she considers it: "Here I am, she mused, a woman, a Negro. Life for me if I were white would be hard enough, but it's going to be doubly so when I have race problems added to my own difficulties as a woman. She toyed idly with the notion as to what her lot would have been if she had been born white—if she were to cross over the line and forget the Negro blood in her body."[28] But as soon as she asks this question, she resolves that even "with all its faults and petty unpleasant features, she would rather remain with her own people. They got, apparently, so much more out of the life they lived, with all its barriers, than those who had more but seemed infinitely less happy with it."[29] That a mulatto could voice such thoughts had apparently never occurred to the designers of the marginal man.

At no point in *Flight* is it suggested that Mimi or any other mulatto character harbors a desperate personal desire for whiteness. Indeed, in this novel especially, the message is clear that Mimi passes for white only reluctantly, and constantly sees throughout the novel that she has left behind the warmth and humanity of the black community for the cold and machine-like existence that is whiteness. Whites are portrayed consistently as mere parts of a giant machine, a machine that while of their own design nevertheless now controls them; or alternatively they are depicted as insects pouring out of buildings and into subway kiosks in the morning and then back again in the evening. Blacks, on the other hand, are represented as sites of warmth, humor, and the humanizing ability to avoid—thus far at least—the dominating effects of technology. In these characterizations, White rejects the descriptions of blackness and mulattoness concocted by the sociologists, and responds in turn with antiwhite stereotypes of his own.

Disappointed and heartbroken by the pettiness and snobbery she finds herself victimized by in Harlem, Mimi reveals to her aunt that she has decided to pass as white: "'I never thought I'd want to leave my own people. I wouldn't leave them now but they've driven me away—driven me to the point where I've either got to drop out of sight where I won't be hounded again or else I'll do something terrible. If that girl can pass I think I can too. My name is French, I speak French—at least well enough to fool anybody who isn't French—I can sew, and they'll never think me anything else but French. I'll see you, of course, but I'm leaving Harlem, leaving coloured people for good. I'll live my own life, make more money than I can here, I'll be able sooner to have Jean with me, and—there's no other way out.'"[30]

Mimi's act of passing is therefore in direct relation to achieving the practical goal of escaping a black society that seeks constantly to impose hypocritical moral standards upon her (the novel contains strong indictments of religious, moral, and national hypocrisies), and to make that escape into a white society where she will, because of her white appearance, not face the racial and racist barriers she otherwise would.

What is most significant here, though, is the reluctance Mimi expresses, the regret she feels at having been forced to go down this path. Most significantly, this regret does not correspond to the desperate longing for whiteness that the marginal man thesis prescribes for mulattoes such as author Walter White and character Mimi Daquin. In fact, it is not inappropriate to imagine Mimi also speaking to persons such as our sociologists, particularly in the sense of them as "those who needed an explanation" when she avers that she, "despite the shortcomings which she saw in her own people, had a loyalty to and an affection for them that was almost an obsession. She never spoke of this feeling, for she felt that to those who understood, explanations were unnecessary, while to those who needed an explanation, whatever she might say would have been obscure and difficult of understanding."[31]

Just prior to passing back into blackness at the novel's end, and considering soberly the life of ease and comfort she has finally won for herself through the act of passing as white (and which she will now relinquish), Mimi wonders "if the somber, cynical companions she met in her home and in other places were worth the price she was paying for these luxuries. People who were playing at enjoying life but whose unhappiness shone through all they did or said."[32] Mimi's decision to renounce her white identity and return to "her own people" answers this question with firmness, and gives the lie to the racist and simplistic *desires whiteness/detests blackness* psychotrauma of the marginal man hypothesis.

I want to now consider two novels by Nella Larsen, *Passing* and *Quicksand*.[33] I shall begin with *Passing* because it is, as the name suggests, a novel about passing, while *Quicksand* is not—at least not in the sense that one normally associates with passing. As mentioned in my remarks on *The Autobiography of an Ex-Colored Man*, I shall return to *Quicksand* in more detail in Chapter 13 when I take up the issue of the mulatto future in regard to undoing biological race. But here, just for a moment, I will look at Larsen's character Helga Crane in *Quicksand*, who, although she does not pass for white, nonetheless is a major mulatto character by a major American mulatto author. Furthermore, and most importantly for our investigation of the marginal man syndrome, Helga appears to suffer a variety of identity crises throughout the novel, and we will want to see whether these crises are attributable to her status as a mulatto. But first, *Passing*.

As in the case of Johnson's work, Larsen's writing is a level above the already very high bar set by the other mulatto writers we have considered in this chapter. Indeed, while all of the works by American mulatto authors that I am reviewing in this chapter offer subtle, complex, and sophisticated explorations of black/white identity and racial passing, Johnson and Larsen's novels can truly be said to, in themselves, be *passing* for novels about passing.[34] After the brief three opening pages of its first chapter, *Passing* begins quite literally with a scene of passing at the start of Chapter 2, as the novel's two main characters, the mulatto women Irene Redfield and Clare Kendry, meet unexpectedly in a double act of passing.[35] They meet in a comfortable, whites-only restaurant high above the brutally hot streets of Chicago in August. As characters, Irene and Clare at first appear to be quite opposite to each other, but as the novel progresses the reader is led to wonder just how different from the other each woman really is.

To proceed, though, and without getting too wrapped up in the novel's plot, in this instance Irene passes as white in order to gain a bit of respite from the heat and humidity of the Chicago street. Indeed, she is about to faint from the heat when she decides to take a cab to a hotel-top restaurant. And she finds there exactly what she wants and what is available only to whites: "Stepping out of the elevator that had brought her to the roof, she was led to a table just in front of a long window whose gently moving curtains suggested a cool breeze. It was, she thought, like being wafted upward on a magic carpet to another world, pleasant, quiet, and strangely remote from the sizzling one that she had left below."[36] This refreshing experience is available to Irene only by passing as white, and while it is perhaps on the trivial side it nonetheless coheres with all that we have seen thus far in terms of mulatto motivation for passing as white—the accomplishment of practical goals as opposed to resulting from some internal blood war deep within the individual's supposed racially fractured psychology.

Irene engages in this sort of situational, *comfort-based* passing on a regular basis, although as an unreliable narrator with "unseeing eyes" she constantly downplays her actions in a variety of respects.[37] On the other hand, Clare, who is Irene's long-lost childhood friend and who recognizes Irene in the restaurant, is herself passing, but in her case she long ago passed permanently over to the white side. Clare's reasons for passing as white are far more pressing than Irene's, and go back to her mysterious and somewhat tortured teenaged years. After the death of her drunkard and illegitimate mulatto father, Clare is taken in by her father's white aunts who give her a "'roof over [her] head, and food, and clothes,'" but who are also religious hypocrites with tendencies toward both racism and cruelty.[38] Apart from her own private excursions to Chicago's South Side, these aunts cut Clare off from Negro life, identifying her to the neighbors as white in the hope of keeping secret the fact that their now-deceased nephew had had an affair with a Negro girl.

Explaining to Irene her motivation for passing as white, Clare reveals her intense dissatisfaction, not with her divided heritage but rather with her material circumstances: "'I was determined to get away, to be a person and not a charity or a problem, or even a daughter of the indiscreet Ham. Then too, I wanted things. I knew I wasn't bad looking and that I could "pass." You can't know, 'Rene, how, when I used to go over to the south side, I used almost to hate all of you. You had all the things I wanted and never had had. It made me all the more determined to get them, and others. Do you, can you understand what I felt?'"[39] Similar to White's Mimi Daquin, Larsen has Clare pass as white due to the fact that she is not allowed to fit into black society. As George Hutchinson explains, Larsen "explicitly identifies [Clare's] motivation for passing, namely a desire for the sorts of things her black friends had. But in pursuit of these things she was barred within the black community by her abject background—a direct inversion of the usual convention in which the passer longs to have what whites have and blackness entails severe deprivation."[40] Yet in the end, Clare's passing is still undertaken for practical reasons, as opposed to divided-blood psychotrauma. Clare's opportunity to escape her material conditions comes when Jack Bellew, a white "'schoolboy acquaintance of some people in the neighborhood, turned up from South America with untold gold.'" Thanks to the racist fastidiousness and hypocrisy of Clare's "honest" aunts, "'there was no one to tell him that I was coloured,'" and on her eighteenth birthday Clare and Jack are married.[41]

One of many sources of tension in *Passing* is the twin relationship between Irene's interest in passing more permanently, an interest aroused by Clare, and the latter's continual pestering of Irene to serve as Clare's conduit to Harlem so that she can reconnect with Negro life. This recurring theme of the richness and warmth of Negro life, expressed with particular strength by White and Larsen, is present in the novels of Johnson and Fauset as well. But at no point does Larsen suggest that either Clare or Irene is torn apart by the bugbear of a racially divided heritage. There is emotional turmoil in great abundance, but such turmoil is not based in divided-blood psychotrauma. Indeed, even Clare's increasing desire to reconnect with Negro life and the danger that particular desire portends for her in the form of her white husband is perfectly understandable in terms of her life history, and has no connection to any marginality-based angst of internal racial division. In fact, it militates rather vigorously against the marginal man precept that mulattoes are predisposed to hate and reject their blackness

I shall offer only a few, brief comments in regard to Larsen's *Quicksand* here in this chapter, as I intend to engage in a much more detailed exegesis of that particular text in Chapter 13. What I want to highlight about *Quicksand* as it relates to the texts I have been discussing in the present chapter is that it presents a mulatto character who appears to have diffi-culty figuring out who she is. Helga Crane moves from identity to identity throughout the text—not racial identity, to be sure, but hers is nonetheless a constant and unfulfilled quest for identity that is continuous from chapter to chapter. Based on this, one might be inclined to exclaim, "Aha! We have found an early twentieth-century text by a mulatto author that supports the marginal man thesis." But such a conclusion would be premature, for none of Helga's continual searching for her place in the world has to do with her divided heritage. As I shall point out in Chapter 13, that unfulfilled search-ing is instead part of Larsen's more general critique of race and racial iden-tity, a sophisticated critique that moves us infinitely beyond the simplistic black/white dichotomy that constitutes the marginal man hypothesis. The perceptive reader of *Quicksand* is made to understand that identity itself is an illusion, that there is no correct and authentic place for anyone, as Helga fails to learn and that leads ultimately to her eternal regret.

Jessie Fauset's *Plum Bun* follows the actions of Angela Murray/Angèle Mory, the main character who passes for white throughout most of the novel. Angela's passing is motivated by two primary concerns: (1) her desire (at times immature and selfish) for wealth, security, and the good things in life, and (2) the fact that she is often taken passively for white, only to have her world upended when her colored ancestry is discovered. Refusing to "placard herself" as colored (an attitude she maintains with consistency throughout the novel), Angela is faced with this situation time and time again: "'Tell you that I was coloured! Why of course I never told you that I was coloured. Why should I?'"[42] Thinking back on these times later in the novel, she reaffirms the propriety of her decision to pass as white by recalling herself "constantly, through no fault of her own, being placed in impossible positions, eternally being accused and hounded because she had failed to placard herself."[43]

Angela's motivation for passing as white, as in the cases of our previ-ous examples, stems from the blunting of opportunity that is coextensive with blackness in a racist America. Before deciding to pass, the narrator re-flects that Angela's "present mode of living gave her little cause for com-plaint except that her racial affiliations narrowed her confines. But she was restlessly conscious of a desire for broader horizons."[44] And even more forcefully, "it seemed to Angela that all the things which she most wanted were wrapped up with white people. All the good things were theirs. Not, some coldly reasoning instinct was saying, because they were white. But because for the present they had power and the badge of that power was whiteness, very like the colours on the escutcheon of a powerful house. She possessed the badge, and unless there was someone to tell she could possess the power for which it stood."[45] Once having made the decision to leave her Philadelphia hometown and move to New York City to pass as a white woman, Angela answers her sister Virginia's query as to her sanity with the practical response that, "'No, I think I'm just beginning to come to my senses. I'm sick, sick, sick of seeing what I want dangled right before my eyes and then of having it snatched away from me and all of it through no fault of my own.'"[46]

At no point does Angela—now Angèle—evidence any psycho-emotional trauma whatsoever associated with her divided ancestry; rather, all of her movement toward passing as white has to do with it being a means to specified, practical ends that cannot be hers if she represents herself as a Negro. Although some readers might take issue with the apparent selfishness of Angèle's attitude for much of the time she is passing—"'Here I am having everything that a girl ought to have just because I had sense enough to suit my actions to my appearance'"—the salient point for my purpose here is that she nonetheless passes as white for reasons that have nothing to do with anything approaching psychological marginality.[47] Indeed, Fauset has Angèle modulate back and forth between attitudes that might be seen as selfish to those that are simply practical. For example, Angèle expresses thoughts concerning her reasons for passing as white that are quite close to those of Chesnutt's John Warwick, who would doubtless applaud Angèle's assertion that "she was free, free to taste life in all its fullness and sweetness, in all its minutest details. By exercising sufficient courage to employ the unique weapon which an accident of heredity had placed in her grasp, she was able to master life."[48]

Fauset has Angèle deal with her passing as white in sophisticated ways that illustrate that race and racial identity are far more complex than the simplistic theory formulated by the creators of the marginal man. For example, though satisfied with her decision to pass as white, Angèle nonetheless "was still conscious of living in an atmosphere of falseness, of tangled implications."[49] She also has Angèle confront an interesting and controversial dilemma in considering what it would take for her to reveal her true ancestry to the unknowing whites around her: "Would it be worthwhile to throw away the benefits of casual whiteness in America when no great issue was at stake? Would it indeed be worthwhile to forfeit them when a great issue was involved?"[50] To her credit, Angèle, at a climactic point of the novel, does indeed find it worthwhile in the latter case. Finally, in the space of a single sentence, Angèle reveals everything that is wrong with the facile, divided-blood nonsense of the marginal man thesis: "'Yet when I begin to delve into it, the matter of blood seems nothing compared with individuality, character, living.'"[51] Would that the sociologists, who were at that very same moment working to impugn the character of all American mulattoes by relegating the full diversity of their different experiences and psychologies to a simple matter of their mixed ancestry, could have been possessed of so keen an insight.

In all of these novels I have reviewed, in each case, the decision to pass as white is based on the achievement of some practical goal. In no case does the melodramatic red herring of divided-blood psychotrauma play any role whatsoever in any character's decision to pass as white, whether temporarily or permanently. In terms of the question of motivation, our American mulatto authors make it clear that the decision is usually also, in some way or other, a forced one. In this they are joined by white author Carl Van Vechten, who in his 1926 novel, *Nigger Heaven,* has one of his Negro characters indicate to his friends his intention to pass with an announcement of "'I'm going white!'" [52] He goes on to explain to his Negro friends the influence of white racism on his decision via the justification that "'they make us do it. . . . They make us. We don't want to. I don't want to, but they make us.'" [53] While some have criticized Van Vechten for sensationalizing certain more prurient aspects of Negro life, in this particular respect at least he is on target in an unimpeachable way.

It is clear that Johnson and Larsen especially, but Chesnutt, White, and Fauset, as well, simply run intellectual rings around Park, Reuter, and Stonequist in terms of presenting sophisticated explorations and evaluations of racial mixture and mixed-race identity. For the latter three it seems to be merely a matter of white superiority, black inferiority, and mulatto appreciation of those salient and "obvious" facts. Indeed, writing in 1933, Sterling Brown's straightforwardly accurate critique of Negro characterizations by white fiction writers might well also apply to the simplistic analyses of our sociologists: "It can be said, however, that all of these stereotypes are marked either by exaggeration or omissions; that they all agree in stressing the Negro's divergence from an Anglo-Saxon norm to the flattery of the latter; they could all be used, as they probably are, as justification for racial proscription." [54] Mulatto writers, however, have a far more sophisticated story to tell, as we have seen. Indeed, it now seems hardly necessary to ask which is more credible as a source of mulatto psychology—the projections of white sociologists or the narrative literature of American mulattoes?

Perhaps these major American mulatto writers did not create characters suffering from a natural, burning, internal desire for whiteness because it did not strike them as a particularly plausible or realistic plot device. Perhaps it also did not match their own lived experiences or the observations they made of the world around them. And in answer to the potential reply that these writers were trying purposely to countervail the marginal man hypothesis by aggressively crafting situations in which mulatto characters provide normative prescriptions for black identity, the fact remains that if the marginal man thesis were true, writers from Chesnutt to Fauset would have included such themes precisely in order to have their characters resolve the dilemma in favor of black identity rather than white. Merely ignoring the divided-blood psychotrauma would have done nothing to combat the marginal man idea.

The only things that would work to combat it—assuming for the sake of argument that it were true in the first place—would be (1) to show mulatto characters gripped in a psychological struggle with it but either always choosing blackness or having those who opt to pass as white suffer permanently harmful fates, or (2) to have characters mention the marginal man thesis, and then show them debating it and ridiculing it for its falseness. But because these major authors chose neither option—because they gave no voice whatsoever to the marginal man thesis, because they simply ignored it—it is safe to assume that not only did these American mulattoes not share Park, Reuter, and Stonequist's certainty that mulattoes desired above all to be white, they did not even find it a credible fictional scenario.

To the potential criticism that these mulatto writers are especially intelligent and therefore are exceptions to the marginal man thesis, the clear rejoinder is that such intelligent mulattoes would have been precisely the prime candidates for marginality in accordance with the theory's own predictions. Therefore, if the marginal man thesis were valid, the writings of these mulatto authors should exude marginality, ambivalence, dissatisfaction, frustration, inferiority, shame, malaise, and rejection of blackness. But of course, their collective writings demonstrate no such things. As but one example, White provides a clear illustration of black unity on the streets of Harlem: "*Black and brown and yellow faces* flitted by, some carefree, some careworn. Mimi sensed the essential rhythm, *the oneness of these variegated colours* and moods."[55] White presents a vision of blackness that includes all hues, hardly the thing to do if he were harboring natural feelings of intense distaste for the Negro group.

Yet the unwillingness, indeed the overt refusal, to admit this reality is what the fantasy of racial superiority does to people. Because these sociologists—Park, Reuter, and Stonequist—were wrapped up so blindly in a racist sense of white superiority, they simply could not conceive of mulattoes willingly and happily accepting hypodescent and, therefore, blackness. These sociologists' own attitudes of white supremacy caused them to suppose that it actually made more sense for mulattoes to undergo divided-blood psychotrauma than to simply accept blackness. The fact is that as a type, the marginal mulatto did not exist in reality; rather, it existed only in the minds of racist white men such as Park, Reuter, and Stonequist. The marginal man is, and always has been, a myth.

Lest I be accused here of misrepresenting the marginal man and its contribution to sociology, let us once again return to Stonequist for additional in-depth investigation of the American mulatto. Focusing once more on the ubiquitous trait of ambivalence, Stonequist offers his analysis that "possibly this ambivalence, together with nervous strain, is at the root of most if not all of the behavior which has frequently been viewed by the biologically minded in terms of 'racial disharmony,' 'the clash of blood,' 'unstable genetic constitution,' etc., when considering mixed-blood persons."[56] From this artless psychoanalysis (for I insist in the strongest possible terms upon calling it by its proper name) Stonequist goes on to muse about the "apparently irrational, moody, 'temperamental' conduct of racial hybrids," noting furthermore that "'inferiority complexes' are a common affliction."[57] Yet insofar as inferiority complexes may be said to go, Brown hits the nail squarely on the head in his comments regarding Negro characterizations by white fiction writers, comments that apply directly to Stonequist as well. As Brown puts it so very succinctly, the mulatto "stereotype is very flattering to a race which, for all its self-assurance, seems to stand in great need of flattery."[58]

How very clearly it can be seen that the marginal man fallacy originates in unabashed and uninterrogated white superiority and in the resultant "obviousness" of white desire on the part of black/white people. Brown's critique of the marginal man's literary precursors is biting, yet white sociologists of the early twentieth century would have been blind to the cynicism in Brown's analysis that in much white fiction the mulatto "is victim of a divided inheritance; he is a 'man without a race' worshipping the whites and despised by them, despising and despised by Negroes, perplexed by his struggle to unite a white intellect with black sensuousness."[59] Indeed, with their racist assurances of mulatto disharmony, irrationality, inferiority complexes, and the ever-present malaise, our sociologists might very likely also fail to see the dripping sarcasm in Brown's lament that "the fate of the octoroon girl is intensified—the whole desire of her life is to find a white lover, and then go down, accompanied by slow music, to a tragic end. Her fate is so severe that in some works disclosure of 'the single drop of midnight' in her veins makes her commit suicide."[60] They might perhaps take it instead for a somewhat extreme but nonetheless reasonable description of a particular subsample of clinical accounts.

Brown saw the manifest fallaciousness—indeed the comical ridiculousness—of the tragic mulatto/marginal man thesis, noting that merely "looking at one of its particulars—that white blood means asceticism and Negro blood means unbridled lust—will reveal how flimsy the whole structure is. It is ingenious that mathematical computation of the amount of white blood in a mulatto's veins will explain his character. And it is a widely held belief. But it is nonsense, all the same."[61] Unfortunately, the fledgling discipline of sociology did not see the obvious nonsense of the harmful theory it was helping raise to the level of unquestioned scholarly truth. Sociology professors and sociology students of the time were all too willing to dismiss the agency of American mulattoes, and to instead subsume the full variety of mulatto individuality under the subordinating and objectifying gaze of white superiority.

Indeed, the objectification impulse is so strong in Stonequist that he is unwilling to grant that mulattoes might actually have opinions of their own worth considering: "In the case of mixed bloods . . . it is a 'deficiency' primarily in the eyes of the dominant race; the group definition precedes the individual's definition of himself. The individual may or may not consciously accept this definition; it influences him none the less."[62] Despite the fact that intelligent and articulate mulattoes were an arm's length away from these researchers and their students, despite the fact that the Harlem Renaissance and its proclamations of a "New Negro" were contemporaneous with the writings of these three, and despite the fact that at least some of the American mulatto writers I reviewed above would have been known to Park, Reuter, Stonequist, their peer reviewers, and their students, the academics who churned out their various marginal man theories never saw fit to view mulattoes as sentient beings who might have something to say about themselves as opposed to being objectified by the Chicago School of Sociology. Daniel McNeil points to this objectification by noting of Robert Park that "rather than investigate the ingenuity of mixed-race actors during the jazz age, he employed what was commonly assumed to be the 'Jewish' field of psychoanalysis and diagnosed the mulatto as a 'marginal man.'"[63]

So what are we to make of the marginal man idea, essentially the tragic mulatto literary stereotype, taken so very seriously by sociology? Sollors thinks it might "be best perhaps if the Tragic Mulatto stereotype were renamed 'Warring Blood Melodrama,' in the understanding that the term be limited to texts (written by anybody) in which the racial composition of a flat, stenciled character (male or female) is expressly and deterministically made accountable for the character's psychology; in other words, if the term were limited to racist kitsch, characterized by such rhetorical features as the 'infusion' topos."[64] Continuing, Sollors offers that "perhaps the image of the 'Warring Blood Melodrama' has worked in the way in which stereotypes often do function—it has served as a mold that has been superimposed upon, and has usurped, the variety of other representations of mixed-race characters. Perhaps the 'Warring Blood Melodrama' should also be called a 'mirage' rather than an 'image' to stress its illusory nature."[65] That Sollors's words would apply just as equally to the marginal man thesis as sketched by Park, Reuter, and Stonequist, is obvious.

In this connection, notice how Brown, though writing about the ways white fiction writers stereotype the Negro, nonetheless provides an acknowledgment of both fallacious schemas of mulatto debility—scientific and sociopsychological—that I catalogued in Chapters 2 and 3. He states, "The stereotype that demands attention, however, is the notion of mulatto character, whether shown in male or female. This character works itself out with mathematical symmetry. The older theses ran: First, the mulatto inherits the vices of both races and none of the virtues; second, any achievement of a Negro is attributed to the white blood in his veins. The logic runs that even inheriting the worst from whites is sufficient for achieving among Negroes. The present theses are based upon these: The mulatto is a victim of a divided inheritance; from his white blood come his intellectual strivings, his unwillingness to be a slave; from his Negro blood come his baser emotional urges, his indolence, his savagery."[66] That the "present theses" for Brown, writing in 1933, are precisely the simplistic analyses that the marginal man sociologists were developing at the same time hardly requires pointing out.

Nor is Brown alone in questioning published portrayals of black characters. Fauset was also concerned during this time with the US publishing industry and its tendency to, in her view, publish works by white writers that provided inauthentic portrayals of black characters. This system had "created a complex of ideologies of race, in fiction and nonfiction alike, that necessitated control by black writers of portrayals of black people."[67] According to Deborah McDowell, Fauset was "skeptical about whether whites could 'write evenly on the racial situation in America.'"[68] Given the simplistic stereotypes we have seen deployed by the sociological "experts" of the time, Fauset was certainly justified in her skepticism, and might as well be addressing Park, Reuter, and Stonequist directly when she states: "'Here is an audience waiting to hear the truth about us. Let we who are better qualified to present that truth than any white writer try to do so.'"[69] It is certain that Afro-American novelist Pauline Hopkins comes far closer to that truth when she has a character, "with a scornful little laugh," state: "'I am not unhappy, and I am a mulatto. I just enjoy my life, and I don't want to die before my time comes, either.'"[70]

Brown, while bypassing for the moment the question of whether any white writers are able to provide accurate portrayals of Negro character, nonetheless offers a critique that goes to the heart of precisely what is so obviously wrong with the marginal man hypothesis by laying bare its simpleminded and racist stereotyping. In Brown's words, the "sincere, sensitive artist, willing to go beneath the clichés of popular belief to get at an underlying reality, will be wary of confining a race's entire character to a half-dozen narrow grooves. . . . such an artist is the only one worth listening to, although the rest are legion"[71] As far as nonfiction writing is concerned, we may with complete confidence place Robert Park, Edward Reuter, and Everett Stonequist squarely at the head of that cliché-ridden latter throng. Indeed, writing more than a half century before these sociologists, and, as in the case of Fauset, seemingly addressing them, Richard Hildreth has the mulatto Archy Moore renounce "that silly prejudice and foolish pride" that had caused him temporarily and mistakenly to believe himself superior to his darker compatriots.[72] Archy attests that he "no longer took sides with our oppressors by joining them in the false notion of their own natural superiority—a notion founded only in the arrogant prejudice of conceited ignorance."[73] Despite pre-dating it by decades, no better anticipation or critique of sociology's marginal man could have been made.

We have seen that of our diverse selection of American mulatto authors writing about mulatto themes prior to and during the promulgation of sociology's marginal man hypothesis, (1) none of them depict madness or suicide on the part of mulatto characters; (2) none of them depict mulatto characters struggling internally with the psycho-emotional malaise that is supposed to be inherent to their personalities; and (3) while they all depict mulatto characters passing for white, in not a single instance of such passing does the motivation have anything to do with divided-blood psychotrauma. In short, the work of the collection of major American mulatto authors I have reviewed provides absolutely no support for sociology's marginal man thesis. Instead, their collective literary output serves to reject the marginal man hypothesis and to suggest that racist fantasies of American mulattoes dreaming of whiteness are a function solely of the white imagination.

Notes

1. Everett V. Stonequist, *The Marginal Man: A Study in Personality and Culture Conflict* (New York: Charles Scribner's Sons, 1937; repr. New York: Russell & Russell, 1961), 145. In an article two years earlier, Stonequist alleges that "increased sensitiveness, self-consciousness, and race consciousness, an indefinable *malaise*, inferiority and various compensatory mechanisms" are "common traits in the marginal man," before stating that "the gifted mulatto, Dr. Du Bois, has analyzed the problem in terms of a 'double consciousness.'" Stonequist, "The Problem of the Marginal Man," *American Journal of Sociology* 41, no. 1 (July 1935): 6.

2. William E. B. Du Bois, *The Souls of Black Folk* (1903, reprinted in *Three Negro Classics*, New York: Avon, 1976), 214. Italics added.

3. Ibid., 215.

4. Stonequist, *Marginal Man*, 145.

5. Tommie Shelby, personal communication, June 25, 2009.

6. Ibid.

7. Ibid.

8. Werner Sollors, *Neither Black Nor White Yet Both: Thematic Explorations of Interracial Literature* (New York: Oxford University Press, 1997).

9. Of course, on a very broad view these kinds of things are part of the general sense of Negro inferiority gestured to by the Chicago School, but I am here distinguishing that more overall stigma from specific incidents of racism and specific reactions to such incidents.

10. William L. Andrews, foreword to *The House Behind the Cedars*, by Charles W. Chesnutt (New York: Houghton Mifflin & Co., 1900; repr. Athens, GA: University of Georgia Press, 2000), x–xi.

11. Charles W. Chesnutt, *The House Behind the Cedars* (New York: Houghton Mifflin & Co., 1900; repr. Athens, GA: University of Georgia Press, 2000), 26.

12. Ibid., 27–28.

13. Ibid., 30. Italics added.

14. Ibid., 127–128. Italics added.

15. Ibid., 164.

16. Ibid., 171.

17. Ibid., 106.

18. Ibid., 128. Italics added.

19. James W. Johnson, *The Autobiography of an Ex-Colored Man*, 1912, reprinted in *Three Negro Classics* (New York: Avon, 1976), 403.

20. Ibid.

21. He undergoes shock and bewilderment, to be sure, but not divided-blood psychotrauma.

22. Johnson, *Autobiography of an Ex-Colored Man*, 510.

23. Ibid., 497.

24. Ibid., 499.

25. Ibid., 507.

26. Walter White, *Flight* (New York: Alfred A. Knopf, 1926; repr. Baton Rouge: Louisiana State University Press, 1998), 300.

27. Ibid., 49.

28. Ibid., 125–126.

29. Ibid., 126.

30. Ibid., 207–208.

31. Ibid., 211.

32. Ibid., 295.

33. Nella Larsen, *Quicksand* and *Passing,* 1928 and 1929 (repr. New Brunswick: Rutgers University Press, 1995).

34. I am certainly not the first to have remarked on this "*passing* as (or pretending to be) a novel about passing" phenomenon in regard to the works of Johnson and Larsen, and certainly do not want to appear to be suggesting that I am.

35. One could raise the case that Irene's husband Brian is also passing in several ways throughout the novel, but I shall not pursue that angle here.

36. Larsen, *Passing*, 147.

37. Deborah E. McDowell, ed., "Introduction," in *Quicksand* and *Passing*, by Nella Larsen (New Brunswick: Rutgers University Press, 1995), xxiv.

38. Larsen, *Passing*, 159.

39. Ibid.

40. George Hutchinson, *In Search of Nella Larsen: A Biography of the Color Line* (Cambridge: Belknap Press of Harvard University Press, 2006), 300.

41. Larsen, *Passing*, 159, 160.

42. Jessie R. Fauset, *Plum Bun: A Novel Without a Moral* (New York: Frederick A. Stokes Company, 1929; repr. Boston: Beacon Press, 1990), 38.

43. Ibid., 243–244.

44. Ibid., 64.

45. Ibid., 73–74.

46. Ibid., 77.

47. Ibid., 123.

48. Ibid., 136–137.

49. Ibid., 271.

50. Ibid., 333.

51. Ibid., 354.

52. Carl Van Vechten, *Nigger Heaven* (New York: Alfred A. Knopf, 1926; repr. New York: Harper Colophon, 1971), 182.

53. Ibid., 182–183.

54. Sterling A. Brown, "Negro Character as Seen by White Authors," *The Journal of Negro Education* 2, no. 2 (April 1933): 180.

55. White, *Flight*, 186. Italics added.

56. Stonequist, *Marginal Man*, 147–148.

57. Ibid., 148.

58. Brown, "Negro Character as Seen by White Authors," 196.

59. Ibid., 195–196.

60. Ibid., 196.

61. Ibid.

62. Stonequist, *Marginal Man*, 149.

63. Daniel McNeil, *Sex and Race in the Black Atlantic: Mulatto Devils and Multiracial Messiahs* (New York: Routledge, 2010), 3.

64. Sollors, *Neither Black Nor White Yet Both*, 243.

65. Ibid.

66. Brown, "Negro Character as Seen by White Authors," 194–195.

67. Deborah E. McDowell, "Introduction," in *Plum Bun: A Novel Without a Moral*, by Jessie Redmon Fauset (New York: Frederick A. Stokes Company, 1929; repr. Boston: Beacon Press, 1990), xxix.

68. Ibid.

69. Ibid., xxix–xxx.

70. Pauline E. Hopkins, *Contending Forces: A Romance Illustrative of Negro Life North and South* (Boston: The Colored Co-operative Publishing Co., 1900; repr. New York: Oxford University Press, 1988), 152.

71. Brown, "Negro Character as Seen by White Authors," 203.

72. Richard Hildreth, *The White Slave. Another Picture of Slave Life in America* (London: George Routledge, 1852; repr. Rye Brook, NY: Adamant Media, 2006), 97.

73. Ibid.

5

Imitations of Life

I now turn to one more literary source, although not a mulatto-authored one, in order to further explore and explain the success of the marginal man hypothesis of Chapter 3 over and against the reality presented by our mulatto authors in Chapter 4. I turn to a source that had much to do with popularizing the marginal man thesis, with assisting its move out of the scholarly realm and into the popular US consciousness in a way that the earlier fiction writers criticized by Sterling Brown were unable to do. This source was and still is a phenomenon that has not only provided that important popularization but has proven to be enduring as well. I am referring of course to the most well-known tragic mulatto work of all, the famous—or infamous, depending on one's tastes—novel, *Imitation of Life* (1933) by Fannie Hurst, and its cinematic adaptations of 1934 and 1959.[1]

Fannie Hurst, while a white, female Jew and not an Afro-American, nevertheless occupies a nearly exclusive place in the US popular consciousness in regard to race mixture and especially to the notion of the tragic mulatto. This is not to suggest that many Americans today even know who Fannie Hurst is, but it is her influence, begun on paper and then translated to celluloid, that is so significant. Hurst's 1933 novel, *Imitation of Life*, neither the first nor the last literary work devoted to the mulatto, must nonetheless be seen as the single most important book dealing with the mulatto as a tragic figure *specifically from the perspective of the work's enduring impact upon the American psyche*. This is so because, when one considers together the 1934 and 1959 cinematic renditions, the book led subsequently to the preeminently influential tragic mulatto film of all time. I therefore undertake an extended analysis of it in this chapter to illustrate its important link to sociology's marginal man hypothesis.

In order to assess the tragic mulatto aspect of *Imitation of Life*—for there are other, equally important ways to interpret the work thematically, ways that do not involve race at all—we need to be conversant with four principal characters: Bea Pullman and Delilah Johnson, who as employer and housekeeper employee are white and black widows, respectively; and Jessie and Peola, their respective daughters.[2] There are a number of interesting symmetries, prominent among them being Bea and Delilah as single-mother widows, each of whom fails to mother her daughter in a proper way. Excess devotion to work in the cases of both women and the ill effects of that devotion also figure importantly, despite the vast differences between the lives of these two characters. In the novel and in the films the mulatto identity theme turns on Peola's rejection of her blackness and her at-times obsessive desire to pass permanently as white. My argument concerning *Imitation of Life* is twofold: (1) that Hurst's novel, if read closely and critically, does not support the tragic mulatto/marginal man thesis, but (2) that the two cinematic adaptations do. Furthermore, despite the fact that *Imitation of Life* was a hugely popular novel in its time, it is the two feature films that have endured in the public consciousness. Put another way, my contention is that while both cinematic versions of *Imitation of Life* are tragic mulatto stories that provided a popular conduit for the marginal man myth, the novel—while, ironically, being the basis of those films—is itself actually not.

My argument regarding the novel is driven in large part by Hurst's atrocious characterization of Delilah, who, to put it bluntly, quite simply has to be the biggest, blackest, most simple-minded, yet irritatingly endearing Mammy one could have the displeasure to imagine.[3] Although Delilah is not a mulatto, her daughter is, owing to Peola's father having been a very light-skinned Negro. Early on in the novel Delilah describes Peola to Bea as "the purfectest white nigger baby dat God ever dropped down in de lap of a black woman from Virginie. Her pap didn' leave her nothin' but some blue-white blood a-flowin' in her little veins. 'Twas de ruination of her pap, dat blue-white blood. 'Taint gonna be hern. We's black, me and mah baby, and we'd lak mighty much to come work for you."[4] Delilah's brief introduction of herself and her daughter Peola to Bea Pullman wraps up the full scope of the tension between black mother and mulatto daughter that will inform all their interactions throughout the remainder of the novel—from, as we shall at any rate see, Delilah's perspective, that is.

As I intimated above, what will surprise readers who have seen either film but who have not read the novel is the interesting fact that if we were to interrogate Hurst's novel for any signs of cause-and-effect regarding Peola's rejection of black identity and desire for white identity, as we did the cases of the mulatto authors in the previous chapter, we would not find the innate, pathological racial tension predicted by Robert Park, Edward Reuter, and Everett Stonequist. Rather, we would discover—despite Delilah's semaphoric revelations of her late husband's disaffection with blackness potentially being inherited by his daughter—some very concrete and practical reasons for Peola's increasing desire to pass as white.[5] For example, from their earliest existence in the Pullman home, her mother sends Peola a clear message that both she and Delilah come second in every way to their white counterparts. Delilah herself grovels continuously throughout the novel and, in every comparison, places Bea's daughter Jessie a step ahead of Peola.

Even in the case where Peola's first teeth are coming in before Jessie's—indeed, Peola already has had two teeth coming in for weeks—Delilah jumps to make an excited though false report to Bea: "'Honey-chile, your young un gonna sprout a tooth! Two weeks younger dan mah 'onery one, and sproutin' fust!'"[6] This sort of second placement of Peola is utterly consistent for Delilah: "In every matter of precedence, including teeth, was the priority of Bea's child most punctiliously observed. The duet of their howling might bring her running intuitively to her own, but the switch was without hesitancy to the white child, every labor or service adhering rigidly to that order."[7] Furthermore, Hurst is clear that this is not to be taken as any sort of clownish but nonetheless subversive act by Delilah, who works sincerely to put Bea and Jessie first in every possible way, regardless of the negative effect it might have on her own daughter or indeed on herself as well. Any question in this regard is certainly laid to rest by Delilah's death scene, in which, having succumbed to the ultimately fatal effects of having hidden her own serious medical condition from Bea, "Delilah, lifting herself out of a hypodermic-induced sleep, began suddenly to pour hot kisses against the bare ankles of Bea, who stood by. In that act she died."[8] Clearly, this scene speaks volumes more than the few words actually comprising it on the physical page.

Beyond the obvious negative effects upon Peola of permanent second-class status in the Pullman household, we could also consider the consequence of the extreme class differentials that are placed before the growing child for comparison. On one side is Delilah, her mother to be sure, but also acting so often more like a mother to Jessie. This maternal disconnect is responsible at least in part for Peola taking on the speech and manners of the home's white occupants as opposed to those of Delilah, which is also no surprise since Delilah gives Peola constant object lessons that whiteness is to be valued far more than blackness. Over time, it would become clearer and clearer to Peola that her mother's speech, mannerisms, and superstitions were of a low-class variety and were not to be emulated: "From her very infancy, Peola, quick as any child to ape, was nevertheless careful to avoid replica of her parent's diction."[9] Moreover, such an attitude on the part of Peola could only be reinforced by Delilah's overt preference for taking care of the needs of her employer's child over those of her own offspring.

Absolutely crucial for a proper understanding of *Imitation of Life* is the fact that Hurst provides a double narrative in regard to Peola's movement away from blackness and toward whiteness; however, one of these narratives is stated explicitly but is unreliable, while the other narrative is there to be seen but is not commented on or acknowledged in any explicit way by the novel's characters. In other words, even though Delilah prophesizes (indeed, if anything it is a self-fulfilling prophecy) that Peola is foreordained to have racial identity problems, the fact is that Delilah's actions themselves are by far the most persuasive rationale for Peola's desires. For instance, prior to Hurst showing Peola actually exhibiting any specific evidence of a racial identity problem, she makes Delilah give the following explanation for Peola's resentment of Jessie, a resentment that, as I have explained, is perfectly understandable purely in terms of her own mother's respective treatment of the two children: "'Shall I tell you what's eatin' out her little heart? Sure as her pap's in de arms of a forgivin' Lawd. It's a curse on her already, lak it was on him. Mah baby hates to be black.'"[10]

To be sure, it is not long before Peola begins manifesting a number of strange behaviors, including among them those involving violent self-destructiveness: "Peola had undergone severe scalp operation, the result of a hot iron simultaneously cutting and burning her as she was secretly trying to iron out an imaginary kink in her straight black hair."[11] Here Hurst presents us with the child undergoing unintended self-mutilation in a futile effort (given that her hair was already straight) to look more white. To appreciate the seriousness of Peola's actions here, one might consider that the modern equivalent of this incident would be the anorexic person believing that she was not thin enough already and then taking self-destructive action to rectify that perceived shortcoming. Clearly, Hurst is impressing upon us that Peola is undergoing some extreme emotional and behavioral challenges, yet despite the fact that Delilah's words point continually toward the "blue-white blood a-flowin' in her little veins" as the cause of this distress, the evidence of the narrative itself points to a far more mundane (i.e., Delilah) source of Peola's problems.

The twisted nature of the parental relationships in *Imitation of Life*, relationships that prove very harmful to Peola and less so to Jessie, can be seen in the following unreliable observation made by Bea: "'I'm away from home so much. Must seem terribly preoccupied by outside worries. Why, Delilah is a better mother to her Peola than I am to mine!'"[12] Yet both women are poor mothers to their own children, for Bea's statement is given the lie a mere two pages later, when she muses that "it was for Delilah, however, that she [Jessie] reserved an almost demonstrative adoration; Delilah, who in turn paid her the perfect tribute of reciprocal devotion by emulating in Peola, as far as her sense of propriety dared, Jessie's clothes, hair-dress, and color schemes."[13] How might we then expect Peola to feel, seeing Jessie favor Delilah over her own mother, and most especially to then see Delilah return that affection, going so far as to turn Peola literally into a replicated human doll of the preferred Jessie?

When one considers the whole of *Imitation of Life*, Peola actually occupies very little of the text, however, those situations in which Peola is featured figure as moments of tremendous crisis and rupture of the narrative. Two crises in particular serve this function, and both occur when Peola is still a small child. The first takes place after Peola is called a "nigger" by Jessie, both children still being of preschool age at this time. Peola's reaction is to respond very understandably: "'I won't be a nigger! I won't be a nigger!'"[14] Interestingly, some of the language Delilah employs in the attempt to comfort her daughter is quite reasonable, and despite Delilah's ever-readiness to wax prophetic over Peola's mixed heritage (which she does in this scene as well), the following key words of hers point not to divided-blood psychotrauma but instead to precisely the same sort of racism to which the characters of our mulatto authors in Chapter 4 were forced to react: "'It ain't de bein' black, honey—it's bein' black in a white world you got to get your little hurtburn quiet about.'"[15] But Delilah's words are to no effect as little Peola literally falls apart in a convulsion directly before Delilah and Bea's eyes:

> "I won't be black! I won't be nig——"
> Off the small lips, which shuddered the word like a defective coupon out of a machine, spun foam.
> "Delilah—the little thing—she's fainted!"
> She had. Quite stiffly and into a pallor that made her whiter than chalk.[16]

A similar, but far more explosive crisis takes place after the revelation of Peola's having passed passively for white for more than two years at the public school she attends, "unsuspected of what she chose not to reveal."[17] Delilah, hurrying to school during an unexpected rainstorm in order bring Peola her "galoshes and mackintosh," ends up revealing Peola's blackness unwittingly to her unsuspecting teacher and classmates.[18] Delilah's reaction to Peola's passing harks back more comfortably to her typical characterization in the novel: "'Lawd help her and Lawd help me to save her sinning little soul.'"[19] Describing, surely accurately, the revelation of little ten-year-old Peola's two-year secret as a "thunderbolt which had smashed a small universe to smithereens," Hurst provides for her readers a scene that deserves to be experienced in its entirety:[20]

> Facing Delilah in the center of the kitchen, her dark lips edged in a pale little lightening of jade green, was fury let loose sufficient to blast the small body that contained it.
> Low-pitched fury, grating along on a voice that was not a child's voice.
> "Bad mean old thing. Bad mean old devil. They didn't know. They treated me like white. I won't ever go back. Bad mean old devil. I hate you!"

"O Lawd! O Lawd! Saw a brown spider webbin' downward this morning. And know'd mah chile was comin' home brown—O Lawd!"

"Go away—you! Yoo—yoo—yoooooo!"

The words out of Peola's fury became shrill intonations of the impotence of her rage, and finally with her two small frenzied fists she was beating against the bulwark of the body in the rain-glossed rubber cape, beating and beating, until her breath gave out and she fell shuddering and shivering to the kitchen floor.

"May de Lawd," said Delilah, stooping to pick her up as you would a plank, the black chinies of her eyes sliding up until they disappeared under her lids, something strangely supplicating in the blind and milk-white balls—, "may de Lawd Jehovah, who loves us black and white alike, show mah baby de light, an' help me forgit mah heart at dis minute lies inside me lak a ole broke teacup."

"Oh, my poor Delilah!"

"Poor Delilah ain't no matter, Miss Honey-Bea. It's poor Peola."

They wrapped her in warm cloths, with memory of methods used in a previous attack similar to this, and chafed her long, slim, carved-looking hands, and, despite dissuading from Bea, there was a smelling muslin bag, with a rabbit foot attached, that Delilah kept waving before the small quivering nostrils.

"Dar's shameweed in dat bag, and asfidity. Shame, mah baby. Lift de curse from mah baby. Lawd, git de white horses drove out of her blood. Kill de curse-shame de curse her light-colored pap lef' for his baby. Chase it, rabbit's foot. Chase de wild white horses trampin' on mah chile's happiness. Chase 'em, shameweed. Chase 'em, rabbit's foot."

"Delilah, that's terrible! That's wild!"

"It's de white horses dat's wild, a-swimmin' in de blood of mah chile. Drive 'em out, Lawd. Drive 'em out, shameweed. If only I had a bit of snail water——"[21]

Needless to say, when a physician is called to examine the convulsed child, his verdict to Bea that, "'You have a highly nervous little organism here to deal with, madam,'" is a tremendous understatement.[22] The above scene is not only intense but also is nearly pornographic in terms of the emotional violence experienced by ten-year-old Peola, regardless of the source of that violence. Defenders of the marginal man hypothesis would doubtless argue that Hurst has here given us an example (if perhaps extreme) of precisely what the theory states. But as I have been pointing out throughout this discussion of *Imitation of Life*, such a conclusion is unwarranted since every bit of Peola's rejection of blackness in favor of whiteness can be laid at Delilah's feet squarely and exclusively.

It is imperative to see the double narrative employed by Hurst as regards the racial-identity theme involving Peola, and to understand that the louder narrative is also the unreliable narrative. Despite Delilah's flamboyant declarations concerning white horses swimming in Peola's blood, it is she who has given Peola every reason for wanting to be white. Consider an incident that takes place prior to either of the aforementioned crises, an incident in which the youngsters Jessie and Peola are observed by Delilah stick-ing pins into the loose folds of skin on the wrists of Jessie's partially para-lyzed grandfather. When Bea returns home from her day of working and is informed of the incident, she at first asks Jessie in a gentle way why she would do such a cruel thing to her grandfather. The situation escalates quickly out of hand, however, when Jessie, pressing close to Delilah for protection, is unrepentant, and Peola, pitifully, tries herself to apologize to Bea. The brief interaction here is nonetheless so very instructive in regard to my thesis concerning whether or not the novel *Imitation of Life* is a tragic mulatto story that it is worth a few moments of close scrutiny.

In the wake of Jessie's open defiance of her mother, Peola says, "'I'm sorry, Miss Bea, even if Jessie won't be.'"[23] To this, Delilah responds al-most comically if not for its damaging implications, "'Peola, will you stop bein' sorry before Jessie is sorry? Ain't you got no way of keepin' yourself in your place?'"[24] Upon an admission by Jessie that she indeed was the one who had initiated the pin sticking, Delilah then says to Jessie, "'Well, you don't need to go cuttin' off your own haid before your own maw.'"[25] One again wonders how Peola would interpret such a remark coming from her own mother, who is seen here going out of her way to place Jessie, the ad-mitted ringleader of this particular cruel incident, on a pedestal when, just previous to Jessie's admission of guilt, Delilah herself had assured Bea, "'No one can put mah chile up to a meanness she ain't thought of fust.'"[26] After Bea instructs Delilah to "'keep out of this,'" and after yet another act of insubordination by Jessie, Peola then says rather pathetically to Bea, "'I sticked pins, Miss Missy,'" whereupon Bea tells Peola to "'hush,'" and con-tinues her unfruitful interrogation of Jessie.[27]

Even though Delilah suggests that she is trying to prepare Peola for racial injustice by saying to Bea that "'taint no use mah chile tryin' to get herself raised on de idea all men is equal,'" if this is truly Delilah's goal, the means she employs to achieve that goal are not only counterproductive but downright cruel.[28] Moreover, it is clear that we are once again faced with unreliable utterances, for all of Delilah's irritating and embarrassing grovel-ing is performed quite obviously for the sake of pure obsequiousness in and of itself and not to teach Peola any particularly useful life lessons. When the now-wealthy Bea asks Delilah what she might do for her financially in ac-knowledgment of Delilah's dedicated service over the years, Delilah's re-sponse is: "'You know what I wants most, honey-chile. Something dat money cain't buy. I wants to drown dem white horses plungin' in mah baby's blood.'"[29] Yet in giving this response she is quite obviously blinded by her own prophesying, for against absolutely everything Delilah has done personally to drive her daughter away from blackness there is not one shred of textual evidence for the suggestion that Peola's mixed heritage has itself anything to do with her racial identity crisis. Beyond even the unreliable narrative, though, is the sheer, unrealistic nature of Delilah's words. Brown, remarking on this line in Hurst's novel, asks rhetorically: "Can one reader be forgiven, if during such passages, there runs into his mind something unmistakably like a wild horse laugh?"[30] We may also rest certain that Jessie Fauset would not have considered the words put in Delilah's mouth by Hurst as representing the truth about Afro-Americans (see Chapter 4).

Near the novel's conclusion, a now-mature Peola, who had moved to a distant city, returns home unexpectedly and announces to Delilah and Bea that she has been passing as white in that city for four years, that she is going to marry a white man who does not know of her racial ancestry, and that they are going to move to Bolivia where her future husband has found work as an engineer. Striking precisely the same note as our mulatto authors, Hurst has Peola gesture toward racism as the impetus for her decision to pass permanently as white: "'There's nothing wrong in passing. The wrong is the world that makes it necessary.'"[31] Any of the mulatto main characters we discussed in Chapter 4 might well have uttered those very same words.

Continuing, Peola lets her mother know that Delilah has not been the only one suffering emotional turmoil: "'You at least can cry. I can't. You've got tears left. I haven't. I've cried myself dry. Cried myself out with self-loathing and self-pity and self-consciousness.'"[32] I cite this last sentence precisely because those who support either the marginal man hypothesis or those who would argue that Hurst's novel is a tragic mulatto story would highlight Peola's words: "self-loathing and self-pity and self-consciousness." However, Peola is not referring to these feelings in the sense that Stonequist, for instance, uses them in attempting to define mulatto personality. Rather than a commentary on divided-blood psychotrauma, Peola's use of these terms is specifically in relation to her struggles with the decision to pass as white. But the key, as I have argued, is motivation. Peola's struggles stem from two discrete causes: (1) the disaffection for blackness that she has been taught (howsoever unwittingly) by her mother, and (2) her understanding that she cannot have the things she wants if she identifies herself as black.

Peola's "self-loathing and self-pity and self-consciousness" are a result of having to make the very difficult choice to pass permanently as white and, as such, are not related in any way to the tragic mulatto trope or the marginal man thesis. Let me be quite explicit here, as some readers may find it difficult to move past Peola's words themselves, and fall subsequently into too facile an analysis of them. If Peola were having these feelings as a result of a natural, internal psychological struggle over her mixed heritage, then the marginal man theory might apply. But it is crucial to see that it is the emotional scarring left by Delilah's poor mothering combined with Peola's desire to avoid racism that are motivating her decision to pass, not any internal blood war within Peola herself. Peola's mixed heritage it-self is relevant only (1) in the sense that she is light enough physically to pass as white, and (2) by way of Delilah's constant and unreliable assertions that her child is doomed to racial-identity unhappiness. But Hurst never shows Peola going through any psychotrauma from the specific cause cited over and over again by Delilah, as every one of Delilah's hysterical pro-nouncements regarding white horses swimming in Peola's blood is a false narrative.

Peola is more than clear that her motivation for passing permanently as white is the unfairness of the racist US society in which she lives, and her fear of having to face that racism: "'But as things go in this world, I have been a good girl, morally or whatever you want to call it. I've worked. I've studied. I've tried to make the best of myself. And all the time with the terri-ble odds against me of knowing I could never get anywhere I wanted to get!'"[33] She challenges Bea to empathize with her situation by asking her directly: "'What do you know about the blight of not having the courage to face life in a black world? You've succeeded in a world that matters to you! Give me that same chance.'"[34] Whether one agrees with Peola's conclusion or gives weight to the strength of her fears, it is nevertheless clear that the greatest motivation for her decision to pass as white is racism. These are mature, rational, and reasonable thoughts coming from a young woman who has suffered tremendous emotional scarring throughout her early life.

In this pivotal scene, one is struck by the stark contrast between Peola and her lucid levelheadedness on one hand, and Delilah's disturbing disinte-gration on the other. Having by this point lost any of the humorous homeli-ness one might have granted them earlier in the book, Delilah's words now serve only to illustrate that she is plunging further and further into uncon-trolled irrationality: "'Lord Gawd Almighty, it ain't mah chile talkin'—it's de horse in her neighin' out through her blood.'"[35] Responding to Peola's cogent statements regarding the circumscribed opportunities for a black woman in a racist America, Delilah utters a pronouncement that would be suited perfectly to the ravings of any number of white Southern politicians a quarter century into the future: "'No, no, no! Gawd don't want His rivers to mix!'"[36] Continuing her descent into absurdity, Delilah offers the harrowing pronouncement that "'Black wimmin who pass, pass into damnation,'" backing up this verdict with the equally stunning declaration that "'Dat's de law-of-de-Lawd talk.'"[37] As Delilah continues to unravel, she also initiates a backward unthreading of the entire fabric of her unreliable "white horses swimming in the blood" narrative.

Preparing to bring to a close Peola's part in the novel, and taking into account the atavistic superstitions of the day, Hurst has Peola relate that she has had herself sterilized against the possible later appearance of a dark child, but that she is nonetheless "'not ashamed. There are millions to populate the world besides me. There is no shame in being sterilized in the name of the happiness of another.'"[38] Peola's levelheadedness is matched by the self-condemnation she feels at not possessing the courage to face life as a black woman in a racist world, and by the heartbreak and grief she is causing her mother to now endure, assuring Delilah that, "'I'm not worth your tears. I'm not worth a single one of them. I'm as vile in my own mind as I must be in yours.'"[39] Pleading with Delilah and Bea to promise never to recognize her should they happen to meet her in the future, and with Delilah agreeing and fainting thereupon from grief, Peola takes her leave of the novel as the narrative's mixed-race theme concludes.[40]

While one important plot line is the theme of mixed-race identity, Fannie Hurst's *Imitation of Life* is not a tragic mulatto story. In regard to its mulatto theme, Hurst's novel rests squarely in that genre of passing novels also occupied by the works of Charles Chesnutt, James Johnson, Walter White, Nella Larsen, and Jessie Fauset. As in the case of Johnson's narrator, Peola embraces rather than renounces whiteness at the novel's end. In that most important aspect by which I have been assessing these works—motivation—Hurst's *Imitation of Life* concurs with the novels by our mulatto authors in that racism is what impels the mulatto character to decide to pass permanently as white, even though in some cases that decision is reversed ultimately. And also as in the novels reviewed in the previous chapter, we do not find the divided-blood psychotrauma predicted by the marginal man hypothesis playing any role in Hurst's mulatto character's decisions. Despite Delilah's constant histrionics concerning the curse of "blue-white blood," we have seen that in Hurst's double-narrative Delilah's words are inert.

How likely is it, though, that most readers of *Imitation of Life* read it properly and understood the unreliable narrative to be a false one? The reality is that Hurst's novel was indeed taken as a tragic mulatto story, Delilah's words were taken to represent prophetic truth, and Peola's desire for whiteness was seen as resulting wholly from internal anxiety over her mixed racial ancestry. Significantly, Brown, in reviewing the feature film (which, as we shall see, is a tragic mulatto story) that soon followed the novel's publication and acknowledging that there are plot differences, nevertheless writes that, "the characterization and ideas, however, are little changed."[41] In other words, Hurst's *Imitation of Life*, while not a tragic mulatto story, was nonetheless taken to be one. Thus, when I state that the novel is not a tragic mulatto tale I am referring to the reality that close reading and close analysis of it reveals it to be a passing novel rather than a tragic mulatto tale, which of course is not the conclusion the general US populace derived from its collective reading. In regard to Brown, I believe that his response to Hurst's novel is very much wrapped up in the latter's horrendous characterization of Delilah, and that his negative reaction to that characterization causes him to accept the unreliable tragic mulatto narrative as given.

Perhaps ironically, Hurst's novel is not the story that most Americans who are familiar with the title *Imitation of Life* know. Even though it was a huge bestseller and spawned two equally popular cinematic adaptations, the novel itself eventually went out of print for many years, taking with it a large portion of Hurst's connection to the US popular consciousness. Although Hurst was once a tremendously popular author, as were a number of women writers in the first half of the twentieth century who were forgotten in subsequent years, she has not been rediscovered or rehabilitated as have many of those other women authors. Instead, her current legacy is the sad and frankly undeserved fact that of those Americans who are familiar with either of the two film versions of *Imitation of Life*, some might possibly also be aware, however vaguely, that someone named Fannie Hurst wrote the novel upon which said films are based. It is to a consideration of those screen adaptations and their significance to the marginal man thesis that I now turn.

As I have indicated, *Imitation of Life* was so enormously popular a novel that it was adapted as a feature film the very next year, 1934.[42] While the basic story is the same, there are differences of a very significant nature in the film's mulatto theme.[43] These differences, while arguably subtle, and doubtless executed by director John Stahl at least in part in order to translate Hurst's lengthy written work to the screen, are nonetheless monumental in terms of the film's treatment of racial mixture. For our purposes here in assessing the film's mulatto theme, the differences serve to alter completely Hurst's interpretation of the Peola character. To put it simply, Stahl's film excises entirely every facet of Delilah's unequal treatment of Peola vis-à-vis Jessie. Stahl's Delilah remains irritatingly naïve, simple minded, and obsequious, but gone are any indications that she places Jessie before Peola, and with them the resultant resentment Peola feels toward Jessie. The effect of this excision is nothing less than a fundamental shift in the film's exploration of mixed-race identity as compared to the novel's. It simply is not the same story; indeed, the film's mixed-race subplot is a story that stands diametrically opposed to Hurst's.

All of the novel's many tortured references to Peola's pap and to the white horses plunging through both her and her father's veins are dispensed with via Delilah's response to Bea's having complimented Peola as a "lovely little girl," with "Yes'm. She's very light; her pappy was a very, very light colored man." This particular bit of dialogue even sounds rushed in the film. And in contrast to Hurst's Delilah referring constantly to Peola as ornery and troublesome, Delilah boasts to Bea that "Peola's a pretty nice brought-up child. She ain't been dragged-up like most of 'em is." While Delilah does later say rather famously (or infamously) of Jessie that "she am an angel," it is in response specifically to Bea's loving and motherly musing that the sleeping child looks like one, and—most significantly—is in no way a comparison to Peola, who is not present in the scene. Additionally, the young children Peola and Jessie are shown as very close friends in the film, and while they are obviously friends in the book as well there is the matter of Peola's resentment of Jessie, which the film omits completely. Delilah even agrees with Bea's observation that "Peola is smarter than Jessie," which Hurst's fawning Delilah would under no circumstances have done, were the observation true or not.

It is important to understand that I do not bring up these differences merely to show that the film deviates from the novel in a variety of trivial details. Rather, I point out these differences specifically because they remove what in the novel are Peola's perfectly understandable motivations for resenting Jessie's being given preference by Delilah, for rejecting blackness, and for desiring whiteness.

As in the novel, the film's first incident of racial crisis occurs when Jessie refers to Peola by a specific term, but whereas in the novel the term is "nigger," in the film it is "black." Interestingly, except for the particular word in question, the film rather faithfully follows the text in this scene, but it is the change in words that makes all the difference. Indeed, it is strange for the film to follow the text so closely since not only does "black" not carry the extreme pejorative connotation that "nigger" does, but Peola is indeed black, a fact that all of the main characters including Peola are well aware of. Instead of declaring "I won't be a nigger," Peola insists "I won't be black," a change of immense proportion, for it short circuits completely the development of Peola's problems that is laid out so carefully in the novel. For the child to state, out of the blue as it were, that she won't be black is simply puzzling to observe.[44] One therefore views this segment of the film wondering what all the fuss is, and I believe that at the very least Afro-American audiences would have had the same reaction to this in 1934 that I have in the present era.

Whereas the reader of Hurst's novel has access to the history of Peola's second-class status, administered and enforced by her own mother, and to the evolution of Peola's rejection of blackness, of which the "nigger" incident was merely one link in that developmental chain, the viewer of Stahl's film simply sees a light-skinned Negro child reject blackness out of hand with no explanation at all, leaving the viewer to conclude that this must be some sort of natural event, a conclusion that is only reinforced by Delilah's reaction of soothing Peola and telling her that she has to learn to deal with it just as in the novel's "nigger" incident.

What Stahl has done here is to set up an equivalence between being a nigger and being black, such that the latter term is to be every bit as despised and rejected as the former. In other words, he has taken a scene from a written text in which there is a violent and perfectly reasonable reaction by a child to having been called a nigger, and then transferred that scene to film completely intact but having changed the offending term from "nigger" to "black." Absent any of the background material of the novel, white audiences of the 1934 film *learned* thereby that a light-skinned Negro child simply and quite naturally rejects blackness and prefers whiteness, a premise that such audiences would likely have found to be every bit as sensible as it was comforting.

To ensure that this point is not missed, Stahl's very next scene is the dreaded rainstorm incident in which Delilah comes to Peola's classroom and "smashes the child's small universe to smithereens" by revealing that the passively passing Peola is actually black. Except for "rubbers and umbrella" taking the place of "galoshes and mackintosh," this scene is faithful to the text, but it hardly matters because Stahl has already perverted Hurst's careful development of Peola's problems, and diverted them from the effects of neglect and jealousy into the natural result of divided-blood psychotrauma. Here Stahl also provides another mention of Peola's father with Delilah's comment when Bea tells Peola to not feel angry about what has happened. Of the following words uttered in response by Delilah, note especially the ones I have italicized: "She *can't help herself* just now, Miss Bea. It's like her pappy was. He beat his fists against life all his days. Just eat him through and through."

What has happened is that while Hurst gives her readers a double narrative, one reliable and one unreliable, Stahl on the other hand gives his viewers only one. However, in the absence of the novel's accounts of Delilah's poor mothering and her harmful preference for Jessie over her own daughter, it is the unreliable narrative that is the only one given, and it is therefore taken by viewers of the film to be the truth.

Peola's next appearance in the film is as a young woman who exhibits unhappiness, anger, frustration, and, yes, malaise, telling Delilah, "I want to be white, like I look." Gesturing toward a mirror, she asks rhetorically: "Look at me. Am I not white? Isn't that a white girl there?" It is a stunning scene, with Peola and Delilah each having essentially the same hair style, and when both women turn toward the mirror, with the camera showing the right sides of their faces, they are eerily similar from the neck up with the one exception of the great difference in their respective skin colors. In true tragic mulatto fashion, the scene ends with Peola leaving the room lamenting, "O, what is there for me anyway?" I do consider it necessary to state here that nothing in my criticism of this scene or of the following scenes featuring Delilah's now mature daughter is meant to in any way detract from the American mulatto Fredi Washington's dignified portrayal of Peola. Indeed, it is Washington's strong performance alone that prevents her role from sinking into what would otherwise have been pure ridiculousness. Additionally, I would advance the same clarification in regard to Louise Beavers's Delilah. Each of these women was forced by the racism of 1930s

Hollywood to play roles that degraded Afro-American women, and it is important to maintain the necessary separation between the women themselves and the roles they embody in this film.

Deviating again from Hurst's text, Stahl has Peola agree reluctantly to attend a Negro college in the South, as Delilah puts it, "one of them high-toned colleges, where only the high-toned goes," only to leave abruptly without returning home or informing anyone of her whereabouts. Bea and Delilah travel by train to Virginia to find Peola passing as white and working as a cashier in a restaurant. Echoing the earlier rainstorm incident, Delilah again reveals her daughter's blackness, despite Peola's refusal to recognize her mother by insisting that "she must be crazy," and effectively ends her newfound job. After this Peola returns home, only to inform Delilah and Bea that she is leaving for good and that they must never recognize her should they chance to meet in the future. She apologizes for her actions in having denied her mother at the restaurant, and then explains that although she has tried to follow Delilah's wishes, she simply cannot remain black. The critical difference here between the novel and the film is that at no time in this scene does Peola mention racism as her motivation for wanting to pass permanently as white. Hurst's novel uses racism as the motivation for passing, and just as with our mulatto authors Hurst uses the mulatto's light-skinned looks as the means to escape that racism. Stahl's film, on the other hand, eschews any mention of racism, and simply portrays Peola as someone who cannot bear being black, no matter what. For Stahl, passing as white is an end in itself, rather than being a means to an end.

Whereas Hurst's Peola challenges Bea by suggesting that she does not "know about the blight of not having the courage to face life in a black world," Stahl's Peola tells Bea that, "You don't know what it is to look white and be black; you don't know." And in one of the most melodramatic lines of the film, Peola, her voice choking with emotion, says: "I can't go on this way any longer." In her final words before leaving, Peola answers Bea's question of how she can make her mother suffer this way, by echoing Delilah's earlier statement about Peola's father, saying (note again my italics), "I'm sorry Miss Bea, but I *can't help it.*" The viewer therefore sees Peola as impelled by a force she cannot control—a natural, internal desire for whiteness that drives her as far as to hurt her own mother. This is different completely from Hurst's Peola, who decides to pass as white because she desires the happiness (importantly, a nonmaterial happiness since she is leaving a situation of immense wealth) that is not available to her as a black woman. It is critical to see that Stahl's Peola wants most of all to have her racial identity match her looks. The Peola of the novel, on the other hand, is concerned about a deeper issue, as illustrated by her words in the equivalent scene: "'I've worked. I've studied. I've tried to make the best of myself. And all the time with the terrible odds against me of knowing I could never get anywhere I wanted to get!'" Hurst's characterization of the mulatto therefore aligns with the characterizations of Chesnutt, Johnson, White, Larsen, and Fauset, while Stahl's represents the essence of the marginal man hypothesis. The two could not be further apart.

Of the many important deviations introduced by Stahl, one of the most crucial is Peola's complicity in the death of her mother. In Stahl's film Delilah dies quite directly of a broken heart soon after Peola's departure, resting on her deathbed and calling out sadly for her daughter, one piece in a dramaturgical sequence of melodrama heaped upon melodrama as the film draws to a close. Essentially, Peola kills Delilah as a result of her selfish desire to be white, a fact reinforced by Peola's exclamation as she is pulled gently away from Delilah's casket: "Miss Bea, I killed my own mother." In Hurst's novel, of course, despite the grief Delilah experiences over Peola's leaving she nevertheless does not die of that heartbreak; rather, she dies of complications from an internal growth she has hidden foolishly and fatally from Bea, who by this time is one of the wealthiest women in the world, and who, given the time to act, could have mustered with no difficulty whatsoever the best medical care possible for her old and dear friend.

The melodramatic, climaxing funeral scene is, as it also is in the 1959 version, by far one of the most remembered in the film. The only significant way the film is not true to the novel in this scene is—as I began describing in the previous paragraph—the critical appearance of Peola, who arrives as Delilah's casket is being borne from the church, too late to even witness her mother's funeral service. Of course, Peola is not present in the novel's funeral scene because she has cut her ties with Delilah, Bea, and Jessie permanently and will soon be in Bolivia with her white husband if they are not already there. Importantly, Hurst does not bring a repentant Peola back, nor does she have Peola renounce whiteness and attend a Negro college, all of which Stahl does. The film's Peola agrees to return to school, and, combined with her remorse over being responsible for her mother's death, we must assume that she has now given up on passing as white as well. Stahl's film thus coheres with the marginal man hypothesis in the sense that it resolves Peola's divided-blood psychotrauma by having her accept blackness. We may note as well the importance in this respect of Peola attending college, particularly a Negro college, which would correspond with her becoming a mulatto leader among Negroes.

Mirroring the novel's success, Stahl's *Imitation of Life* was also hugely popular and was nominated for an Academy Award. I am more interested in the film's relevance to popularizing the marginal man thesis, however. While the architects of the marginal man theory worked in scholarly isolation from the literary and cinematic artists Hurst and Stahl, it is important to notice the way these streams of thought interconnected in the mid-1930s, even if that interconnection went perhaps unnoticed by the parties in question. Of course, as I have noted already in Chapter 3, the tragic mulatto stereotype—as distinguished from the mulatto characters in the passing novels we reviewed in Chapter 4—is an old fixture in US literature. White authors long ago created mulatto characters they envisioned as desiring nothing so much as to possess the whiteness that could never—ultimately, tragically—be theirs. These characters, as noted by Brown, served whites' need to flatter themselves by imagining that partial-white persons were in a state of desperation to achieve full whiteness. This is true even if one acknowledges the fact that many white authors of tragic mulatto literature were abolitionists seeking to inspire sympathy and antislavery action in their white readers. Our mulatto authors and (my reading of) Hurst as well reject the tragic mulatto literary stereotype by providing practical reasons for their mulatto characters' decisions to pass as white, whether permanently or not.

By the early twentieth century, the stereotypical tragic mulatto was becoming less popular in the literary realm, which we might attribute to a number of important reasons, the most primary, of course, being the demise of and growing temporal distance from legalized slavery in the United States. While white authors continued to write "plantation" novels, there was nonetheless and of necessity a reduction in the specific tension that slavery brought along with it. To be sure, the sudden freedom of four million Afro-Americans conjured up other sources of terror for whites, most particularly the now-free and revenge-seeking black male sexual predator. One can see this displacement of danger in the racist novels of Thomas Dixon, for instance, who in his most important works focuses less on the surreptitious threat posed by light-skinned mulattoes infiltrating white society than on the fear of social equality leading to the direct menace of free black men of whatever hue having sexual intercourse with white women, whether by rape or by legal marriage.

While it is undoubtedly more complicated in terms of details, I nevertheless want to advance a chronology in which the tragic mulatto figure was losing literary relevance just as the dawn of sociology as a scholarly discipline was beginning to invoke the marginal man, perhaps as a result of the resonance of those earlier novels and their tragic mulatto stereotypes. Since sociology was an academic discipline, however, its marginal man hypothesis was less likely to enter the broader US consciousness without the assistance of some sort of popular conveyance. In other words, even while the rising marginal man was in essence the fading tragic mulatto, they existed in different idioms of thought.

Consider then the impact of two critical occurrences—the publication of *Imitation of Life* in 1933 and the production of its cinematic adaptation a year later in 1934. My contention is that the novel, if readers failed to notice Hurst's double narrative, and most especially the film, gave a popular boost to sociology's marginal man thesis, which would itself reach a sort of scholarly zenith with the publication only a few years later, in 1937, of Everett Stonequist's magnum opus, *The Marginal Man*.[45] Hurst's novel (if read incorrectly) and Stahl's film would have brought back to popular consciousness the previously fading tragic mulatto figure and would have resuscitated and modernized the stereotype of the black/white person who was desperate to be all white at the very same time that the scholarly world was accepting sociology's marginal man theory as something along the lines of scientific truth. I therefore place added significance on the following words from Brown's review of Stahl's film: "It requires no searching analysis to see in *Imitation of Life* the old stereotype of the contented Mammy, and the tragic mulatto, and the ancient ideas about the mixture of the races."[46] Brown goes on to describe Stahl's Peola as "the tragic octoroon, familiar to novels more than to life."[47] My contention is that we therefore have both literary/cinematic and sociological justifications for the tragic mulatto/marginal man coming onto the American scene at essentially the same time. The fading myth was thus reborn with a vengeance.

And if there was any danger that the passage of time would cause the newly resuscitated myth to fade, that danger was pushed side at least temporarily by Douglas Sirk's 1959 readaptation of *Imitation of Life*.[48] Sirk's effort is far less elegant visually than Stahl's, but while it does contain some important differences that I shall highlight, it is essentially the same film as far as the tragic mulatto theme goes. Because I have already devoted a good bit of space to analyzing Hurst's novel and Stahl's film, I will focus my comments regarding Sirk's film on only those that deal with significant differences or that are otherwise of singular importance. For instance, we may begin by noting that several crucial scenes are essentially the same in both films. These would include the rainstorm incident in which the mulatto child is revealed by her mother to be passing passively at school, the black mother causing the mulatto daughter to lose a job at which she is passing as white, the deathbed scene in which the black mother is dying of a broken heart, and the funeral/casket scene in which the now-repentant mulatto daughter arrives only in time to see her mother's casket being loaded into a hearse.[49]

We need as well to note that the 1959 film uses different names for the principal characters. Bea Pullman is now Lora Meredith, Delilah Johnson is Annie Johnson, Jessie Pullman is Susie Meredith, and Peola Johnson is Sarah Jane Johnson. When Lora and Annie meet initially, Lora assumes that Sarah Jane is white and that Annie is her caretaker. This gives Annie the opening to mention the child's absent father, saying, "It surprises most people. Sarah Jane favors her daddy. He was practically white. He left before she was born." Having thus established early on that Sarah Jane is a white-appearing Negro, the tragic mulatto issue raises its head a mere nine minutes into the film when Sarah Jane refuses the present of a black doll from Susie and instead takes Susie's white doll. When Annie gives the white doll back to Susie, Sarah Jane complains, "I don't want the black one." From the very beginning, then, viewers are meant to understand that Sarah Jane, at only eight years old, is a very disturbed little girl with serious identity problems.

As Sarah Jane prepares to enter the room in Lora's apartment that she and her mother are to occupy, Sirk complicates the tragic mulatto theme somewhat by having Sarah Jane articulate what could be an indirect reference to racism, saying, "I don't wanna have to live in the back. Why do we always have to live in the back?" Dramatically, perhaps over-dramatically, Sarah Jane drops the black doll on the floor outside the room as she enters. Given that the time period of the film is at the very beginning of the still-nascent civil rights era (after the Brown Supreme Court decision, after the Montgomery Bus Boycott, after the Little Rock Nine crisis, but before the student sit-ins, before the freedom rides, and before Albany and the other larger-scale campaigns of the Civil Rights Movement), we might expect a reference to racism, if that is indeed what it is. Nonetheless, it complicates the tragic mulatto theme potentially by, as in the case of Hurst's novel, providing a possible reason for Sarah Jane's rejection of blackness. In this sense, Sirk's film might possibly be closer to Hurst's novel than to Stahl's adaptation.

I point this out because the matter of motivation is how I have, in this and the previous chapter, been assessing the passing theme as it relates to the marginality thesis. Through the reliable one of her two narratives, Hurst establishes early on and clearly, despite Delilah's histrionics about "white horses" and "blue-white blood," that Peola has external reasons for rejecting blackness. It appears that Sirk as well, via the child's comment about always having to live in the back, establishes at least the potentiality of such a reason for Sarah Jane, especially when combined with the facts that at the beginning of the film Annie and Sarah Jane are homeless, and that Annie mentions Sarah Jane not having many friends to play with. One might then be able to take these circumstantial pieces of evidence and construct a reasonable background storyline in which Sarah Jane has been given reasons to understand, not just that she and her mother suffer from antiblack racism, but that in being mistaken passively for white she is herself able, if only temporarily, to escape that racism. Having once established this as a motivation, the subsequent crises over the child's rejection of blackness, desire for whiteness, and passing may possibly be attributed to that particular cause; whereas without this initial motivation those crises may only be ascribed to divided-blood psychotrauma. In contrast, Stahl's 1934 version does not provide even the potentiality of such external reasons, instead presenting the traditional tragic mulatto message that mixed-race identity crisis is internal and natural.

However, we should not be overly hasty in granting that Sirk has abandoned completely the older myth, for there is far more evidence that divided-blood psychotrauma is in fact the driving motivation for Sarah Jane's behavior. Explaining why she wants to continue living with Lora as her maid for only room and board, Annie says to her: "Miss Lora, we just come from a place where . . . where my color . . . deviled my baby." Moreover, in an extremely intense performance, having much more on-screen time and far more dialogue than her 1934 counterpart, Karin Dicker as the child Sarah Jane moves the film back in the other direction. Following the rainstorm incident, she defends her having passed in school by stating forcefully, "But I am white. I'm as white as Susie." As the scene ends, Annie laments to Lora, "How do you explain to your child she was born to be hurt?," a question that resonates with either the racism motivation or the tragic mulatto motivation. Above all, though, it is the intensity of Dicker that gives her performance such a strong sense of internal struggle as opposed to the child dealing with the problem of racism alone.

Fifty-nine years earlier, Charles Chesnutt has young John Walden say naïvely but accurately to Judge Straight: "A negro is black; I am white, and not black," but Walden's statement, while carrying the identical logical force, does not possess nearly the same pathos of young Sarah Jane's.[50] And it is not merely that Sarah Jane speaks audibly in a motion picture while John Walden speaks to us from a printed page; there is a disturbing sadness and uncomfortableness to having a child being distressed so extraordinarily by something she cannot change, at least not legitimately. Indeed, in this respect one might imagine Sarah Jane's anguish as coming rather close to the violent reaction of Hurst's Peola when she faints convulsively following the "nigger" and "rainstorm" incidents.

Additionally, and again a reflection on Dicker's intense performance, the young Sarah Jane closes a discussion of Jesus's race—a discussion that she initiates—by stating with deep conviction: "he was like me, white." It is important to note here that while the mulatto children in the three iterations of *Imitation of Life* all state that they do not want to be black and that it is their black mother who makes each of them black, it is only Sirk's Sarah Jane (both the child and, as we shall see directly, the woman as well) who claims overtly to be white in this way, which is a significant departure. Indeed, it is clear that in this scene Sirk intends for his audience to see Sarah Jane as very disturbed, tragically so, her obsession with whiteness nearly delusional; and it is Dicker's intensity as the child Sarah Jane that makes it possible for Sirk's mature Sarah Jane to exhibit a similar insistent desire for whiteness that is much stronger and far more insatiable than that of her counterparts in either the novel or the earlier film. In situating Sirk's film, then, although there may be an argument to be made that it provides circumstantial evidence of racism as a possible motivation for young Sarah Jane's disaffection with blackness, the child's performance itself suggests instead an innate and unappeasable desire for whiteness that transcends practical considerations, although such considerations may serve to make that desire even stronger.

This is true even though there is a similar gesture toward racism later in the film involving the now mature Sarah Jane. When Susie asks Sarah Jane if her secret boyfriend is a "colored boy," Sarah Jane takes offense, saying, "Well, he's white; and if he ever finds out about me . . . I'll kill myself." When Susie interjects, "But why?," Sarah Jane explains: "Because I'm white too; and if I have to be colored then I want to die. I want to have a chance in life. I don't want to have to come through back doors, or feel lower than other people, or apologize for my mother's color. She can't help her color . . . but I can . . . and I will." I would argue that despite the interjection of racism here, Sarah Jane's manic obsession with whiteness is still the primary motivation, with the racism serving as an additional reason for rejecting blackness. This is because Sirk's Sarah Jane and her reactions are overplayed and exaggerated, which is seen quite easily if we think back to Hurst's Peola or even to Stahl's. Indeed, if we go back to Chapter 4 and consider Jessie Fauset's Angela Murray, and how she undertakes to pass as white and become Angèle Mory because her plans are crushed constantly by white racist responses to her black ancestry, it is clear that the unquenchable desire of Sirk's Sarah Jane for whiteness—her lifelong and life-animating idée fixe—represents not an appropriate reaction to racism but, rather, an overreaction to racism and consequently is sensible only as a result of divided-blood psychotrauma. The 1959 version of *Imitation of Life* must, therefore, be seen as residing in the tragic mulatto tradition rather than in the passing genre.

There are a number of interesting subthemes in Sirk's film that differ from the novel and from the 1934 film, but they do not impact my assessment of the film's status as a tragic mulatto story. Such subthemes would include the more overt bond between Annie and Susie that Sirk revives from the novel and even extends to Annie and the mature Susie, a strong, fictive mother/daughter relationship that Hurst did not continue between Delilah and the mature Jessie. Also, one might point to the explicit sexualization of white and Jewish Susan Kohner's mature Sarah Jane (who, like Karin Dicker as the child Sarah Jane, also has a more substantial role than in the earlier film) vis-à-vis either of the mature Peolas. This, of course, is understandably in keeping with the more liberal sexual mores of 1959 versus those of the early 1930s.

However, although not germane directly to my purposes in this chapter, the overt hypersexuality of the mature Sarah Jane in terms of her physical presence in the film, in terms of her being involved clandestinely with a white boyfriend (who later beats her quite viciously upon discovering her secret), and in terms of her subsequent occupation as an exotic dancer, harks back to the mulatto, most especially the female mulatto, as representing the physical embodiment of illicit sexuality.[51] Finally, unlike Stahl's film, Sirk's is truer to the novel by having Annie suffer from mysterious spells commencing halfway through the film and by having her appear weaker and weaker physically as the film progresses. Thus, in the scene in which the mulatto daughter informs her black mother that she has decided to pass permanently as white, although Sarah Jane's request that Annie not recognize her "if by accident" they "should ever pass on the street" is heartbreaking to her mother, it cannot, as in Stahl's film, be seen as the sole cause of her mother's death.

As in the case of the earlier version, Sirk's directorial effort also resulted in a very successful motion picture, and Americans today who know of *Imitation of Life* are perhaps more likely to be familiar with the 1959 film than with its earlier counterpart. Regardless, most people certainly consider either or both of the cinematic iterations of the *Imitation of Life* franchise as purely and simply tragic mulatto fare. We have seen, however, that the original work, Hurst's novel (if read closely), most certainly was not. Unlike the way that Stahl's film gave a popular boost to the marginal man thesis, though, the same cannot be said of the latter film. Given that by 1959 the Civil Rights Movement had already had a significant impact on the national consciousness and was beginning to gather increasing momentum, a serious work depicting a Negro character desiring to be white would have found the going much more difficult as the movement continued to progress into and beyond Albany, Birmingham, and Selma, to say nothing of the ensuing radicalization of the Student Nonviolent Coordinating Committee and the consequent rise of the Black Power Movement.

Robert Penn Warren's slightly earlier 1955 novel, *Band of Angels*, with its mixed-race central figure, Amantha Starr, supports this analysis. Amantha's racial mixedness, while integral to the narrative, nonetheless is never the source of any internal division or psychotrauma on her part, as her fundamental motivation throughout the novel is to find her own path to personal, emotional, and psychological freedom despite the changing conditions of her life.[52] And even while acknowledging the excessive melodrama of Raoul Walsh's subsequent cinematic adaptation of Warren's novel, the 1957 film *Band of Angels* is no more a tragic mulatto tale than is the novel on which it is based.[53] In this context, then, Sirk's *Imitation of Life* must be seen as representing a closing of the door to serious, popular portrayals of either genre—passing or tragic mulatto—that had the sort of societal impact on the American scene of the *Imitation of Life* trilogy, for instance.[54] This is not to say that Sirk's film did not do a certain amount of mixed-race work, though. The 1959 film certainly reminded Americans of the tragic mulatto myth and, in an important way, did extend and keep that myth alive to a degree, but its impact could not possibly be as significant to its time as the 1934 film's was to that earlier era. In the view of Samira Kawash, "the end of legal segregation and the transformation in racial politics of the 1960s made the theme of passing irrelevant. Passing disappeared from popular racial discourse and representations. By the 1970s, discussions of passing were by and large confined to literary studies of passing fiction."[55]

Although I have devoted a significant bit of space to discussing *Imitation of Life* in its various incarnations, I want to bring that discussion to a close by recalling that my purpose in analyzing it at all is to place it in the context of our mulatto authors on one hand, and the marginal man hypothesis on the other. Despite the fact that Hurst's very popular novel was not actually a tragic mulatto story, it nonetheless was accepted as one and then spawned two equally popular film versions that further embedded the tragic mulatto myth even deeper into the US consciousness, with the 1934 film especially working to popularize sociology's developing marginal man thesis. Unfortunately, American mulatto authors, writing extensively and sensitively on mulatto themes, were ignored when it came to accurate representations of the mulatto. They wrote their own novels, to be sure, but what they had to say in those novels was ignored by white authors, by white filmmakers, and by white social scientists, all of whom preferred a counterfeit representation of the mulatto whose characterizations were designed to flatter whites rather than to illustrate truth.

Thus, and most crucially, it is not that the marginal man thesis was at one time true but that American mulattoes changed over time and grew out of it eventually. No; it must be said with the utmost conviction and with the utmost volume that the marginal man thesis has *never* been true, that it has always been a marginal man myth, and that regardless of the other achievements of Robert Park, Edward Reuter, and Everett Stonequist, it has always and only been based on the racism and the self-projecting flattery of white males.

Notes

1. Fannie Hurst, *Imitation of Life* (New York: Harper, 1933; repr. Durham, NC: Duke University Press, 2004); *Imitation of Life*, produced by Carl Laemmle, directed by John M. Stahl, 111 min. (Universal Studios, 1934), DVD; *Imitation of Life*, produced by Ross Hunter, directed by Douglas Sirk, 125 min. (Universal Studios, 1959), DVD.

2. The 1934 film uses the same names as the novel for the primary characters, while the 1959 film does not. I will give those names when I discuss the latter film.

3. The idea that some of Delilah's attributes may be based on a stereotype of Jewish mothers is interesting, but even if true we are nonetheless still left with the

Delilah Johnson of the text. Daniel Itzkovitz, "Introduction," in *Imitation of Life,* by Fannie Hurst (New York: Harper, 1933; repr. Durham, NC: Duke University Press, 2004), xi.

4. Hurst, *Imitation of Life,* 75–76.

5. One might argue that Peola's father is an example of sociology's marginal man, but since all we have of him are remembrances from Delilah, we cannot determine whether or not a diagnosis of marginality is justifiable in his case. For instance, the words of his that come to us filtered via Delilah may have been the result of any number of experiences and motivations that we, as readers, do not have access to.

6. Hurst, *Imitation of Life,* 82.

7. Ibid., 83.

8. Ibid., 267.

9. Ibid., 98.

10. Ibid., 120.

11. Ibid., 144.

12. Ibid., 173.

13. Ibid., 175.

14. Ibid., 149.

15. Ibid., 150.

16. Ibid.

17. Ibid., 184.

18. Ibid., 185.

19. Ibid.

20. Ibid.

21. Ibid., 185–187.

22. Ibid., 187.

23. Ibid., 100.

24. Ibid.

25. Ibid.

26. Ibid.

27. Ibid., 101.

28. Ibid., 100.

29. Ibid., 216.

30. Sterling A. Brown, "Imitation of Life: Once a Pancake," *Opportunity: Journal of Negro Life* 13 (March 1935): 87.

31. Hurst, *Imitation of Life,* 244.

32. Ibid., 245.

33. Ibid.

34. Ibid., 245–246.

35. Ibid., 245.

36. Ibid., 246.

37. Ibid., 247.

38. Ibid.

39. Ibid., 249.

40. Some words are in order regarding the matter of Delilah's prophecies. Some readers will no doubt point out that several times in the text Delilah forecasts a disastrous end for a young, World War I soldier, Allen Matterhorn, whom she and Bea had nursed back to health from influenza during their early years together, a soldier who after the war goes on to study engineering. Peola refers to her future husband as A. M., and by other aspects of her description of him it is obvious that he is in fact

the same soldier. Given this, some will argue that Delilah was correct that Peola's decision to pass permanently as white would lead to her ruin, and that therefore Hurst's novel is in this sense a tragic mulatto story with Peola playing the role of Brown's stereotypical "octoroon girl." I would reject such an analysis, however, based on the contention that while not every one of Delilah's prophecies is proven wrong, this preeminently important one cannot in fact obtain without it thereby invalidating her very claim to prophecy. Indeed, we may go all the way back to Delilah's introduction of Peola to Bea, when she says that a mixed-race heritage was "de ruination of her pap, dat blue-white blood. Taint gonna be hern. We's black." This is actually the most important of Delilah's prophecies in the novel, and it provides a fascinating philosophical problem. If Delilah is truly a reliable prophet, then regardless of what Peola does or how she chooses to identify, her "blue-white blood" is not going to be her ruination, for Delilah has prophesied that it will not be ("Taint gonna be hern."). Yet this surely conflicts with the final scene involving Peola, in which Delilah pleads with her not to pass as white because it will lead to her "damnation" based on "de law-of-de-Lawd." Although Delilah then embarks on a frantic program of charity giving in order to herself atone for Peola's having passed permanently as white, one is left to wonder just how reliable a prophet Hurst actually intends Delilah to be. This, again, corresponds to the nature of the novel's double-narrative, as, with Delilah especially, it is critical to not accept what is said unless one has determined that the words in question in fact cohere with events that do actually take place within the framework of the novel's events. Finally, the novel concludes with no mention of any misfortune befalling Allen Matterhorn, and as I am unaware of any actual historical event pertaining to Bolivia in 1933 or a few years prior that resulted in a guarantee of danger to American engineers, we are therefore forced into the conclusion that Delilah is simply wrong.

41. Brown, "Imitation of Life," 87.

42. *Imitation of Life,* produced by Carl Laemmle, directed by John M. Stahl.

43. I will admit to having myself failed to distinguish in a proper way the novel from the films in an earlier work, suggesting, erroneously, that Hurst's characterization of Peola was in fact a representation of the tragic mulatto trope. I have rectified that error here. Rainier Spencer, *Spurious Issues: Race and Multiracial Identity Politics in the United States* (Boulder: Westview, 1999), 99.

44. Although Peola does declare once that she won't be black in the corresponding scene in the novel, it is in the context of her stating that she won't be a nigger. In Stahl's film, the only declaration made is that she won't be black.

45. Everett V. Stonequist, *The Marginal Man: A Study in Personality and Culture Conflict* (New York: Charles Scribner's Sons, 1937; repr. New York: Russell & Russell, 1961).

46. Brown, "Imitation of Life," 88.

47. Ibid.

48. *Imitation of Life,* produced by Ross Hunter, directed by Douglas Sirk.

49. Interestingly, the incident in which the white child calls the mulatto child either "nigger" or "black" is omitted from Sirk's film.

50. Charles W. Chesnutt, *The House Behind the Cedars* (New York: Houghton Mifflin & Co., 1900; repr. Athens, GA: University of Georgia Press, 2000), 170.

51. Sarah Jane's employment as a chorus girl at a Hollywood club named the Moulin Rouge carries obvious overtones of old New Orleans with its fancy girls, quadroon balls, and concubinage arrangements. I also want to be clear here that in no sense am I suggesting that Fredi Washington's Peola lacks sexuality. Indeed, her mere walking across the frame exudes sexual energy. Rather, my point is that Susan

Kohner's Sarah Jane is intended to be an overtly sexual being, and Sirk makes sure his audience is well aware of this intention.

52. Robert P. Warren, *Band of Angels* (Baton Rouge: Louisiana State University Press, 1994).

53. *Band of Angels,* produced by Warner Brothers, Directed by Raoul Walsh, 128 min. (Warner Brothers, 1957), DVD.

54. I do not intend to imply that no passing works, or even that no important passing works, have been introduced since 1959. One might list the following recent works as important examples of such, for instance: Philip Roth, *The Human Stain: A Novel* (New York: Vintage, 2001); Danzy Senna, *Caucasia: A Novel* (New York: Riverhead, 1999); Colson Whitehead, *The Intuitionist: A Novel* (New York: Anchor, 2000). My point is that these later works, while significant, nonetheless did not have the same general societal impact as the previous works I have addressed.

55. Samira Kawash, *Dislocating the Color Line: Identity, Hybridity, and Singularity in African-American Literature* (Stanford: Stanford University Press, 1997), 126.

6

Rejecting a
Shared Past

What Part 1 of this book has thus far shown us is that based on notions developed by perpetually insecure and inconsistent white men—most especially the early sociologists—those deleterious and fallacious attributes of the mulatto, sketched initially by pseudoscience and filled-in subsequently by pseudosocial science, were granted folk reinforcement and continued popular life via a variety of literary and then cinematic expressions trading on the tragic mulatto trope. What we see arising from the work of the three prominent sociologists, Robert Park, Edward Reuter, and Everett Stonequist, is a consistent image (or, as Werner Sollors suggests, "mirage") of the mulatto, an image that is centered absolutely on two issues: (1) that mulattoes are the products of biological racial intermixture, and (2) that this biological racial intermixture results in an inner conflict, tension, and malaise that is resolved only by the mulatto adopting a specific (black) racial identity.[1] In other words, mulattoes are born with a natural internal conflict the correction of which requires specific intervention in terms of racial identity development. Unless a Negro identity is accepted and adopted, the mulatto is doomed to eternal ambivalence and alienation. The mulatto is—according to Park, Reuter, and Stonequist—the marginal man.

I will return to this notion in Part 2 when assessing the arguments and justifications for multiracial identity made by the American Multiracial Identity Movement. There, I shall offer a reading of the movement that illustrates its surprising embrace not of the mulatto, but of the marginal man! I want to begin the preparation for that discussion now by establishing in this chapter a link between black/white proponents of multiracial identity today and American mulattoes both past and present.

To do this will require a descent into the logical contradiction that is the American Multiracial Identity Movement—its arguments, positions, and ideologies. This is the domain of Generation Mix. Indeed, contradiction here is far from unusual, a condition perhaps exemplified most instructively by the movement's loud proclamations inveighing against biological race while simultaneously and quite explicitly advocating for federal recognition of a new biological racial identity. Angelique Davis characterizes this contradiction as "the inherent hypocrisy of the multiracial category in drawing a 'biological line' in contradiction of its professed goal of eliminating racial categories altogether."[2] Kerry Ann Rockquemore, David Brunsma, and Daniel Delgado make the similar point that "while Multiracial Movement activists were criticizing classification schemes, they also desired to have their members classified unambiguously 'multiracial.' This burgeoning social movement was simultaneously arguing against the essentialism and inheritability of race and reinscribing essentialism and immutability onto mixed-race people."[3] This most basic contradiction is fundamental to the movement's very being.

What is the relation of the black/white multiracially identifying members of Generation Mix to the mulatto of history? Does the American Multiracial Identity Movement embrace the mulatto as a mixed-race pioneer, as a kindred ancestral spirit, as a lineal precursor? Surprisingly perhaps, or perhaps not, the movement does not do any of these. Indeed, it is important to point out that the specific ideology of the multiracial movement has resulted in its strict refusal to acknowledge a significant relation to the mulatto.[4] Because one of the movement's goals is to maintain a trajectory away from blackness and toward whiteness, a point I will take up in more detail in Part 2, the mulatto is rejected as flawed, degenerate, and retrograde. An explicit linkage with the mulatto is a cost the American Multiracial Identity Movement is not willing to bear, despite the fact that such a link is inescapable both logically and historically. From the perspective of the movement's ideology, the mulatto is incompatible with some of its most important goals. But as I intend to demonstrate in Part 2, it is not the old pseudoscientific and pseudosocial scientific myths that are so incompatible. Indeed, we shall see that some of those very myths are being reinvigorated by the movement, and so can hardly be said to be incompatible at all. As I shall demonstrate presently, the old myths are not the issue when it comes to the mulatto's incompatibility with the movement.

Rather, that incompatibility lies elsewhere, with a major factor being that proponents of multiracial identity have an explicit interest in *not* linking their movement with American mulattoes of the past regardless of whether the old, racist myths are embraced or rejected. Their preference instead is to maintain as much distance as possible from yesterday's mulattoes. This may seem confusing or counterintuitive, so let me be very clear in making this important point. Even if it is acknowledged clearly and unequivocally that the old myths regarding mulatto infertility, debility, and general physical inharmoniousness are completely baseless; even if it is agreed upon by all concerned that the mulatto's alleged yearning for whiteness and the supposed inevitable malaise resulting in virtue of the utter un-attainability of that whiteness are a total fantasy based on white male sociologists' own psychological projections; even if all this is the case—the American Multiracial Identity Movement has a profound and vested interest in denying and rejecting an association with the mulatto at every turn.

Of course, certain highly regarded mulattoes have been appropriated by the movement when convenient. For instance, it is not uncommon for persons such as W. E. B. Du Bois, Walter White, Langston Hughes, or even Malcolm X, for instance—despite their own very clear ideological preferences—to be reassigned retroactively by multiracialists from a black identity to a multiracial identity. In Michele Elam's view, "multiracial advocates have begun a problematic reinterpretation of African American literary history by redefining authors previously identified (or self-identified) and anthologized as 'black' according to the racial discourses of the day, ascribing to them a new multiracial identity. Through this form of presentism, imposing the values and standards of the present moment to the past, these writers and their texts are being 'saved,' redeemed and relieved of their blackness, celebrated and canonized through a process in which bi- and multiraciality become an index of heroic self-definition. . . . Charles Chesnutt, Jean Toomer, W. E. B. Du Bois, Nella Larsen, and many others are all re-presented in this latest canon as misunderstood trailblazers."[5]

As Jared Sexton puts it, "multiracialism wants simply *to lay claim*, by right of force, to erstwhile figures of blackness, and they want to hear no questions, and certainly no lasting protest, from blacks about the matter. They want, in short, to redefine *unilaterally* what or who was once considered 'black' as what or who is now 'multiracial.'"[6] That it is often activist white mothers of black/white children who undertake this kind of appropriation—Susan Graham, executive director of the multiracial advocacy organization Project RACE (Reclassify All Children Equally), being a primary exemplar of this phenomenon—is not without significance. According to Lisa Jones, during a personal exchange with Graham, the latter announced that "if [Langston] Hughes were alive today, he would choose to be multiracial, he would identify first with mixed-race people and the work of her lobbying group."[7]

Such efforts generally represent clumsy attempts to assuage Afro-American resistance to multiracial identity—or to convince non–Afro-Americans that such resistance is groundless—by arguing that certain revered persons in the black pantheon either actually were multiracial, or would be considered or would consider themselves multiracial today. Predictably and inevitably, these efforts backfire as Afro-Americans tend to recognize them for the blatant appropriations they are. Indeed, in witnessing activist white mothers adopting this line of argument in presenting the case that their children are not really black or are *more than* black, one wonders why these mothers would in the first place imagine such arguments being particularly persuasive to anyone but themselves. Notably, however, such retroactive appropriations are reserved exclusively for exceptional mulattoes of the past, and therefore do not impact the movement's general inclination to maintain distance from the mulatto of history.

There is additional acknowledging of the mulatto that we might also note. For instance, reference might be made by multiracial activists and scholars to past censuses and to whether and how these censuses did or did not count mulattoes properly. These census counts and miscounts of mulattoes are invoked to demonstrate unfairness and inaccuracy in regard to US racial categorizations of the past, but significantly do not take the next logical step of linking those past mulattoes with persons living today. In other words, one would expect utilizers of this point to at a minimum make the case for some sort of relationship between mixed-race people of the past who were miscounted and mixed-race people today who claim to be miscounted, at least in terms of those in both cases who have European and sub-Saharan African ancestry. I will note the one exceptional and bizarre case of former multiracial activist Charles Byrd, whose argument requires that yesterday's mulattoes essentially constituted a closed, endogamous population that since the early twentieth century has interbred only with itself so as to continue to be distinguished from Afro-Americans today.[8] So eccentric is Byrd's argument, however, that it has not been taken up by the movement itself in any serious way.

Reference might also be made to a generalized and historically inaccurate claim that mulattoes of the past were not allowed to express their mixture. This is then contrasted with the current, or perhaps incipient, freedom to identify as mixed race, which seemingly needs but federal imprimatur in order to be complete. But regardless of such tactically motivated gestures toward the past, and aside from outlandish cases such as that of Byrd, there is no inclination on the part of the American Multiracial Identity Movement to recognize the traditional mulatto as an ancestor, whether physically or spiritually. There is no connection desired, no embrace of the mulatto as even a distant relative. It is as though at some very high level of abstraction an acknowledgment of past mulattoes is made either because it must be made or because it can be exploited; but it is an acknowledgment that at the same time essentially confers death upon those mulattoes, as if—similar to the early twentieth-century white man's wishful myth concerning Native Americans—all those past mulattoes just died away and today are to be referred to in the past tense only.

This is a key point since such an embrace, such an explicit linkage with mulattoes past—though justified—would serve to work in quite a strong way against one of the main ideological priorities of the movement, which is that today's mixed-race persons represent a new phenomenon in the

United States. By "though justified," I mean that based on acknowledged popular and scholarly understanding of what mulattoes are said to be, they have never ceased existing in the United States. Therefore, if one is to assert a mixed-race identity today, one must not only acknowledge those mixed-race Americans of the past, but one must acknowledge as well their continuing existence through their lineal descendants today. Mulattoes have not died off or gone anywhere; they are still very much here in the United States of America. The specific problem for the multiracial movement is that such acknowledgments of reality then require further acknowledging (1) that all Afro-Americans are essentially multiracial, and (2) that racial mixture in America is an old and ongoing story, both of which the movement is loathe to concede.

I am hard-pressed to make this point strongly enough. In nearly all popular news coverage of the multiracial movement and in nearly all scholarly publications by academics writing in support of multiracial identity, the reader is assured that today's multiracial people represent an historically new event in the US racial narrative. Indeed, this alleged newness is presented as being nearly as important a defining characteristic of the group in question as is racial mixture itself. Multiracial identity is touted as something new and different, not only deserving, but in dire need of, federal recognition. Again, this is not to say that the mulatto is never mentioned by advocates of multiracial identity, but as I have described above, any such references are always tactical. Rather than a lineal ancestor, the mulatto is treated more like an embarrassing cousin, a deranged and closeted uncle—recognized when pressed, exploited when expedient, but not embraced directly as part of the argument for federal recognition of multiracial identity today.

As part of this artificial disassociation from the historical truth of the ancestral past, the fictive newness of the multiracial group is placed precisely at 1967, linking erroneously a supposed subsequent increase in multiracial births to that year's *Loving v. Commonwealth of Virginia* US Supreme Court decision outlawing state antimiscegenation statues, when in fact any such increase is the result primarily of a relaxed national immigration policy enacted two years earlier in 1965 and leading to significantly increased numbers of immigrants from Asia and from Central and South America.[9] The Immigration and Nationality Act of 1965, also known as the Hart-Cellar Act, altered radically the sources of legal immigration to the United States, "making non-Europeans the most significant of all groups migrating to America."[10] Indeed, even prior to the 1965 act, a 1953 amendment to the War Brides Act of 1945—an amendment that extended the waiving of visa requirements to spouses who were Japanese and Korean—had the effect of bringing far larger numbers of Asians into the United States than allowed solely under then-current national immigration policy.[11]

It is reasonable to assume based simply on the demographics of the US military at the time that most of these Japanese and Korean spouses were married to white US military personnel.

Beyond the influx occasioned by the amendment to the War Brides Act, many of the new immigrants resulting from the Immigration and Nationality Act of 1965 married and had children with US whites, but not nearly as many with US blacks, and it is this—a phenomenon involving Asians and Hispanics most specifically—that has been misrepresented by multiracial factions as the so-called *Post-Loving Biracial Baby Boom*, when in fact it had not much to do with *Loving* at all. Consider the numbers provided by Michael Thornton, who offers that the most "visible beneficiaries of the preference provisions [effective beginning in 1968] of the 1965 act have been Asians. Beginning with a population of approximately 490,000 in 1940, there were about 878,000 Asian Americans in 1960, 3.5 million by 1980, and an estimated 5.1 million in 1985."[12] Clearly, the legislative actions of 1953 and 1965 are the impetus for the growing numbers of so-called multiracial births in the United States, not a 1967 US Supreme Court decision that, as in the case of the Emancipation Proclamation, ironically had the very least impact in precisely those areas in which it presumed to alter the de jure status quo.[13] In this regard, it is critical to understand that while *Loving* of course applied to all intermarriages, a review of the states where such marriages were illegal in 1967, as well as an analysis of black/white intermarriage rates in those states today, makes plain that the issue in those states was black/white marriage exclusively.[14] In other words, external to the black/white case, *Loving* was a moot decision; while internal to the black/white case, *Loving* had negligible impact.

Also recognizing that in 1965 "Congress revised the immigration laws in ways that led to substantial growth in the number of arrivals from Asia and Latin America," Rachel Moran points out that although "proponents of multiracialism have attributed the push for a new category to the rise of intermarriage after *Loving*, the picture is more complicated than that. . . . It is no accident that Latinos and the foreign-born are disproportionately represented among those who mark two or more races."[15] Yet, despite these important realities, advocates of multiracial identity, whom Moran refers to as "the self-proclaimed heirs of *Loving*," insist on referring erroneously to today's mixed-race offspring as the "children of *Loving*."[16] Thus, while an increase in so-called interracial marriages and multiracial births is tied to a marked surge in immigration from Asia and Central and South America stemming from the easing of US immigration laws in 1953 and 1965, and while black/white marriages and black/white multiracial births continue to represent the lowest percentages of all, the American Multiracial Identity Movement nonetheless consistently deploys the erroneous message that *Loving* is directly responsible for these purely immigration-fed increases and, further, that black/white marriages and interracial births represent a significant portion of this so-called boom.

While the American Multiracial Identity Movement is replete with falsehoods, the *Loving* legend must be pointed to as being among the most spectacularly fraudulent of its many myths, both in terms of what *Loving* supposedly meant at the time and what it supposedly will bring about in the future. As Peggy Pascoe warns: "If it is wise to resist the tendency to romanticize the heroism of interracial couples, it may be even wiser to question the now commonplace beliefs that *Loving v. Virginia* removed the last roadblock on the road to colorblindness and that colorblindness means the end of racism and white supremacy."[17] According to Elam, "even in post–civil rights era liaisons, power relations are never absent, although the repeated invocation of the Loving Decision as page one of a heroic American narrative about state discrimination overcome often suggests just this. The retroactive scripting of the Loving Decision as the foundational moment in a narrative of love transcending race and nation can distract us from analysis of how interracial unions and the children born of them do, in fact, necessarily participate in the racial, economic, and social economies of a nation."[18] We see the evidence of such ahistorical, "retroactive scripting" in what Daniel McNeil suggests as the real motivation for "prominent multiracial activists," who "tend to be 'white-looking' people with Negro or Native ancestors who longed for a 'respectable' history that they can call their own, or members of black/white marriages in the middle or upper classes, who desired celebratory narratives of a 'biracial baby boom.' This helps explain why so many multiracial activists trace their movement to the Supreme Court's decision in *Loving v. Virginia* (1967)."[19]

The erroneous narrative concerning *Loving* delivers a twin set of false impressions: (1) that *Loving*, although relevant in a technical sense to all intermarriages, had any practical impact beyond the black/white scenario, and (2) that it had any practical impact even in the black/white scenario—that *Loving* was itself a watershed moment in the history of US consensual black/white intimacy. The fact, though, is that excepting black/white marriages, all of the other intermarriages since the loosening of immigration laws in 1965 would likely have taken place even if the *Loving* decision had not been rendered. This is because the good people of Alabama, Mississippi, and the remainder of the 1967 antimiscegenation states who were concerned about intermarriage were concerned specifically about black/white intermarriage. They were not concerned about Native American/white, Hispanic/white, or Asian/white marriage. Only on the west coast was Asian/white intermarriage a major issue historically, and it had been placed well on the way toward resolution seventeen years earlier by the 1948 outlawing of antimiscegenation laws in California.[20] Moreover, *Loving*'s wrongly celebrated significance as an emblem of black/white intimacy is shown to be fallacious by the very fact that black/white intermarriages remain statistically the lowest of all in the United States—and especially in those states whose antimiscegenation laws were thereby overturned—despite the telling reality that blacks have been in this country far longer than the Asian and Hispanic immigrants now welcomed by many whites as marriage partners.

It is absolutely essential to see that any assertions that black/white intermarriage rates are booming or that black/white births are soaring through appeal to national intermarriage and multiracial birth rates is misinformation that depends on conflating a specifically immigration-driven phenomenon involving Asians and Hispanics with a relatively static situation obtaining between whites and blacks in the United States. That this kind of conflation is precisely what popular newsmagazines such as *Time* and *Newsweek* engage in on a consistent basis should come as no surprise.[21] And this is significant since most Americans surely obtain their information on the multiracial identity debate from popular sources such as these, accepting the misinformation with which they have been presented and, as a consequence, believing, wrongly, that they have thereby been educated. As we know, however, it is an increase in Asian, and later Hispanic, immigration to the United States, not any "Post-*Loving* Biracial Baby Boom," that is responsible for the oft-cited increases in the numbers of mixed-ancestry children in the United States.

Nonetheless, it remains a most significant phenomenon because many of these children and their descendants are now moving toward a status of "honorary whiteness" and some even to full whiteness, while their multiracial contemporaries of sub-Saharan African ancestry remain barred from those ivory gates.[22] For instance, Jennifer Lee and Frank Bean report that the racial identity of "Asians has changed over time from 'almost black' to 'almost white,' pointing to the mutability of boundaries for at least some Asian ethnic groups."[23] They also refer specifically to the "post-1965 wave of immigrants, particularly Latinos and Asians," as having a significant effect on changing patterns of multiracial identification.[24] Eduardo Bonilla-Silva emphasizes that "data on racial assimilation through marriage ('whitening') show that the children of Asian-white and Latino-white unions are more likely to be classified as white than the children of black-white unions."[25] In Jenifer Bratter's analysis, "unlike racial mixture involving blacks, which has consistently been defined by a policy of hypodescent, intermixtures between whites and Native Americans, Hispanics, or Asians have at times allowed for a 'white' identity for the offspring."[26] Citing early twentieth-century Southern and Eastern European immigration and intermarriage that "expanded the definition of who is white," Kimberly DaCosta suggests that "Latino and Asian intermarriage seems to be following a similar trajectory."[27] In Kim Williams's view, "like European ethnics before them, contemporary Asians and Latinos could be moving to the white side of the color line. If so, the boundaries of whiteness will expand yet again. . . . The panethnic shift from a smaller to a larger collective—say, from 'Mexican' to 'Latino'—might not stop there. The next stage, presumably most readily available to the native born, could be whiteness."[28] In this sense the multiraciality of these Asian- and Hispanic-descended individuals may be seen—significantly, and with a variety of meanings—as a passing phenomenon.[29]

It is extremely critical to emphasize the historical observations of Da-Costa and Williams here, for while the current trend of near whites distancing themselves from association with blackness and thereby becoming white might seem radical, it is absolutely typical and unremarkable in the broader context of US history. Indeed, even before the phenomenon of Southern and Eastern Europeans transitioning from nonwhiteness to near whiteness and then finally to whiteness, several waves of Irish immigrants went through that very same process. The relative swiftness of this transformation is captured in David Roediger's discussion of the evolving opinion of economist and census director Francis Amasa Walker: "In the post–Civil War years he projected census results to cast the Irish as a looming threat to US civilization and to Anglo-Saxon reproduction. As the century neared its end, he suddenly allowed that the Irish had instead magically assimilated into the 'American race.' The Anglo-Saxon fortress suddenly had a jerry-built Celtic wing."[30] And even before the Irish, in the aftermath of the war against Mexico, California "state law codified race thinking leavened by class, defining Mexican elites as 'white' while proscribing the rights of Indians and propertyless Mexican 'greasers.'"[31]

The strategy for these non- and near-white immigrants was to distance themselves from blackness, both literally and figuratively, as the case of competition over employment illustrates: "The task before Irish Americans was not so much to best black workers in securing jobs as to separate themselves from the stigma of doing the service and hauling work historically associated with African Americans."[32] This they attempted to do by removing those black workers altogether in the hope that the stigma of being associated with blackness would then be removed from that type of work: "Irish workers on the docks and elsewhere attempted to separate themselves from brutally bossed 'nigger work,' as degraded, racialized tasks were then called, by removing black workers."[33] In the phenomenon of becoming white, these immigrant groups—Irish as well as Southern and Eastern European—made a choice. That choice was to eschew solidarity with Afro-Americans at the very time when they were most closely associated with them and to instead distance themselves from that association by reaching for whiteness, a move that succeeded not only in making those immigrants white but also in perpetuating both race and white supremacy. Attention in this regard must be paid to the current phenomenon of "honorary whiteness" and the subsequent transition to full whiteness.

Moran provides valuable insight as to how, in the case of Asians, multiracial identity is leading toward whiteness in a way that could never happen for Afro-Americans: "For Asian Americans, the option to identify as multiracial could offer substantial advantages. In their case, multiracialism does connote intermarriage in the last few generations. As a result, Asian Americans have gained access to the benefits associated with white kinship networks. Indeed, Asian Americans have been so successful at using intermarriage to assimilate that some, like the Japanese Americans, are in danger of losing their distinctive identity altogether."[34] However, as I have been suggesting, and as Moran notes as well, "blacks continue to find that race is a mark of permanent and indelible difference, inescapable even through outmarriage. . . . After all, redefining racial categories is not the same thing as undoing a legacy of racial discrimination and segregation. Blacks are least able to escape race as a marker of segregation and social distance, regardless of how official categories are constructed."[35] Similarly, Bratter finds that "overall, intermarriage and racial classification patterns show that while differences between Asians and whites or American Indians and whites seem to blur, those between whites and black [*sic*] remain relatively distinct."[36]

However, while multiracial identity for black/white Americans moves them away from blackness, and might correspondingly move them toward whiteness, it can never move them *into* whiteness itself, for that option remains foreclosed by knowledge of their sub-Saharan African ancestry. Passing as white can bring ascribed whiteness to the black/white individual, but multiracial identity by itself cannot. Multiracial identity works very differently for Asians, though, for "an approach that recognizes multiple racial origins allows Asian Americans to begin converting their racialized status into one that approximates an ethnic identity. This approach recognizes that race, for them, is not a rigid barrier to integration and intermarriage. At the same time, an acknowledgment of their multiple origins enables Asian Americans to preserve some sense of their heritage despite high rates of exogamy. By converting from a racial to an ethnic identity, Asian Americans can sustain a symbolic recognition of ancestry, reflected in choice of foods or observation of holiday rituals, without giving up the privileges of whiteness through intermarriage."[37] None of these important complexities is taken into account by the overly simplistic paeans to *Loving* so typically encountered.

The misrepresentation of the *Loving* legend is parlayed subsequently into the idea of burgeoning numbers of new, first-time-ever multiracial children in desperate need of recognition precisely as such. At least two problems are glossed over when this idea is put forth. First, the assumption that these predominantly Asian/white and Hispanic/white children are in the first place multiracial plays into the myth of biological race just as much as the assumption of black/white multiracial children does, an error that typically is never considered by any popular media coverage and is without exception or professional excuse ignored completely by multiracial-supporting scholarship. Once acceptance of biological race—whether explicit or implicit—is allowed to enter the debate unchallenged it then realigns the parameters of discussion by transforming a mythic false consciousness (biological race) into a nonproblematic, commonsense, scientific fact. Certainly it seems obvious enough to not even require mentioning, but for a glossy newsmagazine or a respected news source to report that there are growing numbers of multiracial children and young adults who are struggling or otherwise dealing with reconciling within themselves the different races of their parents is for that newsmagazine or news source to undergird its story with the presumption that biological race is an actual scientific reality. In such a scenario it becomes that much more difficult subsequently to inject any semblance of logic and respectable scholarship into the debate.

The following two examples are typical of this practice. In a piece dripping with mawkish and embarrassingly strained attempts at hipness, *Newsweek* writer Lynette Clemetson informs us that in a period of thirty years, multiracial births have gone from a ratio of one per hundred to one per nineteen.[38] MSNBC senior news editor Mike Stuckey goes even further in relating the exact number of multiracial Americans as of July 2007. According to Stuckey, that precise number—4,856,136—represents a gain of 3 percent over the previous year's tally of exactly 4,711,932.[39] These two pieces of popular newsreporting, though written eight years apart, are identical in one critical aspect. Regardless of whether or not these writers are merely parroting figures provided by a respected institution such as the United States Census Bureau, their reporting nevertheless actively and consciously presents a platform in which biological race is normalized and reified in the context of their articles. In doing so, the biological racial foundation of multiraciality is never brought into question, never problematized, never subjected to even minor skepticism, for to do so would be to mute the sensationalistic trendiness of their pieces. Instead, through their work biological race stands as a real phenomenon of the natural world, a scientific truth that is not to be questioned. From that point onward, it hardly matters what reporting is actually then presented for we are already lost in a fantasy world of racial false consciousness.

Second, notwithstanding the fact that any increase in so-called multiracial births is due primarily to Asian and Hispanic immigration, domestic black/white births are nonetheless presented as being the cause of the increase. In addition to offering an inaccurate portrait of the situation in general, this misrepresentation also quite specifically skews the narrative in a direction that favors unjustifiably one particular segment of the American

Multiracial Identity Movement. If we were to give credence to biological race and to multiraciality, Afro-Americans would comprise one of the largest groups of multiracial Americans, since possibly excepting recent immigrants from sub-Saharan Africa or the Caribbean, and their children, Afro-Americans are all always already multiracial.[40] But as I shall continue to describe, just as in the case of the historical mulattoes of America's past, 30 million multiracial Afro-Americans are the last thing the American Multiracial Identity Movement wants to have associated with its ranks. Instead, the movement labors to construct a narrative in which only so-called first-generation persons actually are considered multiracial, and it works as well to present the illusion that the category of black/white children—the slowest-growing by far of all multiracial groups—is itself a burgeoning, exponentially increasing population. A distancing from past mulattoes is therefore matched by a distancing from Afro-Americans of today, and via both of these avenues the myth that first-generation black/white individuals represent a new and exploding population is incubated.

Two factors are at work in this deception, one being the fact that the very loudest multiracial advocacy always and unequivocally comes from activist white mothers of black/white children, who comprise the leadership and the most vocal membership of multiracial advocacy organizations. Williams finds that "multiracial organizations are almost exclusively composed of black-white couples, even though neither group drives interracial marriage trends," that "women tend to become the leaders of these groups more often than men do," and that "consequently, it turns out that the multiracial movement at the grass roots was predominantly led by white, middle-class women living in suburbs."[41] More specifically, in Williams's research on multiracial organizations, "women held the leadership positions by a three-to-one margin over men. . . . Across the country, sixteen out of thirty group leaders were white women, and an additional eighteen white women served on the boards of directors in my four case studies. In comparison, only one black man served as the leader of an organization, and only five additional black men served on the boards of directors in all my case studies combined."[42] And if there is any remaining doubt about it, Williams specifies that these white, middle-class, suburban women who "held the leadership roles in most multiracial organizations" are "married to black men," which further identifies them as the white mothers of black/white children to whom I am referring.[43]

The most emotional testimony, the least appreciation of white privilege and historical context, the greatest overtness in desiring to distance their children from blackness, and a singular unwillingness to consider the implications of their own methods of indoctrination in the racial identity of their children—these are the purview of activist white mothers of black/white children. So pronounced is the activism from this quarter that I have sometimes wondered if there are not perhaps more activist white mothers of black/white children than there are black/white people who personally are themselves advocates of multiracial identity. Their loudness, sensationalism, and extreme emotion (related proportionally, no doubt, to their own discomfort with their children's association with blackness) garner for these white mothers a level of attention that in turn meshes with the second factor—visibility.

The popular media always focus on the black/white case, presumably because black/white miscegenation's historical status as both monumental and abysmal, though suppressed somewhat in the national psyche today, still evokes the strongest level of voyeuristic interest from readers. As Catherine Squires notes of the mainstream press, acting in total indifference to the fact that other groups such as Native Americans and Asians also had very deeply vested interests in the census debates of the 1990s concerning the potential addition of a multiracial category, "dominant press accounts most often used Blacks, Whites, and people of Black and White multiracial families to illustrate the effects of the Census controversy on individuals and how people think about their own racial background."[44] As an example of this, the March 2, 2010, edition of *USA Today* includes an article on multiracial identity and the decennial census in which the photograph that leads the article is of a woman with black/white ancestry who has struggled with her racial identity. This woman is a featured voice in the article, and even though two persons of nonblack ancestry are mentioned very briefly at the very end of the piece, the overall impression given is that multiracial identity is primarily a black/white issue.[45]

This insistence by mainstream print media on presenting the multiracial debate through primarily a black/white lens inflates the significance of the relatively few black/white individuals who are advocates of multiracial identity, and perpetuates the fantasy that the United States has finally overcome its long history of racism. Black/white multiracial children are presented as human bridges capable of healing the nation's principal racial divide, when in fact it is patently obvious that due to the chronic racism Afro-Americans continue to suffer, Asian/white and Hispanic/white intermarriage and childbearing rates far outstrip the black/white case. This racial-bridge notion is clearly a fantasy based on wishful thinking, a fantasy I shall explore in greater detail in Chapter 9. Yet the popular media, who wield such a dramatic influence in actually shaping the stories they purport merely to cover, always prefer the *black/white racial-bridge* narrative regardless of its patent emptiness.

It seems that many whites are perhaps so desperate to believe that race relations are improving that they have bought into the arguments made along this line by multiracial advocates. Squires relates that in the "Reconstruction period and in the decades thereafter, miscegenation and mixed-race peoples were pariahs and symbols of impurity, but today they are reimagined as a natural byproduct of improving race relations by a dominant culture uneasy with the task of conceptualizing race and racism beyond interpersonal interactions."[46] And as DaCosta points out, any improvement in cross-racial interpersonal relations may in fact be limited to family members only, as opposed to the US population in general, which is why "assertions that people in intermarriages and multiracial individuals are less prejudiced natural bridges across the racial divide are problematic. It is easy to make exceptions for one's kin, marking them as the exception to the negative rule for others of a particular group, thus leaving the line of demarcation intact."[47] Quite frankly, "the notion that multiracials cannot be prejudiced is a recurring (if absurd) conceit about multiracialism," yet the fact remains that such nonsense is reiterated constantly and with no critical analysis whatsoever by the popular media.[48]

These two factors—the shrill chorus produced by activist white mothers of black/white children, and the generally unreflective nature of popular media coverage—when combined with the misrepresentation of *Loving* (which was about black/white intermarriage specifically, and not about any other type of intermarriage) lead the uninformed to the assumption that there have been multiple millions of first-generation black/white children born in the United States since 1967 who are distinct in a physical/genetic sense from the general Afro-American population. Activist white mothers of black/white children, taking advantage of the media's ongoing fascination with biological race in general and with black/white miscegenation in particular, do nothing to correct this false impression. Rather, both they and US popular media outlets continue to collaborate in perpetuating the activist myth of an explosion in black/white births when, in fact, as DaCosta reports, "according to Census 2000 figures, multiracial identification is more common among Asians and Latinos than among African Americans."[49]

As I have alluded to previously, these black/white children quite purposely are *not* linked by the American Multiracial Identity Movement to the millions and millions of persons of mixed European and sub-Saharan African ancestry who have preceded them on these shores, and who are their physical, if not spiritual, ancestors. Instead of conceding what is both obvious and extremely relevant to any discussion of *new races*, a delicate balance is maintained in which past mulattoes are acknowledged grudgingly, some even appropriated if they are important enough, but in general a strict distancing from past mulattoes creates space for the illusion of modern multiracial specificity to be planted, to manifest itself, and to grow. This resistance to an explicit linkage with past mulattoes, combined with the unflattering stereotypes of the past, ensures that the trajectory of the multiracial movement is not just away from association with blackness but also away from association with mulattoness in any significant degree.

Were the multiracial identity movement to establish an explicit link with the mulattoes of decades and centuries past, were it to view these mulattoes as psychic precursors, were it to acknowledge them as physical ancestors, it would lead to a conclusion the movement cannot abide. For if it is admitted that mulattoes existed in large numbers in the US past, and if it is acknowledged that these persons merged into the general population of US blacks during the "browning of America" described so effectively by Joel Williamson (or, more precisely, that any remaining unmixed American blacks merged into the growing mixed population via the process of internal miscegenation), then the question must be raised as to how today's black/white persons differ in any appreciable way from (1) those historical mulattoes and (2) the general Afro-American population today.[50]

Of course, there is no satisfactory answer to either of these questions, which is why proponents of multiracial identity from movement leaders to pro-identity academics down to the most grassroots of activists reject this shared past and instead allege so insistently that today's mixed-race Americans represent a *new* phenomenon. The mundane reality of this alleged new population's utter ordinariness is a door that cannot be opened, a path that cannot be taken, a shibboleth that nonetheless cannot be uttered. To acknowledge the nonspecificity of the black/white members of Generation Mix would be to undermine, indeed to eliminate, the most significant element of the ideological foundation supporting the American Multiracial Identity Movement in its continuing quest for recognition of multiracial identity as a new and distinct biological racial identity. And this conclusion impacts not only black/white multiracials but all persons declaring themselves or their children to be multiracial, for if the multiracial movement avers that this new race of multiracials includes both Asian/white and black/white persons, for instance, then the multiracial movement must also include the 30 million members of the Afro-American population. If it does not, it is then guilty of both a fundamental inconsistency and—given the subject matter we are here considering—a decidedly ironic brand of racial discrimination.[51]

Let us recall that what Williamson recounts for us is the absorption by an American mulatto population of the relatively few remaining unmixed blacks, with the result of this internal miscegenation being an ancestrally mixed Afro-American population that could no more make a claim to be black (i.e., unmixed West or Central African) in a genetic sense than it could make a claim to be white. As Gunnar Myrdal makes plain, "*internal miscegenation* within the Negro group between individuals with a varying degree of white ancestry is, and will in the future be, going on. The result is a tendency toward a slow but continuous equalization of Negro and white genes in the Negro people, decreasing the relative numbers at both the black and white extremes and concentrating the individuals ever closer to the aver-

age."[52] These were the *New People*. Afro-Americans became this new people, as distinguished from both the West and Central Africans and the Europeans from whom they were descended. There is therefore no sense in
which today's black/white multiracials are distinct from, more mixed than,
or indeed in any manner *newer* than the already new people who comprise
the general Afro-American population today. Pauline Hopkins recognized
this fact more than a century ago by having one of her characters say: "'My
dear Anna, I would not worry about the fate of the mulatto, for the fate of
the mulatto will be the fate of the entire race. Did you never think that today
the black race on this continent has developed into a race of mulattoes?'"[53]

Let me endeavor to make the same point another way. I want to begin
by reiterating with utmost clarity precisely what it is the multiracial movement in fact claims. The movement itself is based on the notion that since
1967 a new generation of multiracial people has arisen in the United States,
that this population is distinct racially from so-called monoracial populations, and specifically that its black/white members are distinct racially
from Afro-Americans. I, on the other hand, claim first of all that biological
race does not exist, thus rendering the entire notion of monoracial and multiracial people moot. But beyond that very significant scientific fact, I claim
further that there is no distinction to be made between the black/white members of Generation Mix and the general Afro-American population. The
movement claims that the black/white members of Generation Mix are multiracial, thereby distinguishing them from Afro-Americans. I, on the other
hand, claim that the members of the general Afro-American population are
all always already multiracial. In fact, I will claim something much more
specific than this, something that has heretofore not been claimed explicitly
even by opponents of multiracial identity, although it is quite obvious. Not
only are Afro-Americans always already multiracial, but they are in fact—
all of them—mulattoes.[54]

I recognize that I am making an unusual claim here, one that is perhaps
even shocking or explosive to some, but it should by no means be a surprising claim. I actually find it rather surprising that it is not already a common
understanding, but I assume that this is at least partly due to the old and
false mulatto myths we considered in Chapters 2 and 3. Indeed, I imagine
there are many Afro-Americans who would reject my claim out of hand, but
they would be wrong to do so. After all, it is a commonplace that all Afro-
Americans are mixed racially, and that—depending on which particular
piece of research one cites—they have varying but always significant
amounts of European ancestry. It inspires no controversy whatever to state
that all Afro-Americans are multiracial, as even advocates of multiracial
identity will grant this point grudgingly before switching to the argument
that first-generation people represent a different, more exclusive, and more

authentic version of multiraciality. Yet to say that all Afro-Americans are mulattoes seems somehow to be a different kind of statement.

Yet this is precisely what they are. They are the products—either directly, somewhat recently, or farther back in time—of sub-Saharan African/European intermixture. But, one might ask, is it not true that mulattoes no longer really exist, that Afro-Americans now are simply black, that mulattoes have reverted back to the so-called dominant type? No, it is not true at all. The fact is that there is no temporal threshold of *mulattoness* beyond which Afro-Americans cease being mixed racially, although some advocates of multiracial identity might want to argue that there is such a threshold in hopes of thereby disqualifying Afro-Americans from participation in multiraciality. However, if the idea of such a threshold were posited for this purpose by multiracial advocates it would open a door they would not want opened, for it would necessitate that their own supposed alterity qua multiracials would contain essentially a built-in time limit. For if mulattoes cease being mulattoes after some period of time, then multiracials must cease being multiracials after the same period of time. Moreover, such a built-in time limit would bring into even more serious question any remaining justification for establishing a federal multiracial category since the population in question would have an unstable future. Finally, it would very nearly represent a figurative resurrection of the old myth of mulatto infertility, at least in terms of ultimate results, which seems rather a distasteful twist for multiracial ideology to take.

Multiracial advocates would be doing themselves the greatest disservice possible; they would be no less than undermining their own ideology to argue that Afro-Americans are no longer mulattoes due to the passage of time. No, it must be accepted that both mulattoes and multiracials—assuming purely for the sake of argument here that there is any difference between the two—very much continue to exist beyond the first generation, that as far as we are concerned at least for now they continue to exist indefinitely. I want to provide very specific reasoning as to why I make this claim, which I shall do through the examination of a likely counterexample. One might argue, for instance, that over the many years between the beginning of the seventeenth century and the beginning of the twenty-first century, a new Afro-American population developed that should now be considered a monorace in and of itself. If one were to advance this argument, could one not then argue further that the black/white members of Generation Mix are distinct from this Afro-American race? This would appear to open the door to the cherished alterity that Generation Mix so dearly seeks, but it is a false promise, for one could only advance this argument by imposing quite arbitrarily a static and contrived monoracial boundary upon a continually evolving Afro-American people.

How could it be argued that the ancestral mixedness that defines quite literally what it means to be Afro-American can or should be frozen into a faux and artificial monoraciality simply because some subset of Afro-Americans does not wish to be included in the larger group? It is precisely the existence of people such as the black/white members of Generation Mix—mulattoes—that has and continues to be the basis of modern Afro-Americans. How can it be proposed with any seriousness that the direct (miscegenation) and indirect (internal miscegenation) mixing of black and white people over the past four hundred years has produced a particular population, but that the mixing of black and white people today ostensibly produces a different population? This would require the artificial erasure of the massive mixture comprising the current Afro-American population, and the just as artificial sedimenting of that mixture into a completely false monoraciality.

The result of such nonsense would be an assenting to the ridiculous notion that a racially mixed Afro-American population—one that I again point out is defined quite literally by that very population mixture—is recoded as monoracial. People often joke about the power of one drop of black blood to make a person black. Yet multiracial ideology presumes that whiteness is just as powerful, for one drop of white blood in a black/white child is claimed to have the power to take that child's always already-mixed Afro-American parent and recode that parent retroactively as monoracially black. But how does a racially mixed population become a monoracial race? The answer is that outside of existing in complete geographical isolation for several hundred thousand years—a condition and a point we clearly have not yet reached—it does not. So mulattoes continue to exist; they have not turned back into monoracial blacks (or indeed, into monoracial whites). And of course, if mulattoes continue to exist as they most surely do, and if all Afro-Americans are mulattoes, then all black/white members of Generation Mix are mulattoes as well. They are mulattoes in at least one of two ways: (1) by being the offspring or later descendants of one black and one white parent, and/or (2) by being indistinguishable from the always already-mixed general Afro-American population. To be mulatto and to be multiracial are no less than the very same thing.

Moreover, neither is there a sense in which *any* members of Generation Mix, whether of sub-Saharan African ancestry or not, can—qua multiracials in the context of the movement's own ideology—distinguish themselves with any logical validity from the general Afro-American population in terms of membership in the multiracial grouping the American Multiracial Identity Movement is attempting to establish. What I mean is that if the members of Generation Mix recognize themselves to be members of a racially mixed group, then they must also recognize *regular* Afro-Americans to be racially mixed members of the very same group. If they do not, they then reveal themselves to be logical charlatans, special pleaders, and, quite frankly, racial opportunists. In other words, when an Asian/white constituent of Generation Mix celebrates herself and proclaims her co-membership in a biological multiracial group with a black/white constituent of Generation Mix, basic and undeniable logic then requires her to also incorporate all Afro-Americans within this group as well. Failure to do so is fatal—in terms of logic, validity, consistency, and intellectual legitimacy—to the multiracial identity thesis. Failure to do so reveals the basis of the American Multiracial Identity Movement to be nothing more than a bogus and expedient kind of personal celebration and aggrandizement at the expense of generations of past and present American mulattoes. And of course, acceptance of the a priori fact that all Afro-Americans are mulattoes and therefore multiracial also deals the multiracial identity thesis a fatal blow from the other direction, at least insofar as black/white multiracials are conceived as being distinct from Afro-Americans.

And this is not a mere question of choice, for if multiraciality is said to exist then people either are or are not multiracial. It is not a question of asserting that those people of mixed ancestry who actively grasp and don a multiracial identity are multiracial, while those people of mixed ancestry who choose to not do so are monoracial. Yet this is the convenient and simplistic answer from the movement—that mixed-ancestry people who identify as multiracial are multiracial while mixed-ancestry people who identity as monoracial are monoracial. Graham illustrated this fundamental inconsistency quite plainly when testifying about black/white identity before Congress in 1997: "If you identify yourself as multiracial, then you would be multiracial. If you identify as black, you would be black."[55] But persons who identify as the latter cannot be monoracial if—as should by now be abundantly clear—they are already multiracial, for how could a person possess both predicates simultaneously? What significance would each presumably important predicate have in that case? And if they are not monoracial, what then are they?[56] Unless multiracial identity is based completely on individual caprice, and not at all on biological facts—which would bring seriously into even more doubt that particular identity's significance—the question of personal preference may be interesting to sociologists or psychologists but is quite irrelevant as to whether an individual is or is not multiracial.

I have brown eyes. Whether or how aggressively I choose to identify as brown-eyed is irrelevant completely to the fact that I have brown eyes. Regardless of whether I might wish that my eyes were green or hazel, they are brown. Leaving surgical alternatives or colored contact lenses out of account, I cannot choose to not be brown-eyed any more than I can choose to be a fish or a protozoan. It is not that I am brown-eyed *because* I choose to identify that way, as if merely stating that I were green-eyed would make it so. Yet, multiracial scholars and activists stake much—indeed, it would appear, everything—on how Generation Mix opts to define itself (or, significantly, how its younger members are indoctrinated by their parents in regard to self-definition). I would argue that what people in fact *are* is far more important than what people say they are, what they might think they are, or what their parents have told them they are.

Some might envision a difficulty for my thesis here, and I want to devote some space to addressing it. To take a typical line of argument, Kathleen Korgen claims in quite a specific way that since the end of the civil rights era in 1965, "a transformation has occurred in the racial self-identification of Americans with both an African American and a white parent," that "most young adult offspring of black/white couples define themselves as biracial."[57] To put it bluntly prior to going forward, Korgen's work suffers from a multitude of problems stemming from poor methodology and also from presumptions of "obviousness" similar to those I addressed in Chapters 2 and 3, although in Korgen's case the obviousness leans decisively toward multiracial superiority rather than mulatto debility. These methodological problems in turn lead Korgen to numerous unjustified generalizations that tend to plague as well most pro-identity academics, in particular those who base their published work on interviews generated by snowball sampling.[58]

While these problems represent serious credibility issues, I am less interested in the structural flaws of Korgen's research than I am in her assertions regarding the self-identification preferences of the black/white members of Generation Mix, especially since her work is characteristic of pro-identity scholarship in general. Although her conclusion is a gross overgeneralization, applicable primarily to affluent Northeasterners attending elite colleges and universities, it nonetheless represents both the public ideological face of the American Multiracial Identity Movement as well as the general trajectory of the uncritical coverage the movement receives via the popular media.[59] As such, a reader might be inclined to agree that if young black/white persons (or some subset of them) are identifying as multiracial, then they in fact are a new people. Such agreement would be a mistake, however.

If there is a difference vis-à-vis some black/white mixed-race Americans who are now calling themselves biracial or multiracial, and some black/white mixed-race Americans who are not identifying in that way, if that is the key point, then what sort of difference is it really? In what, beyond the mere appellation itself, does this alleged difference consist? Is Korgen—and let me again be most clear that she is typical of the general line of pro-identity argument in this regard—not really saying that nonmultiracially identifying Afro-Americans are in fact mixed racially but merely choose not to identify as such? If this is so, if the only difference lies in the inconsequentiality of what people are calling themselves as opposed to any actual difference in their respective biological constitutions, then there is no difference at all. There is only confusion in the best case, or a calculated rejection of the reality of a shared past in the worst.

Korgen refers specifically to those with "both an African American and a white parent," which is an example of the selective hypodescent that pervades the multiracial identity position, a selective hypodescent that works to efface the long history of population mixture among Afro-Americans. It is a selective hypodescent that in an ahistorical way retrofits always already-mixed Afro-Americans as pure blacks for the specific purpose of facilitating the assertion of multiracial children. Because of this, it is absolutely critical to unmask multiracial ideology and precisely what its positions and supporting arguments entail. This is a responsibility the popular media as well as academics who are supportive of multiracial identity have in general eschewed. To put it most straightforwardly, the multiracial identity position is yet another privileging of whiteness as pure, yet another affirmation of whiteness as an essence that is superior to blackness and that is corrupted by contact with blackness. In this regard the American Multiracial Identity Movement positions itself squarely in the tradition of the racist nineteenth-century natural scientists and the racist early twentieth-century sociologists who held precisely the same views concerning the "obvious" superiority of whiteness over blackness.

It is therefore decidedly ironic that an ideology opposed so strongly to the application of hypodescent in the identification of black/white children would itself be undergirded absolutely and unequivocally by that very same hypodescent. We ought to be very wary of multiracial ideology's claims to cultural unity and to be ushering in the end of race when its very existence and acknowledgment require absolutely the reification of biological race and the continued devaluing of blackness vis-à-vis whiteness. This fact is inescapable. One may attempt to avoid it consciously, as the popular media and academics who support multiracial identity do quite consistently; but if one pulls one's head out of the sand and bothers to actually reflect upon the American Multiracial Identity Movement's absolute entwinement with hypodescent, this damning conclusion simply cannot be ignored.

Recognizing this, we must also realize at once that having a so-called black parent is no different from having a so-called black/white parent, thereby minimizing—indeed, eliminating—the specificity of Korgen's foundational equation. In other words, even as Korgen attempts to justify the existence of black/white multiracial children by placing their respective parents into separate black and white racial categories, she is immediately guilty of crafting a false distinction between the always already-mixed Afro-American parent and that parent's indistinguishably mixed child. She can accomplish this *only* by applying hypodescent to the mulatto, multiracial, always already-mixed Afro-American parent—by recasting that racially mixed parent as monoracially black.

Yet if both groups are in fact mixed—mixed-race Afro-Americans who choose to identify as multiracial and mixed-race Afro-Americans who do not choose to identify as multiracial—what is the actual, significant difference between them? I want to be clear in pointing out that what Korgen is attempting is to invoke the fabrication of first-generation multiraciality, a contrivance that depends absolutely on the selective hypodescent I have just described. By this maneuver, Korgen seeks to create an artificial distinction between the always already-mixed Afro-American population and the black/white members of Generation Mix. The idea behind the first-generation thesis is that the black/white members of Generation Mix are somehow more mixed, more recently mixed, or more significantly mixed than *regular* Afro-Americans, all being propositions which fail miserably the most meager tests of philosophical and biological consistency one might care to apply. Even the notion of more recent mixture fails, for how can something that is already mixed be mixed any further by the addition of whiteness, yet *not* be mixed any further by the addition of blackness? This is a question that multiracial advocates, whether academics or activists, do not dare address because the answer reveals the absolute veneration of whiteness that exists at the very core of multiracial ideology.

Let us consider a perhaps easier-to-follow example. If an always already-mixed Afro-American conceives a child with a white partner, that child is considered multiracial. But if that same Afro-American conceives a child with an Afro-American partner, the child is not considered multiracial. But why not? In either case, at least one of the parents is mixed racially. Indeed, in the latter case both parents are mixed racially. Let us be clear that we are not in any sense dealing with a situation of monoracial individuals, because there is no such thing—not even among whites, regardless of their imaginings to the contrary. But even if we pretend that the whiteness in our example is monoracial, we know very well that the blackness is not. It is always, already, most thoroughly mixed with whiteness. So if the addition of whiteness to that mixedness produces multiraciality, why then does the addition of blackness not also produce multiraciality?

If the answer is that multiraciality is not produced in the latter case because Afro-Americans are always already multiracial, then quite obviously there can be no justifiable distinction drawn between Afro-Americans and the black/white members of Generation Mix. Moreover, on this view, neither then should the addition of whiteness be responsible for producing multiraciality in the former case, for again, one of two the parents is already mixed racially. In other words, the resulting child's multiraciality in the former case would not be caused by or depend in any way upon her or his white parentage, for the child would be multiracial regardless of that second parent's race. Clearly, this is not the answer the American Multiracial Identity Movement would invoke to explain why the addition of whiteness to mixedness produces multiraciality, whereas the addition of blackness does not.

If, however, the answer is that multiraciality is not produced in the latter case—but *is* produced in the former case—because whiteness is somehow more pure, less diluted, or essentially more easily corrupted than blackness, we will then have unmasked a critical ideological support of the Generation Mix phenomenon—a support operating at the very deepest levels of structure. We will have unmasked the white supremacist underpinning of the American Multiracial Identity Movement via its dependence on the twin operating principles of hypodescent—white purity and black impurity. These are the only two possible answers: (1) that there really is no distinction after all, or (2) that a distinction is only possible through acknowledgement of the superiority of whiteness vis-à-vis blackness. Because this fundamental issue is ignored purposely by activists, multiracial-supporting academics, and the popular media alike; and because whatever issues are addressed typically receive sophomoric analyses geared to stimulate the emotions rather than the intellect; this absolutely perverse spectacle of *other people*—often white mothers and white academics—deciding which Afro-Americans are multiracial and which Afro-Americans are merely black is hidden from view.

The bottom line is that Korgen, along with the academics and activists who hold similar views, cannot afford to admit the truth that there is no functional difference between the two groups, that Generation Mix is in no sense a new people. She and they simply *want* the black/white members of Generation Mix to be distinct from *ordinary* Afro-Americans, regardless of the reality that they are not. The words of one white mother attest to this intense desire at least as well as I could put it: "I am a white mother of biracial children and I don't care if my child is darker than his black father, they are bi-racial!!! We teach others around us how we want our kids to be viewed. Before each school year, we meet with their teachers and let them know that they are bi-racial. Whenever we fill out forms, if we can't check a black and a white box, then we check the 'Other' box and write in bi-racial or multi-cultural. Society can see my kids as black all they want . . . but they aren't. They know that, I know that, their father knows that and we make it a point to let anyone who miscategorizes them for any reason know that. We educate others on how we want to be viewed as a family. It's really not that difficult!"[60]

We have been assured, then, that this white mother has taught her black/white children that they are not black. What this mother's fusillade of emotion does not tell us, however, is exactly how these children are *not* black in a way that always already-mixed-race Afro-American children (or, indeed, her children's own father) *are* black. Elsewhere, I have broached in an explicit way the usually taboo topic of activist white mothers of black/white children, and of white academic supporters of multiracial identity who have familial ties to black/white children.[61] I hereby link that discussion expressly to the present one, and repeat very clearly my contention that these individuals very simply and very desperately *want* Generation Mix to be distinct. Given the obvious vacuousness of the claim to multiracial specificity, the intellectually honest thing to do would be to admit as much, and to admit as well the operative dynamic of white superiority driving that desire for distinction.

Nor do I want to leave the impression that Korgen is alone in crafting a false dichotomy between Afro-Americans and black/white multiracials, or that her approach is the only method by which it is done. Barry Edmonston, Sharon Lee, and Jeffrey Passel attempt to accomplish the same goal, albeit by different means. In making population projections for the next one hundred years, the authors presume that each subpopulation they consider in doing this, including the black population, is composed of two different kinds of people—those who are a single race or ethnicity and those who are multiracial or multiethnic: "First, we assume that the 2000 population includes persons of single and multiple racial and ethnic origins."[62] Before proceeding any further it must be stated with no ambiguity and in the strongest terms possible, at least as far as Afro-Americans are concerned, that this is complete and utter nonsense. Afro-Americans are always already mixed, so there is no legitimate basis for separating them into fallacious unmixed (single race) and mixed (multiple race) groups. As is so very typical, the recoding and reassignment of Afro-Americans from mixed to monoracial is accomplished without concern, as yet another attempt to erase their variegated history is set in motion.

Embarking on what is essentially a fool's errand, Edmonston, Lee, and Passel recode those racially mixed Afro-Americans who do not declare a multiracial identity overtly as unmixed black, and those racially mixed Afro-Americans who do declare a multiracial identity overtly as mixed black, when of course both groups are mixed racially: "The single-origin population includes only persons who have single racial or ethnic origins: they represent the population who reported only one race or ethnic origin in the 1990 census and their descendants who marry within the same race or ethnicity group. The multiple-origins population includes persons who reported multiple race-ethnicity origins in the 1990 census, their descendants, and the offspring of racial-ethnic intermarriages in the future."[63]

There are two related errors in this massive inconsistency. First, when the authors write that "the single-origin population includes only persons who have single racial or ethnic origins," it is a meaningless statement as far as it relates to Afro-Americans, for no Afro-Americans have "single racial origins." Second, the authors then create—completely artificially—

their monoracial black population by defining it as representing "the population who reported only one race or ethnic origin in the 1990 census and their descendants who marry within the same race or ethnicity group." Yet of course none of this has anything to do with the historical and physical reality that, far from having "single racial origins," the average, rank-and-file Afro-American is among the most ancestrally mixed persons in the United States. How is it possible to take this massively mixed grouping of people and with a straight face recode it as a "single-origin population"? But this recoding is the key, for once that preliminary step is undertaken, the illegitimate consequences are then able to flow unimpeded.

As an illustration of the practical effect of such thinking, consider that the *New York Times* deemed worthy of front-page coverage the news of a genealogist's determination that Michelle Obama, wife of President Barack Obama, has white ancestry.[64] According to the article, "these findings . . . substantiate what Mrs. Obama has called longstanding family rumors of a white forebear."[65] Yet substantiation of such "rumors" by a professional genealogist was unnecessary, for any traditional Afro-American (as opposed to recent immigrants or their children) can be certain that she or he has white forebears. The identity of such persons may not be known or even recoverable but they are there, for the alternative—a family tree spreading backward exponentially and consisting of only *unmixed* sub-Saharan Africans—is absurd. But via this story, the *Times* suggests that it requires the efforts of a professional genealogist to move an Afro-American from the unmixed to the mixed, or from the "single-origin" to the "multiple-origin," group. It might certainly be satisfying personally to be able to fill-in the blanks of one's family ancestry with specific names if one has the resources to do so, but the fact that a particular Afro-American has white forebears or slave ancestry is simply not news in any significant sense. The *Times* seeks to make the admittedly significant historical point that someone with slave ancestry has finally made it to the White House as the president's spouse, but the same would be true for any traditional Afro-American who made it to the White House—with or without the benefit of professional genealogical authentication.

Again, let us contemplate the implication of what the innocent-sounding term "single-origin population" really means—namely, that not only do the Afro-Americans in this category have no European ancestry, but that their own ancestry is an unbroken and ever-expanding tree of *unmixed* West and Central Africans going back over four hundred years! How else could they be understood sensibly as being of "single origin"? The ridiculousness of it is simply stunning, and is surpassed only by the sad fact that, excepting the all-too-rare efforts such as my own argument, such assertions remain for the most part unchallenged in the scholarly literature as well as in the popular media. The illegitimacy of such approaches is made clear by Rockquemore, Brunsma, and Delgado, who warn that "we must be careful, however, not to confuse racial identity with racial category, as is frequently done in the use of census data where we hear estimates of the 'multiracial population' that are in fact only a small subset of mixed-race people who checked off more than one race as their racial category."[66] Kevin Binning, Miguel Unzueta, Yuen Huo, and Ludwin Molina also point out the fundamental error in the simplistic approach taken by Edmonston, Lee, and Passel: "Much previous research on multiracial identity has tended to operationalize multiracial identity using check boxes representing traditional, monoracial categories. Those who check off more than one racial group are subsequently coded as multiracial; those who check off only one racial group are coded as monoracial. . . . A potential problem with this operationalization of multiracial identity is that multiracial individuals' awareness of their racial lineage might be distinct from the way they psychologically interpret their multiple group memberships."[67]

Edmonston, Lee, and Passel go on to note specific "increases in the multiple-origin black population" from the year 2000 to the year 2100, "under the assumptions made in this population projection. By 2100, there is a single-origin black population of 66 million and a multiple-origin population of 39 million."[68] This then is the concrete consequence of the massive fallacy countenanced by the authors—a wholly unjustified distinction drawn between two indistinguishable groups of racially mixed Afro-Americans. From here it is but a small matter eventually to conceptualize the mixed group as being fundamentally different from the unmixed group, thereby lending support to the cause of a federal multiracial category. Finally, according to the authors, "the reported black population could vary between 66 and 105 million in 2100, depending upon the self-identification of multiple-origin black persons," even though it is obvious that said "multiple-origin black persons" are no more mixed racially than the "single-origin black population."[69] We have here, as in the case of Korgen's somewhat different approach, an object lesson in how the dangerous nonsense of multiracialism becomes legitimated and institutionalized, for none of this ought to depend on the self-identification of anyone. People are what they are. They either are mixed racially or they are not; and in the case of Afro-Americans we know that they are always already mixed.

As Sexton points out, "it is argued that current classification schemes, both official and unofficial, efface the reality of contemporary race mixture, denying the very existence of 'racially mixed people in America' to the latter's express detriment."[70] Yet it is the American Multiracial Identity Movement itself that is denying the "very existence of 'racially mixed people in America.'" It engages in a denial that racially mixed people exist in America every time it asserts that its black/white members are distinct from American mulattoes of the past and from the Afro-American population today. It engages in a denial that racially mixed people exist in America every time it deploys a selective hypodescent to recode racially mixed Afro-American parents of black/white children as monoracially black. It engages in a denial that racially mixed people exist in America every time it refuses to include today's 30 million always already-mixed Afro-Americans within the membership of its multiracial ranks. Consider the spectacle of multiracial-supporting author Sundee Frazier offering examples of biblical biracial characters and consoling today's multiracial people to "be encouraged that you're not alone in your struggle but are joined with biracial people through the ages," when Frazier's "biracial people through the ages" of course excludes today's always already-mixed Afro-American population.[71]

Let there be no doubt that I consider it especially important to reject the endlessly recycled claim that today's Generation Mix represents a new people, a rejection I have argued in this chapter's preceding pages. I also feel it important to critique the haughty and self-congratulatory attitude that generally accompanies this claim. Some Afro-Americans chafe at a certain sense of rejection felt when the black/white members of Generation Mix or their advocates proclaim a distinction from the general Afro-American population, a perceived rejection that is at the very least understandable regardless of one's position on the multiracial identity question. Beyond that, however, there is another rejection at work in this ongoing debate. It is a rejection that typically goes unnoticed, and it is at the same time particularly offensive—most especially since the objects of this rejection have no voice.

In addition to a perceived rejection of Afro-American confraternity, there is a clear rejection of a relation to the mulatto of history. While I have been making this point in various ways throughout the chapter, I want very specifically to dwell for a moment on this rejection and why it strikes me as so offensive. The distinction I draw between these two cases of rejection revolves specifically around the fact that Generation Mix devotes such energy to proclaiming itself to be a new people. In this sense, and although the two are related, it is the false newness as well as the false distinction that I find objectionable. Both the newness and the distinction are ahistorical and unjustifiable attempts to rewrite history, and I again emphasize the point that such a rewriting comes at the expense of a voiceless community. Having devoted some space to arguing against the false distinction being put forth by Generation Mix, I will endeavor to address the false newness as well by placing it in the historical context of real people's lives.

Toward that end I want to dedicate some additional space here, as I begin to close this chapter and Part 1, toward bringing an explicit awareness of these voiceless people to light, for it is not sufficient to acknowledge them only as statistics or with a mere, discursive wave of the hand. I want to emphasize the physical existence, the humanity, of these persons—an existence and a humanity that are trampled upon and erased in the unreflective rush to anoint Generation Mix as a new people. In Chapter 4 I considered the literary works of American mulatto authors and the mulatto characters they created. These characters were critical to establishing the falseness of the racist marginal man myth, but we must now move beyond fictional characters. I am referring here to real people who lived real lives, some of them quite miserable and harsh, and who would doubtless be astonished to hear the black/white members of Generation Mix proclaiming themselves to be a new people.

We might travel back to the mid-nineteenth-century slave South with Frederick Law Olmsted in order to recapture a portion of this necessary awareness. "It was not uncommon," according to one plantation overseer with whom Olmsted spoke, "to see slaves so white that they could not easily be distinguished from pure-blooded whites."[72] Regarding such white-appearing but racially mixed slaves, this particular overseer reported never before having been on a plantation that "had not more than one on it."[73] Pointing out one particular slave girl, the overseer said to Olmsted: "'That one is pure white; you see her hair?' (It was straight and sandy.) 'She is the only one we have got.'"[74] "'Now,'" replied Olmsted, almost rhetorically, "'if that girl should dress herself well, and run away, would she be suspected of being a slave?' (I could see nothing myself by which to distinguish her, as she passed, from an ordinary poor white girl.)"[75]

Who was this slave girl? What sort of life did she lead? Was she freed from slavery before the end of the Civil War? Assuming she lived, how did she fare through Reconstruction and Redemption? Did she live to experience the beginnings of Jim Crow? And, most significantly for my purposes here, what would have been her reaction to the black/white members of today's Generation Mix rejecting Afro-American confraternity with her, and declaring themselves to be a new people? The historical examples of such persons as this slave girl, whether they melded into the constantly browning Afro-American population or passed into white society, put the lie to any claims of today's Generation Mix as representing some kind of new, racially mixed population. There indeed is something distinctly disturbing about the insistence of Generation Mix upon its multiracial newness and specificity in the face of the true historical reality.

Harriet Jacobs describes in a very poignant way another mixed-race person and the real implications life held for that person: "I once saw two beautiful children playing together. One was a fair white child; the other was her slave, and also her sister. When I saw them embracing each other, and heard their joyous laughter, I turned sadly away from the lovely sight."[76] Jacobs turned away because, based on her own personal experience, she could imagine readily how the mixed-race slave child's life would diverge eventually and significantly from that of her free, white sister. Moving on from this depressing image to close her chapter with an antislavery plea directed at her readers, Jacobs asks that "God bless those, everywhere, who are laboring to advance the cause of humanity."[77] And while some will doubtless take issue with the particular use to which I shall put Jacobs's words here, I nonetheless ask whether Generation Mix, in celebrating itself so falsely and so extravagantly as it does, is advancing the cause of humanity or merely engaging in an historically revisionist spectacle of solipsistic reverie.

The source of Jacobs's sadness can be seen readily in Solomon Northup's heart-wrenching account of the separation of the slave woman Eliza from her young, mulatto daughter, Emily. When William Ford offers to purchase both Eliza and Emily in order to keep mother and child together, the slave-trader Theophilus Freeman refuses, noting of seven- or eight-year-old Emily that there were "heaps and piles of money to be made of her . . . when she was a few years older. There were men enough in New Orleans who would give five-thousand dollars for such an extra, handsome, fancy piece as Emily would be, rather than not get her."[78] Northup completes the horrific scene as the young child is torn from her mother: "'Don't leave me—mama—don't leave me,' screamed the child, as its mother was pushed harshly forward. 'Don't leave me—come back, mama,' she still cried, stretching forth her little arms imploringly. But she cried in vain. Out of the door and into the street we were quickly hurried. Still we could hear her calling to her mother, 'Come back—don't leave me—come back, mama,' until her infant voice grew faint and still more faint, and gradually died away, as distance intervened, and finally was wholly lost. . . . Eliza never after saw or heard of Emily."[79]

We might, if we cared, ask what happened to little Emily. Did she end up in New Orleans? Did she become a fancy girl? Did she somehow find her way out of slavery and to a quadroon ball, becoming perhaps fortunate enough to receive an offer of plaçage concubinage from a rich, young white man?[80] Or was she simply raped every day of her sexually useful life by any white man who could afford to either rent or own her body? And we should also acknowledge the fact that a man such as Theophilus Freeman could no doubt find more than enough ways to satiate his own desires in abusing young Emily without damaging her future sexual value. We might ask such questions and wonder about such things if we could manage to tear ourselves away from the endless drumbeat of modern mixed-race celebration that rejects association with people such as seven- or eight-year-old Emily. I would offer that the narcissistic celebration of Generation Mix both as new and as distinct from Afro-Americans is an affront and an insult to young Emily as well as to untold generations of American mulattoes.

Frederick Douglass, writing of the white slave-owner who "in cases not a few, sustains to his slaves the double relation of master and father," and who is "frequently compelled . . . to sell his children to human flesh-mongers," provides yet more proof of the absolute historicity of mulattoes in America's past.[81] I realize that I have already made this case, but I am here striving to capture the actual human dimension of the argument, with testimony from and about people who were themselves mulattoes, and whose existence as mixed-race Americans must not be displaced from view by what is essentially a contemporary social fad. Speaking to us more than a century-and-a-half removed in time, Douglass makes this important point as plain as it might be made today: "If the lineal descendants of Ham are alone to be scripturally enslaved, it is certain that slavery at the south must soon become unscriptural; for thousands are ushered into the world, annually, who, like myself, owe their existence to white fathers, and those fathers most frequently their own masters."[82] I shudder to imagine the reaction of the great Frederick Douglass to the assertion that today's black/white members of Generation Mix are not ancestrally mixed Afro-Americans and are instead a new people—different even from him. Douglass would doubtless have much to say in response. Yet this sort of relevant analysis is lost completely in the shallow and never-ending celebrations by and about Generation Mix.

Criticizing white Southerners' deployment of the fear of miscegenation as a red herring against arguments for emancipation, Lydia Maria Child points out that "the outcry about amalgamation, as the result of emancipation, is simply ridiculous, in view of the swarms of mulattoes, quadroons, and octoroons, produced by slavery."[83] Moreover, she writes, "a careful computation of the proportions shows thirteen times more amalgamation at the South than in the North; but in making this estimate an important fact is kept out of view, viz: that very many of our colored citizens originated in the South, and a large proportion came to us already bleached to various shades of brown or yellow, by plantation processes."[84] Charles Chesnutt strikes a similar note in reference to colored men and women "whose complexion is white or nearly white," noting that "more than half of the colored people of the United States are of mixed blood; they marry and are given in marriage, and they beget children of complexions similar to their own."[85] It is clear that there is no Generation Mix distinction or newness; there is only the noxious and self-serving rejection of a shared past.

The two principal purposes of Part 1, somewhat separate threads that will be joined together in Part 2, have been to (1) recover a brief outline of the American mulatto that illustrates not only the falseness, but also the racist underpinnings of sociology's marginal man thesis regarding said mulatto; and (2) demonstrate that, beyond whatever people may want to call themselves or whatever they may have been taught to call themselves, there is in fact no appreciable difference between the mulatto of history, Afro-Americans today, and the black/white members of Generation Mix. Much of

Part 1 of this book has dealt with racist myths directed at the mulatto, myths that stemmed from the psychological projections of white men in their inability to reconcile their own deep investment in the miscegenation they claimed so much to despise. I will return to some of these myths in Part 2 when I demonstrate that they have been revived—albeit perhaps unknowingly—in the very ideology and arguments of the American Multiracial Identity Movement. What this historical review of mulattoes has done is confirm that from the perspective of biological race, upon which multiracial ideology depends so necessarily, black/white multiracial Americans have existed and have been studied for centuries. They are in no sense new or distinct.

This chapter has been concerned with arguments over precisely which racially mixed Afro-Americans are and are not multiracial today. Clearly, the existence of black/white racially mixed Americans over the last four centuries is not in question. What has been attempted by the American Multiracial Identity Movement, and what I have endeavored to challenge and correct in this chapter, however, is a strategic erasure of portions of that history—an erasure having the goal in mind of presenting today's black/white multiracially identifying members of Generation Mix as different from, more mixed than, and—as we shall see in Part 2—better than *regular* Afro-Americans, all of whom are always already mixed racially and are, therefore, mulattoes. The implications of this erasure are significant, as I began to elucidate in this chapter's discussion of "honorary whiteness," and which I shall continue in Chapter 7.

Notes

1. Werner Sollors, *Neither Black Nor White Yet Both: Thematic Explorations of Interracial Literature* (New York: Oxford University Press, 1997), 243. Reuter is the most direct of the three in regard to advising mulattoes to adopt a Negro identity. While not stating this in an overt way as Reuter does, both Park and Stonequist present precisely the same equation as Reuter: that mulattoes are a biological mixture of Negro and white, a mixture that leads necessarily to inner conflict. Obviously mulattoes cannot identify as white, unless by racial passing, since white society would not allow it. Therefore, the only way to resolve their tension is to identify as Negro, which, though they might find it distasteful, they nonetheless can do.
2. Angelique M. Davis, "Multiracialism and Reparations: The Intersection of the Multiracial Category and Reparations Movements," *Thomas Jefferson Law Review* 29, no. 2 (Spring 2007): 181.
3. Kerry Ann Rockquemore, David L. Brunsma, and Daniel J. Delgado, "Racing to Theory or Retheorizing Race? Understanding the Struggle to Build a Multiracial Identity Theory," *Journal of Social Issues* 65, no. 1 (2009): 25.
4. Writing about the mulatto debility theses of previous generations, Kim Williams makes note of the fact that the founders of the foremost multiracial advocacy organization, AMEA (Association of MultiEthnic Americans), "made no ex-

plicit reference to this past." Kim M. Williams, *Mark One or More: Civil Rights in Multiracial America* (Ann Arbor: University of Michigan Press, 2006), 10.

5. Michele Elam, "The Mis-education of Mixed Race," in *Identity in Education,* ed. Susan Sánchez-Casal and Amie A. Macdonald, 137–138 (New York: Palmgrave Macmillan, 2009).

6. Jared Sexton, *Amalgamation Schemes: Antiblackness and the Critique of Multiracialism* (Minneapolis: University of Minnesota Press, 2008), 149–150.

7. Lisa Jones, *Bulletproof Diva: Tales of Race, Sex, and Hair* (New York: Doubleday, 1994), 61. Scholars also go down this path, as in the case of Paul Spickard in "Does Multiraciality Lighten? Me-Too Ethnicity and the Whiteness Trap," in *New Faces in a Changing America: Multiracial Identity in the 21st Century,* ed. Loretta I. Winters and Herman DeBose, 294–296 (Thousand Oaks, CA: Sage, 2003). Spickard's appropriation is much more measured and is in the context of a scholarly argument; however, I nonetheless highlight it as another example of this sort of arrogation. I would also point out what is in my opinion a subtle difference between what Spickard does in this reference, and Naomi Zack's analysis of how certain Harlem Renaissance Era mulatto elites confronted their racial identities in *Race and Mixed Race* (Philadelphia: Temple University Press, 1993), 95–111.

8. Rainier Spencer, "New Racial Identities, Old Arguments: Continuing Biological Reification," in *Mixed Messages: Multiracial Identities in the "Color-Blind" Era,* ed. David L. Brunsma, 92–93 (Boulder, Lynne Rienner, 2006).

9. I say a "supposed" increase because in the Afro-American context especially, the presumption is made that the parent is monoracial when in fact Afro-Americans are all already mixed. This realization throws into serious doubt any claim that a black/white child's black parent is not already multiracial, undermining in turn the notion of multiraciality itself, most particularly the notion of it as a new phenomenon.

10. Michael C. Thornton, "The Quiet Immigration: Foreign Spouses of U.S. Citizens, 1945–1985," in *Racially Mixed People in America,* ed. Maria P. P. Root, 69 (Newbury Park, CA: Sage, 1992).

11. Ibid., 67, 68.

12. Ibid., 68–69.

13. In the midst of noting these drastic changes to immigration policy, it is important to keep in mind, as David Roediger points out, that the opening up of immigration from Asia and Latin America was not the result of moral anguish over past policy. Roediger argues instead that legislators "had their sights much set on intra-European matters," and that "the eventual 1965 legislative reforms thus paid little attention to the bill's possible effects on immigration from Latin America, the West Indies, and Asia. The openings created for additional entry from those areas were more a result of miscalculations about potential immigrants' facility to relocate than a mark of considered and dramatic liberalization of immigration policy as it applied to migrants from beyond Europe." David R. Roediger, *How Race Survived U.S. History: From Settlement and Slavery to the Obama Phenomenon* (New York: Verso, 2008), 191.

14. As a contemporary example of how black/white intermarriage still evokes strong negative feelings, Renee Romano reports that during the mid-1980s in "Mississippi, South Carolina, and Alabama more than 40 percent of the voters cast ballots to retain their state's symbolic constitutional bans on interracial marriage." *Race Mixing: Black-White Marriage in Postwar America* (Cambridge: Harvard University Press, 2003), 253. See also Rachel F. Moran, *Interracial Intimacy: The Regulation of Race and Romance* (Chicago: University of Chicago Press, 2001), chap. 6.

15. Rachel Moran, "*Loving* and the Legacy of Unintended Consequences," *Wisconsin Law Review*, no. 2 (2007): 255, 258.

16. Ibid., 256, 257.

17. Peggy Pascoe, *What Comes Naturally: Miscegenation Law and the Making of Race in America* (New York: Oxford University Press, 2009), 313.

18. Elam, "The Mis-education of Mixed Race," 144.

19. Daniel McNeil, *Sex and Race in the Black Atlantic: Mulatto Devils and Multiracial Messiahs* (New York: Routledge, 2010), 11.

20. Rebecca C. King-O'Riain, *Pure Beauty: Judging Race in Japanese American Beauty Pageants* (Minneapolis: University of Minnesota Press, 2006), 46, 202.

21. John Leland and Gregory Beals, "In Living Colors," *Newsweek*, May 5, 1997, 60; Connie Leslie, Regina Elam, Allison Samuels, and Danzy Senna, "The Loving Generation: Biracial Children Seek Their Own Place," *Newsweek*, February 13, 1995, 72; Jack E. White, "'I'm Just Who I Am,'" *Time*, May 5, 1997, 33. These several articles are typical. Even though the graphs in such pieces may indicate that black/white intermarriages or birthrates are far lower than those of other groups, the overall message, nonetheless, is that interracial marriages and births are skyrocketing in a way that is shaking the foundation of race in the United States and that the black/white component is significant.

22. For an in-depth discussion of this phenomenon see Eduardo Bonilla-Silva, "'New Racism,' Color-Blind Racism, and the Future of Whiteness in America," in *White Out: The Continuing Significance of Racism*, ed. Ashley W. Doane and Eduardo Bonilla-Silva (New York: Routledge, 2003); Charles A. Gallagher, "Racial Redistricting: Expanding the Boundaries of Whiteness," in *The Politics of Multiracialism: Challenging Racial Thinking*, ed. Heather M. Dalmage (Albany: State University of New York Press, 2004); and Jennifer Lee and Frank D. Bean, "America's Changing Color Lines: Immigration, Race/Ethnicity, and Multiracial Identification," *Annual Review of Sociology* 30 (2004).

23. Lee and Bean, "America's Changing Color Lines," 234.

24. Ibid., 235.

25. Bonilla-Silva, "'New Racism,'" 281.

26. Jenifer L. Bratter, "Will 'Multiracial' Survive to the Next Generation? The Racial Classification of Children of Multiracial Parents," *Social Forces* 86, no. 2 (December 2007): 824.

27. Kimberly M. DaCosta, *Making Multiracials: State, Family, and Market in the Redrawing of the Color Line* (Stanford: Stanford University Press, 2007), 9.

28. Williams, *Mark One or More*, 32.

29. I will have more to say about multiraciality's stability for the future in Part 3.

30. Roediger, *How Race Survived U.S. History*, 136, 137.

31. Ibid., 76.

32. Ibid., 150–151.

33. Ibid., 151.

34. Moran, *Interracial Intimacy*, 167.

35. Ibid., 174.

36. Bratter, "Will 'Multiracial' Survive to the Next Generation?," 825–826.

37. Moran, *Interracial Intimacy*, 167.

38. Lynette Clemetson, "Color My World: The Promise and Perils of Life in the New Multiracial Mainstream," *Newsweek*, May 8, 2000, 70.

39. Mike Stuckey, "Multiracial Americans Surge in Number, Voice," MSNBC.com, May 28, 2008, http://www.msnbc.msn.com/id/24542138/.

40. In fact, the simple notion that such immigrants would themselves be un-

mixed black is not sustainable. But even so, and acknowledging recent increases in sub-Saharan African immigration to the United States, as soon as those persons intermarry or merely interbreed with either American blacks or even American whites, they become part of the same mass of multiracial Afro-Americans.

41. Williams, *Mark One or More,* 86.

42. Ibid., 96.

43. Ibid., 112.

44. Catherine R. Squires, *Dispatches from the Color Line: The Press and Multiracial America* (Albany: State University of New York Press, 2007), 137.

45. Haya El Nasser, "Multiracial No Longer Boxed In by the Census," *USAToday,* March 2, 2010, http://www.usatoday.com/news/nation/census/2010-03-02 -census-multi-race_N.htm?csp=hf.

46. Squires, *Dispatches from the Color Line,* 150.

47. DaCosta, *Making Multiracials,* 185–186.

48. Ibid., 166.

49. Ibid., 9.

50. Joel Williamson, *New People: Miscegenation and Mulattoes in the United States* (New York: Free Press, 1980), chap. 3. It is critical to remember as well that my referring, for the purpose of illustration, in the current instance to "unmixed American blacks" is, properly speaking, inaccurate, since it presumes that there was no population mixture between sub-Saharan Africans and Europeans in West and Central Africa, on the West African coast, on slave ships, in the Americas, and, especially, in the Caribbean, whence many slaves were exported to North America, or any subsequent internal miscegenation even among the parents of darker-complected people. Such a realization only serves to further reinforce my foundational argument concerning the falseness of biological race. Additionally, granting this "unmixed" status for the sake of argument demonstrates the falsity of any claim that modern-day multiracials are in any sense "newer" than either the mulatto population of the past or the general Afro-American population today.

51. It is a question worth pursuing to ask whether this discrimination is not only racial, but racist as well.

52. Gunnar Myrdal, *An American Dilemma: The Negro Problem and Modern Democracy* (New York: Harper & Brothers, 1944), 135. It is absolutely critical to recognize that even in the case of a sexual union between a mulatto and a presumptively unmixed black, internal miscegenation still occurs. European genetic material is still being transferred to the resulting children in such a case, even in the physical absence of a fully European parent.

53. Pauline E. Hopkins, *Contending Forces: A Romance Illustrative of Negro Life North and South* (Boston: The Colored Co-operative Publishing Co., 1900; repr. New York: Oxford University Press, 1988), 151.

54. There may be an argument for making the case that some Sea Islanders may be exceptions, but this would still not evade the general problem revolving around claims that the West and Central Africans brought to the Americas were themselves unmixed.

55. House Subcommittee on Government, Management, Information, and Technology, Committee on Government Reform and Oversight, *Hearings on Federal Measures of Race and Ethnicity and the Implications for the 2000 Census,* testimony by Susan Graham on May 22, 1997. 105th Cong., 1st sess., April 23, May 22, and July 25, 1997, 371.

56. Of course, no people are either monoracial or multiracial, but I am here engaging the premises upon which the American Multiracial Identity Movement has constructed itself in order to analyze the movement's philosophical validity.

57. Kathleen O. Korgen, *From Black to Biracial: Transforming Racial Identity Among Americans* (Westport, CT: Praeger, 1999), 3.

58. Rainier Spencer, *Challenging Multiracial Identity* (Boulder: Lynne Rienner, 2006), chap 1.

59. For a study that quite literally explodes such generalizations, first by examining a research sample from the US South, and second by recognizing and taking into account the important differences between how people might identify themselves racially to others and how they actually internalize their racial identities personally, see Nikki Khanna, "If You're Half Black, You're Just Black: Reflected Appraisals and the Persistence of the One-Drop Rule," *The Sociological Quarterly* 51 (2010): 96–121.

60. Anderson Cooper CNN Blog, "I Am Neither Black Nor White. I'm Both," July 25, 2008, http://ac360.blogs.cnn.com/2008/07/25/i-am-neither-black-nor-white-im-both/.

61. Spencer, *Challenging Multiracial Identity,* 11–13, 22, chap 3.

62. Barry Edmonston, Sharon M. Lee, and Jeffrey S. Passel, "Recent Trends in Intermarriage and Immigration and Their Effects on the Future Racial Composition of the U.S. Population," in *The New Race Question: How the Census Counts Multiracial Individuals,* ed. Joel Perlmann and Mary C. Waters, 244 (New York: Russell Sage Foundation, 2002).

63. Ibid., 244–245.

64. Rachel L. Swarns and Jodi Kantor, "First Lady's Roots Reveal Twisty Path from Slavery," *New York Times,* October 8, 2009, A1.

65. Ibid.

66. Rockquemore, Brunsma, and Delgado, "Racing to Theory or Retheorizing Race?," 29.

67. Kevin R. Binning, Miguel M. Unzueta, Yuen J. Huo, and Ludwin E. Molina, "The Interpretation of Multiracial Status and Its Relation to Social Engagement and Psychological Well-Being," *Journal of Social Issues* 65, no. 1 (2009): 38.

68. Edmonston, Lee, and Passel, "Recent Trends in Intermarriage and Immigration," 245.

69. Ibid.

70. Sexton, *Amalgamation Schemes,* 155.

71. Sundee T. Frazier, *Check All That Apply: Finding Wholeness as a Multiracial Person* (Downers Grove, IL: InterVarsity, 2000), 153.

72. Frederick L. Olmsted, *The Cotton Kingdom: A Traveller's Observations on Cotton and Slavery in the American Slave States* (1861; repr. New York: Modern Library, 1984), 458.

73. Ibid.

74. Ibid.

75. Ibid., 458–459.

76. Harriet A. Jacobs, *Incidents in the Life of a Slave Girl, Written by Herself* (1861; repr. Cambridge: Harvard University Press, 1987), 29.

77. Ibid., 30.

78. Solomon Northup, *Twelve Years a Slave,* 1853, ed. Sue Eakin and Joseph Logsdon (Baton Rouge: Louisiana State University Press, 1968), 29, 58.

79. Ibid., 59–60. Adding to Eliza's unbearable pain, her only other child, ten-year-old Randall, had been sold away from her a mere two weeks and two days earlier. Although Northup refers to Randall as Emily's half-brother, there is circumstantial evidence that Randall might have been her full brother and a mulatto as well, particularly Northup's revelation that Emily's white father separated from

the white wife with whom he was quarreling and took up residence with Eliza "soon after the birth of Randall" (29, 31, 55).

80. For an explanation of plaçage, see Williamson, *New People,* 23.

81. Frederick Douglass, *Narrative of the Life of Frederick Douglass, an American Slave,* 1845, reprinted in *The Classic Slave Narratives* (New York: Signet Classics, 2002), 341.

82. Ibid., 342.

83. Lydia M. Child, "A Letter from L. Maria Child: Emancipation and Amalgamation," 1862, in *A Lydia Maria Child Reader,* ed. Carolyn L. Karcher, 264 (Durham: Duke University Press, 1997).

84. Ibid., 266.

85. Charles W. Chesnutt, "What Is a White Man?," 1889, in *Charles W. Chesnutt: Stories, Novels, & Essays* (New York: Library of America, 2002), 843, 844.

Part 2
The Mulatto Present

7

Postraciality, Multiraciality, and Antiblackness

I devoted the last chapter to initiating a discussion of what the black/white members of Generation Mix are (indistinguishable from mulattoes) and of what they are not (a new phenomenon on the US racial scene). The context for that discussion was the past, particularly in the sense of comparing yesterday's and today's mulattoes with today's black/white multiracials.[1] I shall continue that discussion in this chapter and in Part 2 generally, but with a focus on the present. In other words, I will still be arguing that the black/white members of Generation Mix cannot distinguish themselves from mulattoes and that they are in no sense a new people, but here the argument will be in the context of the implications of the multiracial identity debate in the contemporary moment.

As I have already intimated in the previous chapter, the arguments and positions I am presenting in this book go against the grain of much public opinion and practically all popular media reporting/shaping of thought on this issue in the United States. It also does not sit well with me on a personal level to stand by idly while fallacious new biological race fantasies are deployed—particularly when those deployments come at the expense of American mulattoes. And we should be clear that they do in fact come at the expense of mulattoes, as we are dealing with a zero-sum game of who is and who is not mixed racially. Every attempt by black/white multiracials to set themselves at a distance from the always already-mixed American mulatto population that they are an indistinguishable part of represents an artificial and arbitrary (one might even say unnatural) fracturing of the American mulatto reality. The very nature of the American Multiracial Identity Movement's goal of racial exclusivity, and the specificity of that exclusivity's concomitant distancing from blackness, abets this continuing process of fragmentation.

Moreover, since all Afro-Americans are themselves mulattoes, the broadening acceptance of black/white multiracial identity comes directly at

139

the expense of Afro-Americans in general. There is a sense, then, in which my position may be read as an acknowledged and unambiguous charge that the American Multiracial Identity Movement is engaged in nothing less than an antiblackness project, as Jared Sexton has argued quite effectively.[2] Kerry Ann Rockquemore, David Brunsma, and Daniel Delgado, in considering the current trend of multiracial research, assess it as being encumbered with "epistemological problems coupled with a class bias and a flair for identity politics."[3] In their view, it overemphasizes "the agency of mixed-race people (particularly those that self-identify as multiracial), ignoring structure in favor of an individualistic stance."[4] Importantly, they describe this stance as containing "a palpable disdain for Blackness and an eye toward Whiteness."[5] Minkah Makalani is especially direct in calling the multiracial identity movement "a racist project."[6] Although the charge of antiblackness is often derided as sour grapes or as an exaggeration, if not a complete fabrication, unpopularity in and of itself does not stand in place of valid argument as I intend the ensuing discussion to demonstrate.

As part of this antiblackness project some contemporary mulattoes are denying their mulattoness and in so doing are attempting to move upward in the US racial hierarchy by climbing over their (for lack of a better term) racial siblings. And here is a key point—the issue is not that the black/white members of Generation Mix are denying their blackness, as has been alleged for years by some segments of both the Afro-American lay and scholarly communities. Rather, regardless of whether or not they are denying their blackness overtly, the deeper and more primary issue is that the black/white members of Generation Mix are denying their mulattoness by rejecting their intimate connection to both historical and contemporary American mulattoes. The result of that denial, and of the denial's fervent embrace by American whites and the popular media, is the further isolation of Afro-Americans and their concerns on the periphery of contemporary American life.

I want to ensure that I am absolutely clear regarding what I intend here, as it might seem to be an obscure point. By displacing the denial of blackness argument with a denial of mulattoness argument, I am striving to bring clarity to some essential facts that tend usually to become lost in this debate. While one might appeal to semantic or definitional reasons for objecting to the denial of blackness charge—however persuasive or unpersuasive such reasons might be—it is simply impossible logically to provide a coherent defense against the denial of mulattoness accusation. Moreover, even if one determines at the end of the day that denial of mulattoness reduces ultimately to denial of blackness, there nonetheless are important reasons to linger in the dialectic of the present discussion before settling on that particular conclusion.

My own view is that denial of blackness is not a particularly useful path to follow, in part because of the intense emotion found on both sides of the argument. This emotion limits the opportunity for real, reflective analysis, leading instead to an unfortunate descent into childish name calling and bruised feelings—again, on both sides—whether in the lay or scholarly realms. Charges of not being black enough, answered in turn by counter-charges of racial policing are unproductive and unsophisticated. Denial of mulattoness, however, is a much subtler notion, with far richer opportunities for deep philosophical investigation that move us away from the overly personal confrontations of the usual approach. So even in the context of my raising the general charge of antiblackness against the American Multiracial Identity Movement, I want to stress that my interest here lies in proceeding along the specific avenue of denial of mulattoness rather than the seemingly more direct route of denial of blackness. Finally and before proceeding, we should be clear as well that although they are related in the context of the multiracial identity debate, denial of blackness and antiblackness are not the same thing.

Far from the abominable and abhorrent status accorded to black/white multiraciality in previous centuries, which I detailed in Chapter 2, black/white interracial heterosexual relations in the contemporary era—or, more precisely, the reproductive products of such relations, as black male/white female interracial sex itself still remains problematic at multiple levels—are regarded by many as portending the approaching dawn of an age of racial paradise in the United States. Nor is it a minor point that black/white multiraciality—the slowest-growing variety of all—is touted so very loudly as being the very physical evidence of racism's impending end, for as long as they are disconnected successfully from the larger body of American mulattoes the black/white members of Generation Mix remain a miniscule threat to whiteness and to white supremacy.[7] Indeed, far from representing any kind of threat at all, their cooptation by the US political right, as well as by the mainstream media, renders them a chief collective abettor of continued white domination, as white purity and white superiority are advanced every time acknowledgment is given to black/white multiracial identity as a new and positive phenomenon. Nonetheless, it must still be noted at this point that our new-age multiraciality represents nothing less than a remarkable and fascinating alteration (I would call it an *apparent* alteration at this point) of white attitudes toward limited black/white racial mixture, even if in the end the new view supports white supremacy just as much as did the old.

Yet precisely who benefits from this radical revisionist reading of multiraciality, and who is disadvantaged by it? When viewed from a critical perspective, as opposed to the far more prevalent viewpoint of enthusiastic and unreflective cheerleading, contemporary multiraciality assumes a very different dimension. The difficulty lies in bringing this dimension to the table for discussion, as the national infatuation with Generation Mix creates an almost fundamentalist environment in terms of even suggesting that there could be something less than wonderful about contemporary multiraciality, an environment that relegates the skeptic to the margins prior to the start of any real discussion. For instance, much of the challenge to multiracial identity, though by no means all of it, comes from the Afro-American quarter that, in response, is then castigated as being hopelessly retrograde and still engaged in a longstanding pursuit of victimhood and handouts. Afro-American dissenters from multiraciality are seen as jealous, bitter, and as holding racial attitudes that are dangerously behind the present times and are therefore a menace to the national future.[8]

I want to emphasize that this is no mere conspiracy theory. Readers will particularly note my continual criticism of the popular media in regard to its coverage of multiracial identity.[9] It is a criticism that rests on two points: (1) the simplistic and often bathetic approach taken in pieces concerning multiracial identity, and (2) the even more disturbing fact that gross misinformation, as well as a particular ideological orientation, is conveyed by these outlets. This ideological orientation is neither left wing nor right wing, and might be best referred to as *white wing*. Michael Thornton, reviewing elite media accounts of multiraciality from 1996–2006, finds that "often backing this 'America becoming' are mass media, notably newspapers, the second most important news source in America."[10] According to Thornton, mainstream newspapers favor multiracial identity and envision blacks as impediments to the achievement of America's postracial future: "Typically, mainstream papers focus on Black Americans, who do not see the error of their ways, and who stand in the way of others (i.e., multiracial people and America) trying to achieve personal freedom."[11] For the mainstream press, in the context of the quest for a postracial America, "Black-American attitudes are archaic for they adhere to racial identity politics; multiracial people are their antidote."[12]

These reactions to Afro-American views regarding multiracial identity are but part of a large-scale marginalization of blackness taking place currently in the United States. Not all of it can be laid at the feet of Generation Mix, to be sure, but there are external factors that mesh quite well with the Generation Mix recipe of racial progress through multiracial identity and therefore give that recipe more power than it would possess normally. Notable among these might, for example, be the rise of a few, privileged persons of sub-Saharan African descent to previously unheard of positions of power and influence in US political circles, a rise of select individuals that transmits the erroneous (but very much welcomed) signal that significant racism directed against Afro-Americans is therefore no longer a serious problem in the United States. Colin Powell (Chairman of the Joint Chiefs of Staff and Secretary of State), Condoleezza Rice (National Security Adviser and Secretary of State), and, of course, Barack Obama (President) represent profound personal success stories and historically important symbolic victories, but many Americans are far too eager to make the unjustified leap from the facts of such individual successes to the attractive non sequitur that US racism is no more (or indeed, that it has even changed at all). As Eduardo Bonilla-Silva, writing in 2003, points out, one of the central elements of the structure of "new racism" that he identifies is "the incorporation of 'safe minorities' (e.g., [Supreme Court Justice] Clarence Thomas, Condoleeza [*sic*] Rice, or Colin Powell) to signify the nonracialism of the polity."[13]

Certainly, some readers will be inclined to the view that the aforementioned successes are in themselves proof absolute that racism must surely be in its death throes, but the reality is far more complicated than this. Without diminishing the personal triumphs that these important successes represent, treating this subject in an honest way nonetheless requires engaging in an impolitic conversation that up to now has had few participants. This conversation would interrogate the interesting fact that the first black person elected president of the United States is not a descendant of the West and Central Africans who were enslaved in British North America and the United States but is instead the son of an East African. And I stress that I am in no sense attempting to malign or otherwise take anything away from Barack Obama and his political success; rather, my comments are directed very specifically toward white liberals, who (if they could take a moment to stop congratulating themselves on having finally overcome their racism so that their decades of white guilt might finally be laid to rest) might ask why the first person of sub-Saharan African descent to gain the presidency is a man whose personal ancestry sidesteps the entire history of Afro-Americans in this country.

Consider the reality that had Colin Powell chosen to run for president in 2000 or 2004 he would have enjoyed tremendous white support, perhaps as much or even more than Obama in 2008. Powell's tenure as Chairman of the Joint Chiefs of Staff was applauded nearly unanimously, and he enjoyed national hero status after the first Gulf War. Yet he chose not to run. However, if national white support for a specific and exceptional black man is to be taken as proof of racism's death, why did racism not begin to die significantly in 2000 or 2004 when white approval of Colin Powell was sky high? Had Powell run in 2000 or 2004 he would likely have defeated George Bush, Al Gore, or John Kerry handily. On the current thesis that white national support for Obama entails the end of racism, white national support for Powell—and the support was there regardless of his decision to not run—should have meant the end of racism as early as a full decade ago. Clearly, the "end of racism" thesis as based on white national support for specific and exceptional black people does not hold. When we force our-selves to move beyond celebrating Obama's victory in 2008, we must ask ourselves not just what it means, but also what it does not mean, for it is certainly possible for whites to support a black man for president (and most especially so if the opposing party's candidates for president and vice president do not have the full support of their own party) and yet still not want their daughters to marry one.

Had Hillary Clinton been elected president of the United States on November 4, 2008, would we have seen a similar headlong rush to declare that sexism was dead, or would we in a much more sober way have understood that even though a woman had finally been elected president, sexism never-theless was every bit as entrenched as ever, possibly to become even more entrenched as a reactionary result? Yet, in a manner that departs in a signifi-cant way from the problem of sexism, white liberals seem especially pos-sessed with the need to exploit the election of Obama as a way to move beyond the conundrums of race and racism without ever having really dealt with them. In this they join hands happily with white conservatives, who have the same desire to circumvent the problem of race. As David Roediger points out, "we hear often that race is almost spent as a social force in the US, eliminated by symbolic advances, demographic change, and private choice, if not by structural transformations or political struggles. Nowhere is this line of argument more forcefully, or more contradictorily, made than in analyses of Barack Obama's 2008 campaign for US president."[14] In Roediger's view, "careening representations of the Obama campaign" hav-ing moved the nation beyond race "reflect an overwhelming desire to tran-scend race without transcending racial inequality, as well as the impossibility of doing so."[15]

Recognition of this reality led *New York Times* columnist Bob Herbert, a mere ten months after Obama's election as president, to refer derisively to "those who contended when Mr. Obama was elected that we had achieved some Pollyannaish postracial society."[16] Herbert's fellow *Times* columnist Charles Blow concurs, noting that in an analysis of Federal Bureau of In-vestigation hate crimes statistics, "if you look at the two-year trend, which would include Obama's ascension as a candidate, anti-black hate crimes have risen 8 percent, while those against the other racial groups have fallen 19 percent."[17] Moreover, in light of the simplistic narrative that has been ad-vanced in which Barack Obama has been anointed as the harbinger—in-deed, as the very instantiation—of US postraciality via multiracialism, what are we to make of the fact that on his 2010 US Census form he identified himself as black?[18] From the perspective of multiracial activism most espe-cially, Obama's self-identification as black exposes the wrongheadedness of invoking him as the herald of US postracialism, convenient though such in-vocation might be.

In the context of premature projections regarding the impending demise of US racism, it bears noting at the very least that the three very unique persons mentioned above—a nonthreatening man from the Virgin Islands, a nonthreatening woman scholar of Soviet studies, and a nonthreatening son of a Kenyan—have been supported and embraced by whites in ways that do not extend to less unique persons of sub-Saharan African descent in the United States. We might ask ourselves how far apace this is really from the often-heard *compliment* that some particular person of sub-Saharan African descent is "not like other black people," and whether it is any more progressive an impulse when enacted on the national level than on the personal. Nevertheless, Americans prefer to not be bothered with such annoying questions as these, and so the triumphs of Powell, Rice, and Obama are exploited in a somewhat desperate effort to proclaim that racism is dying.[19]

Inasmuch as multiracial ideology supports and is supported by this trend, it should and must be confronted rather than taken as unjustified proof of a newfound racial reconciliation that does not in fact come close to obtaining today. Frank Bean and Jennifer Lee are certainly correct to point out that "because boundaries are loosening for some non-White groups, many observers might erroneously conclude that race is declining in significance for all groups, and moreover, that race relations are improving at the same pace for all racial/ethnic minorities."[20] More specifically, they argue that "the emergence of multiraciality in American society suggests a loosening of rigid racial boundaries and thus the prospect that the negative kinds of race relations the country has so long endured might be weakening. A similar optimism permeated the legal banishment of discrimination during the 1950s and 1960s. However, as we have subsequently learned, the strong tendency for Black economic disadvantage to persist suggests the powerful legacy of slavery and its aftermath in the United States continues to endure."[21] To give voice to these realities, however, and particularly from the Afro-American perspective, puts one in opposition to popular opinion and suggests that one simply does not desire to accept the end of racism as such.

Sexton offers that in undertaking its assault on blackness, "multiracialism suffers from this conundrum: wanting to condemn identification with racial blackness as the source of social crisis, seeking to locate a politicized blackness as the barrier to a postracial future, while affirming 'mixedness' in ways that reinforce and expand notions of racial purity and the concomitant hierarchies of value that underwrite white supremacy and antiblackness."[22] Yet while certainly a logical conundrum, it is a practical conundrum only if people care to take notice of its inherent inconsistency; as we have seen, Generation Mix has been given carte blanche in respect to avoiding critical scrutiny. As Generation Mix attempts to create itself, or, to be more precise, as it attempts to persuade others that it exists already, "two operations are executed: one, blackness is negatively *purified* insofar as mixedness and blackness are strictly demarcated; and two, whiteness, whose purity remains intact, is *revalorized* by a people of color contingent flying the banner of antiracism, awarding themselves the proper legacy of the civil rights movement."[23]

Through an elaborate ideological shell game, Generation Mix, with the eager support of an uncritical media, creates itself both from and decidedly apart from blackness. Of course, this approach leaves the American Multiracial Identity Movement open to significant charges that it is inconsistent on the questions of whether biological race does or does not exist and whether it indeed serves as the basis for the movement's own instantiation. "In fact, the problem that this oscillation institutes—claiming that race *is* and *is not* a fact of biological data seems to be indispensable, a conceptual doubletalk that makes room for the simultaneous discrediting of race-based politics for blacks and the promotion of race-based politics for the multiracial contingent."[24] Michele Elam gestures specifically to an overt defensiveness on the part of some multiracial advocates, suggesting that this "embattled sense of identity limits critical self-reflection and thus does little to discourage commercial and political co-optation of their 'mixed' image, at the expense of their darker-skinned brethren, in often unwitting support of a color-struck status quo. In this way, not more carefully theorizing their experience can lead to complicity with the very status quo that mixed race advocates claim to challenge, and to perpetuate and extend unknowingly institutionalized systems of inequity."[25] This overly defensive attitude, along with an unreflective brand of politics on the part of the mixed-race movement, plays into the hands of the current power structure.

As Thornton points out, "for mainstream papers, we are in a new era, sans racial determinants, and in this context multiracial people embody a color-blind America where core values and personal desires are the norm. Opposing this trend are Black Americans, who are obstinately irrational, adhering to antiquated ideas about group identity. The unstated implication is that—despite strong evidence that race remains an important aspect of American life—White Americans know better what race means than those suffering most from its presence."[26] Yet any critique of this process from the Afro-American quarter, any suggestion that inconsistency can only beget yet more inconsistency, any suggestion that there are many things requiring repair on the racial inequality front before we as a nation declare "mission accomplished," is met with the charge that blacks simply do not want to admit that the old racism is dead, or at least terminally ill. Sadly, rather than face the harsh reality, the US public is much more willing to countenance such simplistic assessments as that of multiracial-supporting author Stephanie Bird that the "tan [multiracial] area" is a place where "character, personality, and deeds outweigh appearance and geographic origin."[27]

In making the case for rejecting such simplistic analyses I would, along with Sexton, also take note of the ubiquitous rise of "people of color" language wherever one turns these days. While purporting to provide more power to marginalized minorities through a combining of effort and numbers, the "people of color" approach is always likely to marginalize the Afro-American component because, speaking generally, that component will always be at the extreme end of oppression as compared to the other groups. In the words of Bean and Lee, "such omnibus terms combine all non-White groups on the basis of presumed racialized minority status, thus connoting that the individuals to which they refer share a similar subordinate status vis-à-vis Whites. By homogenizing (and thus reifying the experiences of all non-White groups), the 'people of color' rubric indicates the boundaries among non-White groups are less distinct and salient than the boundary separating Whites from non-Whites."[28] Since the result of this methodology is necessarily a blending and averaging of problems (and solutions) among "of color" groups, whatever is proposed is unlikely to have a strong enough relevance to specific Afro-American concerns.

As was the case with Stokely Carmichael and Charles Hamilton's still relevant admonition against Afro-Americans entering into coalitions from a position of relative weakness, the "people of color" phenomenon provides a similar danger of being subsumed by the agendas of more powerful *allies*.[29] Yet, any reticence on the part of Afro-Americans regarding this strategy is perceived as selfish isolationism, which is precisely the same reaction given to Afro-American reluctance to endorse multiracial identity. As Sexton puts it, "black community—assumedly beholden to a retrograde separatism and therefore uninterested in interracial intimacy—has been found wanting, to the point of criminality, in the project of 'Building One America for the Twenty-First Century.'"[30] "Blacks are thus depicted in the multiracial imagination as a conglomerate anachronism, perpetuating disreputable traits of antebellum slave society and presenting a foremost obstacle to the progress of liberal society today; white supremacy in blackface, antiblackness turned upside down."[31] Moreover, "this new oppressive black power is figured as an *internalization* of white supremacy (its rules of definition, codes of conduct, and overall frame of mind) that amplifies its effects insofar as it is now projected against victims who are more vulnerable and less powerful than blacks were once thought to be."[32]

From this there results an isolating of the Afro-American critique and of Afro-Americans themselves from the national debate insofar as only commentary hewing to the received wisdom (i.e., that multiracial identity is the progressive cure to the race problem in America) is granted significant voice. This in turn meshes with the inaccurate declaration that racism is dying, and also with the current realigning of the US racial paradigm that allows for the limited expansion of whiteness and also for honorary whiteness (see Chapter 6), but that maintains the historical and seemingly perpetual status of Afro-Americans at the bottom of the hierarchy. A number of factors, then, are working in concert, with the result that however much things might change or be rearranged above them, Afro-Americans nonetheless continue to view the US racial landscape from the bottom upward.

And this is far from being a new problem, as the lure of whiteness and the stigma of blackness serve to explain "why 'not-yet-white' ethnic immigrants historically strove to become white as well as why immigrants of color always attempt to distance themselves from dark identities (blackness) when they enter the United States' racial polity."[33] Even though they might have been considered nonwhite initially, the persistent attempts of Irish and Southern and Eastern European immigrants to distance themselves from blackness (see Chapter 6) bore fruit eventually in the forms of gradual acceptance and political power that "enabled new immigrants, although victims of 'Nordic' supremacy, to become in time also the beneficiaries of white supremacy."[34]

Intermarriage and multiracial identity, far from ameliorating this alarming situation, only make it worse in the case of Afro-Americans. According to Rachel Moran, "the quest for multiracialism cannot address the growing asymmetry of the underlying racial categories on the census. If current patterns of intermarriage persist, there will be one group, blacks, who remain maritally isolated from all other groups. Race will mark a significant social divide, one that does not exist to the same degree for Asian Americans, Latinos, and Native Americans. As the Asian American and Latino populations continue to expand, blacks will become an increasingly small and isolated group, even among nonwhites. As a result, the color line itself could shift. The critical divide may no longer be between whites and nonwhites but between blacks and nonblacks."[35]

While others in addition to Moran, most particularly Bonilla-Silva via his "triracial system," have characterized this ongoing alteration of the paradigm as one that is moving from a white/black or white/nonwhite dynamic to a nonblack/black dynamic, or a dynamic of whites/honorary whites/collective blacks (the latter category of the triracial system consisting of other groups in addition to Afro-Americans, including "Filipinos, Vietnamese, Hmong, Laotians, Dark-skinned Latinos, Blacks, New West Indian and African immigrants, and Reservation-bound Native Americans"), I believe that such reconfigurations, while useful to a certain extent, nonetheless obscure the vital power that whiteness continues to exert on the paradigm as a whole, as well as the stigma of sub-Saharan African-ancestried blackness—the respective power and stigma that give the paradigm its life.[36] Rather, I see the realignment of the paradigm as moving toward a white/nonblack/black dynamic in which both the white and nonblack categories are seen as being far above the black category. On this view, then, there would be whites (including honorary whites and those mixed-race people deemed fit to enter the white category); nonblacks (Asians, Hispanics, and mixed-race people not able to enter the white category, including those black/white people who disassociate themselves successfully from mulattoes); and blacks (the always already-mixed Afro-American population, all alone again at the bottom of the hierarchy).[37]

In this arrangement, of course, all members of Generation Mix regardless of ancestry (excepting those who are able to and pass as white or who otherwise are granted entry into the expanded white category) imagine themselves in the nonblack category. I am, however, quite receptive to Bonilla-Silva's triracial system, and offer my own version only because I tend to think that blackness is and will continue to be considered so repellant that even the "collective blacks" in Bonilla-Silva's system who are not of sub-Saharan African descent (Filipinos, Hmong, Laotians, etc.) will attempt to distance themselves from *regular* US blacks. I could also see expanding my version and replacing the "nonblacks" with the two separate categories of (in hierarchical order) "honorary whites" on one hand (moving them out of the white category) and "collective non-sub-Saharan African-descent nonwhites" on the other. The differences between these systems, though, are relatively minor in the context of the larger picture. Commenting on Bonilla-Silva's system, Steve Garner illustrates the danger inherent in such realignments becoming actualized: "In this structure, a continuum of racialized positions is complicated by increased mixing and variable identification by Hispanics and Asians. However, at the bottom, socio-economically, remain those with darker skin. The middle of the spectrum is thus extended but the principle lines remain intact. Some lighter-skinned people may become 'honorary Whites,' but changing where the boundaries are established does not mean that the boundaries disappear."[38]

It is in regard to this phenomenon, whichever realignment system one prefers, that my previous comment concerning a zero-sum game was intended, as it should be clear that even in the case of an altered paradigm the black category remains in its seemingly never-ending state of axiological deficit, a situation now abetted by the denial of mulattoness of the black/white members of Generation Mix. It is therefore important to understand that the problem I am here outlining is not a quantitative issue of gross numbers, but rather a qualitative issue of isolation and marginalization. While many commentators over the last two decades have warned of a South African apartheid-like or a Brazilian-style racial dynamic involving a multiracial buffer group developing in the United States should multiracial identity receive broad—and most especially, federal—recognition, these have in fact been wrongheaded concerns. Also wrongheaded have been alarms raised over the negative public policy effects of the black community's losing significant numbers of former and potential members via the gross defection of large numbers of black/white multiracials. While there certainly are a number of important effects to be taken into account regarding these concerns, these fears nevertheless do not represent what should be the primary concern regarding the spread of multiracial ideology.

The notion of a discrete, mixed-race buffer group standing between whites and blacks in the United States is not likely, and becomes less likely with each passing day. The connections to South Africa and Brazil come easily to mind, but they should be rejected on the basis of the serious unlikelihoods they represent, especially considering the huge historical and demographic differences obtaining between these two nations and the United States. Likewise, it is not the simple idea of gross numbers of black/white persons leaving the black category that is the real issue, but instead something a good bit more subtle than that. There is something else going on; it is not merely the gross numbers but rather the disassociation, the movement away, in qualitative rather than purely quantitative terms. Thus, the simple *defection in terms of numbers* concern misses the point.

However, the idea of mixed-race individuals augmenting a developing nonblack group composed of people who for whatever reason are not white enough to be categorized as white but who nonetheless seek distance from blackness is taking place before our eyes. And this coalescing of nonwhite groups into either a new, nonblack *supergroup* or two separate groups of honorary whites and non-sub-Saharan-ancestried nonwhites does not represent the birth of a buffer race, for it does not operate in the way a buffer race does. Rather, it is a simpler but no less problematic situation in which either of these new, nonblack groupings are—along with whites—among several distinct categories standing apart from and above the black group, each, to some degree, defined by its relative distance from the bottom of the well.[39] The major concern, in my view, should be neither buffer-race fantasies nor category-defection paranoia, but rather the further marginalization of Afro-Americans in the context of an altered US racial order—or, perhaps more accurately, a US racial order that remains unaltered *only* for them.

Such is the structural backdrop against which I intend, in the remainder of Part 2, to evaluate the American Multiracial Identity Movement in contemporary terms. This evaluation will proceed along two general and occasionally overlapping lines: (1) an analysis of the present-day movement's relationship to the negative and pathological assessments of the American mulatto of history that I detailed in Chapters 2 and 3, and (2) a critical examination of the way some of those old myths have been revived by the movement today for the purpose of supporting arguments for multiracial identity.

Notes

1. Of course, my thesis is that there is in fact no difference between these groups. The notion that there is any relevant difference is what I am arguing against.

2. Jared Sexton, *Amalgamation Schemes: Antiblackness and the Critique of Multiracialism* (Minneapolis: University of Minnesota Press, 2008).

3. Kerry Ann Rockquemore, David L. Brunsma, and Daniel J. Delgado, "Racing to Theory or Retheorizing Race? Understanding the Struggle to Build a Multiracial Identity Theory," *Journal of Social Issues* 65, no. 1 (2009): 24.

4. Ibid.

5. Ibid.

6. Minkah Makalani, "A Biracial Identity or a New Race? The Historical Limitations and Political Implications of a Biracial Identity," *Souls* (Fall 2001): 74.

7. Let me be clear that by "slowest-growing," I am referring specifically to so-called first-generation births, as of course internal miscegenation continues its centuries-old work of population mixture both endlessly and silently.

8. Sexton is of immense help in illuminating the ways this particular critique, as leveled against Afro-Americans, is conceived as a problem of national scale, as a very threat to what the United States purportedly could otherwise aspire to.

9. Indeed, it is perhaps no longer accurate to refer to the present discussion as a "multiracial identity debate," for the US popular media has already determined that multiracial identity is legitimate.

10. Michael C. Thornton, "Policing the Borderlands: White- and Black-American Newspaper Perceptions of Multiracial Heritage and the Idea of Race, 1996–2006," *Journal of Social Issues* 65, no. 1 (2009): 106.

11. Ibid., 110.

12. Ibid., 111.

13. Eduardo Bonilla-Silva, "'New Racism,' Color-Blind Racism, and the Future of Whiteness in America," in *White Out: The Continuing Significance of Racism*, ed. Ashley W. Doane and Eduardo Bonilla-Silva, 272 (New York: Routledge, 2003).

14. David R. Roediger, *How Race Survived U.S. History: From Settlement and Slavery to the Obama Phenomenon* (New York: Verso, 2008), 213.

15. Ibid., 217.

16. Bob Herbert, "The Scourge Persists," *New York Times,* September 19, 2009, A17.

17. Charles M. Blow, "Black in the Age of Obama," *New York Times,* December 5, 2009, A19.

18. Sam Roberts and Peter Baker, "Asked to Declare His Race for Census, Obama Checks 'Black,'" *New York Times,* April 3, 2010, A9.

19. I again stress, against any misinterpretation whatsoever, that I am not here saying anything against Powell, Rice, or Obama, but am instead reflecting on white liberal acceptance and embrace of these three vis-à-vis white liberal acceptance and embrace of other persons of sub-Saharan African descent.

20. Frank D. Bean and Jennifer Lee, "Plus ça Change . . . ? Multiraciality and the Dynamics of Race Relations in the United States," *Journal of Social Issues* 65, no. 1 (2009): 215–216.

21. Ibid., 216.

22. Sexton, *Amalgamation Schemes,* 65.

23. Ibid., 66.

24. Ibid., 71.

25. Michele Elam, "The Mis-education of Mixed Race," in *Identity in Education,* eds. Susan Sánchez-Casal and Amie A. Macdonald, 145 (New York: Palmgrave Macmillan, 2009).

26. Thornton, "Policing the Borderlands," 121–122.

27. Stephanie R. Bird, *Light, Bright, and Damned Near White: Biracial and Triracial Culture in America* (Westport, CT: Praeger, 2009), 15.

28. Bean and Lee, "Plus ça Change . . . ?," 211.

29. Stokely Carmichael and Charles V. Hamilton, *Black Power: The Politics of Liberation in America* (New York: Vintage Books, 1967), chap. 3.

30. Sexton, *Amalgamation Schemes,* 5.

31. Ibid., 51.

32. Ibid., 56.

33. Bonilla-Silva, "'New Racism,'" 271,

34. Roediger, *How Race Survived U.S. History,* 167.

35. Rachel F. Moran, *Interracial Intimacy: The Regulation of Race and Romance* (Chicago: University of Chicago Press, 2001), 175.

36. Bonilla-Silva, "'New Racism,'" 278. See also Eduardo Bonilla-Silva and David G. Embrick, "Black, Honorary White, White: The Future of Race in the United States?," in *Mixed Messages: Multiracial Identities in the "Color-Blind" Era,* ed. David L. Brunsma, 33–35 (Boulder: Lynne Rienner, 2006).

37. Despite some ambiguity in the name, the nonblack group does not contain whites. I simply consider a name such as "nonwhite nonblacks" too cumbersome to use.

38. Steve Garner, *Racisms: An Introduction* (Thousand Oaks, CA: Sage, 2010), 100.

39. The reference is to the title of Derrick Bell's book, *Faces at the Bottom of the Well: The Permanence of Racism* (New York: Basic Books, 1992).

8

Resurrecting Old Myths of Mulatto Marginality

In Part 1, I related that white men in the late nineteenth and early twentieth centuries developed a portrait of the mulatto that divided generally into physical debility on the one hand and psychological/emotional debility on the other. The physical incapacity was confined mostly to the earlier time frame and the psychological/emotional weakness to the latter. The notion of mixed-race physical debility is, of course, more difficult to sustain in the present day, and so we find it unsurprising that there is far more to say today on the emotional/psychological front. Nevertheless, there are some important ways that physicality stands out as an issue of difference for Generation Mix, and we may examine those aspects. Indeed, we would do well to heed the words of John Mencke, written thirty years ago but still relevant today, who offers the useful caution that "certainly it is questionable whether even today all of the late nineteenth-century suppositions and superstitions about race, racial differences, and the effects of race mixture have disappeared from the mind of white America."[1]

While it is not as direct as pure debility, the often repeated and always wrong multiracial medical fallacy stands as a primary example of the assertion of modern-day debility, albeit coming ironically from the multiracial camp itself. Often the case is made by lay advocates of multiracial identity, and occasionally even by multiracial-supporting scholars (whom we would expect to know better), that multiracial persons have special healthcare needs.[2] This is corollary to a similar claim made in regard to special emotional/psychological needs, but more on those later. It is also corollary to a generalized tendency toward a clear sense of self-pity/special pleading integral to multiracial ideology itself, a function of the ideology's inclination to reclaim and internalize the marginal man pathology paradigm of decades past, regardless of outwardly spirited but nonetheless insincere denunciations of that same paradigm.

When multiracial activists and scholars argue that there are special healthcare needs pertaining specifically to multiracial persons, two related points call for our attention. First, when they do this we can quite rightly recognize it as a hopeless quest for distinctiveness without distinction, an impossible search for an alterity that does not exist, a fruitless hunt for an invented specialness that is every bit as chimerical as it is constructed. In other words, the medical argument is merely yet another faux terrain upon which the special pleading for multiracial difference is mapped. Second, and what is perpetually missed in this discussion, is the significant fact that there is no single healthcare issue that can be pointed to as affecting multiracial people in particular, not even one important medical condition that applies only to multiracial persons.

One would think that after nearly two decades of agitation appealing to precisely such mawkishly alarmist reasoning we would have been provided with at least one documented example of how putative multiracial people are genetically distinct from putative monoracial people, such that a specific medical condition exists affecting only them (or that there exists a general medical condition pertaining to all people but that nonetheless affects multiracial people in some distinct way), but there is no such condition because there cannot be. There cannot be because we are not talking here about closed, endogamous societies such as Hasidic Jews who, because of their nondiverse ancestry, are subject to serious medical ailments such as Tay-Sachs disease. Rather, we are talking about people—especially, but not just Afro-Americans—who have considerable ancestral mixture, both known and unknown. Given that no persuasive argument can be presented for multiracial physical difference in general, there is therefore no persuasive argument to be made for a nonexistent multiracial medical difference.

While rank-and-file activists and certain lax academics may repeat the false warnings of the medical fallacy with misinformed sincerity, the shrewder activists and scholars are well aware when they parrot these claims that they are in fact orchestrating a campaign of major misdirection, for the true goal has never been to uncover and treat specific medical conditions that apply only to multiracial persons. The multiracial medical fallacy has instead always been targeted specifically toward establishing a federal multiracial category via the false assertion that in the absence of such a federal category a host of (nonexistent) multiracial medical conditions will continue to ravage the multiracial community without intervention.

Commenting on the multiracial movement's foundational logical fallacy of claiming to reject biological race on the one hand while simultaneously advocating for a new biological racial category on the other, Kim Williams notes that "one finds a similar contradiction in the multiracial claim that misdiagnoses in health applications represented a grave problem that a federal multiracial category would solve. And why, in the case of the [multiracial advocacy organization] Project RACE proposal, would it be more accurate to lump responses into a catchall multiracial category?"[3] There is then a clear sense in which the old myth of mulatto physical debility is modernized and put to use by contemporary multiracial activists in the service of generating sympathy for the establishment of a federal multiracial category, and most specifically *not* for uncovering any medical conditions that in the first place *cannot* be uncovered because they do not exist.

At the opposite end of the spectrum, in terms of seriousness, from the falseness of the multiracial medical fallacy is an equally false concern regarding the more trivial topic of the hair of multiracial people, especially black/white people, especially children, and most especially girls. Kimberly DaCosta remarks on a line of hair-care products named Curls that purports to be a solution for the alleged special problem of mixed-race hair. DaCosta, however, questions the very premise of the Curls agenda: "In order to accept the rationale that mixed-race women have unique hair care needs, one must believe that the kind of curly hair such women have is different *in a generalizable way* from the curly hair of *non*racially mixed women and girls. As we know, however, lots of women (including African American women) have curly hair and have managed to 'care' for it all these years without Curls or the statistics necessary to identify a multiracial market. Such a claim relies for its impact on the folk belief that there is an inherent bodily difference between the races that expresses itself in *predictable* ways when the races mix (without ever needing to say so directly). While it may be true that many people of partial African descent have corkscrew curls, it's also true that many do not."[4]

DaCosta concludes that Curls is essentially attempting in an *invalid* (my interpretation) way to "delineate a characteristic fairly widespread among people of partial African descent (curly hair)," and convince black/white women or the white mothers of black/white girls to buy its product, by "capitalizing on the desire of those who purchase it to believe that they [or their daughters] are part of a definable, knowable group of women."[5] DaCosta's analysis makes plain the link between the seeming triviality of hair-care products and the deeper narrative regarding multiracial difference/uniqueness that I explore and criticize in this chapter. In the end, Curls stands as yet another example of multiraciality exposed as distinction without difference.

Also in terms of the physical, among the old myths were a few ostensibly positive traits to go along with the more strongly represented debilities. Prominent among these were the notions that mulattoes were more intelligent than blacks and that they were more attractive than blacks as well, both notions stemming from the mulatto's status in-between blacks and whites. Although the former of these notions is not raised today in an open way, the latter is all too common, from activist white mothers who boast of their multiracial children ("How could we not love them?" "They're so cute") to the glossy magazine advertisements and television spots that use young people, and especially young women, to sell merchandise through the exploitation of an image of racial mixedness.[6]

In the case of aesthetics, though, we need to delve beneath the immediate surface in order to see what is actually going on, as the "cuteness boast" may seem at first to be merely an innocuous and perfectly reasonable expression of motherly love and pride when in fact it is much more than just that. The comment is, first of all, not a comment about all children; were it a comment about children in general, it would be perfectly unproblematic. Rather, it is a comment specifically about multiracial children, and given the context of the particular source cited (Lisa Jones writing about activist white mothers of biracial children), and considering also that the demographics of the American Multiracial Identity Movement are dominated by white mothers of black/white children, it is most assuredly a comment about black/white children. The idea that black/white children are "cuter" than ordinary black children is a long-running subtheme in the narrative concerning contemporary mixed-race identity in the United States, although the comment above is likely as overt as it is put typically. Nonetheless, it is a perfect complement to all the many other claims about the purported *specialness* of multiracial children.

I have suggested elsewhere that there exist certain forbidden corridors within multiracial discourse, corridors that are taboo, corridors that have mainly to do with white mothers of multiracial children.[7] And here as well it is necessary for me to raise a question that will surely be considered impolitic at best. When white mothers brag about the cuteness of their black/white children—which is a bragging not merely about them as these mothers' children, *but specifically about them as black/white children*—it is clear that the comparison intended is to ordinary black children. Any apologetics to the contrary would require a complete and concerted evasion of the weight of nearly four centuries of Anglo/sub-Saharan African contact in North America. So the question is this: Given that white mothers of black/white children see their children as being cuter than ordinary black children, do they also see them as being cuter than ordinary white children? The answer is that of course they do not; indeed they cannot, for the privileging of whiteness that serves as the foundation of multiracial ideology does not and cannot sanction such an outcome.

I am not so naïve as to fail to anticipate that my assertions regarding this matter will be met with an outraged cry of "Foul!"; however, I challenge anyone to argue persuasively and with a straight face that when white mothers speak gushingly of the beauty of their black/white children (*as* black/white children and *in* the context of a discussion of multiracial identity) they are doing anything other than what I am here suggesting—namely, using ordinary black children as an axiological reference point for comparative statements about their own black/white children's beauty. This is both obvious and uncontroversial; however, as is often the case with pointing out that someone has spinach stuck between her or his teeth, a critique is usually not uttered out of a misplaced sense of politeness.[8] But I certainly find it to be a perverted sense of politeness that at the same time enables these mothers to engage in speech degrading black children, whether overtly or under the surface.

From the microlevel of parental boasting about multiracial cuteness we may move to the more macrolevel phenomenon of explicit marketing of multiracial beauty as a racially transcendent and politically progressive zeitgeist and, upon doing so, we again find serious problems behind the celebration. In this case the showcased mixedness typically is actually no more than a fad, while it masquerades as something much more powerful and significant than it really is. In elevating a self-indulgent social fad to the status of a socially conscious, transgressive politics, the advertisers succeed in prostituting the manufactured exoticness of Generation Mix in order to sell a false image of progress against the racial superstructure while at the same time prevailing perversely in cementing that very superstructure ever more firmly into place. Readers might wonder why the assertion and proliferation of mixed-race identity and imagery do not weaken the US racial paradigm. As I intend to demonstrate, the answer has to do with the difference between real structural change at the foundational level of the racial order and purely cosmetic adjustments on its surface, such that despite the celebration of mixedness and the postracial equality it might be presumed to imply, a motivation of increasing distance from blackness and increasing nearness to whiteness is very much at work here.

Something that has failed to generate adequate attention is the fact that it is a very specific type of mixed-race imagery that is proliferating lately in the commercial world—an imagery that is often part Asian or otherwise considered nonwhite, and *if* partaking in blackness is usually of a very much lighter-skinned variety. And even while the imagery in these thoroughly nontransgressive and nonpolitically conscious advertising campaigns tends for the most part to be either part Asian or nonwhite, the narrative articulated by local and national multiracial identity organizations and support groups is—owing to the principal membership and leadership of those organizations, which tends to be white mothers of black/white children—overwhelmingly a message about black/white mixture and its supposed transformative effect on the structuring of race in the United States. In highlighting this divergence, I am arguing that there is a sense in which that heavily promoted black/white narrative is riding a wave of part Asian/nonwhite multiracial imagery and part Asian/nonwhite upward movement within the US racial paradigm, and taking advantage of the content of a particular conversation that it is actually not a party to.[9]

Sushi Das, writing in an Australian publication about marketing trends in global perspective and also making several specific references to the United States, notes that "ambiguity, it seems, is in vogue and the current fascination with racial hybrid is reflected in the myriad ethnic looks eagerly adopted by models and other trend setters."[10] She finds that "ad campaigns for top-end brands such as Louis Vuitton, YSL, and Lancome all use models with racially indeterminate features, and the look is also being embraced in the music world."[11] Das conveys the words of a Melbourne modeling agency executive who "knows exactly what advertisers want" and who "reports a hike in demand for mixed-race models."[12] Speaking of a world trend Australia is attempting to catch up with, this executive asserts that "over the last couple of years, there has been an increase in using Asian people in advertising, and also a lot of people like the mixed-race look as well: not too Asian, but with a bit of a Western feel. We handle a lot of Asian and Eurasian models."[13]

Linking specifically these kinds of advertisers with the rising general trendiness of multiracial identity, Das opens the door for questioning which is cause and which is effect here, and also for an assessment of how deeply rooted either in reality or in any sort of progressive politics this display of multiracial imagery is: "Cheekily referring to themselves as the 'remix generation,' this group of young people sees a future born out of a mixed-race heritage. And while models, superstars and pop idols chase the latest 'look,' advertisers and marketing teams are frantically pumping out images that they say reflect a multicultural society."[14] Yet if this frantic pumping out of multiracial imagery in search of the most recent popular "look" is nothing more than pure marketing, if it contains no element of political consciousness, then it is subject to the same critique Caroline Streeter makes in regard to a Levi-Strauss US billboard advertisement featuring a mulatto woman that, in her view, "relies on celebratory and ahistorical rhetoric that elides the vexed strategies that racially mixed subjects have deployed to negotiate hierarchies of race and color."[15]

In Streeter's view, "this kind of multicultural imagery makes racially mixed people symbolic embodiments of antidiscrimination while using their images to mask persistent inequalities."[16] It is a view that meshes nicely with that of Julie Matthews, who, in analyzing the supposed transgressiveness of Eurasian mixed-race identity politics through the lens of performativity, discovers that "its vacant hollowness overflows with alluring impressions of cosmopolitan transnational/transcultural attributes and embodied visual aesthetics. Fear and antipathy to miscegenation is smoothed over, rather than effaced, when the mixed-race other is recoded as 'cosmo chic'—familiar, knowable, sophisticated and worldly."[17] Steve Garner suggests that "we may already have passed the point at which mixed-ness stops being a threat to the racial order, given the ideological work that such bodies perform in advertising."[18] DaCosta would appear to concur with Streeter, Matthews, and Garner in averring that "too often, advertisements featuring images of multiraciality repeat rather than challenge racial stereotypes. The images of multiracials now put forth by advertisers echo older images of the mulatto, but include only those elements that are putatively positive in the age of hip consumerism."[19] Nor should we soon expect any progressive change to this kind of apolitical exploitation, for DaCosta is surely correct to remind us that "as long as mixed race maintains its air of hipness and authenticity, marketers will continue to exploit it."[20]

Multiracial-supporting author Sundee Frazier gestures toward this exploitation in warning multiracial people against thinking themselves "superior to those 'monoracials.'"[21] Frazier counsels multiracials against "arrogance, especially now that being multiracial is considered chic. Our visages are flashed all over the place to sell clothes, cars, cell phones—you name it. We're the faces of the future, very vogue and of course *always* good looking. We have the best of both worlds—Anglo features *and* that Coppertone tan everyone covets. It's tempting to take in marketers' messages and have an inflated and false sense of esteem."[22] It is difficult, though, in reading Frazier's words, to detect a clear sense of what one would hope is sarcasm. Rather, it appears that she agrees with the premise that multiracials do indeed possess aesthetic superiority over monoracials, but advises that they should not gloat about that inherent superiority.

Ronald Sundstrom provides a somewhat similar sort of advice to black/white multiracial people in respect to their superior looks vis-à-vis monoracial blacks: "What remains then, is the obligation of multiracial individuals not to harm monoracial groups in their representations and celebrations of mixed-race looks."[23] But Sundstrom goes further even than Frazier in his patronization, suggesting that "this response would necessarily involve a willingness to generously listen, the humane recognition of loss, and the promise to be responsible."[24] One can almost visualize here the beautiful multiracial person, patting the head of and consoling the irredeemably ugly monoracial black.

Whether in reference to individuals who are black/white, part Asian, or some other combination, the notion (or perhaps multiple notions) of a relatively superior mixed-race aesthetic (or aesthetics) is clearly operative in contemporary US society. Indeed, one view holds that multiracial people are more attractive because they are more symmetrical than monoracial people.[25] But whether based on questionable notions of symmetry, on simplistic conceptions of improving blackness by adding whiteness to it ("They're so cute") or on equally troubling modes of sexual exoticization and fetishization, the contemporary mixed-race figure, especially when female, brings forward into modernity the old myth of the mulatto's aesthetic desirability over (and this is often a lost point) the *lesser* half of her or his ancestry. This is most especially so in the case of black/white mixture, given that such cases represent the antipodal extremes of the US racial paradigm, and play back into the monumental and abysmal interracial sex act of black and white parents. So when the aesthetic superiority of Generation Mix (a superiority that is always relative to nonwhiteness of some kind or other) is trumpeted—whether by white mothers of black/white children or by exploitive advertisers—it is an old story, albeit modified and thereby augmented by the enhancements of modern communications media and the overly willing consumption of the US public.

The aesthetic superiority of whiteness vis-à-vis blackness is what led in the American past to the unbalanced terminology for quadroons and octoroons. I refer to that terminology as unbalanced because it takes only half of the potential combinations into account—those with continuing white admixture; and I refer to it quite self-consciously in the present tense ("it takes only half") because even though the terms themselves might now be considered archaic, the idea behind that lack of balance remains in full force. To illustrate this imbalance, let us consider two simple questions. First, using the old terminology, what would one call a person with one black grandparent and three white grandparents? Such a person would be a quadroon. Now, what would one call a person with three black grandparents and one white grandparent? Of course, there is no specific term for this person, for the category is nameless. Simply put, white men cared about mulattoes because they represented the direct results of the illicitness of white male desire for, and white male consummation of, interracial sex.

But after this, white men cared only about the descendants of mulattoes who had continuing white admixture, since these—most especially those who were female—approached nearer and nearer to whiteness while their receding black ancestry served as a sort of exotic icing on the aesthetic cake, as exemplified by the words of one particularly unsavory white male character in Dion Boucicault's 1859 play, *The Octoroon*, who says, "that one drop of black blood burns in her veins, and lights up her heart like a foggy sun. Oh, how I lapped up her words like a thirsty bloodhound! I'll have her if it costs me my life!"[26] But those descendants in the other direction on the continuum, those with continuing black admixture, were deemed unimportant enough to be categorized in a similar way. They were simply black or vaguely mulatto. The United States has always been more interested in the idea of blackness moving toward whiteness through several generations of offspring (even though those offspring may never become white legitimately) than it has been interested in whiteness moving toward blackness. Indeed whiteness does not in any case really move toward blackness, since whiteness as a pure and coherent essence is in fact subsumed and consumed by blackness in the first generation of offspring. Therefore, even though either side of the continuum is every bit as mixed as the other, historically it has only been the whiter side that has been deemed to be mixed racially.

Today we are witness to precisely the same phenomenon in terms of the black/white members of Generation Mix and the American Multiracial Identity Movement's views as to who is and who is not multiracial. As I illustrated in Chapter 6, multiracial ideology holds that the addition of whiteness to mixedness (mixedness in the form of an always already-mixed Afro-American parent) produces mixedness, but that the addition of blackness to that same mixedness does not produce mixedness but instead produces monoraciality. This is why the modern multiracial identity movement, while of course not utilizing the term octoroon and while of course preferring first-generation mulattoes most of all, will nonetheless embrace the person with one black great-grandparent and seven white great-grandparents while rejecting from its ranks the person with seven black great-grandparents and one white great-grandparent. Just as white men of yesterday gave the descendants of mulattoes who had white admixture the names quadroon and octoroon because they considered such persons more important than those nameless unfortunates having the reverse ancestry, the American Multiracial Identity Movement today likewise (and quite stunningly, in my view) considers the contemporary equivalent of yesterday's quadroons and octoroons to be more important, and therefore more deserving of membership in the ranks of contemporary multiraciality. Not only is the mulatto more pleasing aesthetically than the black, but adding further whiteness to the mulatto only increases this aesthetic superiority while adding blackness moves back in the opposite direction toward nameless, indeed unnameable, ugliness.

Through false notions of bodily vulnerability such as the multiracial medical fallacy, or equally false ideas of aesthetic superiority, Generation Mix has positioned itself so as to be entwined comfortably with centuries-old racist myths of mulatto physicality that are hardly as forgotten as one might have thought or hoped. In these resuscitated physical myths the marginal mulatto is reincarnated. As fascinating as these correlations certainly are, the more obvious, more salient, and more powerful connection between Generation Mix and marginality comes via the way of emotional/psychological debility. Here, more so than even in the case of the old myths of physical incapacity, Generation Mix and the academics who provide its scholarly support attempt to make the case for multiracial exceptionalism by drawing directly upon racist and biological notions of blackness, whiteness, and mulattoness from deep within the most troubled recesses of our national past. The overarching motif in regard to emotional/psychological debility is that multiracial people (most especially children) have special emotional and psychological needs that must be addressed if they are to attain completeness in terms of their emotional and psychological maturity. Readers will see very readily the ironic and, indeed, twisted, relationship of such claims to the work of the early twentieth-century sociologists whom I discussed in some detail in Chapter 3.

We will recall that those racist, white male sociologists—compelled by their own commonsense and "obvious" notions of white superiority and Negro inferiority and by their narcissistic assumption of an unquestioned desire on the part of mulattoes to be white—developed an elaborate program of mulatto emotional and psychological debility based on these profoundly bankrupt premises. According to this analysis, mulattoes were born with a terrible problem, one that was likely irresolvable without specific intervention geared toward convincing mulattoes to accept their blackness and to give up on the futile and mentally crushing quest for the whiteness they could never hope to attain. My earlier critiques of this sociopsychological assessment in Chapters 3 and 4 stand, and I do not intend to rehearse them here in the present chapter. However, I do intend to offer an important connection to those critiques by interrogating what might be the strangest artifact of contemporary multiracial ideology—namely, that while activists within and supporters of the American Multiracial Identity Movement will generally react with intense disdain to suggestions such as those of our racist early twentieth-century sociologists that impugn the emotional and psychological stability of black/white people, the movement has nonetheless itself erected an essentially parallel paradigm in which only the polarity of the normatively prescribed desire for blackness has been reversed.

Consider, as an example of this reversed parallel, the words of multiracial activist Marvin Arnold, testifying before Congress in support of a stand-alone multiracial identifier for federal statistics. In Arnold's view, "racial identification" as multiracial, "is important for the Multiracial person because of the perceived psychopathology engendered as a result of his/her inability to identify with a specific racial category. . . . Because he/she cannot identify with a specific racial group the conclusion is that dysfunction will ensue."[27] Arnold invokes an explicit warning of psychological danger and damage to multiracial people who do not adopt a multiracial identity. "Psychopathology" and "dysfunction" are not minor issues, and regardless of whether or not Arnold was exaggerating in order to win favor for his argument, his alarming words nonetheless were considered by the congressional panel before which he testified and now stand as part of the historical record.

It is important to point out that Arnold speaks explicitly in regard to black/white children. In the course of his testimony he makes clear that he is interested in this particular population through not only direct references but also by invoking specifically offensive terms such as "Zebra" and

"Oreo."[28] He also indicates that he is a "member of a Multiracial family," has two daughters, and that his interest in this subject stemmed from a "dilemma that emerged for [him] with [his] own children."[29] One could, of course, using Arnold's framework, provide the counterargument that black/white persons could resolve their "inability to identify with a specific racial category" simply by identifying as black, but that clearly is not an acceptable option to the American Multiracial Identity Movement. In that vein, however, it is crucial to understand that when proponents such as Arnold argue for black/white multiracial identity, they are effectively arguing *away from blackness*, which as I am endeavoring to point out is merely the reverse of the early twentieth-century *toward-blackness* solution for resolving black/white mixed-race identity problems.

Fascinatingly, ironically, and indeed dangerously, Arnold's words could just as easily have been those of Robert Park, Edward Reuter, or Everett Stonequist arguing that mulattoes must accept black identification or else risk psychological dysfunction. The only difference is that today the polarity of therapeutic normativity has been reversed from *toward blackness* to *away from blackness*. In every other sense, however, the Generation Mix paradigm for mixed-race emotional/psychological stability as articulated here by Arnold in particular and by the American Multiracial Identity Movement in general is perfectly parallel to the marginal man paradigm developed by racist, white male sociologists in the early twentieth century. Clearly, one would suppose that this development should represent a serious problem for the American Multiracial Identity Movement in terms of its moral and antiracist standing at a very minimum. That it seemingly is not a concern at all speaks volumes about how the movement positions itself in regard to whiteness, white superiority, and antiblackness.

This parallel, both ironic and perverse as I shall demonstrate in some detail, follows the same pervasive pattern of internal contradiction that so plagues the American Multiracial Identity Movement whenever it can be extricated from its protective cocoon of hip, media-supported favor and subjected to even a minimum level of critical intellectual inquiry. Just as in the under-examined cases of unpersuasively rejecting biological race while lobbying actively for a new biological racial category, and hypocritically rejecting hypodescent for black/white children while applying it continuously to their always already-mixed Afro-American parents, the movement involves itself in yet another logical contradiction in regard to the emotional/psychological needs of its seemingly perpetually vulnerable constituents.

This approach is a staple among the lay activist group, and can be found with regularity in the writings of the multiracially supporting academic contingent as well. For example, Ursula Brown argues that multiracial people lack "self-esteem" in the absence of an ability to proclaim publicly both portions of their identities.[30] Not content to stop at such hyperbolic nonsense—nonsense that highlights Brown's own questionable self-positioning as a white woman presuming to pass judgment on the self-esteem of black/white people—Brown goes so far as to warn that white parents' "biological and psychological connection" to their black/white children "is wiped out with the provision of a black label."[31] Unsurprisingly, Brown leaves us in the dark as to the specific scientific details of how a contingent racial label is able to "wipe out" an actual, biological, parent-child connection. But in today's gadarene rush to valorize Generation Mix, such traditional academic considerations as providing at least a modicum of evidence for controversial claims seem to be of little import.

Continuing the trope of marginality, Sundstrom avers that to be multiracial in today's society results in "anguish and alienation."[32] Similarly, G. Reginald Daniel speaks of "psychological oppression" stemming from the lack of a federal "multiracial identifier" for mixed-race people to select.[33] It is all too easy to allow the words to glide by without much thought, but "psychological oppression"?—in regard to filling out paper forms? As should by now be clear, supporters of multiracial identity, both lay and academic, demonstrate a tendency to exaggerate; however, exaggeration or not, it is crucial to hold these commentators—and most especially to hold the scholars—to their printed words. So from an activist testifying before Congress, and three respected scholarly supporters of multiracial identity, we see such dire warnings as psychopathology, dysfunction, lack of self-esteem, the severing of parental-child psychological *and biological* connections, anguish and alienation, and psychological oppression being bandied about as the certain effects of failing to legitimize multiracial identity. It is doubtful that Park, Reuter, and Stonequist in their day did any better than these modern-day supporters of the American Multiracial Identity Movement at advancing the impression that black/white people are born with a serious problem that needs explicit psychosocial intervention in order to rectify it.

If there is some aspect of emotional/psychological weakness that goes along with contemporary black/white mixed-race identity in the United States, it is a weakness that is neither natural or biological, nor inevitable. If such a weakness exists it is a weakness that instead is taught and learned. Indeed, it is a weakness that is part and parcel of the inculcation of multiracial ideology in the United States, and as such differs completely from the unequivocal *acceptance as black* that has taken place traditionally (and that still does when it is not rejected) in the context of Afro-American communities. I therefore advance the claim that, generally speaking, being taught that one is black/white multiracial today brings with it this weakness, creates and installs it, so to speak. Somehow, in the process of indoctrination to a multiracial identity, the indoctrinators—whether white mothers or some other agents—establish this originary psychosocial debility as part of what it means to be black/white in the United States. Thus is the new millennium marginal man born.

As in the case of the physical question, there is also a two-pronged approach to the emotional/psychological side, as we find both positive and negative traits or conditions being deployed in the effort to present the argument in support of multiracial identity. There is no comprehensive, mixed-race sociopsychological profile driving this ascription of traits. Rather, it is very much a *kitchen-sink* type of strategy in which anything that will generate sympathy or otherwise make the case for multiracial superiority is appealed to regardless of whether or not it coheres with the remainder of the evidence in the sink. And we shall see that, as in the case of physicality, the pieces of evidence offered on the emotional/psychological front—both the positive and the negative pieces—have direct analogues to the long-discredited mulatto myths detailed in Chapter 3.

We will recall from Chapter 3 our review of early twentieth-century sociologists' racist analyses that led to such ridiculous (but to them quite "obvious") conclusions as Robert Park's assertion that mulattoes are "often sensitive and self-conscious to an extraordinary degree."[34] This "sensitivity" derived supposedly from the mulatto's fractured and fragile psychology stemming from having been cursed to live an impossible existence somehow combining—simultaneously—intimate connections to the most highly developed and the most depravedly degraded two races on earth. Significantly, and seemingly either unaware or unconcerned about the racist and hegemonic positioning that Park presumed to occupy in his writings about mulattoes, Kathleen Korgen resuscitates Park's notions about cosmopolitanism in arguing that "biracial men and women possess a broader and more objective view of society than nonmarginal persons."[35] Indeed, Korgen goes so far in validating Park as to declare of her research sample that the "vast majority of the under-thirty interviewees agree with Park that they are more 'cosmopolitan' than non mixed-race persons."[36]

We see in these statements a bizarre inversion of negative and positive over the seven decades of temporal distance between Park and Korgen; although, for her part, Korgen does not seem to consider Park's analyses to be at all problematic or negative. Yet it is clear that Park's judgments in regard to the mulatto have no meaning outside the framework of his whiteness, his inherent racism (regardless of whether or not understood or acknowledged by him), and his mistaken and projected belief that mulattoes reject blackness and desire most of all to be white. All of these factors combine to ensure that Park's work on mulattoes is interesting only for what it tells us about the racist projections of early twentieth-century white male sociologists, and that it is certainly unable to relate to us any meaningful sociological facts regarding early twentieth-century mulattoes themselves, as shown through our review of mulatto writers in Chapter 4. Nonetheless, Korgen embraces Park's negative comments about mulattoes and resurrects them as positive statements in reference to the supposed specialness of modern-day black/white people.

As Minkah Makalani puts it, "the most obvious methodological problem is Korgen's failure to analyze her respondents' responses. Rather than demonstrate their broader worldview, she merely accepts their word that they possess such a worldview. This approach stems from a more serious theoretical problem: Korgen's failure to critique, modify, or bring into the current historical era Robert Park's seventy-two-year-old idea of the marginal man. As she accepts Park's essentialist, racialist, and masculinist premise, it is no wonder that she exemplifies . . . a tendency to view people of mixed parentage as intellectually superior to 'unmixed' Blacks, a reformulation of the antebellum 'mulatto hypothesis' that makes a social constructionist argument that hopelessly dovetails into a morass of essentialism. Korgen's argument would make people of mixed parentage race seers, purveyors of a new racial order based solely on their mixed parentage and date of birth—which presumably signals their distance from the Black community and proximity to the white community."[37]

Korgen reports approvingly of her respondents' self-elevation through the mythology of mixed-race superiority that in their cases merely replaces the old, negative racist stereotype with a new, positive racist stereotype. Devoid completely of anything resembling critical commentary, one sees quite easily that Korgen's work reads very much like the typical fluff piece on multiracial identity that we have come to expect from the likes of *Time* or *Newsweek*. And while Korgen takes care to use such terminology as "such and such respondent feels that" and "biracial persons believe that they," her decision to eschew completely any critical comment on these assertions makes plain that she is in perfect agreement with these myths of multiracial superiority. For example, she relates her respondents' preposterously self-serving claims that a "mixed racial background has prevented them from being racist," that they "could never be racist," and that it "would be impossible for them to be prejudiced."[38] Yet nowhere is found the least suggestion that these narcissistic and self-serving assertions might possibly be mistaken. And what are we to make of Korgen's report that "today young black-white persons feel not only different but, in some ways, wiser than monoracial persons"?[39] The only thing missing from Korgen's statement is the honest inclusion of the words "racially superior." Commenting on the fact that Korgen's research is based on testimonials, Makalani cautions that while not devaluing "personal experiences," nevertheless "they must be viewed as data for scholarly analysis, not as the analysis itself."[40]

Margaret Shih and Diana Sanchez take us down a similar slippery slope of Generation Mix racial superiority by offering that "multiracial people, on average, tend to challenge the validity of race itself and tend to view race as a social construction more than those of monoracial descent. Viewing race as a social construction tends to put multiracial people at an advantage because racial stereotypes lose their meaning and fail to affect multiracial people's performance."[41] There are at least three serious problems with this brief statement. First, it should be clear that multiracial persons do nothing to "challenge the validity of race," as the best way for them to challenge race would be to reject rather than embrace their alleged biological multiraciality. Second, if multiracial people actually view "race as a social construction," they would in fact not claim in the first place to be multiracial since it is the sexual, as opposed to the social, union of their parents that is the cause of their putative multiraciality. Finally, we are faced with yet another iteration of the false idea that the members of Generation Mix are less prone to racial bias. Indeed, one thing that is becoming clearer and clearer in regard to this population is a pointed racial bias *toward* multiracial people and their alleged superiority—both aesthetic and intellectual—over mere monoracials.

There is a smugness associated with this valorization of contemporary racial mixture that is palpable if one is not party to the celebration, a smugness that is a complement to the rejection of the mulatto of history that I considered toward the end of Chapter 6. It is in that regard a double insult to American mulattoes today and to their voiceless precursors of past decades and centuries. I am therefore moved to provide a name for what has thus far been only a feeling, something I have responded to and reacted against, but that until now has remained nameless. I therefore introduce the concept of *miscentrism*, by which I mean an ideology that holds multiraciality to be superior to all monoraces with the exception, naturally, of whites. This exception is necessary to note, for the American Multiracial Identity Movement is invested at a deep philosophical level in the perpetuation and veneration of whiteness as purity and superiority. In a perverse way, the American Multiracial Identity Movement's clear stances of mulattophobia and Negrophobia are counterpoised against its own miscentrism in a kind of isometric logical fallacy.

An even more far-fetched version of the argument for mixed-race specialness and superiority comes by way of broadcast journalist Elliott Lewis, who ascribes to the members of Generation Mix such as himself the veritable super power of detecting by sight alone not just multiracial people but first-generation multiracial people! To avoid any misperception of my having put words into Lewis's mouth, it will be best to allow him to speak for himself: "I call it 'MULTIRACIAL RADAR.' It's some sort of sixth sense that members of interracial families learn to develop over the years. It allows us to spot other multiracial people who share similar experiences of living between two worlds."[42] Following a weak passage in which he suggests that multiracial radar may not always work perfectly, Lewis then reverts immediately back to grand announcements of its awesome power: "My multiracial radar is what told me that Sundee Tucker Frazier was biracial."[43] Indeed, so effective is Lewis's multiracial radar that the first time he was introduced to Frazier's family he "wasn't the least bit surprised by their racial makeup. They were just how [he'd] pictured them."[44] Thus, despite Lewis's disingenuous sowing of mild doubt it is clear that he intends for us to understand that his multiracial radar is a strong and consistent super power available to all members of Generation Mix. Unaccountably, however, Lewis's trusty multiracial radar failed him completely when he met Irene Johnson, with him noting that "I had no idea she was biracial until she brought it up."[45]

Lest I be accused wrongly of failing to see that Lewis's comments about multiracial radar are intended by him to be some sort of humor, his actual seriousness about this particular Generation Mix super power is revealed when, in bringing up an historical point made by Daniel concerning segregation-era Afro-Americans who were hired by white business owners to "spot" other Afro-Americans passing as white, Lewis writes that "in other words, spotters were people who had finely tuned multiracial radar."[46] So I am inclined to take Lewis at his word when he makes the assertion that as a multiracial person he possesses multiracial radar. Or, in other words, I think Lewis actually believes he does in fact have the super power to detect first-generation multiracial people by sight, its puzzling failure in the aforementioned case of Irene Johnson notwithstanding.

To ensure that I am not perceived as delivering an excessive critique at Lewis's expense, let us be clear that is not only him claiming to have multiracial radar. DaCosta reports on another mixed-race individual with, apparently, the very same super power: "'I had that mixed person's radar,' said Kanji Uyematsu 'where I would just leave my shit if I found somebody that was mixed. I just went up to them, "Oh my God, you know what it's like."'"[47] DaCosta goes on to explain that "Kanji's 'radar' was tuned to pick up the signals of other mixed people in public. That his radar was tuned in this way is telling of the extent to which he was seeking similarly situated others whom he felt would understand him."[48] However, that Kanji Uyematsu's "mixed person's radar" super power is an actual scientific fact and that mixed-race people give off "signals" that can be detected in public by others is, significantly, left unquestioned.

Certainly, one can be forgiven for an inclination to dismiss Lewis and Uyematsu's nonsensical super power as well as Korgen's self-serving super-cosmopolitanism (self-serving since she happens herself to be the aunt of a presumably super-cosmopolitan black/white child); but dismiss them as we might, these sorts of inanities continue to collect around and to be drawn into the vortex of Generation Mix celebratory hype.[49] It is a hype that has been manipulated by the American Multiracial Identity Movement in order to bend concrete reality in an illegitimate way and replace it with ethereal perception. For example, Lewis's claim of being able to "spot" multiracial people has connections to a larger fallacy regarding race and appearance that continues to gain a foothold in both the scholarly and popular realms despite its patent artificiality. In fact, it is a tendency that is related to nineteenth-century literature introduced first by white writers, and later lampooned by Afro-American writers, that asserted with surety that it was always possible to detect that hidden tinge of African blood in the mulatto (see Chapter 2). Only now, the tinge is apparently no longer hidden, but fairly shouts out loud in announcing itself—at least to those whose personal "radar" can detect it, at any rate.

Kerry Ann Rockquemore, David Brunsma, and Daniel Delgado engage this narcissistic tendency of Generation Mix in a critical way by noting that "*Multiracial* is at times equated to racially ambiguous and uncategorizable phenotype that binds individuals into 'Generation E. A.' (ethnically ambiguous); however, the empirical reality of phenotype in the mixed-race population is one of striking variation and heterogeneity, not similitude and homogeneity."[50] DaCosta also exposes this particular fallacy, an error that is rampant in the literature on Generation Mix, when discussing the tendency of multiracials to construct symbolic markers of multiraciality so as to make the case for a singular multiracial identity and experience: "One indicator of the extent to which ambiguous appearance was seen as emblematic of mixed experience is evidenced by the frequency with which respondents described someone as 'typically mixed looking,' which for many meant being unable to easily situate that person in dominant racial categories."[51] I have elsewhere commented on this error, but the fallacy is such that it will do to provide a more extended elucidation of it here.[52]

I would begin by raising the question of precisely how—most especially in the Afro-American case—DaCosta's respondents imagine themselves to be delineating a legitimate boundary between "typically mixed looking" persons of sub-Saharan African and European descent and "typically unmixed looking" persons of sub-Saharan African and European descent, the latter of course referring to *ordinary* Afro-Americans as members of the "dominant racial category" *black*. What, precisely, are the specific parameters involved in being "typically black looking," and how do those parameters then differ in the case of a "typically mixed looking" black/white person? Even the slightest reflection upon the vast continuum of Afro-American appearance—including skin color, facial features, and hair texture, to name only a few of the most prominent points of typical focus—reveals the notion of the "typically mixed looking" person as being far beyond preposterous. In fact, it is clear that there is significant analysis required before we ought to accept the notion that someone can be "typically mixed looking," that the term actually has any useful content at all.

The truth is that we have, in the case of race and racial mixture over the last nearly four hundred years on the North American continent, what might be called a temporal sliding scale, whose operation seems to be all but invisible to nearly everyone in the contemporary moment. The ultimate effect of this sliding scale is to continue the simultaneous broadening and lightening of what is considered black in North America, a phenomenon pointed out decades ago by both Gunnar Myrdal and Joel Williamson (see Chapter 6). Although all sorts of combinations are possible, considering the darkness of the first sub-Saharan African people in British North America (whether having arrived directly from Africa or via the Caribbean), and the paleness of the English colonists, the very first black/white persons here must have been relatively brown-skinned people who today would in no sense be considered "obviously mixed." However, decade by decade and century by century, blackness has expanded its breadth such that what was too light to be considered obviously black in one century becomes unproblematically black in future centuries. Or, to put it another way, the Afro-American who in 1710 appeared to be "obviously mixed" would in 2010 appear to be unproblematically black.

This is the reality, that over the centuries the average skin color of Afro-Americans, to consider but a single parameter, has become ever lighter and lighter. If we were to calculate the average skin color readings of all people of sub-Saharan African ancestry on the North American continent in the years 1710, 1810, 1910, and 2010, we would find a consistent lightening from that earliest century to the most recent. This is a concrete effect of the enforcement of hypodescent, to be sure, but it is also a potent refutation of the current "obviously mixed looking" falsehood. Today's "obvious mixedness" is in fact standing on the back of centuries of "obvious mixture," such that the assertion that some person today is "obviously mixed" stands as a completely meaningless and completely false piece of commentary. Today's "obvious mixture" relies on the imposition of a static and arbitrary falseness that in a most self-interested way disregards the dynamism of centuries of Afro-American population mixture in this matter. What the apologists for Generation Mix fail to appreciate (or, rather, what they find in their interest to ignore) is the surety that what appears "obviously mixed" today will at some future time be seen as unproblematically black.

The very serious problem that presents itself when we are inattentive to this phenomenon is that each unchallenged instantiation of "obvious mixedness" thereby erases or otherwise obscures a portion of the massive mixture that preceded it, which in turn serves to convey the false impression that there is in fact a "mixed look," and that what one is seeing is therefore "true and authentic mixedness." But if there truly is a "mixed look," it is the look of any Afro-American; indeed, it is the look of every Afro-American. The brown-skinned daughter of a Central African freeman and a white indentured servant-woman in the colonial Chesapeake would doubtless stand be-mused at the assertion today of what supposedly does and does not consti-tute a person's being "obviously mixed looking." But as we saw in Chapter 6, respect and concern for the historical mulattoes of America's past is nowhere on the Generation Mix agenda.

What passes in many cases for research on multiracial identity often contributes to this fallacy. In an article investigating the way mixed-race in-dividuals code faces and place them into racial categories, Kristin Pauker and Nalini Ambady add to the confusion over multiracial looks. According to these authors, "the categorization of multiracial individuals is often diffi-cult because of the ambiguity in their racial appearance. Precisely because of this ambiguity, multiracial individuals are frequently bombarded with the question, 'What are you?'"[53] I want to make clear precisely what I am in-tending here since readers may not see an immediate connection between a "visibly mixed-race look" and the appearance of "racial ambiguity." These notions are in a sense taken to be equivalent; they are an attempt to state that mixed-race people have a particular appearance. And this is often the problem with such research. It is not necessarily only the basic methodol-ogy or other factors of the research project itself, but rather also the mis-taken and unchallenged presumptions the researchers build into the body of the project. Addressing this problem in connection with studies of race in general, Barbara Koenig, Sandra Lee, and Sarah Richardson point out that sometimes "researchers' commitments function in a way that obscures the tautologies at the core of their methods and practices—building race 'in' to the analysis leads inevitably to finding race as a salient 'outcome' variable."[54] The same point may certainly be made in regard to unchal-lenged assumptions concerning the ubiquity of mixed-race people's visual ambiguity.

Pauker and Ambady believe that multiracial people are ambiguous vi-sually. The authors do not qualify their statement by suggesting that some multiracial people are ambiguous visually or that certain combinations are more ambiguous visually than others. They simply take for granted that multiracial persons are ambiguous ("*the* ambiguity in their racial appear-ance" [italics added]). It is a small mistake, but one that then infects their entire project, for the unchallenged presumption of ambiguity is bogus, to put it plainly. Pauker and Ambady report on their specific work with Asian/white respondents, but since their statement about *the* ambiguity of multiracial persons appears in the very first line of their article, it is clear that they intend that statement to refer to all multiracial persons. Moreover, they also state—of multiracial people in general—that "their shared experi-ence of dealing with having an ambiguous appearance in a world obsessed with categorization may lead to conceptions of race and compensatory strategies unique to their experience, and wholly different from that of monoracial individuals."[55] The two authors' unquestioned assertion that all multiracial people experience a "shared . . . ambiguous appearance" is close—bizarrely and perversely so—to the idea that *they all look alike*, even though what is actually being asserted is that they all look *unlike* monoracial persons.

It requires no great effort to see how the black/white case exposes the wildly invalid nature of this assumption. Is there a monoracial Afro-American visual appearance in the United States? If so, what does that appearance look like? Of course, we know at the outset that the always already-mixed Afro-American population contains within it every conceivable skin shade, hair texture, and eye color that could possibly come as a result of black/white intermixture. We also know that it is nothing particularly special for two Afro-American parents to conceive a child who is lighter in skin color than a supposed first-generation black/white multiracial child is. These are commonplace facts of life in the United States that point to the ridiculousness of claiming that some black/white people have an ambiguous look that other black/white people do not have. Yayoi Winfrey points to the absurdity of this claim in reporting that "recently, a group called Multi Generation Multiracials (MGMs) challenged First Generation Multiracials (FGMs). Although both groups have mixed ancestry, FGMs have one white and one black parent while MGMs may have two parents, or even grandparents, that are mixed. MGMs who aren't able to 'officially' claim a biracial heritage, argue that they are often more mixed looking than FGMs who, because of their parents' visibility, can automatically declare a dual ethnicity."[56]

The fallacy of "obvious mixedness" is related to an interesting phenomenon also involving visual acuity, and it will be useful to take a brief detour through that particular issue before proceeding. Ironically, for nearly two decades multiracial advocates have shed crocodile tears over so-called eyeballing, the complaint of being scrutinized visually in order to determine the race of multiracial persons, yet they now claim the ability—indeed, as we have seen, the unique super ability—to themselves "eyeball" the difference between monoracial and "visibly mixed" persons, only now they rejoice in it. As with so much of multiracial ideology, there is actually no consistent principle that is appealed to. When eyeballing can be used as a means to generate sympathy for multiracial persons (as when they are eyeballed by menacing monoracials), it is so deployed; but when eyeballing can be proffered as evidence of multiracial special ability and community building, it is deployed in the opposite way.

Let us ensure quite carefully that in the matter of eyeballing the American Multiracial Identity Movement has indeed expressed outrage at the idea of monoracials engaging in the practice, usually schoolteachers for the purpose of completing forms required by federal civil rights compliance monitoring if the student or parent has refused to provide the information requested. As DaCosta notes, "in administrative settings such as schools and medical facilities, someone other than the person being classified often records race. Multiracial activists explicitly objected to this practice, which they dubbed 'eyeballing' because it violated the ethos that individuals should determine their own identity."[57] According to Susan Graham, executive director of Project Race (Reclassify All Children Equally), "'eyeballing' by a teacher, employer, census enumerator, or *anyone* is subjective, highly inaccurate, and probably a violation of civil rights. No one should be allowed to 'guess' a person's race based on the perceived color of their skin, on their surname, or on any other criteria."[58] Testifying before Congress, Graham referred to eyeballing as "totally subjective" and "unfair."[59]

Also appearing before Congress, Carlos Fernández, former president of the Association of MultiEthnic Americans (AMEA), found it "especially offensive as well as a violation of privacy" for teachers to perform this required task, testifying that it "has more in common with the sorting of animals than it does with the ordinary respect supposed to be accorded human beings."[60] He also calls it "probably the most onerous and outrageous enforcement of the one-drop rule."[61] Deploying the exaggerated, overplayed, and emotionally charged weapon of there being an imminent danger to children, all too common during the census debates of the mid-1990s, Nancy Brown and Ramona Douglass (the latter also a former president of AMEA) link eyeballing to the denial of multiracial children's dignity, writing that the "'eyeball test' is still being used in many classrooms across America by teachers whose own racial baggage may further depreciate the self-esteem of the young minds entrusted to their care."[62] Finally, questioning the accuracy of eyeballing, Jane Chiong considers it an "antiquated practice."[63]

Lest I leave the impression that multiracial resentment at eyeballing is a relic of decades past, DaCosta's contemporary research reveals that her respondents "were intimately familiar with experiences like being 'eyeballed' by others (stared at) that many felt was objectifying and demeaning."[64] Yet DaCosta also reports that "one respondent said she 'loved looking at [other] multiracials.'"[65] And this I think is the key, for the obvious inconsistency of the American Multiracial Identity Movement on this issue is that eyeballing is construed as invasive, insulting, and threatening—unless it is a situation where it is multiracial people who are doing the eyeballing. Indeed, *"nearly all"* of DaCosta's "respondents of mixed descent . . . describe being drawn to other multiracials, *captured in stories of not being able to take their eyes off the multiracials they saw in public.*"[66] Let us be clear that DaCosta's respondents are simultaneously averring that they find being stared at by others to be "objectifying and demeaning" but that they themselves are not "able to take their eyes off the multiracials they [see] in public." So much for the crisis of eyeballing. Let us return then to the issue of "obvious and visible mixedness."

Lewis's account of attending a multiracial college student conference embodies precisely the fallacious thinking that I have been criticizing in regard to a supposed "visibly mixed-race look": "To walk into a room and find a sea of visibly mixed-race people—folks who looked like me—was overwhelming. 'These are my people,' I remember thinking."[67] As I have been suggesting throughout this book, and in this chapter in particular, there is a peculiar Generation Mix dynamic in which unchallenged wishful thinking is allowed to stand as established fact. This dynamic is then abetted by multiracial-supporting scholars and by popular media outlets, adding yet another layer of fantasy to the myth of contemporary mixed-race specialness and exceptionalism. Thus, far from eliciting the least bit of critical challenge, we may be sure that Lewis's words will instead be taken as proof in and of themselves that there is, indeed, such a thing as "visibly mixed-race people."

Lewis, a black/white individual, would have us believe that now, abruptly, in this moment, it is possible to place people accurately into discrete biological racial categories; and that furthermore it is reasonable to wipe away nearly four hundred years of population mixture's physical history in order to declare that blackness has suddenly become static and can be differentiated from so-called visible mixedness. Aside from contradicting the bogus notion that the American Multiracial Identity Movement does not support the idea of biological race—for the assertion of "visibly mixed-race people" clearly requires that there also be "visibly unmixed-race people"—Lewis also advances the absurd idea that the general Afro-American population is a monoracial one against which Lewis's "people" may be manufactured.

The fact is that if we took a "white," indigenous person from England and a "black," indigenous person from West or Central Africa and placed them at either end of a line, and then placed the 30 million Afro-Americans between them, the vast majority of the 30 million would look "obviously and visibly mixed" as compared to the two persons at either end. But people who are determined to prove a fallacious point see only what they want to see. The multiracial advocate says that a particular first-generation person of European and sub-Saharan African ancestry appears "visibly mixed," while someone else looks at that very same person and says she looks "obviously black." In the case of Afro-Americans—that is, persons of European and sub-Saharan African ancestry—their appearances range to all skin tones, hair textures, and facial features, such that there is no black/white Generation Mix "look" that is not always already an Afro-American "look." To assert otherwise is simply to ignore both history and present reality.

We may put the lie to such self-serving ignorance by going back more than a century in time to Pauline Hopkins's 1900 novel, *Contending Forces*, in which she has a character state with conviction that "'it is an incontrovertible truth that there is no such thing as an unmixed black on the American continent. Just bear in mind that we cannot tell by a person's complexion whether he be dark or light in blood, for by the working of the natural laws the white father and black mother produce the mulatto offspring; the black father and white mother the mulatto offspring also, while the *black father* and *quadroon* mother produce the black child, which to the eye alone is a child of unmixed black blood. I will venture to say that out of a hundred apparently pure black men not one will be able to trace an unmixed flow of African blood since landing upon these shores!'"[68] Hopkins's point—that it is impossible to utilize "looks" as an index of mixedness—is even more true today than when she made it over one hundred years ago, for in the case of Afro-Americans there simply is no connection between appearance and a fallacious monoracial purity. Indeed, the additional century of internal miscegenation alone has ensured that there is far, far less of an excuse for insisting on such a nonsensical connection today than even in Hopkins's time. Writing just a few years later, Hopkins goes even further than this in rejecting any essential physical difference between blacks and whites: "The slogan of the hour is 'Keep the Negro down!' but who is *clear enough in vision* to decide who hath black blood and who hath it not? Can any one tell? No, not one; for in His own mysterious way He has united the white race and the black race in the new continent. . . . No man can draw the dividing line between the two races, for they are both of one blood!"[69]

As Deborah McDowell sees it, Hopkins's argument, "propounded throughout the narrative in various guises, is that the blood has flown so freely between the races that any attempt to sort and separate them was inevitably confounded. . . . Thus the narrator's question in *Of One Blood*— 'Who is clear enough in vision to decide who hath black blood and who hath it not?'—posed an implicit challenge to the visual logics on which biological understandings of race depended, particularly the 'one drop rule' that made ancestry the unimpeachable determinant of 'blackness.'"[70] What must be pointed out, and in the strongest terms, is that Lewis's "visible mixedness" is precisely the sort of "visual logics" on which depend the "biological understandings of race" that Generation Mix—based on its racial presumptions and its acceptance of selective hypodescent—cannot possibly move us beyond. Rather than imbibing the opiate of visible mixedness, science and logic require that we accept all three of Hopkins's premises: (1) that race in general is a fallacy, (2) that mixed-racial difference is a fallacy as well, and (3) that the notion of such nondifference being detectable visually is a complete absurdity.[71]

One therefore wonders how Lewis, an experienced broadcast journalist, can with a straight face and his professional integrity intact promulgate the nonsense that there exists a "visibly unmixed" Afro-American look that can be contrasted, as if in a relationship of binary opposition, with a "visibly mixed" Afro-American look. Has he never bothered to take the time to actually look at Afro-Americans and see the infinite array of skin colors, facial features, and hair textures they possess? What Generation Mix advocates do, then, is not only revivify the ancient notions of *Natus Æthiopus* and *Natus Albus* (born black and born white, respectively) in a distinctly visual sense, but then add to these archaisms a new visually defined category, *Natus Miscerus!*[72] Perhaps we may surmise from this that multiracial support groups engage in a ritual of fingernail inspection behind closed doors, gleefully showing off their lunulae to each other, or possibly searching each other's eyes for that indistinct, telltale darkish tinge around the iris.

Mirroring Lewis's wishful thinking, one young-adult multiracial activist describes his first experience of joining a mixed-race organization in a similar fashion: "There was something about stepping into a room and seeing 30 other kids that kind of looked like you."[73] It is necessary to question what is going on in these recitations, however. Frankly, I think it is either (or both) a pre-experience expectation or a postexperience reformulation that coheres happily and conveniently with the desire of multiracial persons to see themselves and those who identify as they do as different (from monoracial people) and as special. After all, it is as easy to imagine a room full of light- and brown-skinned Afro-American members of the local college's Black Student Solidarity Club as it is to imagine exactly the same grouping as members of the same college's Multiracial Support Group. But would Lewis or our commentator above be likely to extol the "visible mixedness" of the former group? One thinks not, for such honesty would not advance the multiracial message.

This sort of double standard is reflected as well in the overly dramatized issue of the "What are you?" question that has become a staple of the multiracial position, as exemplified by Stephanie Bird, who refers to it as "*the* question."[74] One group of multiracially biased researchers has gone so far as to refer to this question as a case of "overt racism" specifically "targeting multiracial people."[75] However, we can put this rather overstated remark in context by noting that these same researchers, in discussing the lack of a specific federal multiracial identifier on institutional forms, aver—rather incredibly, to my thinking—that "not having a racial designation on institutional forms is one of the most invidious experiences of racism that occurs to multiracial people."[76] Once again, it is made clear in quite an obvious way that multiracial advocacy, whether in the nonscholar activist arena or deep within academia itself, is apparently at some pains to express itself without engaging in what we might for the sake of tact call exaggeration. Frazier adds to the "What are you?" double-standard when she complains that "fielding these comments and inquiries gets old after awhile," just before negotiating a deft about-face to aver that "I kind of like it that people are thrown off by my ambiguous appearance."[77] One can indeed have it both ways, apparently, if the issue is multiracial identity.

As with "eyeballing," instances of being asked the "What are you?" question are represented as uniformly insulting, demeaning, and, at least according to some academics, "overt racism." But is it really this bad, even among multiracial people, to be asked a personal question of this sort? In returning to Lewis having discovered "his people," he writes: "Here the question wasn't, 'What are you?' It was, 'What's your mixture?'"[78] Perhaps I might be forgiven in failing to detect a shred of difference between the two questions qua questions. Similar to the hypocrisy of the eyeballing double standard, the only difference here appears to be in who is asking the question. Missing then, of course, is the feigned personal outrage that erupts supposedly from the first question (which is in fact precisely the same inquiry as the second question) when posed by a monoracial person.

Given that Lewis himself expresses frustration with being asked the irritating "What are you?" question, one would expect him, at least, to be sensitive to asking such irritating personal questions of other people as a matter of internal consistency if nothing else.[79] However, Lewis recounts for us that when he first met Geetha Lakshminarayanan, he did precisely that to her in asking how long it took her to learn to spell her last name, which strikes me as being rather along the lines of asking a tall person what the weather is like up there.[80] At one point he even started counting—*out loud*—the number of letters in her name: "one, two, three—," before she was moved to provide the answer of "sixteen."[81] Even in writing about this event after the fact, and noting that his response to her name was "a reaction Geetha has experienced, by [his] guess, about a million times," Lewis nonetheless remains blind, completely, to the irritating and personal nature of his inquiry, as well as to its equivalence with the "What are you?" question, ending his story with the jaunty comment: "Yep, she had definitely been through that conversation before."[82]

Against the potential criticism that I am making far too much of a trivial and heartwarming incident, let me insist in the strongest terms possible that there is absolutely no difference whatsoever between Lewis being asked the dreaded "What are you?" question and Lewis himself asking Geetha Lakshminarayanan how long it took her to learn to spell her last name. In fact, there is one very significant difference—in the latter case it is Lewis who is asking the question, going so far as to make light of it. One thing that apparently never crosses the minds of the outraged members of Generation Mix is that on those occasions when they are asked the "What are you?" question, perhaps those menacing monoracials are merely curious and mean no harm. Or could it be that some members of Generation Mix are simply looking to be insulted? In any case, if multiracial persons want to be consistent and want to avoid hypocrisy there very clearly needs to be a rearticulation of both the "eyeballing" and the "What are you?" controversies such that monoracial persons who stare at multiracials and multiracial persons who stare at multiracials—however endearingly—garner the same reaction, and such that irritating personal questions along the lines of Lewis's "What's your mixture?" or even his "How long did it take you to learn to spell your last name?" invoke the same response regardless of whether the questioner is monoracial or multiracial. In my view, such activities and questions must in themselves, and in a prima facie sense, either be "objectifying and demeaning" or not; it cannot depend on the questioner.

Lest I be accused of being unfairly dismissive of or insufficiently sensitive to these concerns, let me address my point through an example. Imagine two persons who eyeball or stare at multiracials, and who also ask them the "What are you?/What's your mixture?" question. Person One is a light-skinned black/white person who identifies as monoracially black, and Person Two is a dark-skinned black/white person who identifies as multiracial. Should the multiracial target of staring/questioning by Person One not be insulted because she might take Person One to be multiracial (which according to Lewis and according to DaCosta's respondents would make it acceptable)? Should she be insulted because Person One has done these things and identifies as monoracial (and, according to multiracial ideology, therefore *is* monoracial), or since she does not know Person One but might think he is multiracial, should she be insulted only if she happens to actually discover that Person One identifies as (or is) monoracial? The same questions might be raised in the case of Person Two with, one supposes, opposite results. Clearly, the fact that "eyeballing" and the "What are you?" question are objectifying and demeaning only if monoracials (whether real or perceived) engage in them, but not if multiracials (whether real or perceived) engage in them, leads to a host of logical absurdities that reveal the special pleading taking place.

Such special pleading is a component of the miscentrism that animates modern multiracial advocacy. This miscentrism has resurrected and embraced many of the myths of marginality that were used to deprecate American mulattoes from the late nineteenth through the early twentieth centuries. The significant difference today is that miscentrism switches the polarity of the solution for resolving mixed-race identity from *toward blackness* to *away from blackness*. In Chapter 9, I shall take up one of the most often deployed but also one of the most flagrantly fallacious myths of the American Multiracial Identity Movement—namely, that Generation Mix possesses a unique super power of racial bridging that will bring about the end of race and that will usher in an American postracial future.

Notes

1. John G. Mencke, *Mulattoes and Race Mixture: American Attitudes and Images, 1865–1918* (Ann Arbor: UMI Research Press, 1979), 49–50.
2. Kathleen O. Korgen, *From Black to Biracial: Transforming Racial Identity Among Americans* (Westport, CT: Praeger, 1999), 105.
3. Kim M. Williams, *Mark One or More: Civil Rights in Multiracial America* (Ann Arbor: University of Michigan Press, 2006), 44.
4. Kimberly M. DaCosta, *Making Multiracials: State, Family, and Market in the Redrawing of the Color Line* (Stanford: Stanford University Press, 2007), 162.
5. Ibid.
6. Quoted in Lisa Jones, *Bulletproof Diva: Tales of Race, Sex, and Hair* (New York: Doubleday, 1994), 58–59.
7. Rainier Spencer, *Challenging Multiracial Identity* (Boulder: Lynne Rienner, 2006), chap 3.
8. Beyond this is also the secondary possibility that these white mothers are endeavoring to normalize the interracial erotics of their children's genesis by emphasizing their cuteness as black/white children, somewhat along the lines suggested by Jared Sexton, who writes that "since it is understood by multiracial advocates that criticism of or opposition to interracial relationships is based in large part on concerns about potential offspring, the creation of positive images for multiracial people is, in circular fashion, taken to be an exoneration of interracial relationships as well." Sexton, *Amalgamation Schemes: Antiblackness and the Critique of Multiracialism* (Minneapolis: University of Minnesota Press, 2008), 159. Still, though, I believe the primary impulse to be a much simpler comparative to ordinary black children that serves to establish the same kind of distancing from blackness as does so much else within multiracial ideology.
9. A less charitable assessment would be that it has hijacked that conversation.
10. Sushi Das, "They've Got the Look," *The Age,* April 20, 2004, http://www.theage.com.au/articles/2004/04/19/1082357106748.html.
11. Ibid.
12. Ibid.
13. Ibid.
14. Ibid.
15. Caroline A. Streeter, "The Hazards of Visibility: 'Biracial' Women, Media Images, and Narratives of Identity," in *New Faces in a Changing America: Multiracial Identity in the 21st Century,* ed. Loretta I. Winters and Herman DeBose, 308–311 (Thousand Oaks, CA: Sage, 2003).
16. Ibid., 311.
17. Julie Matthews, "Eurasian Persuasions: Mixed Race, Performativity and Cosmopolitanism," *Journal of Intercultural Studies* 28, no. 1 (February 2007): 43.
18. Steve Garner, *Racisms: An Introduction* (Thousand Oaks, CA: Sage, 2010), 100.
19. DaCosta, *Making Multiracials,* 170.
20. Ibid., 182.
21. Sundee T. Frazier, *Check All That Apply: Finding Wholeness as a Multiracial Person* (Downers Grove, IL: InterVarsity, 2000), 86.
22. Ibid.
23. Ronald R. Sundstrom, "Mixed-Race Looks," *Contemporary Aesthetics Special* 2 (2009), http://www.contempaesthetics.org/newvolume/pages/article.php

?articleID=540. Sundstrom's argument is not limited to black/white multiracials, but every example he deploys in the contemporary context is a black/white example.

24. Ibid.

25. Alon Ziv, *Breeding Between the Lines: Why Interracial People Are Healthier and More Attractive* (Fort Lee, NJ: Barricade, 2006), 90.

26. Dion Boucicault, *The Octoroon,* 1859, reprinted in *Plays by Dion Boucicault,* ed. Peter Thomson (London: Cambridge University Press, 1984), 148.

27. House Subcommittee on Census, Statistics, and Postal Personnel, Committee on Post Office and Civil Service, *Hearings on the Review of Federal Measurements of Race and Ethnicity,* testimony by Marvin. C. Arnold on June 30, 1993, 103d Cong., 1st sess., April 14, June 30, July 29, and November 3, 1993, 162.

28. Ibid., 161.

29. Ibid.

30. Ursula Brown, *The Interracial Experience: Growing Up Black/White Racially Mixed in the United States* (Westport, CT: Praeger, 2001), 3.

31. Ibid., 65.

32. Ronald. R. Sundstrom, "Being and Being Mixed Race," *Social Theory and Practice* 27, no. 2 (April 2001): 285.

33. G. Reginald Daniel, *More Than Black? Multiracial Identity and the New Racial Order* (Philadelphia: Temple University Press, 2002), 190; Daniel, *Race and Multiraciality in Brazil and the United States: Converging Paths?* (University Park: Pennsylvania State University Press, 2006), 281.

34. Robert E. Park, "Mentality of Racial Hybrids," *American Journal of Sociology* 36 (1930–1931): 545.

35. Korgen, *From Black to Biracial,* 79.

36. Ibid.

37. Minkah Makalani, "A Biracial Identity or a New Race? The Historical Limitations and Political Implications of a Biracial Identity," *Souls* (Fall 2001): 94.

38. Korgen, *From Black to Biracial,* 78.

39. Ibid., 79.

40. Makalani, "A Biracial Identity or a New Race?" 92.

41. Margaret Shih and Diana T. Sanchez, "When Race Becomes Even More Complex: Toward Understanding the Landscape of Multiracial Identity and Experiences," *Journal of Social Issues* 65, no. 1 (2009): 7.

42. Elliott Lewis, *Fade: My Journeys in Multiracial America* (New York: Carroll & Graf, 2006), 55.

43. Ibid.

44. Ibid., 55–56.

45. Ibid., 176.

46. Ibid., 118.

47. DaCosta, *Making Multiracials,* 135.

48. Ibid.

49. Korgen, *From Black to Biracial,* 3–4.

50. Kerry Ann Rockquemore, David L. Brunsma, and Daniel J. Delgado, "Racing to Theory or Retheorizing Race? Understanding the Struggle to Build a Multiracial Identity Theory," *Journal of Social Issues* 65, no. 1 (2009): 25.

51. DaCosta, *Making Multiracials,* 140.

52. Spencer, *Challenging Multiracial Identity,* 100–102.

53. Kristin Pauker and Nalini Ambady, "Multiracial Faces: How Categorization Affects Memory at the Boundaries of Race," *Journal of Social Issues* 65, no. 1 (2009): 69.

54. Barbara A. Koenig, Sandra Soo-Jin Lee, and Sarah S. Richardson, "Introduction: Race and Genetics in a Genomic Age," in *Revisiting Race in a Genomic Age,* ed. Barbara A. Koenig, Sandra Soo-Jin Lee, and Sarah S. Richardson, 10 (New Brunswick: Rutgers University Press, 2008).

55. Pauker and Ambady, "Multiracial Faces," 82.

56. Yayoi L. Winfrey, "In the Mix: Issue of Mixed Race Stirs Controversy for Census," *International Examiner,* January 21, 2010, http://www.iexaminer.org/category/issue/volume-37-no-02/.

57. DaCosta, *Making Multiracials,* 41.

58. Susan R. Graham, "The Real World," in *The Multiracial Experience: Racial Borders as the New Frontier,* ed. Maria P. P. Root, 46 (Thousand Oaks, CA: Sage, 1996). Italics added.

59. House Subcommittee on Census, Statistics, and Postal Personnel, Committee on Post Office and Civil Service, *Hearings on the Review of Federal Measurements of Race and Ethnicity,* testimony by Susan Graham on June 30, 1993, 103d Cong., 1st sess., April 14, June 30, July 29, and November 3, 1993, 109.

60. House Subcommittee on Census, Statistics, and Postal Personnel, Committee on Post Office and Civil Service, *Hearings on the Review of Federal Measurements of Race and Ethnicity,* testimony by Carlos Fernández on June 30, 1993, 103d Cong., 1st sess., April 14, June 30, July 29, and November 3, 1993, 130.

61. Carlos A. Fernández, "Government Classification of Multiracial/Multiethnic People," in *The Multiracial Experience: Racial Borders as the New Frontier,* ed. Maria P. P. Root, 27 (Thousand Oaks, CA: Sage, 1996).

62. Nancy G. Brown and Ramona E. Douglass, "Making the Invisible Visible: The Growth of Community Network Organizations," in *The Multiracial Experience: Racial Borders as the New Frontier,* ed. Maria P. P. Root, 325–326 (Thousand Oaks, CA: Sage, 1996).

63. Jane A. Chiong, *Racial Categorization of Multiracial Children in Schools* (Westport, CT: Bergin & Garvey, 1998), 63–64.

64. DaCosta, *Making Multiracials,* 198.

65. Ibid., 135.

66. Ibid. Italics added.

67. Lewis, *Fade,* 230.

68. Pauline E. Hopkins, *Contending Forces: A Romance Illustrative of Negro Life North and South* (Boston: The Colored Co-operative Publishing Co., 1900; repr. New York: Oxford University Press, 1988), 151.

69. Pauline E. Hopkins, *Of One Blood; Or, The Hidden Self* (1902–1903; New York: Washington Square Press, 2004), 178. Italics added.

70. Deborah E. McDowell, "Introduction," in *Of One Blood; Or, The Hidden Self,* by Pauline E. Hopkins (New York: Washington Square Press, 2004), xi–xii.

71. I stand on this interpretation of Hopkins even while acknowledging the contradictions in *Of One Blood* that have Hopkins averring that all humans are of one blood while seeking at the same time to distinguish in a special way ancient and modern-day Ethiopians (the latter term including American blacks) through bloodline descent. For an explication of this, see Susan Gillman, *Blood Talk: American Race Melodrama and the Culture of the Occult* (Chicago: University of Chicago Press, 2003), chap. 2.

72. For a discussion of *Natus Æthiopus* and *Natus Albus,* see Werner Sollors, *Neither Black Nor White Yet Both: Thematic Explorations of Interracial Literature* (New York: Oxford University Press, 1997), chap. 2.

73. Quoted in Kimberly M. DaCosta, "Mixing It Up," *Contexts* (Fall 2005): 16.

74. See, for instance, Teresa Kay Williams, "Race as Process: Reassessing the 'What Are You' Encounters of Biracial Individuals," in *The Multiracial Experience: Racial Borders as the New Frontier,* ed. Maria P. P. Root, 191–210 (Thousand Oaks, CA: Sage, 1996); Stephanie R. Bird, *Light, Bright, and Damned Near White: Biracial and Triracial Culture in America* (Westport, CT: Praeger, 2009), xii. I myself have never been asked the dreaded "What are you?" question.

75. Marie L. Miville, Madonna G. Constantine, Matthew F. Baysden, and Gloria So-Lloyd, "Chameleon Changes: An Exploration of Racial Identity Themes of Multiracial People," *Journal of Counseling Psychology* 52, no. 4 (2005): 514.

76. Ibid., 511.

77. Frazier, *Check All That Apply,* 33.

78. Lewis, *Fade,* 230.

79. Ibid., 5.

80. Ibid., 259.

81. Ibid.

82. Ibid.

9

The False Promise
of Racial Bridging

Another major analogue to the discredited mulatto myths of the past—and, also, yet another super power—is the notion of modern-day multiracial persons serving as bridges between the races. As is the usual case, the black/white example is the most salient and the one most appealed to by the movement and its supporters. In Catherine Squires's description of this particular viewpoint, the "multiracial citizen is often described as a bridge, linking disparate racialized sections of the public."[1] Naturally, this viewpoint is related to, indeed is an extension of, the simplistic and erroneous view that multiracial persons are necessarily less prejudiced merely because of their parentage.

Something one notices quite readily is that this conceptualization requires a tremendous amount of work to be laid upon the shoulders of multiracial persons, most especially so in the case of black/white persons. As Tavia Nyong'o puts it: "Racial mixing and hybridity are neither problems for, nor solutions to, the long history of 'race' and racism, but part of its genealogy. Racisms can emerge, thrive, and transform quite effectively without ever being undone by the magical, privatized powers we invest in intimacy and reproduction. The impossibly burdened figure of the biracial child cannot conceivably do the work of utopia that we repeatedly impose upon her."[2]

The motivation for the wishful thinking that leads to the racial bridging daydream is simple enough. In mixed-race children, from the perspective of white liberals and white conservatives both, is seen an easy way out of the difficult and uncomfortable work of engaging a centuries-old racial animosity, a way that would allow the nation to avoid actually dealing with the problem directly. Instead, and quite conveniently, black/white persons—simply because of who (or, indeed, what?) they and their parents are—are tasked to serve as racial ambassadors, engaging in a frenzied shuttle diplomacy back and forth between the races until they solve the race problem with something akin to the aplomb of professional mediators. That such an outcome is not actually expected ever to obtain goes without saying, which is in no sense a disappointment to those for whom race is an annoying distraction. The important point is that someone else would now be delegated to work on the problem.

And from the general perspective of the members and supporters of Generation Mix (the latter whether white or not), this idea is yet another special plea for the utility of multiracial identity. It is another facet of the kitchen-sink strategy of claiming and embracing anything, regardless of how outlandish, that garners support from some corner or other. One need look no further than the nauseating and fairly pornographic mid- to late-1990s public romance between the American Multiracial Identity Movement and the political far right, including such notable figures as Newt Gingrich and Ward Connerly, in order to see that the Generation Mix strategy of soliciting and accepting support from any quarter, regardless of that particular support's own corporate agenda, is anything but a new phenomenon.[3]

But what of the notion that black/white persons are *in themselves* natural bridges for the facilitation of racial healing and reconciliation? It should come as no surprise that this is a biological argument dressed up in sociological attire. The simplistic presumption is that black/white persons, having one black and one white parent, are—because of that mere factor alone and regardless that it is, of course, biological nonsense—themselves somehow immune to racism and prejudice, and are motivated personally to act as ambassadorial bridges between their constituent races. This notion operates on two different levels, one biological and the other social. Certainly it is easy to see that on our everyday, low-level, glossy newsmagazine stratum of understanding, the biological approach is accepted without question or hesitation. Sad though this reality might be, it is nonetheless true. An American public that first of all remains invested deeply in biological race will have little difficulty believing that persons of purported biologically mixed racial descent are constituted quite naturally to act as healing bridges between their parental races.

In keeping with my thesis throughout Part 2, the reaffirmation of the old mulatto myths of the early twentieth century may be seen as operative in the racial bridge notion as well. It might not appear evident at first but, as I shall describe, the same basic principles are functioning here even though the old schema did not, of course, contain any suggestion of direct racial reconciliation via mulattoes. However, while that older schema did not contain any advice or overt expectation for mulattoes to serve as a mediative element between blacks and whites, nonetheless such was the intended practical result of that particular arrangement, although unrealized ultimately because it was part of the erroneous marginal man mythology. In other words, the hope or expectation of early sociologists such as Robert

Park, Edward Reuter, and Everett Stonequist was that by aligning themselves with and serving as the leaders of Negroes, mulattoes would provide some element of mediation between the races, a mediation to be understood primarily in terms of safe distance.

This is not to be confused with the idea of a buffer race, which I discussed in Chapter 7 and eliminated from contemporary consideration. Rather, the more intelligent, more serious, more highly tensioned, more reflective mulattoes—with their presumed natural affinity for whiteness—would, while not being an actual buffer race, nonetheless still provide distance from blacks, at least from the perspective of whites. I would be remiss here in failing to include one important caveat, which is that at least in Reuter's program, which is the most explicit in terms of manipulating mulattoes for white advantage, he points specifically to Southern as opposed to Northern mulatto attitudes as a normative guide to be followed by these hoped-for leaders of the Negro race.[4] So even though not a buffer race in the traditional sense of standing somewhat equidistant between whites and blacks while not being part of either group, as was the case with the black/white "Coloureds" in apartheid South Africa, for instance, Reuter's mulattoes would still—as the recognized leaders of the Negroes—stand in an important sense between whites and Negroes, thereby providing the increased distance from Negroes that has been sought by whites in a continuous way for centuries. Clearly, a critical question would be whether the Generation Mix version of mixed-race distinctiveness also provides increasing distance between whites and blacks, and the answer is that it does.

But in making this connection and arguing thus am I not implying, then, that the contemporary notion of the black/white members of Generation Mix serving as racial bridges is in fact an instrument for generating distance between whites and blacks, and would this not represent a contradiction? Yes, indeed, as I am so arguing; however, it is not nearly as contradictory as it might at first appear to be. Understood in its proper context of white supremacy and antiblackness, it is in no sense contradictory at all. First, as I intimated above, no one beyond low-level activists and poorer-quality scholars expects the racial bridge idea to actually work. White power brokers certainly do not, regardless of political ideology. And multiracial activists and scholars of a more perceptive bent realize full well that just as in the case of the multiracial medical fallacy (see Chapter 8), the racial bridge misdirection is also merely a means to the specific end of garnering sympathy and support for federal recognition of multiracial identity.

Yet even so, how can the concept of Generation Mix racial bridges be thought of as generating distance between whites and blacks? The answer lies in the fallaciousness of the racial bridge notion itself and in a kind of false advertising—of the bait-and-switch variety—involving that notion. Since Generation Mix cannot and therefore will not in fact be a racial bridge between whites and blacks, the recognition and ensuing elevation of Generation Mix serves, as I foregrounded in Chapter 7, to further isolate Afro-Americans and their legitimate concerns on the periphery of what is seen as the current, substantive, and constructive dialogue on race in the United States. In this arrangement Afro-American concerns are considered old-hat, illegitimate, and tied to ossified attitudes on the part of blacks that are no longer relevant to where the nation is now and to where it must go in order to achieve its postracial destiny.

Relevant here also is Jared Sexton's criticism of the American Multiracial Identity Movement's motivations when, as considered in Chapter 6, it appropriates certain Afro-Americans of the past and recodes them unilaterally as multiracial: "Here blackness is defined of necessity as the *negative residuum* of the interracial encounter, left over and distilled, the difference subtracted not only from the mythic purity of whiteness but also from the sanctified 'impurity' of the multiracial contingent. On this score, the multiracial camp would like to disentangle its incorporation of figures of 'false' blackness from its inevitable expulsion of figures of 'true' blackness, an annexation that is at the same time a distancing. Distancing *through* annexation: this is a differentiation installed by the new border, the new color line . . . *the re-racialization of blackness*."[5] Blackness is something to be used for a purpose and then discarded once that purpose has been fulfilled. In this, both the movement and the nation in general share a wish to move past blackness into not so much a postracial future as a postblack future.

Clearly, purging itself of and finally moving beyond the *black problem* will be a great and necessary aid to the nation in its quest. This national impulse is driven by the attraction of achieving postraciality without actually dealing with the Afro-American problem, by simply bypassing it instead. In this it is clear that Generation Mix and the American Multiracial Identity Movement have been assigned, and for all that can be ascertained, have accepted, an absolutely key role to play. In being representative of a *good minority*, in proclaiming loudly and in no uncertain terms that they are *not* black, in attempting to navigate away from blackness and toward whiteness, the black/white members of Generation Mix especially perform the dutiful service of continuing the isolation of Afro-Americans from both Generation Mix and from the larger US body politic.[6] Indeed, most Afro-Americans fail to recognize that the present heady rush toward a postracial American future (a rush they should view with sharply critical eyes) contains a downside for them that will result in a far worse state of affairs than the already unacceptable situation obtaining for Afro-Americans.

That the public form of this looming downside is the seemingly friendly face of multiracialism may be ironic, but that irony makes it no less alarming and no less dangerous to the prospects of Afro-Americans who either cannot or do not care to attain the new postracial mixed-race status.

What is lost in the contemporary Generation Mix narrative is, as I have been endeavoring to illustrate, the important reality that "multiracialism not only proves complicit with white supremacy and antiblackness but goes on in that respect to announce itself as avant-garde."[7] It is this faux avant-garde progressivism, accepted wrongly on so many fronts, that blinds nearly all commentators (albeit some quite willingly) to its far more sinister and wholly self-interested underside of biologically based multiracial superiority over *regular* (but nonetheless always already mixed) Afro-Americans.

As I argued in Chapters 7 and 8, the Generation Mix phenomenon impels a concerted movement away from blackness, a movement that results in Afro-Americans remaining in an isolated and bottom-of-the-barrel position in the US racial order. In the case of the black/white members of Generation Mix it is specifically a personal rejection of confraternity with their fellow mulattoes and a personal movement away from blackness and toward whiteness. In the case of the nonblack/white members of Generation Mix it is a more general distancing that makes possible the white/nonblack/black restructuring of the paradigm I detailed in Chapter 7. Either way, distance is opened between Afro-Americans and the next higher group in the paradigm, a distancing that quite necessarily results in helping to realize the goal of increased distance between whites and Afro-Americans as well.

Thus, even though contemporary mixed-race Americans, especially those who are black/white, are touted as racial bridges, everything about the American Multiracial Identity Movement's ideology and operation is actually structured to have the opposite effect, at least in terms of any connection to blackness. As the black/white cohort of the mixed-race movement gains in recognition and momentum it redoubles its growing impulse to move away from blackness. Regardless of the enticing lure of the racial bridge promise, that promise is an empty one, for there is no effort, no intention, no inclination to in fact perform the difficult work of racial bridging, as the far stronger desire is to achieve distance from blackness.

In Janus-like fashion the movement extols enthusiastically the utility of its black/white members' ability to serve as racial bridges while working simultaneously to encourage a view of those same members as being so distinct from Afro-Americans as to very nearly be unrelated at all. If one listens to the collective black/white voices of Generation Mix, one hears a much louder chorus of "I am not black, so stop calling me black," than anything along the lines of "Allow me to be a racial bridge that helps you make a connection to the other side." Seen from this perspective the point is decidedly clear, and the racial bridge fantasy decidedly inert. If any bridge is being built by the black/white members of Generation Mix, it is a bridge toward whiteness, for the mixed-race movement has already set afire the bridge that lies in the other direction. The bridge toward blackness is already burning.

So whereas for Reuter and his co-architects of the marginal man, acceptable distance was hoped to be achieved via mulattoes serving as humble leaders of the Negro race, in the contemporary moment the same goal of distance is achieved by the incessant valorization of Generation Mix—especially of its black/white members—as being distinct from, superior to, and far less troublesome than the mass of retrograde Afro-Americans. Therefore, with every subsequent elevation of Generation Mix, additional distance is generated between it and regular Afro-Americans; but even more fundamentally and far more importantly, additional distance is thereby generated between whites and regular Afro-Americans. This is so regardless of fanciful and contradictory enticements of racial bridging that are so very far from being attained and not even desired enough to be actually attempted.

But beyond even this, there is yet another reason why the racial bridge formulation is erroneous. It relies on an unthinking, accepted presumption that is as false as it is unexamined. Indeed, this erroneous presumption is so very much taken for granted that what I am about to argue may at first glance seem quite shocking. In contradistinction to the claim that the black/white members of Generation Mix are suited especially to serve as racial bridges, I contend instead that black/white persons cannot serve as racial bridges because they are completely unqualified to. Or, to be more precise, they are no more qualified to be racial bridges than supposedly monoracial whites, monoracial blacks, or anyone else. But how can this be if black/white persons partake of both blackness and whiteness? Is it not true that black/white persons are situated uniquely in terms of an intimate connection to both races? Do they not partake of both races, both biologies, both essentialities?

In fact, all of these presumptions are false, for they rely on an error so sloppy and so profound as to be unforgivable from a scholarly perspective. Indeed, they rely on nothing more than the very same unquestioned wishful thinking that underlies so much of the American Multiracial Identity Movement and its uncritical championing by the US popular media. Let us be clear on what the actual claim is. In a variety of forms the basic argument is that multiracial persons, including and especially black/white persons, are, precisely because of their multiraciality, situated uniquely to serve as human bridges in terms of mediating racial conflict. This argument is heard alike from the lips and pens of multiracial activists, multiracially supporting scholars, and rank-and-file members of Generation Mix.[8] Multiracial activist Carlos Fernández makes the claim when testifying before Congress that the multiracial "community is uniquely situated to confront these issues [of race and interethnic relations] because of the special experiences and understanding we acquire in the intimacy of our families and our personalities."[9] Making exactly the same point, multiracially supporting scholar Kathleen Korgen assures us that having "an open mind" is "something that comes with a biracial background," and that therefore "biracial persons can act as mediators between black and white persons."[10]

Paul Rosenblatt, Terri Karis, and Richard Powell aver that "biracial children . . . have major advantages over children who are not biracial," including "advantages that come with knowing two worlds and having dual perspectives."[11] Writing about US popular engagement with black/white romantic intermixing, Renee Romano reports that "interracial love in these accounts is an, or even *the*, answer to how to improve American race relations. Some focus on the importance of multiracial children, whose very existence not only will undermine racial categories, but who also may have a unique ability to serve as racial ambassadors, shuttling back and forth between each of their racial homes in an effort to make peace."[12] Ellis Cose remarks that "many advocates of the new [multiracial] designation see multiracial individuals as ambassadors between groups."[13] He cites one such advocate who "argues that society would benefit from having multiracial people who are uniquely positioned to be 'sensitive, objective negotiators of inter-group conflict.'"[14] Multiracially supporting author Sundee Frazier claims that multiracial people "possess the potential to bring together the groups to which we belong," and that "metaphorically, multiracial people display the life that flows from racial reconciliation."[15] Heather Dalmage finds that "multiracial family members often say that they perceive themselves as a bridge between blacks and whites."[16] Finally, Rachel Moran's work uncovers the phenomenon that "mixed-race individuals are sometimes celebrated as ideal mediators between different races."[17]

The foregoing was a sampling of the variety of means by which the racial-bridging claim is articulated in remarkably similar, remarkably consistent ways by various elements of the American Multiracial Identity Movement. There is no doubt that this claim about the skill of racial mediation is a central tenet of the Generation Mix argument for recognition and acceptance. There is also no doubt that it is wrong, and wildly so, in at least two related ways: (1) by sloppily treating race and culture as the same thing, and (2) by making the mistake of assuming that being associated with someone—even closely—is the same thing as being able to adopt that particular person's racial mindset. The first fallacy is a category error, while I shall label the second a *marriage error*, which I shall explain directly after addressing the first.

Race is not culture and culture is not race; the two terms are not interchangeable in any sense. It is, however, a general failure of US epistemological practice to treat them as if they are the same thing when they most obviously are not. Race, for one thing, does not exist. Biological race is a fallacy, an error of clear thinking that science has debunked conclusively in various ways again and again over the past six decades. Culture, though, does exist, both incorporeally and materially. It exists in the beliefs that people inculcate, in the clothes they wear, in the foods they eat, in the rituals they enact, and in the attitudes they adopt as part of their particular societal groupings or subgroupings. In fact, one could say that belief in race is itself a cultural phenomenon, even if such belief is in the end a false consciousness.

If we conceive of a society as a living, physical group of people, we can think of culture as the shared values and ideals that define those persons' standards of behavior in the context of that society. Here we can also consider at least two levels of culture, which we may label respectively culture and subculture. Speaking properly and in a formal, anthropological sense, culture would refer to major collective operating principles in terms of worldview, underlying cosmological grammars, and overarching modes of societal organization. In this sense, cultural difference might be compared by analogy to the difference between two societies of people, one strictly carnivorous and the other strictly vegetarian. Both groups eat, of course, but the foods they eat differ significantly—in terms of type—from that of the other. The analogical example I provide here purely for the sake of illustration is an extreme one, in which the food of one group is incompatible with the other, but some cultural differences are quite easily this stark even while others fit more comfortably within the confines of a slowly shifting continuum. Subculture, on the other hand, would be more along the lines of the concept of some lower-order distinction. It would be a situation in which we are considering two groups (indeed, subgroups) that are both carnivores, but in which one subgroup very much prefers seafood and the other subgroup very much prefers land animals. In other words, subcultural differences are relatively minor (in the large scale of things) preferences of flavor in the context of the same overarching culture.

To now move this distinction away from the realm of the hypothetical and closer to reality, one cultural difference is that between the United States and Germany on the one hand, and Saudi Arabia and Iran on the other, in regard to the place of women in society. Few would attempt to argue that the two different systems under consideration here do not deviate hugely along a fundamental fault line on the subject of women. Another cultural difference is the divergence between the United States and Vietnam in terms of the veneration of ancestors. Clearly, the idea of engaging one's deceased kin in an active way so as to have an impact on the way those kin continue to affect the living is for the average American a completely foreign notion. Finally, a third example of a cultural difference is the elemental divide between the general Judeo-Christian tradition in the United States, and the varieties of animism practiced in sub-Saharan Africa. So wide is this particular divide that many Americans would have no problem in withholding the title of *religion* from those animist beliefs. These are examples of large-scale differences that have to do with operational grammars far above the level of active thought. They are examples of cultural distinctions.

Subcultural differences are relatively minor variations (again, in the large scale of things) under the same general culture. The American example is again useful here. Certainly there exist certain communities in the United States that would prove to be exceptions to the general rule, from certain Native American groups (though not all) to extreme religious cults to anarchist antigovernment groups that would constitute separate cultures in themselves, but it is nonetheless completely uncontroversial to describe general US culture as highly racialized and highly stratified racially, Judeo-Christian, capitalistic, materialistic, individualistic, male-dominant sexist, homophobic, and since the terrorist attacks of September 11, 2001, fairly xenophobic.[18] For the average American these are underlying cultural grammars that inform her or his interactions in society. However, under this generalized US culture are minor variations or flavorings. Subcultural differences would be the variance one finds in different regions of the country or among different age cohorts, for example. Indeed, subculture can on occasion be so nebulous that it appears sometimes to break down and scatter even as one attempts to investigate it.

A nonregional, non-age-related example comes to mind here. One could consider evangelical Christians, mainline Protestants, Catholics, and Jews in the United States and argue that while they all fit comfortably under generalized US culture, as subgroups they each have significant-enough specific variances that justify differentiating them based on those variations. While some might contend that these variant religious interpretations should make for different cultures in themselves, such a criticism would miss the point that all four profess belief in the same type of general theological framework and in the same type of God. Indeed, depending on which group's members one asked, some would even claim it is the same God while others might not. The point is that in terms of cultural grammar, the four religious movements considered in this example, while distinct enough from each other to justify being seen as subcultures, can nonetheless be grouped together easily under Judeo-Christianity and distinguished quite readily from religions that are animist or that stress ancestor veneration, for example. So, the differences between evangelical Christians, mainline Protestants, Catholics, and Jews in the United States are in this sort of structural analysis subcultural differences, not cultural differences.

Some might argue that US culture as I am using it is not, speaking properly, a culture, but is instead itself a subculture of Western culture. Such a view does not impact my general argument, however, as I have elected to take the more generous route. In other words, on that even more restrictive view of culture, my arguments that follow would thereby be made that much stronger. The most important point is that when we speak of culture, we are (or should be) speaking in terms of large-scale, underlying cosmological and structural grammars that order societies and in turn determine the ways that those societies assemble themselves and then adapt to change as they move forward through time. Even subcultures have strong organizing principles, although on a far, far lower scale than cultures proper. We are not (or should not be) speaking of trivialities along the lines of what people look like physically or whether they prefer listening to the musical stylings of Snoop Dogg or Barry Manilow.

Finally, if it were to be countered that my use of culture is far too structured and rigid, that what is meant by culture in the writings of multiracially supporting scholars and activists is something far less demanding and more in line with the inconsequential musical example I lampoon above—sort of a little "c" culture or subculture as opposed to my big "C" Culture or sub-Culture—my response would be that such a trivial concept of culture is far, far too weak to have the great significance that is imputed to it by those very writers. In other words, if such a weak concept is what those writers have in mind when invoking culture, then it cannot possibly do the work they intend it to do, reducing essentially instead to the banal difference between sprinkling salt or sugar on one's grits.

Having laid out briefly what culture in fact is, we may return now to the question of the relationship between race and culture in the ideology and rhetoric of the American Multiracial Identity Movement. In returning to this question, let me state first of all and with no equivocation whatsoever (albeit perhaps counterintuitively at this point), that when it comes to the vast majority of whites and blacks in the United States, there are no differences between them such as I described above—not of the cultural type, nor even of the subcultural type. In much the same way that human beings cannot be categorized consistently into biological racial groups, black Americans and white Americans cannot be categorized into two discrete groups on the basis of culture, regardless of the level. Indeed, I had anticipated arguing originally that any differences between the two were not cultural, but were in fact subcultural and therefore insignificant, but in thinking about this in even more detail I hold that there are not even subcultural differences that delineate black Americans and white Americans from each other. Rather, whatever differences might distinguish particular subgroups of black Americans from particular subgroups of white Americans cannot even be called subcultural differences. And even here the assertion of coherent subgroups is very much a less than certain enterprise.

But, might it not be objected, is it not a commonplace that Afro-Americans are more religious and more family oriented than white Americans, and that in terms of cognition they are oriented in a circular way while whites are oriented linearly? And is it not true that Afro-American male behavior is driven by a strong impulse toward a demand for respect on one hand and avoidance of disrespect on the other that stems from its steady cycle of creation and consumption of hip-hop and rap music? And finally, do we not know that their African ancestors' development under the smiling sub-Saharan sun makes Afro-Americans less individualistic and less obsessed with controlling nature than whites with their dog-eat-dog heritage of ice-age struggle? It should be obvious that the foregoing are just as wrongly and every bit as inaccurately stereotypical as older myths concerning Afro-Americans' natural proclivity for dancing and aptitude for sports. That these more modern myths are repeated today as if they are actual cultural factors is unfortunate but not at all surprising.

There are arguably a number of things on which one might agree with Tommie Shelby when he refers to "black forms of cultural life," but it is surely a long leap from such an acknowledgment to the romantic notion that there is a distinct black culture in the United States.[19] Nevertheless, commentators often conjure up simplistic and unjustified accounts that "generally characterize black culture as fundamentally oral, communal, harmonious, emotive, spontaneous, spiritual, earthy, experiential, improvisational, colorful, sensual, uninhibited, dialogical, inclusive, and democratic. White culture, by contrast, is often viewed as essentially logocentric, individualistic, antagonistic, rationalistic, formal, materialistic, abstract, cerebral, rigid, bland, repressed, monological, and hegemonic."[20]

That these nonsensical and, indeed, racist notions of black circularity and white linearity filter down to society in general may be seen in Frazier's personal comparison of white and black cultures in the United States. Pointing out the "great strengths of European American culture and traits" she sees in herself "to a degree," she mentions that her mother's "thoughtful preparation shows others that she cares and makes for better presentation."[21] Frazier also cites her mother as "a planner who values attention to detail."[22] In contrast to this stereotypical portrait of white culture as organized and in control, of the "great strengths of African American culture and traits" she sees in herself "to a degree," Frazier is able to come up with her father's "going with the flow," his "spontaneity," and his being able to "make things work with whatever he has."[23]

To the potential objection that I am wrongly generalizing the traits of Frazier's parents to whites and blacks, I reply that it is Frazier herself who promotes precisely such an overt generalization by offering her parents' examples *not* as individual idiosyncrasies but explicitly as "cultural differences."[24] It is Frazier who describes European American culture as "a culture that expects the expected," and Afro-American culture as "a culture that expects the unexpected."[25] In this stereotypical binary-opposition is a reflection of the hierarchy of the US racial order, with Frazier conceiving of whites as "expecting the expected," implying both that they know what to expect and that they know what to do about it; and blacks as "expecting the unexpected," implying that they are not in control of themselves and therefore operate continually in a reactionary mode—in response presumably to the directed and controlling actions of whites.

Beyond these offensive stereotypes, there is an unthinking tendency to postulate competing varieties of singular Afro-American cultures as if all Afro-Americans can be placed into one particular cultural framework. One such postulation has it that Afro-American culture is essentially urban, violent, and interested in getting rich quickly outside of normal occupational channels. There surely are Afro-Americans for whom this would ring true, but the fact is that there are likely far more whites—especially suburban, white, teenage males—who adopt in a conscious way all or significant portions of this persona, and what are we to make of them? Are such white teens partaking in black culture? If so, are they as a result, then, black? Another model suggests a singular Afro-American culture that is rooted in "giving back to the community," even if one did not come from or take anything from "the community," and that stresses a continuing connection to the traditions of the Southern slave experience, even if one has no relevant personal connections to the American South.

In an article contending that the ideology of colorblindness on the one hand, and the racialization of poor blacks on the other, affect the racial identity choices of biracial Americans, Korgen first of all postulates a dominant "'gangsta' culture" for blacks, but then hedges her bets as to precisely whom this culture applies.[26] Korgen avers initially that "many young well-to-do Black Americans feel the need to act as if they were raised on the streets of poor urban neighborhoods in order to be seen as 'really' Black," but then a mere four pages later she asserts quite contradictorily that "many middle-class . . . Black Americans . . . resist the notion that they can't be Black if they are not poor or do not share the cultural traits of poor Black Americans."[27] The reader is left to wonder which statement should be understood as being Korgen's position on what constitutes "real" blackness.

Such cultural universalizing and assignation aside, it hardly needs stating that Afro-Americans are every bit as diverse in terms of their contemporary lives as whites or any other group, but it serves the interests of those who would keep them at the bottom of the US racial order that Afro-Americans remain mysterious and insular. The postulation of a separate and strange black culture is merely the modern and more acceptable equivalent of the past imposition of biological racial difference. As Shelby warns, "the sad fact is, some whites would be quite content, some would be enthusiastic, if blacks were to insist on remaining 'different,' as this would buttress white privilege and exacerbate black disadvantage."[28]

The fact is that to speak of these flavorings, these styles, as culture (or even subculture) is nonsensical. Shall we conclude that celebration of

Kwanzaa makes one an authentic practitioner of black culture? Or perhaps Kwanzaa plus verified love of barbeque chicken combined with the ability to dance the Electric Slide would suffice.[29] And even if we were, somehow, for the sake of argument, to agree that this or that particular trivial style corresponded to even a subculture, it would be every bit as impossible to place many blacks in such a supposed black subculture as it would be to keep many whites out, which would in turn invalidate the very claim to it being a black subculture in the first place.[30] But such debates usually escape our view since we never in the first place arrive at this level of analysis when dealing with Generation Mix or the overly simplistic coverage it garners from popular media outlets.

Not only is it impossible to place a supposed black racial group into a distinct black culture or subculture, but we must deal as well with the complication that people can very easily have more than one subculture to which they adhere simultaneously. Certainly there are many, many leanings strong enough to merit the designation of subculture. For some persons, surely, religion would constitute a very salient subculture. Yet one could easily imagine a mainline Protestant who was also a member of the gay subculture in the United States.[31] Indeed, our imaginary person could in addition to these two subcultures be part of a fiercely dedicated environmentalist movement that might qualify as a subculture as well. So subcultures are not necessarily mutually exclusive, and they cut across other lines of organization, such as gender and class. It should be clear, then, that as in the cases of gender and class, race is not equivalent to culture or subculture. Rather, persons of supposed different racial groups do not entail discrete subcultures qua racial groups, but instead all partake of the practically limitless possibilities that subcultural affiliation offers.

Indeed, it is far more defensible to postulate an American hip-hop subculture than any singular Afro-American subculture. Even though a hip-hop subculture would likely be populated mostly by Afro-Americans it would certainly not be exclusively Afro-American by any means. It would include sizable Asian, white, and Hispanic elements as well. And even if one were to argue that the basis of hip-hop is some aspect of the many Afro-American experiences in this country, such a conclusion in no way entails that a hip-hop subculture would itself be constituted as exclusively Afro-American. The very catholicity of hip-hop makes this plain enough. Therefore, we will find that some Afro-Americans are part of a hip-hop subculture, while many are not; likewise, some Asians, whites, and Hispanics are part of a hip-hop subculture, while many are not. The hip-hop example is yet another means of demonstrating that it is simply impossible to argue successfully that there is a black culture or subculture in the United States and that such a culture or subculture is synonymous or coextensive with racial blackness, however the latter might be constituted.

If race is not culture, then, it clearly would be a significant problem for the American Multiracial Identity Movement to treat it as though it were. So let us turn to the voices of the movement—scholarly, activist, and rank-and-file voices—to determine if indeed such a huge mistake is made in support of arguments on behalf of Generation Mix. Romano provides an initial indication as she reports on one black woman's plan for how she and her white husband will raise their soon-to-be-born multiracial child: "We're going to teach you both cultures, your black side and your white side, and you're not going to have to choose, if we can help it."[32] This example demonstrates, as will those that follow, an unquestioned and overt substitution of race for culture and culture for race that is as contradictory as it is umproblematized. The sticky problem, though, is that were multiracialism to disengage itself from its wrongful embrace of culture it would then have only the false consciousness of biological race with which to state its case.

Broadcast journalist Elliott Lewis writes that multiracial families are "insisting on identifying as multiracial to better reflect their multicultural upbringing."[33] One wonders, though, why such families are not therefore insisting on identifying as *multicultural* rather than *multiracial* if, as Lewis implies, multiculturality is the relevant distinction. But there is no cultural difference, and the subcultural difference—if conceived of as ethnic difference—is irrelevant to the racial issues put forth and the racial arguments being claimed here. To ensure that we are not misunderstanding Lewis we may turn to his account of one woman's embrace of multiraciality, in which he notes that there is "more to Amanda's embrace of her Japanese heritage than the racist actions of others."[34] But of course, Amanda's Japanese heritage is ethnicity, which has to do with culture, not race. Considering another woman's "attitude when it comes to identifying as multiracial," Lewis nonetheless cites her speaking of "'all my cultures, all my heritages,'" which, again quite obviously is ethnicity—and therefore culture—not race.[35]

Writing about yet another member of Generation Mix, Charles Yesuwan, Lewis touts this person's "ethnic background."[36] Acknowledging the contradiction, Lewis then offers Yesuwan's explanation that although he is a "multiethnic Asian," he nonetheless considers himself racially "mixed because [he is] a product of those different cultures and heritages and customs."[37] Yet whither multiraciality as raciality? Despite the clear ethnic—and thus cultural—concepts invoked, Yesuwan was nevertheless "taking part in a national awareness tour on the mixed-*race* experience."[38] Similarly, and also blurring the differences between race, culture, and ethnicity, Frazier claims that multiracial people "easily move in and out of different racial and ethnic settings because of our *multicultural* upbringing."[39] Are these no more than yet additional examples of the kitchen-sink strategy of simply throwing arguments into the ring? Is the issue multiracial identity, is it multiethnic identity, is it multicultural identity, or can we simply label as *multiracial* anything we want to feel special about? This is no small point, for the black/white mixed-race dynamic is distinctly different from these dilemmas of ethnic identity—particularly those having an Asian component—yet all are rolled unproblematically into the same argument for Generation Mix multiracial identity.

From a scholarly perspective, Ursula Brown offers that "biracial children are not just black or white; rather they incorporate both black and white identity parts in one body and one self."[40] Yet Brown does not describe or otherwise quantify these "identity parts" for us. However, since she mentions both "one body and one self" it is fair to assume that she intends for biological race to have a prominent import here. Commenting on the switch in federal policy regarding the collection of race information that replaced the previous instruction to *mark one only* with the current instruction to *mark all that apply*, Brown writes that "hopefully this change will enable mixed-race parents to teach their children that they are, and *culturally* can be, part of both racial groups."[41] Yet here we are again mixing race and culture in such a way that they become interchangeable, indistinguishable from each other. Speaking in general terms, anyone can be, subculturally, part of nearly any racial group, for culture has nothing to do with race. So declarations that this or that black/white teenager is comfortable in both white and black alleged cultural settings are irrelevant completely to any proper analysis of multiracial identity as a racial identity.

Marion Kilson writes that her multiracial survey participants "value not only their ability to move comfortably within and between different *cultures* but their insights into different *cultural* worlds, which they perceive derive from their *multicultural* experiences as Biracial Americans."[42] Yet again, is the issue biraciality or biculturality? It is plain to see that Kilson is blurring race and culture quite consciously here, for she does it more than once: "Many [multiracial people] attribute their ability to move comfortably between *cultures* to their Biracial heritage. Several people spoke of viewing themselves as 'bridges' between *cultures* and valuing that role, while others talked of moving easily between *cultural* worlds."[43] Finally, Kilson again conveys very clearly the notion that multiracial persons are human racial bridges because of culture when she writes that "Biracial Americans, then, perceive themselves to be facile cross-*cultural* navigators and take pride in that role."[44] The contradiction here is stunning, surpassed only by the fact that so few commentators have made the effort to point it out. Moreover, in the midst of this exaggerated excitement over cultural bridging we would do well to consider Shelby's rather rational observation that "it must nevertheless be relatively rare that dialogue breaks down because blacks fail to understand the cultural ways of white folk."[45]

It should also go without saying that the concept of racial bridging cannot refer to mere linguistic code switching, which is something completely different than the purported skill of being a natural racial mediator. Code switching, or altering one's speech patterns depending on one's immediate environment, might be seen as a useful skill for a racial mediator, but it certainly does not constitute racial mediation in and of itself. Afro-Americans have been code switching between Standard English and Black Vernacular English for centuries—and quite extensively and quite exponentially since at least the early twentieth century—and yet it has not had the least effect on bridging the racial divide between them and whites.

Given the sloppy substitution of race for culture, and culture for race, that we have seen is endemic to multiracial rhetoric, it will come as no surprise, then, to learn that one of Kilson's respondents boasts of possessing expertise in racial mediation with the startling revelation that "I change my speech."[46] Given what has already gone before in my critique of the racial-bridge notion, this admittedly is a trivial example, but I utilize it nonetheless because it so very well illustrates the tone of the Generation Mix intellectual endeavor that I have been framing and critiquing. Another respondent, in describing the art of racial shuttling, reveals that "when I'm with my White family, the terms are okay; 'now I'm with my White family, what do I do with all this other stuff?' When I'm in my Black community, 'What do I do with all this other stuff?'"[47] However, the "stuff" referred to here is no more the essence of blackness than are a hooded sweatshirt, a taste for soul food, or a Kwanzaa greeting card.

This is yet another example of the confusion between what might be called emblems of blackness (emblems that might be appropriated by anyone, however) with the concept of blackness itself. And whether blackness is in the end a false consciousness or not, the "stuff" that Kilson's respondent believes is racial "stuff" is surely nothing of the sort. Indeed, when one considers the words of Generation Mix activists, scholars, and rank-and-file members, one finds no real arguments as to precisely how *multiraciality* as a specific kind of *raciality* grants to its members any sort of special skill at racial mediation. Rather, all the arguments presented revolve consistently around shuttling between cultures, straddling cultures, and the overly hyped transgressivity of linguistic code switching.

Nikki Khanna points out the enormous error made by these researchers in failing to distinguish what respondents are really saying when they talk about culture and race. According to Khanna: "When describing differences between black and white 'cultures,' respondents frequently describe characteristics that appear related less to a race's 'culture' and more to social class."[48] Writing of her own black/white interview subjects, Khanna notes that "they often reduce 'black culture' and 'white culture' to oversimplified, one-dimensional images (e.g., white people speak Standard English, listen to rock and roll, drive trucks, value education; black people speak Ebonics, listen to hip-hop or R&B music, do not value education)."[49] Additionally, she finds that "for some biracial respondents, their perceptions of 'white culture' and 'black culture' reflect social class disparities found between blacks and whites in the larger American society."[50] What therefore distinguishes Khanna from the researchers I have critiqued above is her astute understanding that "what is often described by these biracial respondents as 'cultural' differences between blacks and whites arguably reflect differences in social class, not race alone."[51] As we recognize the necessity of refusing the simplistic bait of equating race with culture, we would do well to heed Samira Kawash's advice that "if we are to take seriously the idea that race is not a biological but a cultural fiction, then we must confront not only the fictionality of the biological way of understanding race but also the fictionality of the cultural way of seeing race."[52]

The second way the Generation Mix claim regarding the skill of racial mediation is wildly wrong has to do with what I termed above the *marriage error*. Even apart from questions of the gross misuse of the concept of culture, the Generation Mix argument for racial mediation hangs on the presumption that being related closely to a person of another race and spending considerable time with that person (such as growing up under said person's parental care) will result in one having access to, being able to understand, and being able to replicate that other person's racial mindset. This is, again, the sort of inane fluff that glossy newsmagazines dispense to an unreflective readership whenever it is time to do another story on the perils and pitfalls of mixed-race identity.

Contrary to popular opinion—and realizing full well that what I am about to give voice to is supposed to remain unspeakable—if a black/white child grows up believing she is not white (whether believing she is black or mixed-race), that child will not have access to whiteness. The child may have a white parent and may spend considerable time with white people, but unless the child believes she is white and grows up as white, she will not have access to whiteness. When I mention "access to whiteness" in this context I am referring specifically to the sort of unique entrée, insider understanding, or special knowledge that is being touted as the exclusive domain of multiracial individuals, especially black/white persons, in regard to their alleged expertise as racial bridges. And let there be no doubt that such exclusive dominion is precisely what is being claimed or else it would not in the first place be ballyhooed as so very, very noteworthy a skill as to distinguish multiracial people from everyone else.

There is a very simple truth that has somehow escaped notice in both the popular and scholarly discussions concerning racial bridging. That simple truth is the reality that neither looking white nor being taken for white occasionally are the same thing as experiencing life as white—or, speaking more properly, experiencing the false consciousness of whiteness—for there are far deeper ideological considerations and ingrained expectations than that. To assert that a black/white person (who does not identify as white) understands whiteness simply because of her home life is to diminish grossly and irresponsibly the tremendous power of race and racism in the United States. It is to trivialize the oldest and longest-lasting (along with sexism) self-induced scourge this nation has yet to free itself of. And the US racial structure itself is far from accommodating this idea of bidirectional racial flexibility. After all, one unchanging fact of life in the United States is that black/white persons are free to be mixed or black, but they are not welcomed into whiteness as long as their sub-Saharan African ancestry is known.

Recognizing that it nonetheless is a false consciousness, what we might call participation in whiteness consists in a particular state of mind (believing that one is white) that coheres with a particular experience (being perceived by others as white), and that carries with it both observed and unobserved white privilege. Absent one or the other of these two states (belief plus experience), one does not partake in whiteness. It is the reciprocality of these internal and external states that brings true participation in the false consciousness of whiteness. Merely living with a white parent or white siblings does not. Therefore, the person who believes she is multiracial, regardless of how she is perceived by others, does not participate in whiteness any more than does the person who believes he is black but is perceived by others as white.

Seeing, talking with, and living with someone who identifies as white may give one important insights into that person's personality and psychology, but the point I will stress over and over (because it so very crucial) is that such contact, however intimate, does not by itself grant one unique access to understanding the nature of whiteness in a way that then results in an ability to mediate racial conflict. This purported ability has been asserted time and again by multiracial persons, by movement activists, and by scholars who support multiracial identity, but the fundamental and always unrecognized key point is that despite the endless assertions, it has not been supported by the least bit of anything approaching actual argument or proof.

Let us once again reorient ourselves in terms of the specific claim being advanced. Multiracial persons, including and especially black/white persons, are said to be situated uniquely to serve as racial bridges because of their mixed racial parentage. We should first of all ensure that this is not a biological claim—that we are not talking about a claim to a genetic kind of racial imprinting that for all practical purposes operates at the level of instinct. Such a conceptualization of the factors behind racial bridging would leave us with the absurd conclusion that a black/white person who did not know she was mixed racially, perhaps having been adopted and raised as black by a black couple, would nonetheless possess the skill of racial mediation purely because of her genetic heritage. I am unaware of any multiracial advocate—even on the fringe of the farthest fringe—making such a claim, and so we may feel comfortable in retiring it at this point.

But if the special power of racial bridging does not have a genetic basis, it must then have a social basis. It must be, therefore, that the unique form of racial mediation being advanced by the multiracial movement, if not inherited biologically, is instead a skill born of social interaction and social experience. Yet how sensible is this? In asking the question I want especially to maintain an emphasis on the assertion that mixed persons are talented *uniquely* in this way. It is critical to not elide the distinction between just anyone being good at racial mediation and multiracial persons being *very* good at it, for the central claim under consideration is that multiracial persons are especially good at racial mediation, precisely because they are multiracial.

On this view, one supposes that children adopted transracially would be just as good as multiracial persons at being racial mediators, for this special trait stems from social contact and not from biology. Naturally, children fostered transracially would also fall into the same category and would therefore also possess the same cross-racial mediatory skills. Or perhaps only some would be, for such children might be adopted or fostered, as the case may be, by a monoracial parent set and, if so, they would not have parents of two different races. Indeed, outside of celebrities and other famous people, we do not expect white children to be adopted by Afro-American parents. But is there any reason—beyond our being told so, always sans evidence—to suppose that this racial-bridging phenomenon actually takes place? It has certainly been declared time and time again, as we have seen above, and quite apparently with complete certainty; however, I am of the opinion that we might perhaps think about and examine this proposition before accepting it as truth.

Structurally, the argument being proffered by the American Multiracial Identity Movement is that growing up with one parent who is in some significant way different from the other parent gives one access to the essentiality of that parental difference, such that one is then able—specifically from the perspective of either parent's particular difference—to interact empathetically with other people from either parental group, and that in the multiracial case specifically one is able to do this in a distinctive way not available to monoracial persons or, one supposes, to multiracial persons who for whatever reason have parents of the same race. Therefore, as the argument is deployed, if one has one black parent and one white parent, one is thereby situated uniquely to mediate conflict successfully between blacks and whites; and one is able to accomplish this precisely because one is the child of these differently raced parents. But, I dare ask, why so? Surely we are not speaking simply of the mundane notion that being acquainted with someone, as a friend, classmate, or work colleague, means that one possibly comes to know that person better as a result. This is something that anyone is certainly capable of, and it happens every day. No, the Generation Mix racial-bridging argument goes much deeper than this, and is expressly about a *unique* skill in regard to racial mediation, a skill that is based expressly on one's status as multiracial.

It therefore must be something significantly more than talking to a workmate over lunch every day and hearing that person give her side of things. It therefore must be something significantly more than working on a semester-long group project with a classmate and having him explain his perspective. If it were merely something along the lines of these trivial examples it would be nothing special and it would not require a multiracial identity in order for the skill to be conferred. Yet Frazier says just as much in making the racial-bridging claim: "I have friends in both worlds. I see things from a different perspective that enables me to see both sides of a situation. I can understand where a black person might be coming from, but I can also understand where a white person might be coming from. And that enables me to be a person to help the two sides understand one another."[53]

Frazier's structuring of the claim, by placing the point about friends first, implies that it is her having "friends in both worlds" that makes all this possible, rather than multiraciality itself. This would make anyone with "friends in both worlds" a potential racial mediator. On the other hand, if that is a misinterpretation on my part, and the point about having such friends is meant to be subordinate to multiraciality, Frazier would of necessity then have to be arguing that it takes being multiracial in order to have "friends in both worlds," which, ignoring its patent falseness, would perhaps represent yet another Generation Mix super power. But the argument breaks down even before we arrive at this point, for according to racial-bridging logic it is clear that one need not have a multiracial identity in order to have this skill. I am thinking here of a black/white interracial couple who have a multiracial child and subsequently adopt a black child. On the assumptions of the racial-bridging schema, that black child should be as proficient at black/white racial mediation as his mixed-race adopted sibling. Indeed, we need not even posit a black child, for should this same couple adopt an Asian child, that Asian child should also develop the special skill of mediating racial conflict between blacks and whites. Presumably, in accordance with the logic of the racial-bridging claim, both the black child and the Asian child will undergo the same processes of parental interaction or, indeed, mere observation, that would grant black/white racial bridging skills to the multiracial child, for it is social interaction and not biology that brings about the purported special skill, although one would then have to do what has yet to be done, which is to provide a coherent argument that such parental social interaction is different significantly from the trivial examples given above.

Note that I am not claiming that the black or Asian child adopted by a black/white couple will in fact have the same experiences as that couple's black/white children by birth. What I am pointing out is that according to the logic of the racial-bridging claim, if the special skill of racial mediation is not based in biology but is based instead in social interaction, then both the black child and the Asian child adopted by a black/white interracial couple will go through the same processes that grant the skill of racial mediation between blacks and whites, whatever those processes may be. The key is that, if one takes the logic of the racial-bridging argument seriously, one then of necessity affirms that racial mediation expertise derives simply from living with parents of different races, such that the adopted Asian child of a black father and a white mother will possess in a unique way the skill of mediating conflict between blacks and whites. It is the simplistic logic of the racial-bridging claim that leads to such absurd conclusions as this.

What is holding this entire fallacious structure in place is the erroneous idea that family life somehow confers an access to race that is beyond—and in a very significant way—that conferred by the more trivial friendship, school, or workplace associations mentioned above. I do not think that it does, however, for this is yet another one of those uninvestigated and always unproblematized *commonsense* assertions that the American Multiracial Identity Movement has become expert at tossing into the kitchen sink of multiracial special pleading. With neither the popular media nor multiracially supporting scholars inclined to acknowledge or otherwise contend with these sorts of errors, merely floating such ideas is all that is required in order to see them seated firmly into popular discourse. Yet I nonetheless question expressly the heretofore uncritiqued assertion that being multiracial and having parents of two ostensibly different races gives to one a set of racial mediation skills significantly above and beyond the trivial examples of friendship, school, and workplace associations. I can surely anticipate the criticism that the racial-bridging claim was never meant to be held to such logical scrutiny, that I am overanalyzing it, but I reject such counterarguments in the strongest terms. If a claim is made, particularly an important claim such as this, then it ought to withstand rational examination or otherwise be withdrawn summarily.

Much as in the case of the somewhat related and just as smarmy assertion that interracial marriage is emblematic of harmony between the races (as if monoracial marriage were emblematic of harmony *within* the races), the commonsense notions about multiracial life in an interracial family require serious unpacking before they are accepted. In addition to the complication that members of such families may very easily hold thoughts and feelings about their own particular family members that diverge wildly from their thoughts and feelings about said family members' groups in general, we have also the fact that family life and parental influence are not the overarching factors that simplistic analysis would have us believe. In terms of the former, there is nothing impossible about a white person who is married to a black person but who nonetheless is an antiblack racist. Nor is there anything impossible about the reverse case, as people have a remarkable capacity for selfishly inconsistent behavior. One's spouse, partner, parent, or child may very easily be set apart as an exception to a generalized racist outlook.

And in terms of parental weight, there is the reality that peer influence becomes a larger and larger factor as one's development progresses. As the individual expands her horizons by attending school and going outside to play unsupervised with friends, those other associations compete with and eventually supplant parental influence. All of which is to state that parental and family influence—as they are conceived specifically in the racial-bridging schema—are exaggerated to quite a strong degree. To be sure, parental and family influences, when present, account for their fair share of a child's development; however, the flowery assumption fostered by the racial-bridging argument is far too naïve. Put simply, it is much more complicated than that, despite multiracial advocates' insistence on proffering those extraordinarily simplistic analyses.

Writing about multiracial people and intimate interracial relationships, Courtney Bonam and Margaret Shih overlook completely the foregoing inconvenient facts and instead offer the sentimentalized and unproblematized view that "Multiracial youth often grow up in interracial families in which they observe people of different backgrounds living together in harmony, contradicting society's messages about the inevitability of racial conflicts."[54] Their study, though, contains no evaluation whatsoever of this claimed harmoniousness of interracial households. To merely state it, apparently, is enough. I will, however, continue to insist that when these kinds of unverified presumptions are built into a research model, that particular model cannot help but be tainted either by the careless failure to substantiate such a key presumption or by the specific bias of the presumption itself, or, very likely, by both.

It is not only academics who stand guilty of attempting to wish the racial-bridging thesis into reality. For example, Frazier sees the possible salvation of the nation itself as being bound up with racial mixing when she avers that "American social problems may increase if mixing *doesn't* happen. Racial tensions are as high as they've ever been. Interracial families, however, ameliorate tension by bringing diverse people together."[55] Given that racial tensions were a good bit higher, and demonstrably so, during, say, the years leading up to the American Civil War (the Compromise of 1850, the Kansas-Nebraska Act, Bloody Kansas, the Dred Scott Decision, John Brown's Raid, etc.), during the Reconstruction and Redemption periods, during the horrendous decades of lynching and Jim Crow, as well as during the Civil Rights and Black Power Eras, one could be forgiven for supposing that Frazier is engaging in significant exaggeration here—exaggeration that extends as well to her unsupported thesis concerning the ameliorative effects of race mixing.

Since, as is usual in the cases of pro-multiracial assertions, there is absolutely no actual empirical evidence to support the racial-bridging claim, what is the best similar case we might be able to use in order to obtain a sense of the argument's validity? The best and most obvious case is the institution of marriage, which involves persons of different sexes (overwhelmingly, despite new laws and court challenges here and there) living together in close intimacy. Importantly, given that we are investigating an argument involving racial difference, sexual difference is likewise taken to be a primary difference, a fundamental difference, an elemental difference—much as racial difference is taken to be—and so it should serve therefore as a very useful indicator of the validity of the racial-bridging argument.

If simply living together is supposed to confer a privileged access to essentialist racial empathy, then we should expect the most significant act of living together to bring about the same results in the area of sexual difference. If living with parents of two different races grants to the multiracial individual a unique ability to bridge the races, then living with a spouse of the opposite sex should grant to men a unique ability to mediate conflict with women, and it should grant to women a unique ability to mediate conflict with men. Indeed, if the structural presumptions of the racial-bridging argument are valid, then married households of opposing sexes should see an absolute minimum of intersexual misunderstanding and tension. This is the marriage error I mentioned earlier.

It hardly requires pointing out that far from married couples in the United States representing anything approaching the state of mediated, blissful and "harmonious" understanding we would expect were the racial-bridging structure to actually be valid, the US institution of marriage is more accurately conceived as a disaster of endlessly replicated serial monogamy driving the nation's horrendous divorce rate continually in an ever upward direction.[56] Moreover, based on this simplistic view of marriage and on interracial marriage as a symbol of extra-special love, black/white couples should never divorce. However, a glance through any of the survey research shows quite a different story, for in that literature we tend to find significant numbers of black/white individuals with divorced parents. Indeed, if any such naïve theory of racial bridging accomplished by the progeny of interracial marriage were actually true, it might have to be based most ironically on many multiracial individuals growing up with only one parent present in the home.

Indeed, there is a reason for the gaping absence of anything approaching evidentiary justification by the champions of racial bridging who claim "harmonious" interracial marriages (and especially black/white marriages) as a cause. And that is the inconvenient fact that actual research reveals quite the opposite to be true. In an article investigating "the relative marital stability of interracial and same-race marriages," Jenifer Bratter and Rosalind King report two conclusions that are particularly relevant to the present discussion. The first conclusion is that "generally, non-Whites who intermarry experienced less marital stability than their same-race married coethnics," and that even taking into account differences between the various groups in question (a complication the apologists for "harmonious" interracial marriages and racial bridging never trouble themselves to consider), "interracial marriages overall are more prone to divorce."[57]

The second very significant conclusion is that "compared to White/White couples," interracial marriages involving white women and black men "were more prone to divorce."[58] Indeed, the authors reiterate their finding that black/white marriages, "specifically those involving Black men and White women, have the highest likelihood of disruption of any White/non-White marriages."[59] Insofar as black/white marriage is concerned, the black man/white woman combination represents the predominant pattern in the United States. As Khanna reports: "In 2000, black men had white wives 2.65 times more often than black women had white husbands," a fact that, when considered in the context of Bratter and King's research, quite simply proves fatal to any claim suggesting that the "harmoniousness" of black/white intermarriages leads to the unique skill of racial bridging on the part of multiracial offspring.[60]

Moreover, in an article discussing the relative psychological distress experienced by interracially married partners, Bratter again, this time with Karl Eschbach, finds "a significantly increased rate of distress" for white women married to black men.[61] They conclude that in the case of black/white marriage, "the increase in distress for persons in these relationships is specific to the white partner, and especially white wives with African American husbands."[62] We may therefore draw two very significant conclusions from the research of Bratter, King, and Eschbach: (1) that claims concerning interracial marriage that fail to take into account the differences within and among the various groups in question are flawed inherently, and (2) that generalized and oversimplified celebrations concerning the "harmoniousness" of interracial marriages, black/white marriages in particular, are based on nothing more than wishful thinking and unreflective fantasy.[63]

But even apart from these devastating empirical revelations, the racial-bridging model fails the most basic tests of logical consistency. If living with someone is supposed to result in special understanding with regard to racial difference, then it is absolutely reasonable to infer that it should also result in special understanding with regard to sexual difference. If living with someone of a different race is supposed to result in a unique ability to serve as a mediator for people of that race, then living with someone of a different sex should likewise result in a unique ability to serve as a mediator for people of that sex, since the driving idea is that living with essentialist difference results in special understanding and access to that essentialist difference in a way that qualifies, equips, and practically deputizes the individual to serve in a mediative way between the groups in question.

To be as direct as possible, this is complete nonsense, regardless of how often it might be repeated and accepted blindly over and over again. Merely living together does not bring women and men together in this way, it does not give them access to each other's essentialities, and it certainly does not equip them uniquely to mediate conflict between the sexes. Indeed, in many cases marriage actually intensifies and worsens that sexual conflict. So the blanket, unquestioned, commonsense assertion that living together grants one this specific kind of access and mediatory skill—whether in terms of sex or in terms of race—while popular and accepted, is patently false. As is the case with so much of multiracial ideology, the claim of racial bridging is merely stated without the least bit of critical backing, while no one inside the movement, and precious few outside it, care to point out the inconsistency. It is no more than an unproven desire, a case of wishful thinking, based on a supposed alterity of multiracial people that harks back to the marginal man.

In order to place the racial-bridging claim in context, it will be useful to return to Robert Park's declaration of mulatto superiority over Negroes—a superiority based on intimate contact with white people: "The mulatto and the mixed blood are, for the reasons I have described, the product of a double inheritance, biological and cultural, that is different from that of the black man. If the mulatto displays intellectual characteristics and personality traits superior to and different from those of the black man, it is not because of his biological inheritance merely, but rather more, I am inclined to believe, because of his more intimate association with the superior cultural group."[64] The modern-day claim that Generation Mix has a racial-bridging super power based purely on social contact is precisely the kind of superiority that Park attested to mulattoes possessing over monoracial blacks nearly eight decades ago. Is this the extent of the progress we have made since 1931?

While admittedly anecdotal, I nonetheless think it very useful and perfectly appropriate here to close this chapter's discussion by reflecting on my own experience of living at home with a white mother for the first twenty-two years of my life. In undergoing this reflection I can state quite honestly and for the record that being putatively black/white racially mixed and living with a white mother did not give me any special access to whiteness nor did it render me in any way qualified—whether uniquely or not—to serve as a racial bridge between whites and blacks any more than it qualified me to serve as a bridge between females and males, between Germans and Americans, between persons with blue eyes and persons with brown eyes, or between persons whose first names begin with the letter "L" and those whose first names begin with the letter "J."

While I am quite obviously satirizing the idea of racial bridging through the use of the latter facetious examples, I want to make it clear that I do not take racial identity itself to be a trivial status in US society. It is a false consciousness, to be sure, but hardly trivial nonetheless. The simple reality is that the members of Generation Mix put forth the nonsensical myth of the racial-bridging super power because they want desperately to believe this about themselves. They want to believe that being mixed racially confers upon them the power to serve as racial bridges, and so they say that it does. And they are facilitated in this wish by pro-multiracial academics such as Kilson and Korgen, who record such desires during their interviews of multiracial youth, and then report those desires as fact while neglecting conveniently their academic duty to apply scholarly objectivity and critical tools to their published work. It is much easier to assume the role of scholarly cheerleader and pretend that multiracial identity will lead to the deconstruction of race in the United States, than to actually engage in something along the lines of academic work in pursuit of proving that particular claim.

Sexton is correct in pointing out to us that the assumption that racism is "undermined by the proliferation of now permissible race mixture and the correlated growth in multiracial self-identification requires, at the very least, gross historical amnesia and acute political naïveté."[65] As no less a giant than James Baldwin has stated, blacks know whites; indeed, that has never been a problem. Knowing them has not done anything to lessen racism, however. "The American Negro has the great advantage of having never believed that collection of myths to which white Americans cling. . . . Negroes know far more about white Americans than that; it can almost be said, in fact, that they know about white Americans what parents—or, anyway, mothers—know about their children."[66] "Ask any Negro what he knows about the white people with whom he works. And then ask the white people with whom he works what they know about *him*."[67]

Moreover, as Moran writes, "the idea that intermarriage will serve as a natural melting pot for the races is an insidious myth, one that masks the magnitude of the marriage gap for blacks as compared to Asian Americans, Latinos, and Native Americans."[68] Indeed, in Moran's view, "multiracialism is apt to work best at mediating race relations where it is needed least. Groups already intermarrying in substantial numbers will produce offspring who can bridge an ever narrowing social divide."[69] And we will note here with some significance that Moran writes specifically of bridging a "social divide," not a "racial divide."

Notes

1. Catherine R. Squires, *Dispatches from the Color Line: The Press and Multiracial America* (Albany: State University of New York Press, 2007), 187.

2. Tavia Nyong'o, *The Amalgamation Waltz: Race, Performance, and the Ruses of Memory* (Minneapolis: University of Minnesota Press, 2009), 174–175.

3. See Rainier Spencer, "Census 2000: Assessments in Significance," in *New Faces in a Changing America: Multiracial Identity in the 21st Century,* ed. Loretta Winters and Herman DeBose, 105–108 (Thousand Oaks, CA: Sage, 2003).

4. Although an actual analysis would be far more complicated, the standard view contrasting Booker T. Washington and W. E. B. Du Bois, for example, provides a useful sense of Reuter's thought here in regard to Southern versus Northern mulatto attitudes.

5. Jared Sexton, *Amalgamation Schemes: Antiblackness and the Critique of Multiracialism* (Minneapolis: University of Minnesota Press, 2008), 150.

6. As Squires points out, "indeed, as has happened sporadically with Asian Americans, multiracial people seem to be moving into a 'model minority' niche in mainstream news media accounts of their rise to visibility and demographic critical mass." Squires, *Dispatches from the Color Line,* 2.

7. Sexton, *Amalgamation Schemes,* 31.

8. In reading the citations that follow, it is important to note that some are the objective reports of careful scholars on what other people are thinking and saying in regard to multiracial persons supposedly serving as racial bridges, while others are the pronouncements of decidedly less careful scholars who personally support that same flawed premise.

9. House Subcommittee on Census, Statistics, and Postal Personnel, Committee on Post Office and Civil Service, *Hearings on the Review of Federal Measurements of Race and Ethnicity,* testimony by Carlos Fernández on June 30, 1993, 103d Cong., 1st sess., April 14, June 30, July 29, and November 3, 1993, 128.

10. Kathleen O. Korgen, *From Black to Biracial: Transforming Racial Identity Among Americans* (Westport, CT: Praeger, 1999), 77.

11. Paul C. Rosenblatt, Terri A. Karis, and Richard Powell, *Multiracial Couples: Black & White Voices* (Thousand Oaks, CA: Sage Publications, 1995), 195, 196.

12. Renee C. Romano, *Race Mixing: Black-White Marriage in Postwar America* (Cambridge: Harvard University Press, 2003), 288.

13. Ellis Cose, *Color Blind: Seeing Beyond Race in a Race-Obsessed World* (New York: HarperPerennial, 1998), 18.

14. Ibid.

15. Sundee T. Frazier, *Check All That Apply: Finding Wholeness as a Multiracial Person* (Downers Grove, IL: InterVarsity, 2000), 131, 135.

16. Heather M. Dalmage, *Tripping on the Color Line: Black-White Multiracial Families in a Racially Divided World* (New Brunswick: Rutgers University Press, 2000), 169–170.

17. Rachel F. Moran, *Interracial Intimacy: The Regulation of Race and Romance* (Chicago: University of Chicago Press, 2001), 159.

18. I acknowledge that some readers may take issue with one or more of these adjectives. Some are expressed more intensely than others, but I hold that all still apply.

19. Tommie Shelby, *We Who Are Dark: The Philosophical Foundations of Black Solidarity* (Cambridge, MA: Belknap Press of Harvard University Press, 2005), 167.

20. Ibid., 163–164.

21. Frazier, *Check All That Apply,* 96.
22. Ibid.
23. Ibid., 95, 96.
24. Ibid., 95.
25. Ibid.
26. Kathleen O. Korgen, "Black/White Biracial Identity: The Influence of Color-blindness and the Racialization of Poor Black Americans," *Theory in Action* 2, no. 1 (January 2009): 24.
27. Ibid., 31, 35.
28. Shelby, *We Who Are Dark,* 187.
29. The Electric Slide is an omni-generational line dance that is popular with many Afro-Americans.
30. As Shelby asks most incisively: "Are there distinctly black norms of etiquette or black social values? Is there a black ethics, epistemology, or aesthetic? Are there uniquely black styles of dress, hairstyles, or modes of speech? While some of these are no doubt interesting questions, there is no reason to believe, and in fact every reason to doubt, that blacks can achieve anything like consensus on such matters." Shelby, *We Who Are Dark,* 225.
31. I could certainly see a similar objection to there being a gay subculture as such, just as I have argued that there is no black subculture in the United States, that gayness is perhaps an attribute much like blackness, as opposed to constituting a discrete culture or subculture. I would not take issue with such a position if argued for competently.
32. Romano, *Race Mixing,* 280.
33. Elliott Lewis, *Fade: My Journeys in Multiracial America* (New York: Carroll & Graf, 2006), 116.
34. Ibid., 257.
35. Ibid., 365.
36. Ibid., 265.
37. Ibid., 265–266.
38. Ibid., 265.
39. Frazier, *Check All That Apply,* 139. Italics added.
40. Ursula Brown, *The Interracial Experience: Growing Up Black/White Racially Mixed in the United States* (Westport, CT: Praeger, 2001), 45.
41. Ibid., 113. Italics added.
42. Marion Kilson, *Claiming Place: Biracial Young Adults of the Post–Civil Rights Era* (Westport, CT: Bergin and Garvey, 2001), 55. Italics added.
43. Ibid., 81. Italics added.
44. Ibid. Italics added.
45. Shelby, *We Who Are Dark,* 182.
46. Quoted in Kilson, *Claiming Place,* 145.
47. Ibid.
48. Nikki Khanna, "Country Clubs and Hip-Hop Thugs: Examining the Role of Social Class and Culture in Shaping Racial Identity," in *Multiracial Americans and Social Class: The Influence of Social Class on Racial Identity,* ed. Kathleen O. Korgen, 54 (New York: Routledge, 2010).
49. Ibid., 65.
50. Ibid.
51. Ibid., 61.
52. Samira Kawash, *Dislocating the Color Line: Identity, Hybridity, and Singularity in African-American Literature* (Stanford: Stanford University Press, 1997), 129–130.

53. Quoted in Lewis, *Fade,* 287.

54. Courtney M. Bonam and Margaret Shih, "Exploring Multiracial Individuals' Comfort with Intimate Interracial Relationships," *Journal of Social Issues* 65, no. 1 (2009): 88.

55. Frazier, *Check All That Apply,* 26.

56. Jenifer Bratter and Rosalind King report that "over the past few decades, the rate of divorce (per 1,000 married women aged 15 years and older) rose from 14.9 in 1970—the year before the introduction of no-fault divorce laws—to a peak of 22.6 in 1980 and then declined and stabilized to around 20.0 during the 1990s." Jenifer L. Bratter and Rosalind B. King, "'But Will It Last?' Marital Instability Among Interracial and Same-Race Couples," *Family Relations* 57 (April 2008): 161.

57. Ibid., 169.

58. Ibid., 160.

59. Ibid., 169.

60. Nikki Khanna, "If You're Half Black, You're Just Black: Reflected Appraisals and the Persistence of the One-Drop Rule," *The Sociological Quarterly* 51 (2010): 105.

61. Jenifer L. Bratter and Karl Eschbach, "'What About the Couple?' Interracial Marriage and Psychological Distress," *Social Science Research* 35 (2006): 1035.

62. Ibid., 1040.

63. This is not to say that all black/white marriages are in distress or that all such marriages are doomed to failure. Rather, the larger point is that both the popular and the academic literature that takes for granted the "harmoniousness" of interracial marriage in general is simply wrong.

64. Robert E. Park, "Mentality of Racial Hybrids," *American Journal of Sociology* 36 (1930–1931): 547.

65. Sexton, *Amalgamation Schemes,* 51.

66. James Baldwin, *The Fire Next Time* (New York: Vintage International, 1993), 101.

67. Ibid., 103.

68. Moran, *Interracial Intimacy,* 178.

69. Ibid., 178.

10

Assessing the New Millennium Marginal Man

Although it makes for a bizarre kind of irony, the claims of the American Multiracial Identity Movement for mixed-race exceptionalism place it squarely within the ideological orbit of sociology's marginal man—a laughable caricature that is nonetheless appealed to by way of physical debility in the form of special healthcare needs, by way of emotional/psychological debility necessitating a concerted movement *away from blackness*, and by way of a racial superiority that gives the members of Generation Mix certain super powers unavailable to monoracial blacks. These conceptions are facilitated by modern-day incarnations of Robert Park, Edward Reuter, and Everett Stonequist, who do their part to breathe life into the desiccated corpse of the marginal man, whether by invoking Park directly as does Kathleen Korgen (see Chapter 8) or by simply substituting liminality for marginality as in the case of G. Reginald Daniel.[1]

Daniel attempts to explain away the "problem" approach to marginal man theory by arguing that persons who took this perspective did so "based on misinterpretations of sociologist Robert E. Park's theories," arguing, for example, that Stonequist "distorted, or at least misinterpreted, Park's actual theory of marginality."[2] I would refer to my assessment of Park and his theory in Chapter 3 and invite anyone to find any misinterpretation whatsoever in terms of Park's clear orientations of white superiority, Negro inferiority, and a nearly insatiable mulatto desire for whiteness. Indeed, Kerry Ann Rockquemore, David Brunsma, and Daniel Delgado refer specifically to Park's marginal man theory as the "'problem approach' to theorizing multiracial identity."[3] They write regarding Park's theory that "despite the fact that mixed-race individuals possessed both Black and White ancestry, they were doomed to a permanent state of crisis in which their mental state was marked by turmoil that reflected a deeply racist and eugenic epistemology."[4] The authors explain further that "Stonequist went on to more fully explain and expand upon Park's general theory."[5] Making refer-

213

ence to Stonequist, Daniel McNeil notes that "Park had also encouraged one of his students to publish an analysis of the 'mulatto mind.'"[6]

There is no misinterpretation of Park or of "'problem' marginality" here. Rather, it would appear that the only misinterpretation in this matter is on the part of Daniel in his vain attempt to rehabilitate Park. One may certainly present a case for "'positive' marginality" if one is so inclined, but it cannot be done legitimately—not in terms of American mulattoes at least—by invoking the racist, white superiority–inspired fantasies of Robert Park, as Korgen and Daniel attempt to do.[7] Nor are Korgen and Daniel alone in advancing this sort of specious validation. Simon Cheng and Kathryn Lively, in an article in which they endorse the marginal man thesis as a "common" and "popular" theoretical framework for understanding multiraciality, announce that "self-identified multiracial adolescents, overall, display outcome profiles that fit well within the purview of the marginal man perspective and/or the subsequent elaborations of the theory."[8]

The American Multiracial Identity Movement, in its own words, demonstrates that it endorses the "problem approach" to the marginality it embraces quite openly. We will recall Rockquemore, Brunsma, and Delgado's assertion of Stonequist's argument that "mixed-race people's awareness of the conflict between the two races created some level of identification with both groups resulting in an internalization of the group conflict as a personal problem."[9] In his own words, Stonequist says of the marginal man, that "in looking at himself from the standpoint of each group he experiences the conflict as a personal problem."[10] Adding yet more confirmation that Generation Mix is in fact the embodied reincarnation of sociology's marginal man, Sundee Frazier, a black/white person and popular author within multiracial identity circles, states that as long as "black and white people remain separated and hostile, I've got to live with that tension."[11] But one wonders why; why in the world should someone internalize so personally the battles of others, both living and long dead? Yet Frazier is quite clear that in donning the garb of the marginal (wo)man—with its racist-inspired projection of internalized group conflict—the "problem approach" to that marginality is indeed a perfect fit: "I felt the longstanding war between two people groups raging inside myself."[12] This is part of a kind of self-pity that is coextensive with contemporary multiracial identity, a need to be suffering constantly. Here we see a frankly bizarre internalization of white/black racial strife that can serve no purpose other than to begin and end in a quite circular generation of self-pity, and, it must be added, malaise. In Frazier, Stonequist could not have asked for a better disciple.

I have devoted a good deal of space to arguing that the black/white members of Generation Mix are not a new phenomenon on the US racial scene, that it is not possible to differentiate them legitimately from the general Afro-American population. I want to close Part 2 by probing a bit deeper into the question of what the black/white members of Generation Mix are and are not. Prior to doing so, though, I shall consider two additional and related ways that the American Multiracial Identity Movement attempts to distinguish its constituents as a new and separate racial category. Both of these approaches share the interesting logical invalidity that the basis of multiracial identity has to do not with the multiracial subject itself, but rather with things external to that subject.

The first of these approaches is exemplified by Kimberly DaCosta's respondents, who "drew the boundary between multiracial and monoracial on the basis of a set of experiences that had to do with having differently raced *parents*."[13] For her respondents, the experience of feeling "'out of place' in their families" and also "'out of place' in the ethnoracial communities of their parents" leads to "the desire to create 'multiracial community.'"[14] But is this a valid basis for multiracial identity, or is it merely another blind avenue to pursue given that every other approach has thus far been proven to be logically invalid or a contradiction internally?[15] Notice that DaCosta's respondents do not claim a multiracial identity on the basis of having parents of different races, which might at least be valid within the framework of a fallacious belief in biological race. Rather, they base their multiracial identity on a "set of experiences" stemming from having such parents.

The counterexamples begin queuing-up immediately, and I shall consider only a few. Since multiracial identity is here based on a "set of experiences," the first problem to arise is the question of what would happen should a particular mixed-race individual not have those qualifying experiences. Would that mixed-race person therefore not be mixed race? Indeed, one supposes on this view that an individual with parents of different races is actually not herself or himself mixed race until that certain set of experiences takes place, leading to the bizarre conclusion that a child of differently raced parents would not be born mixed race, and would not in fact become mixed race until those experiences had indeed obtained. To illustrate the outlandish nature of this way of defining multiracial identity, the equivalent case would be to claim that black identity is based on having racist experiences, and that a child of two black parents is therefore not actually black until having undergone those particular experiences.

How, we might ask quite reasonably, can the essentiality of being multiracial depend on something other than multiraciality itself (i.e., "a set of experiences"), and how can this set of experiences constitute a valid "boundary between multiracial and monoracial"? The logical implication is that the salient difference between being multiracial and monoracial is not whether one is in fact multiracial or monoracial but whether or not one has these particular experiences. Therefore, a child of differently raced parents who is adopted by two same-race monoracial parents is not and will never be multiracial, whereas a monoracial child who is adopted by two differently raced parents may become multiracial eventually, presuming she has the requisite qualifying experiences later in life. As we can see, the reductio ad absurdum possibilities for this definition of multiraciality are quite extensive to say the least and reveal that, rather than encountering anything approaching a valid framework for contemporary multiracial identity, we are instead facing nothing more than ordinary special pleading.

Ronald Sundstrom advances another variation of the argument from experience via his claim that "multiracialism cannot be largely a genealogical matter; rather, it is an experience."[16] According to Sundstrom, not only does multiracial experience vary temporally, but even within a particular unspecified time period, "each multiracial experience is tied to a particular site—to a particular social forces network that gives the identity presence and effect—rendering it distinct."[17] Sundstrom, though, falls victim to the same problem as the previous argument, for by de-linking multiracial identity from biology he must then demonstrate (although he merely states rather than demonstrates) that each multiracially identifying person in fact has this particular experience, and, in addition, he must concur that said person is not multiracial until this experience has taken place.

Moreover, though, Sundstrom entangles himself in yet an additional complication, for unlike the previous example in which the criterion was said to be "a set of experiences that had to do with having differently raced *parents*," Sundstrom's is simply the overly broad criterion of "experience" itself. But if for Sundstrom, "each multiracial experience is tied to a particular site—to a particular social forces network that gives the identity presence and effect—rendering it distinct," then must not this site specificity cause each individual experiencer to be a member of a distinct multiracial group consisting of only herself or himself—multiracial$_1$, multiracial$_2$, multiracial$_3$, etc? Or perhaps the site specificity would allow for categories such as West Coast multiracials and East Coast multiracials, or Berkeley multiracials and Cambridge multiracials.

But even this is not satisfying, for it presumes that all of the multiracials within a particular site at a given time have precisely the same experience of being multiracial, which, according to Sundstrom, is what gives the category its distinctive "presence and effect." Of course, this would be both absurd and an objectifying insult to the persons in question, rendering Sundstrom's *experience over genealogy* formulation quite ridiculous. All of these problems are due to Sundstrom's unsuccessful attempt to evade the absolute foundation of multiracial ideology and identity, which is biological race. What we see is that evasions based on experience, whether conceived broadly or narrowly, are doomed to logical failure.

The final means of delineating multiracial identity that I will discuss is related to the idea of experiences, but rather than an amorphous "set of experiences" or a broad but unspecified notion of "experience," focuses specifically on one particular area of experience. This approach presents the notion that today's multiracially identifying black/white people are somehow different, qua black/white people, from all those past generations of black/white people and from today's racially mixed Afro-Americans because their families are now public and they are therefore free to identify as they wish. Yet just as in the "set of experiences" definition, this is a logical error as well, for in this case the subject (black/white people) remains unchanged even with the assumption that there is a difference in environment.

It is not clear how the black/white person is different merely because the situation she finds herself in is different. If a mulatto finds her family rejected one day, but discovers sudden recognition and acceptance of that family the next day, does that mulatto thereby transform into a nonblack, black/white member of Generation Mix? If one takes a fish from one's indoor fish tank and places that fish in a backyard pond, is the fish changed as a result? The important question is not whether the fish's situation has changed, but specifically whether the fish itself has changed. Even if there are things the fish can now do in the pond that it could not do while in the fish tank, is it not still the same fish? The subject, whether a mulatto or a fish, may indeed act differently given a new environment, but such changed opportunities and changed actions are completely distinct from the essence of the thing itself, a critical reality that is lost conveniently in this unsuccessful attempt at multiracial definition. Moreover, if one counters that the individual was always multiracial, then the definition under consideration is therefore invalid since that definition states specifically that it is the new situation of family recognition that makes one multiracial.

What the "family recognition" argument is really about is the imposition of a predicate, an adjective that modifies the subject (although only in terms of its environment) but does not alter its essentiality. Unlike the "set of experiences" definition, this delineation does seem to posit the prior existence of multiracial individuals regardless of any particular set of qualifying life occurrences. But, contradictorily, it also does not allow for the instantiation of multiracial identity until such time as the individual's family is recognized, a situation that is said to be incipient at the moment. The very serious logical problem, though, is that if we posit the existence of the multiracial individual prior to the moment of "family recognition," how then is the multiracial individual changed—qua a multiracial individual—as a result of that moment of recognition? The person's situation has changed, her environment has changed, but has the essentiality of her multiraciality itself been changed? If she was already multiracial, how does family recognition alter her such that multiracial identity is now valid for her in a way that it was not valid previously?

It is important to keep in mind in this case, as in the case of the "set of experiences" argument, that these are intended as definitions of multiracial identity, justifications of multiracial identity (recall, for instance, that Da-Costa's respondents "drew the boundary between multiracial and monoracial" based expressly on their definition), not explanations of why people might or might not want to identify multiracially. As such, both kinds of definitions are devoid of logical validity; neither type comes any closer to reality than an outright biological race justification of multiraciality. There is tremendous difference between the definition of a category and an explanation of why someone might be drawn to that category. Desire to be different and special, to want to separate oneself from other people, no matter how intense, is not the same thing as legitimate justification for that purported separation. This is especially so when the bases of that supposed justification are none other than the discredited myths of biological race and the marginal man.

If we compare them, the marginal man and the black/white member of Generation Mix represent nearly the same thing. Both the marginal man and the black/white member of Generation Mix take biological race to be a reality, a reality that makes the mixed-race person a separate racial entity distinct from either parent's racial essence. Biological race is the foundational principle of the American Multiracial Identity Movement, for if the movement did not maintain a dependence on biological race it would not aver that there are, in the first place, multiracial people. Addressing this inherent contradiction, DaCosta notes that "while activists and parents describe their use of multiple terms for indicating their racial identity as 'revolutionary' or simply 'accurate,' it is also true that the logic of mixed race stems from the same underlying logic that preceded it—that individuals have race, and when they combine sexually we get 'racial mixture.'"[18] Jared Sexton is again crucial in illuminating both the deception and its purpose: "If multiracialism reinforces the idea of biological race in general, it does so by negatively 'purifying'—which is to say *quarantining*—racial blackness in particular as the centerpiece of a vaster re-racialization of U.S. society in the post–civil rights era. After resurrecting the tenets of a long-debunked scientific racism, multiracialism then renders black resistance to its dubious goals as an intransigent, unthinking force of political *repression*."[19] In this reliance on the fallacy of biological race there is no essential difference between past and present iterations of the marginal man.

Both the marginal man and the black/white member of Generation Mix reject blackness and, to an arguable degree, desire whiteness. One need not look far to find this often quite loud rejection of blackness, whether in the shrill voices of white mother-indoctrinators or in the hip and often smug pronouncements of the black/white members of Generation Mix themselves, despite empty promises of racial bridging. One may argue about how much the black/white members of Generation Mix desire whiteness; and while such desire certainly seems to not be in the range of the original marginal man's purported desire, at the same time we must acknowledge and account for their rejection of blackness and its parallel to the marginal man's similar rejection. In comparing yesterday's to today's marginal man, it is not the equally strong rejection of blackness that is in question, merely the relative intensity of any desire for whiteness.

Both the marginal man and the black/white member of Generation Mix are in grave danger of deep psychological and emotional damage if their respective divided-blood psychotraumas are not addressed. They each require specific retraining and reorientation in order for the biological racial differences within their bodies to be reconciled appropriately. Lest I be accused of exaggerating the claimed danger to today's black/white people, the words of Marvin Arnold ("psychopathology," "dysfunction"), Ursula Brown ("lack of self-esteem," "the severing of parental-child psychological and biological connections"), Sundstrom ("anguish and alienation"), and Daniel ("psychological oppression") from Chapter 8, will remind us that these very extreme dangers are precisely what the American Multiracial Identity Movement is propagating in defense of its antiblackness objectives.

The single aspect in which the marginal man differs from the black/white member of Generation Mix is that while the remedy for identity confusion and pathology in the former case was to move *toward blackness*, in the latter case the remedy is to move *away from blackness*. In all other regards, the two personality frameworks are essentially the same. Finally, in considering Generation Mix's revivified marginal man, one notices once again the prominence of white researchers presuming to circumscribe and demarcate the psychologies and life trajectories of black/white persons by prescribing a normative identity for them. Only now, women have taken the lead, as Robert Park, Edward Reuter, and Everett Stonequist have been replaced by Ursula Brown, Marion Kilson, and Kathleen Korgen, among others.

When we look at Generation Mix, and most especially at its black/white members, it is important to understand that we are not seeing anything new. First of all, race mixture is an old story, as we know. Persons of sub-Saharan African/European descent are among the nation's oldest inhabitants. Second, I have shown that the American Multiracial Identity Movement has chosen to embrace the marginality doctrine of Park, Reuter, and Stonequist. Thus, we are essentially seeing a return onto the American scene of the tragic mulatto story, albeit this time with a slightly different ending. Generation Mix is based on marginality, but reverses the therapeutic polarity such that the former *cure* involving a movement *toward blackness* is now reconceived as a movement *away from blackness*. As with the former version, there are both negative and positive traits associated with black/white identity. That this identical structure is resurrected—regardless of the traits themselves, or that the *cure* now merely lies in the opposite direction—should throw into serious doubt any assertions of the movement's progressiveness, and, I daresay, its apparent capacity for imagination or creativity. Generation Mix, despite its hipness, its narcissistic celebration, and its embrace by the popular media, is at heart the same old story of mixed-race turmoil until such time as the proper psychological remedy can be effected.

That the American Multiracial Identity Movement has opted to take this route is strange and ironic. It seems especially retrograde in the present moment, particularly after the discussion in Chapter 4 concerning how American mulatto authors, decades and decades ago, rejected the badge of marginality imposed upon them by their era's racist sociologists. This retrogression may be explained at least partially by the dominance within the movement of white mothers of black/white children, who embrace that badge of marginality in an effort to generate sympathy for a reclassification of their children *away from blackness*. Their extreme emotionality and their near vehemence in asserting that their children are not black (for we never do and never will hear that level of outraged passion should the same children be mistaken for white) are likely responsible for the pathological approach that the new marginal man (the liminal man?) represents. Also, the fact that the movement began and is very much still directed by activists entails a necessary failure on its part to appreciate white privilege, white superiority, and the endless contradictions inherent in the movement's own ideology.[20] One need only think back to that ill-fated, mid-1990s seduction of Newt Gingrich and Ward Connerly by the multiracial movement in order to appreciate this point. Finally, the effects of antiblackness, however much hidden or repressed, hardly need stating.

If the black/white members of Generation Mix are not a new phenomenon on the US racial scene, if they are not something different and special, if they are not an entity separate from the always already-mixed Afro-American population, what are they then? It is a fair question, and deserves an answer, although that answer will surely not be satisfying to those who embrace and support that particular identity. The reality is that precisely because they are not anything new or special, because they are not a distinct category in and of themselves, there is nothing in particular that they in fact are. Am I therefore asserting that the black/white members of Generation Mix are black? Am I thereby joining that old chorus of "You're black; so just get over it"? No, I am not. Indeed, that is the last thing I would assert since biological race is a myth. There is nothing, racially, that anyone in fact is, including the purported black/white members of Generation Mix.

What I am asserting, however, and what I want to state in as careful a way as possible, is that whatever the black/white members of Generation Mix want to call themselves, there is no legitimate way for them to distinguish themselves physically, biologically, or genetically from Afro-Americans. And the biogenetic connection here is absolutely critical, for race as a social construction is not to the point. The black/white members of Generation Mix take themselves to be multiracial not because their parents are considered to be members of different social races (as if the notion of a *social race* in the first place makes the least bit of sense anywhere outside the discipline of sociology), but rather, quite bluntly, because their particular parents had sex with each other and through that sexual union brought them into biological existence. Thus, what I am asserting is that regardless of what they choose to call themselves, the black/white members of Generation Mix cannot differentiate themselves in a valid way from American mulattoes/Afro-Americans.

When the black/white members of Generation Mix say that they are not black, when they say that they are distinct racially from Afro-Americans, when they say that they are a new and different racial phenomenon apart from Afro-Americans—when they say such things—they are simply wrong. They want to be distinct; oh how very desperately and how very intensely they want to be different, but the fact is that they are not. They are part of a long tradition of sub-Saharan African/European population mixture going back nearly four centuries in British North America and the United States. If the American Multiracial Identity Movement wants to invoke biological race—which it does by its very existence—then it must live with the consequences of that decision. If the black/white members of Generation Mix are asserted to be anything racially, Afro-Americans must by definition be asserted to be the very same thing. It would be far more honest for the black/white members of Generation Mix to eschew an approach based on (multi)racial identity and instead admit the truth: "We are a subgroup of Afro-Americans who have decided to pursue a sociopolitical ideology that results, whether directly or indirectly, in support of antiblackness."

As I began Part 2 by discussing, the assertion of a new, nonblack, black/white, multiracial identity contributes to the marginalization of Afro-Americans that is currently taking place. The black/white members of Generation Mix are seen and appropriated by the United States and its mainstream news outlets as something to be brought closer even as *regular* Afro-Americans (always already mixed, of course) are pushed further and further away. In a sort of self-fulfilling prophecy, then, when those *regular* Afro-Americans object to being relegated to the periphery in favor of the Generation Mix mirage, the United States and its mainstream news outlets respond by perceiving that objection as an additional reason to bring Generation Mix even closer and to push *regular* Afro-Americans even further away—a cycle that replicates itself in seemingly endless fashion as the nation seeks to step over its Afro-American problem on the way to the beckoning illusion of a postracial future.

The issue in question is desire—desire on the part of Generation Mix to be different and separate, desire on the part of the nation in general to move beyond the thorny Afro-American problem without having to get its hands dirty by actually dealing with it. It is the substitution of euphemism for harsh reality, and the foolishly hoped-for evasion of troubles that will not go away unless they are dealt with in an honest manner. It is, in essence, a desire to become postracial without first, or indeed ever, becoming postracist. Yet if we insist on pretending that some persons of mixed sub-Saharan African/European descent are different and more special than other persons of mixed sub-Saharan African/European descent, we are only succeeding in fooling ourselves—and to our own detriment as well.

An often-heard sentiment concerning Generation Mix, as well as an ever-present undercurrent whether spoken out loud or not, is that its new version of multiraciality represents a revolutionary element, an insurgent force against the power of the US racial superstructure. Even beyond the empty nonsense regarding racial bridging, Generation Mix is presumed to be the vanguard of a new (non)racial order in the United States. In Chapter 11 I shall consider the insurgent nature of Generation Mix and assess how it does or does not represent a revolutionary threat to the US racial order. It is important to determine whether Generation Mix and the American Multiracial Identity Movement are truly bringing about the demise of race and its attendant evils or whether, in the words of Rockquemore, Brunsma, and Delgado, "We see the construct *race* falling apart at the seams, while racism and group-level inequalities persist."[21] If it is the former, it should be supported without question. If it is the latter, however, it is merely a sort of shell game, an illusion that threatens to leave Afro-Americans once again on the periphery and out of account. We shall want to see, therefore, if the place Generation Mix says it is taking us is in fact its destination.

Notes

1. G. Reginald Daniel, *Race and Multiraciality in Brazil and the United States: Converging Paths?* (University Park: Pennsylvania State University Press, 2006), 163–169.

2. Ibid., 164.

3. Kerry Ann Rockquemore, David L. Brunsma, and Daniel J. Delgado, "Racing to Theory or Retheorizing Race? Understanding the Struggle to Build a Multiracial Identity Theory," *Journal of Social Issues* 65, no. 1 (2009): 16.

4. Ibid.

5. Ibid.

6. Daniel McNeil, *Sex and Race in the Black Atlantic: Mulatto Devils and Multiracial Messiahs* (New York: Routledge, 2010), 3.

7. Daniel, *Race and Multiraciality in Brazil and the United States,* 164.

8. Simon Cheng and Kathryn J. Lively, "Multiracial Self-Identification and Adolescent Outcomes: A Social Psychological Approach to the Marginal Man Theory," *Social Forces* 88, no. 1 (September 2009): 61, 65, 84.

9. Rockquemore, Brunsma, and Delgado, "Racing to Theory or Retheorizing Race?," 16.

10. Everett V. Stonequist, "The Problem of the Marginal Man," *American Journal of Sociology* 41, no. 1 (July 1935): 6.

11. Quoted in Elliott Lewis, *Fade: My Journeys in Multiracial America* (New York: Carroll & Graf, 2006), 287.

12. Sundee T. Frazier, *Check All That Apply: Finding Wholeness as a Multiracial Person* (Downers Grove, IL: InterVarsity, 2000), 92.

13. Kimberly M. DaCosta, *Making Multiracials: State, Family, and Market in the Redrawing of the Color Line* (Stanford: Stanford University Press, 2007), 127.

14. Ibid.

15. For previous critiques of multiracial identity see Rainier Spencer, *Spurious Issues: Race and Multiracial Identity Politics in the United States* (Boulder: Westview, 1999), chap. 3; and Spencer, *Challenging Multiracial Identity* (Boulder, Lynne Rienner, 2006), chap. 4.

16. Ronald R. Sundstrom, *The Browning of America and the Evasion of Social Justice* (Albany: State University of New York Press, 2008), 114.

17. Ibid., 114–115.

18. DaCosta, *Making Multiracials,* 183.

19. Jared Sexton, *Amalgamation Schemes: Antiblackness and the Critique of Multiracialism* (Minneapolis: University of Minnesota Press, 2008), 51.

20. Multiracially supporting academics are significant in propagating multiracial ideology, to be sure, but they follow the lead of the activists. When the activists make a new claim for multiracial exceptionalism—regardless of how ridiculous the claim might be—the academics then attempt to build the scholarly case, as in the example of the multiracial medical myth discussed in Chapter 8, for instance.

21. Rockquemore, Brunsma, and Delgado, "Racing to Theory or Retheorizing Race?," 26.

Part 3
The Mulatto Future

11

Whither Multiracial Militancy?

"Multiracial Solidarity!" "Multiracial Power!"
—*From a flyer announcing the Multiracial
Solidarity March of July 20, 1996*

What would a truly militant US politics of multiraciality look like? By this I mean a politics of multiraciality that did not merely *declare* its militancy, but one that actually *was* militant. Precisely what would it be militating against? Exactly what would it be protesting for? As might already be evident by the preceding few sentences as well as by Parts 1 and 2 of this book, I do not consider multiracial activism in the United States to be a militant project. In fact, I do not think the American Multiracial Identity Movement possesses a single militant bone in its entire ideological body. To be sure, current versions of multiracial identity politics are at times scrappy, bellicose, and belligerent; however—and this is a most critical point—those versions of multiracial identity politics are at no time scrappy, bellicose, or belligerent in opposition to the idea of race or to the basics of the US racial order. As I shall argue in this chapter, multiracial ideology is far more complicit with than it is subversive of current deployments of race in the United States. This, to my thinking, renders it a decidedly nonmilitant enterprise, and also renders its purported future utility to the dismantling of race in the United States very questionable indeed.

As we have thus far seen, current popular wisdom asserts that we are in the midst of a paradigm shift concerning the way race is constructed in the United States. According to this view, individuals of mixed race—most specifically, so-called first-generation multiracial persons—are confounding the US racial paradigm by virtue of their ambiguous phenotypes and their supposedly more cosmopolitan cultural outlooks. This perspective is reflected in television and magazine advertising, in popular newsmagazine coverage, and in books both academic and nonacademic. Kathleen Korgen provides a typical rendition of this standpoint with her announcement that "today mixed-race Americans challenge the very foundation of our racial structure."[1] *Newsweek* writer Lynette Clemetson concurs with Korgen, reporting that demographic changes in the United States "give many teens a chance to challenge old notions of race," and quoting in an affirmative light one high-school student's startling declaration that race "doesn't even really exist anymore."[2]

We hear that today's multiracial young adults accept a multiracial identity in far greater proportion than did their predecessors, but precisely what are they assenting to and what does it mean, if anything, beyond the pronouncement of a parentally indoctrinated fad? Advocates of multiracial identity have long argued that their position is destructive of race, that acceptance of multiracial identity will bring about the demise of the US racial order. The arguments of scholars who favor multiracial identity, as well as the sentiments expressed via popular media outlets by members of the multiracial movement, suggest that multiracial identity possesses an insurgent character, that advocacy of multiracial identity is therefore a militant stance for one to assume vis-à-vis the idea of race in the United States.

I as well as others have argued in turn that such a claim is without merit, that indeed it is quite self-contradictory since the very assertion of multiracial identity requires prior belief in biological race. If it is true that multiracial identity is a real and valid identity, then such an identity is sensible only *as* a biological racial identity. If words are to mean anything, and I very seriously believe they should, it quite obviously simply cannot be that a multiracial identity is somehow *not* a biological racial identity. If the issue were ethnicity, we would be debating the idea of multiethnic identity. If the issue were nationality, we would be debating the idea of multinational identity. If the issue were cultural affinity we would be debating the idea of multicultural identity. But as we are debating the idea of multiracial identity, the nature of that identity is made clear by the very wording in which the debate is framed. Nor is there any escape from this contradiction through asserting that racial identities are socially designated and not biological, since it is the sexual (and thereby biological) union of ostensibly differently raced parents that supposedly produces multiracial children. They are what they are said to be due to biological mixing, not social designation.

Multiracial identity activists and the scholars who provide intellectual support for them share a belief that multiraciality is a militant project. Maria Root opens her second anthology on multiracial identity, *The Multiracial Experience: Racial Borders as the New Frontier*, with a chapter titled "A Bill of Rights for Racially Mixed People."[3] The major subheadings for this chapter are "Resistance," "Revolution," and "Change," with Root averring that the "affirmation of rights" in her bill "reflects *resistance, revolution,* and ultimately *change* for the system that has weakened the social, moral, and spiritual fiber of this country."[4] Moreover, Root offers this set of "affirmations or 'rights' as reminders to break the spell of the delusion that creates race to the detriment of us all."[5] Based on the clear intent of its author's own words, Jill Olumide is certainly correct in describing Root's bill as a "programme of resistance," as is Kimberly DaCosta in terming it "a manifesto of sorts."[6]

Philosophically, it seems to me that this manifesto stands on two primary presumptions: (1) that multiracial activism is a militant cause ("resistance," "revolution," and "change"), and (2) that this activist project is corrosive of ideologies of biological race (such ideologies being marked by the manifesto as constituting delusional spell that ought to be broken). These presumptions undergirding Root's manifesto are also the primary presumptions of the multiracial movement at large, as the latter has been constructed consciously and conspicuously upon the former.

Root's Bill of Rights is somewhat dated, but nevertheless nothing has since come along to displace it. Rather, it has solidified and achieved for itself a sort of cult status within the ideology of the American Multiracial Identity Movement, and therefore must be said to still be very much alive in a deeply pervasive sense. Indeed, G. Reginald Daniel reports that "ritualistic practices within the multiracial community include the reading of Maria Root's 'Bill of Rights for Racially Mixed People' at support group meetings and conferences."[7] In addition, Marion Kilson and Loretta Winters close their respective book and anthology on multiracial identity by reprinting the complete text of Root's Bill of Rights in the Epilogue of each.[8]

Kim Williams highlights further the continuing significance of Root's bill by noting that "perhaps the most extensively reproduced statement exemplifying the movement's broad goals can be found in Maria Root's 'Bill of Rights for Racially Mixed People,' which has become something of a charter statement within the activist multiracial community."[9] Because of the status of Root's bill within multiracial activist circles and its continuing impact on the movement as a whole, I want to hold its two premises (that multiracial activism and advocacy is a militant project, and that this militant project works to undermine race) as central to my overall analysis of the movement's purported militancy and its likelihood to lead us toward a postracial US future.

My thesis in Part 3 of this book generally, and in this chapter specifically, is that the multiracial movement, which congratulates itself so continuously and so effusively for its success at being militant and at working against notions of biological race, is not at all successful in accomplishing these two goals. In fact, critical analysis reveals quite clearly that it is engaged in neither task in an active way. Indeed, due to the nature of its true goals the movement cannot undertake these tasks with anything approaching sincerity and integrity. Rather, the American Multiracial Identity Movement is a self-indulgent social enterprise whose primary aim is to bend—but not break—the bars of race just enough to move its adherents upward from lesser- to more-privileged positions within the structure of the US racial paradigm.

This might not seem evident if one's information about the multiracial movement comes from the voices of movement leaders and adherents via the generally unreflective pages of popular newsmagazines such as *Time* and *Newsweek*, or through academic works written by movement scholars such as Daniel, Kilson, Korgen, and Ursula Brown, or nonscholar movement authors such as Elliott Lewis and Sundee Frazier, for instance.[10] Significantly, discussing pro-movement academics whose work was utilized by multiracial organizers during the federal multiracial category debates of the mid-1990s, DaCosta makes the important point that "the messages in some of the writings by these academics, most of whom identify as mixed race or are themselves intermarried, are indistinguishable from those of activists," noting further that Root's Bill of Rights "illustrates the extent of this parity."[11]

The writings of these scholar-activists, alongside a consistent brand of popular media coverage that can only be described as overwhelmingly bathetic, are responsible for the remarkable success of the multiracial movement; however, the remarkable success to which I am referring is not at all related to the stated goals of the movement (militancy and the undermining of race), which, as I have noted, have been neither achieved nor even attempted. Rather, the remarkable success—indeed, one might argue, the only success—of the multiracial movement has been in conflating in a highly effective way those stated goals with what are in reality the de facto goals of the movement (enhancement of personal self-esteem and a concerted movement *away from blackness*). In the most basic sense it is a case of stating one thing while actually doing the opposite, a logical flaw with which the multiracial movement has found itself ensnared from the very beginning of its existence. Its consistent response to that flaw has been to emphasize the stating of the one thing and to ignore or camouflage the doing of the exact opposite.

When introducing her Bill of Rights, in a discussion about the multiracial person's not having to justify her or his existence in this world, Root, referring to invasive questions posed by people (by monoracial people, quite obviously), mentions a few of the "stereotypes that make up the schema by which the *other* attempts to make meaning out of the multiracial person's existence."[12] What is most intriguing to me in reading this passage, however, are not the stereotypes Root mentions, but rather her instructive choice of language in situating monoracials as the "other" in the context of a discussion in which she also rather inconsistently advises multiracial persons to refuse to "uncritically apply to others the very concepts that have made some of us casualties of race wars."[13]

This leads quite obviously to the question of what the multiracial person is to do. Does she heed Root by refusing to take part in categorical stereotypes that facilitate the construction of racial boundaries, or does she heed Root by imagining the diverse collectivity of monoracial persons as a stereotypical and unitary category of "other" against which she then constitutes her own identity? Moreover, given that one of the true operative dynamics of the multiracial movement is the attempt to move its constituents upward within the racial hierarchy toward whiteness and, most especially, *away from blackness*, it is reasonable to assume that the monoracial "other" Root imagines here is a nonwhite other. In any case, engaging in the former would seem to preclude the latter and vice versa, highlighting the logical contradiction inherent in saying one thing and doing the opposite.

This sort of logical contradiction has been and still is being reproduced continuously through the ideology of the multiracial movement that looks to Root's Bill of Rights for Racially Mixed People as a foundational document. As an example of this reproduction, Erica Childs, writing about major multiracial websites, reports that "despite fostering a sense of community and place of acceptance for multiracial individuals and families, a sense of 'us versus them' is created, pitting the multiracial community against the 'enemy,' who is readily identified as people of color who identify with traditional racial and ethnic communities."[14] Given that such websites are often a person's initial encounter with organized multiracial activism, their influence should not be underestimated in terms of how they shape perceptions of what authentic multiraciality entails and of how this identity should be constituted vis-à-vis outsider "others." The influence and the double nature of Root's bill are clear in this example, where the natural consequence of the multiracial impulse may be seen to have played itself out.

In making the case for the movement's militant character, advocates of multiracial identity politics often pronounce themselves to be free of race, to be beyond race, to have transcended the American fixation on and paranoia about race. Certainly this would be a most worthy accomplishment but, as I and others have argued many times, multiracial identity is unintelligible without the foundation of biological race upon which it depends. Thus, the celebratory tones in which adherents of multiracial identity trumpet their freedom from the chains of race are every bit as self-conflicting as they are self-congratulatory.

Regardless of one's standpoint, race in the United States is not breaking down or otherwise being deconstructed. Rather, it is evolving, as it has done for centuries, in response to new pressures. As Eduardo Bonilla-Silva describes, "systems of racial domination . . . are not static. Much like capitalism and patriarchy, they change due to external and internal pressures."[15] As whites become a numerically smaller proportion of the US populace, race is evolving so as to allow some persons of Asian and Hispanic descent to enter through the coveted door to whiteness (see Chapters 6 and 7). And while this surface modification occurs, others who are not as close to whiteness as these—including those with sub-Saharan African ancestry but who are nonetheless not perceived to be 100 percent black—are moving *away from blackness* toward an intermediate status. For activist white mothers of black/white children especially, this coveted intermediate status is multiracial identity.

Recent research has captured this shift.[16] This research points out the relatively new freedom for some Asians to become "honorary whites," and for their part-white children and grandchildren to become accepted fully as white—even though their Asian ancestry is known. This phenomenon, relatively new for Asians, has long been operative for Native Americans and since it is already the case that Hispanics may be either white or nonwhite, it quite obviously applies to them as well. However, this experience of "honorary whiteness" and of racially mixed children and grandchildren being accepted fully as white—despite their nonwhite ancestry being known—is simply not possible in the Afro-American context. Regardless of the newfound upward mobility within the US racial order of some persons of Asian and Hispanic descent, acknowledged sub-Saharan African ancestry disqualifies black/white persons from participating in whiteness. If whiteness is truly desired in their cases, racial passing as white remains the only full solution. Short of passing as white, the best that may be hoped for is a movement away from blackness, a movement upward and into that intermediate multiracial status.

But it is critical to understand that none of these moves toward whiteness and away from blackness serve to disrupt the race concept. The US racial order evolves continually but is in no sense ever deposed or even challenged, because at its most elemental level of structure lies a simple binary equation of white purity and black impurity. Everything else regarding race in the United States is erected upon this structure. Without a significant alteration of this most basic equation—an equation requiring the deployment of hypodescent—any other changes to the US racial paradigm are essentially cosmetic only. In other words, until such time as it is no longer accepted that a white woman may give naturally conceived birth to a black child but a black woman may never give naturally conceived birth to a white child, white purity and race in the United States remain unchallenged and unchanged. This is the only truly relevant test of racial change, and in various forms it has been in place for centuries. David Roediger reminds us that during the period when slavery began to be consolidated via law in British North America, "'white' women could only give birth to free children," while "enslaved African women, on the other hand, could only legally give birth to property."[17] When considered in the context of the typical demographic of black/white parenthood in the United States, as well as the shrill and often frenzied chorus of white mothers in their capacity as the activist leadership of the American Multiracial Identity Movement insisting on the nonblackness of their children, Roediger's historical point takes on added meaning in the present as well.

That the continuing maintenance of whiteness requires that it now accept the occasional incorporation of some measure of Asian or Hispanic ancestry is no threat to whiteness, for white purity—which has always been merely illusory anyway—has simply been rearticulated accordingly. We must remember, after all, that biological race is in the first place hardly a logical enterprise, and that such a rearticulation therefore incurs no penalty in the thought process of the US imaginary. As a simple confirmation of this, we might consider the certainty that many white Americans of decades and centuries past would have been incredulous at the proposition of Greeks, Italians, or the Irish being considered white; yet these groups are unproblematically white today.

The only development that could serve to actually shake the foundation of race in the United States would be a clear and total rejection of hypodescent, but no such clear and total rejection has been demanded in the protests and purported militancy of multiracial activists, and no such clear and total rejection will be forthcoming. Despite their claim of despising hypodescent, multiracial activists cannot reject it for they require monoracial black parents in order to create the false consciousness of first-generation black/white mixed-race children, and those monoracial black parents are made possible expressly through the selective application of hypodescent. Multiracial activists will howl in complaint if a black/white child is made subject to hypodescent; yet these activists demonstrate no concern whatsoever in making the same child's always already-mixed Afro-American parent subject to a selective hypodescent that effaces completely that parent's substantial history of population mixture. Due in part to the work of these multiracial identity activists, hypodescent—the popularly understood illustration of the foundational black/white binary upon which the US racial order is based—remains very much alive and well in the United States.

In emphasizing the centrality of the black/white binary to the construction of race in the United States, I want to be especially clear that this in no way implies that Asians do not endure racism or that Native Americans and Hispanics lead unproblematic lives in a racist America. Rather, it is to point out quite specifically that the fundamental underpinning of the race concept in the United States goes back hundreds of years to the creation of whiteness in constitutional opposition to blackness. This binary relationship is the foundation of race as Americans know it. In the simplest sense, it is to say that although whiteness has expanded its previous limits and can now be a bit Asian, somewhat Hispanic, or partly Native American, it can in no sense be slightly black and still remain white. That is the fundamental predicate, the defining characteristic, of the US racial order. Multiraciality, regardless of its seemingly endless and self-congratulatory celebration, does nothing to contest or disrupt this deep structure.

A few elemental questions therefore follow from this reality. Do the solemn recitation of Root's Bill of Rights for Racially Mixed People, the self-conscious exhibitionism of Generation Mix hipness, and the politically vacant exoticization and eroticization of mixed-race advertising models rise to the level of militant activism? Does the constant pleading of white mothers of black/white children to free their children from blackness and move those children nearer to whiteness represent a motivation or intention to challenge the US racial paradigm and its primary operative dynamic of white purity and black impurity? How can the surface alteration of the paradigm, so that some former nonwhites may become "honorary whites" and so that their children and grandchildren may become full whites, be taken seriously as anything related remotely to "resistance," "revolution," and "change"? Where is the militancy in begging to be part of a paradigm of biological race as opposed to working actively to destroy that paradigm? In what sense is a paradigm of biological race undermined, deconstructed, or even challenged if one's desperate goal is to become a recognized constituent of it via the formal advocacy of multiracial identity within the structure of that very paradigm?

There is no revolutionary suicide in the American Multiracial Identity Movement, for it is instead a movement of reactionary accommodation and nothing more.[18] In Charles Gallagher's view, "rejecting the monoracial categories imposed on multiracial people is taken as an act of revolution and ultimately such insurgency can bring about positive social change by acknowledging how the idea of race as a socially constructed category reflects power, politics, and the maintenance of white privilege."[19] Yet according to Gallagher, this revolution has not taken place. Instead, "what appears to be taking place is a reconfiguring of existing racial categories."[20] This reconfiguration is one in which proximity to whiteness and the consequent distancing from blackness are what is valued. Assessing descriptions of multiracial people conceived as ushering in the deconstruction of race, Rebecca King-O'Riain finds that "key in all of these predictions is the importance of not visually sticking out and being able to blend in with whiteness as the basis of equality."[21]

In the view of Jennifer Lee and Frank Bean, "at this time, America's shift in color lines points to the emergence of a new split that replaces the old black/white divide and one that separates blacks from nonblacks, or what sociologists refer to as a black/nonblack divide. In a black/nonblack divide, Latinos and Asians fall into the nonblack category."[22] Bonilla-Silva comes to a similar conclusion in what he terms the "Latin-Americanization of Whiteness in the United States."[23] Regardless of whether one favors these reconfigurations or the alternate variations I presented in Chapter 7, one nonetheless struggles in vain to discern evidence of any revolutionary character in this alarming development, one in which moving away from blackness is a principal motivation.

In the same vein, and specifically examining the black/white case, Minkah Makalani's work "raises serious doubts about the biracial project's claim to be a progressive social movement. Rather than seeking to overthrow the racialized social system, it is a reactionary political response to the racialization of people of African descent in the United States as Black. Specifically, it uses whiteness to distinguish PMP [people of mixed parentage] from African Americans as a new race that would be positioned between Blacks and whites in a reordered, racialized social system."[24] The fact that the multiracial movement operates from within the structural organization of the US racial order as opposed to challenging that order necessitates, indeed guarantees, this reality.

The multiracial movement's accommodation to, as opposed to any opposition to, white purity and selective hypodescent is tied to the movement's unquenchable desire for distance from blackness and its absolutely comfortable positioning within America's racial and racist structure. As Jared Sexton describes, "it is because the position of the multiracial does not break from the assumptive logic of antimiscegenation that it can be accommodated by white supremacy. It threatens the racial schema from within but does not seek to challenge the regime of meaning, reason, interpretive capture, and definition that white Anglo racism paints in such bold strokes. It merely seeks to refine or reconfigure the apparatus, to establish a space for the full play of a multiracial identity or a race-transcendent human identity. It is, in other words, a battle within the bounds of the strategic field, contained by the fear of being undone or losing itself in the struggle."[25]

One therefore asks: Is it progressive and militant or is it retrograde and discriminatory for a movement to advocate the continued veneration of white purity via acceptance of biological race and selective hypodescent? There is a clear sense of superiority—and, one supposes, it would have to be a racial superiority, *miscentrism*—in the transcendent celebrations of Generation Mix. The idea seems to be that these young people are mixed and mixing with abandon and that such mixing is in itself some sort of revolutionary act deserving of celebration.[26] But precisely what is being celebrated? If the mere fact of population mixture is being celebrated, it is already an old story that certainly does not begin with Generation Mix. It has been done before, both coercively and consensually, and is at least centuries old.

Discussing the threat that may be posed by unstable identities, Martha Cutter notes that "a player who refuses to play by the rules calls those rules into question, suggesting that they are not permanent, fixed, and closed but changeable, unstable, and open."[27] In what way, we might ask, does the advocacy of multiracial identity accord with the latter as opposed to the former? To be sure, most Americans may take it as a commonplace that mixedness destabilizes and undermines the racial structure. This is, after all, the consistent message from scholars writing in favor of multiracial identity as well as from popular media sources. So our questions are these: Does Generation Mix in fact refuse to play by the rules? Is it true that these youthful purveyors of multiracial identity call the system of racial categorization into question by confounding the possibilities for the assignation of racial identities?

Playing by the rules in regard to race consists of assenting to belief in biological race, in biological racial groups, and in the assignment of persons to particular biological racial groups.[28] This is the racial superstructure that the American Multiracial Identity Movement is supposedly bringing down to a crashing ruin. Yet in celebrating their mixedness, the members of Generation Mix are celebrating precisely the fact—not that they are transcending biological race at all—but that they are engaged in a very active way in the race work of instituting a new biological racial category in the United States. The celebration of a new multiracial identity is nothing less than a celebration of the active construction of biological race. As Minelle Mahtani notes, "clearly, 'mixed race' people have been made intelligible in ways that maintain racial hierarchies."[29]

As was made clear in Part 2, this reality marks it as a retrograde movement in the sense that it resurrects the otherwise long-dead marginal man of sociology's past. Of course, the American Multiracial Identity Movement does not claim the marginal man(tle) overtly; to do so would expose the reality that this marginality is donned for the specific purpose of generating sympathy for its adherents. However, under the guise of rejecting and transcending biological race, Generation Mix brings the marginal man—the tragic mulatto—back to life, but without tragedy. Indeed, far from tragedy, the Generation Mix version of the marginal man is celebrated as a racially superior being insofar as belief in biologically multiracial people living among biologically monoracial people is privileged over belief in biologically monoracial people only, to say nothing of the multiracial super powers we reviewed in Chapter 8.

Moreover, this new millennium marginal man is not only black/white, but may encompass all varieties of biological racial mixture. In a sense, then, the marginal man concept is being resurrected even though people are not embracing a tragic mulatto identity in an overt way. In other words, if one asked the members of Generation Mix if they were adopting a new marginal man identity, they would surely say they are not. Yet, the structure they are erecting is precisely the resurrection of the marginal man—the mixed-race person who is distinct racially from either ostensibly pure parent, and who therefore is doomed to suffer from divided-blood psychotrauma unless a specific racial (in this case, multiracial) identity is adopted. This resurrected marginal man is no more than a confirmation of the logical reality that mixed-race advocacy depends absolutely on acceptance of biological race. Regardless of how many empty manifestos one might recite, there is no separating biological race from the quest for multiracial identity, which once again highlights the logical contradiction inherent in saying one thing and doing the opposite.

Interrogating the US mixed-race movement, including mention of Root's Bill of Rights, Stephen Small reaches a similar conclusion in his observation that "it is clear that 'race' remains central to their enterprise."[30] That race occupies this central position in the movement is confirmed by Root herself. One of the affirmations listed in Root's bill is the right "not to keep the races separate within me."[31] Given that in the same piece of writing she also refers to race as a delusion whose spell ought to be broken, it is difficult to see how that ostensibly revolutionary goal is to be accomplished in the context of an acknowledgment of biological races that are "within" people. The truly radical position would be to deny that any races—whether separate or mixed—are "within" anyone.

According to Root, "the multiracial person's existence challenges the rigidity of racial lines that are a prerequisite for maintaining the delusion that race is a scientific fact."[32] Root's statement turns out to have been crafted rather superbly, however, since her seemingly deconstructive and seemingly radical words actually only allow for a very specific and very limited reading of racial revolution. It is a faux militancy that is reflected in the movement itself, for the racial project of the multiracial movement and of Generation Mix is very specifically to challenge the "rigidity" of racial lines only; it is not to challenge the racial lines themselves. In other words, what the members of Generation Mix work to do is to bend those lines so as to blend themselves more comfortably into the US racial order—either through the successful infiltration to whiteness or through the construction of multiracial identity as a discrete biological racial identity both distinct from and superior to blackness. Steve Garner puts it quite succinctly in noting that "mixed-ness per se really challenges only the existing sets of categories, not the category of 'race' itself."[33] The only militancy deployed in this effort by Generation Mix is militancy directed against a connection to blackness, which hardly represents a revolutionary stance in the United States either yesterday or today, and certainly bodes no better for the future.

In response to the criticisms I have levied, advocates of multiracial identity will argue that, far from being retrograde, their movement does in fact represent a militant stance against the US racial paradigm. But how true would such a claim be? Let us take seriously King-O'Riain's timely questions: "But do mixed-race bodies really call into question racial concepts?

Do they actually transgress racial boundaries and the materiality of race?"[34] Her questions are especially important because we will not find them asked in the glossy pages of *Time* or *Newsweek*, nor will we find them addressed at all in the academic writings of multiracially supporting scholars. They are inconvenient questions because so many people would prefer to assume that they are unnecessary, that multiraciality does do all the race-transcendent work that its adherents claim for it. But as we have already seen, it does not do the things it is presumed to do. In fact, what it seems most good at is making self-serving and unjustified assertions from multiracial radar to racial bridging to any number of other outrageous and unproven claims (see Chapters 8 and 9).

I contend that multiracial identity is a retrograde and essentially copy-cat enterprise—yet another (and, at that, quite passé) racial essentialism. One rarely hears the question raised as to how, if it is supposed to be the avant-garde vehicle that will move us beyond race, the imposition of one more (multi)racial essentialism is in any sense possibly fitted to such a task. Consider DaCosta's comment concerning the comforting environment of multiracial identity: "In this hierarchy [of multiracial relatedness], one feels more of a sense of belonging, affinity, and closeness with those who are of their same mix, where 'same' is defined in racially and ethnically specific terms."[35] Clearly, the American Multiracial Identity Movement is not actually serious about transcending race if in the first place it defines itself in "racially and ethnically specific terms." This, again, goes to the foundation of multiracial activism in biological race regardless of how many times that fundamental connection is denied. As Susan Gillman puts it: "We hear so many announcements, invocations, and prophetic calls willing a postmodern 'beyond' race, spoken by academics, activists, and politicians alike on both the Left and the Right. Such institutional changes as the category *mixed race* on the 2000 U.S. census are another index of the rising call against the continued use of *race* as an analytic, social, or legal category. Yet so many of these pronouncements continue, willfully or willy-nilly, to depend on the old, supposedly outmoded racialisms for their political and ethical utopian force."[36]

Moreover, we find in Generation Mix the same, old, ordinary, exclusionary impulses that it is supposedly transcending: "In their critique of authenticity tests for granting racial inclusion, some multiracials have substituted their own understandings of an authentically *mixed* position."[37] Frankly, it is more than merely "some multiracials" who are guilty of this variety of hypocrisy as it is clear that this purportedly race-transcending movement is focused precisely on the creation of a new biological racial boundary. Although writing about white male construction of racial difference, Abby Ferber's point works in regard to the construction of multiracial identity as well: "The construction of racial identities, then, requires a policing of the borders, maintenance of the boundaries between 'one's own kind' and others. . . . It is through the construction of boundaries themselves that identities come into existence."[38] Why in the world should we expect multiracial identity to be any different, especially since it carries such a heavy, built-in complement of antiblackness? Given that the multiracial movement is grounded in belief in biological race as well as the rejection of blackness in support of its boundary making, we should not be the least bit surprised by Childs's nonetheless disturbing discovery that "most multiracial websites simply reproduce the racial hierarchy by further demarcating a separate multiracial community and vilifying blackness."[39]

According to DaCosta, writing about Generation Mix, "there is an inescapable irony of group making that in seeking to undermine the foundations of American racial thinking, they reaffirm racial thinking as well."[40] Unsurprisingly, she finds that the movement's insistence on federal recognition represents "a striking acceptance of the racial state, in and through which the category of race was created and through which it is reproduced."[41] This contradiction at the heart of the multiracial project illuminates the reality that there is no desire to transcend the racial state, whether militantly or meekly. What we see instead is nothing more and nothing less than classic collaboration with the existing power structure. Specifically, "it [the construction of multiracial community] creates new racial subjects while conforming to the preexisting U.S. racial order."[42] Where then in this explicitly racial field is one to find "resistance," "revolution," and "change," to say nothing of the red herring of transcending race? How does the construction of a new racial identity move us away from race?

Despite all the talk about the transcendent future that Generation Mix is purportedly leading us toward, no one has really envisioned anything specific about that future beyond nebulous and empty promises that it will be postracial. I would like to investigate one aspect of such a future, however. Or, to be more precise, I propose investigating the future implications of accepting multiracial identity today by focusing specifically on the progeny of multiracial people. Much has been made of first-generation multiraciality in the arguments for the racial exceptionalism of Generation Mix. But—assuming the sensibility of the "first-generation" label only for purposes of argument—what would be the status of the children of those first-generation multiracials? For instance, if a first-generation black/white person has a child with a black person, would the resulting child be multiracial or black? If the same first-generation black/white person has a child with a white person, would the resulting child be multiracial or white?

Ellis Cose asks an interesting question along these very lines: "If the designation applies only to the first generation, will these children (like many light-skinned 'blacks') become monoracial by the second generation? Or will their children, twenty years from now, be fighting for yet another redefinition of race?—for, perhaps, a new box labeled 'old multiracial' as opposed to 'new multiracial' or even 'part multiracial' (which, of course, raises the question of how much multiracial one has to be to be considered truly multiracial)."[43] I would like to take up the issues surrounding Cose's question in a serious way by postulating three scenarios. I will keep these scenarios simple in order to allow us to better see the basic implications of the multiracial future. Indeed, as we shall observe, while a variety of complicating factors would make things considerably murkier, even the three simple scenarios that I present are themselves fraught with troubling implications.

To begin, let us posit a hypothetical first-generation black/white person. Next, let us posit that this person, a male, has three different children with three different women. In the first instance, our hypothetical person has a child with a black person, that child has a child with a black person, that grandchild has a child with a black person, that great-grandchild has a child with a black person, and that great-great-grandchild has a child with a black person. This last child will be our individual's first great-great-great-grandchild, a non-first-generation black/white person. In the second instance, our hypothetical first-generation black/white person has a child with a white person, that child has a child with a white person, that grandchild has a child with a white person, that great-grandchild has a child with a white person, and that great-great-grandchild has a child with a white person. This last child will be our individual's second great-great-great-grandchild, a non-first-generation black/white person. Finally, in the third instance, our hypothetical first-generation black/white person has a child with a first-generation black/white person, that child has a child with a first-generation black/white person, that grandchild has a child with a first-generation black/white person, that great-grandchild has a child with a first-generation black/white person, and that great-great-grandchild has a child with a first-generation black/white person. This last child will be our individual's third great-great-great-grandchild, a non-first-generation black/white person.

Again, I am focusing only on the generations between the one great-great-great-grandparent and each of the three great-great-great-grandchildren in order to try to maintain focus. Obviously, real human experience would likely lead to the introduction of a good many complicating factors such as infidelity, incest, and other combinations of parents including Asians, Hispanics, Native Americans, as well as all manner of intermediate mixtures, for instance. Of note as well is the fact that in these hypothetical examples I will be positing four types of people: black, white, first-generation black/white, and non-first-generation black/white. As I have been arguing, all the black people concerned would of course be always already mixed (as would many of the whites, whether knowingly or unknowingly), but for the sake of making this illustration we will gloss over that reality and pretend that people really can be placed consistently and exclusively into those four categories.

How then do these three hypothetical great-great-great-grandchildren, these distant cousins, relate to each other and to their great-great-great-grandfather? How do we assess their various racial statuses? Before beginning this assessment, it will provide a useful perspective for us to diagram the lineages of each cousin back through to the level of their shared great-great-great-grandfather. Cousin One has 32 great-great-great-grandparents. Of these, 1 is first-generation black/white and 31 are black.[44] Of the 62 persons comprising the direct line of descent from the level of her great-great-great-grandfather to Cousin One, 57 are black, 1 is first-generation black/white, and 4 are non-first-generation black/white. Cousin Two also has 32 great-great-great-grandparents. Of these, 1 is first-generation black/white and 31 are white. Of the 62 persons comprising the direct line of descent from the level of her great-great-great-grandfather to Cousin Two, 57 are white, 1 is first-generation black/white, and 4 are non-first-generation black/white. Lastly, Cousin Three has 32 great-great-great-grandparents. Of these, 15 are black, 15 are white, 2 are first-generation black/white, and none are non-first-generation black/white. Of the 62 persons comprising the direct line of descent from the level of her great-great-great-grandfather to Cousin Three, 26 are black, 26 are white, 6 are first-generation black/white, and 4 are non-first-generation black/white. Interestingly, for Cousin Three, 36 of these persons have sub-Saharan African ancestry and 36 have European ancestry, owing to the particular population mixture of this line, a population mixture that marks it as thoroughly Afro-American (which is to say that it is comprised of persons of European and sub-Saharan African ancestry). Indeed, let us recall that for the sake of this example we are for the moment ignoring the fact that all 26 who are black also have European ancestry.

Are all three cousins multiracial; are all three members of the same race? Even on the most bathetic *feel-good* interpretation it is clear that they would not be considered to be the same race. I am not here taking into account each cousin's personal racial identification nor any ways that they may have been indoctrinated toward racial identity as children—whether such indoctrination might have been to a black identity, a white identity, or a multiracial identity. Rather, I am proposing that we assess how they would be viewed racially, by the American Multiracial Identity Movement and by Americans in general.

Let me commence this exercise by suggesting that there is no circumstance in which anyone who believes in race would consider Cousin One to be anything other than black. This reality has immediate implications for the American Multiracial Identity Movement and its promises and predictions of a postracial American future should its desires for multiracial recognition, most especially federal recognition, be met. If the multiracial movement avers that Cousin One is black (and not multiracial), then we are once again back to the issue of the movement's deployment of selective hypodescent, its exclusionary tendencies, and indeed, its antiblackness. If the movement views Cousin One as black it simply cannot defend itself against the charge that it engages in the very same hypodescent that it hypocritically rails against at every other opportunity.

If, on the other hand, the movement grants that Cousin One is not black but is instead multiracial it thereby opens a veritable hornet's nest of self-contradictory hypocrisy. This is so because should the American Multiracial Identity Movement offer that Cousin One is multiracial (and not black) it would then have to explain how Cousin One—with 1 black/white and 31 black great-great-great-grandparents—differs from the average Afro-American that the movement now rejects most firmly from inclusion in its exclusionary ranks. This is no small point, for the crucial fact is that there is no racial difference between black/white multiracials and the average Afro-American. Our example here merely provides a very clear illustration of what I have been arguing throughout this book. As we move further away from our original first-generation black/white person in this first example—moving forward through time from that person to the present—we approach the very same situation of many Afro-Americans today (i.e., ancestral population mixture that people who believe in biological race would nonetheless not be disposed to call mixed, most especially if the predominant race is black). Most Americans would conclude that Cousin One is not multiracial but is instead merely black, having reverted back to type, so to speak. When we look at the example of Cousin One it is exactly the situation of the vast majority of Afro-Americans today.

We appear then to be lodged on the horns of a dilemma with Cousin One. If Cousin One is considered black, it is yet another validation of the charge that the American Multiracial Identity Movement engages in hypodescent; practices an exclusionary ideology, especially in regard to blackness; and that its assurances of a postracial future have no substance. If Cousin One is not black, however, and is instead multiracial, the movement's hypocrisy stands exposed in the full and direct sunlight of truth since—with 1 black/white and 31 black great-great-great-grandparents—Cousin One is indistinguishable from the general Afro-American population, especially if we step back and lift for a moment the artificiality of presuming that these 31 great-great-great-grandparents are in the first place monoracially black, which they of course could not be. It seems to me that in order to maintain any logical consistency, the American Multiracial Identity Movement would have to conclude that multiraciality is a highly volatile and not a permanent sort of essence vis-à-vis blackness and, I daresay, most especially whiteness. But even this is no real solution, for it would then be difficult to put forth the case that such a volatile and impermanent racial identity is in any sense deserving of federal recognition. Clearly, the case of Cousin One presents significant problems for validating the Generation Mix postracial promise.

Let us see if the example of Cousin Two will result in a better outcome. The immediate question is whether Cousin Two is white or multiracial. Since most Americans would view Cousin One as black would they therefore view Cousin Two as white? The answer is not so straightforward, however, even though the situations represent a reverse parallel, for there is a key complication in the form of hypodescent. Regardless of the fact that only 1 of Cousin Two's 32 great-great-great-grandparents is part black, that information—if it is known—determines everything about race in US society. Despite the fact that some of today's Asians and Hispanics are moving to a status of honorary whiteness, that same privilege is not accorded to persons of known sub-Saharan African descent. And as we know, the American Multiracial Identity Movement is itself one of the most active purveyors of hypodescent by way of its selective application in the cases of Afro-American parents vis-à-vis their black/white children. Moreover, it is not likely that we will begin to see serious discussions about whether this or that particular and exceptional person with black ancestry might be granted entry to the privileged status of whiteness, for such discussions would in turn open the door to even more promptings, thereby raising the unacceptable specter of potentially large numbers of Afro-Americans charging the gates of whiteness. Regardless of its current willingness to incorporate certain Asians and Hispanics into whiteness, its protectors have demonstrated with firm consistency that whiteness cannot likewise incorporate sub-Saharan African ancestry and still remain white.

When it comes to black/white mixture in the United States there is only hypodescent; there is absolutely no *hyper*descent. Blackness is maintained by hypodescent, while whiteness is maintained by the reverse side of hypodescent, by what we might term usefully the "no drop rule." In other words, while it takes only a single metaphorical drop of black blood to make a person black, that same single metaphorical drop is all it takes to make a person nonwhite. As we have seen, whiteness may incorporate metaphorical drops of Asian and Hispanic blood, but it cannot incorporate blackness and still be white. We might say that nonblackness is what makes whiteness what it is.

Given all this, how does the American Multiracial Identity Movement view Cousin Two? Since the movement's ideology is based in biological race, in the antiblackness of selective hypodescent, and in a corresponding veneration of whiteness, it of necessity must view Cousin Two as multiracial or perhaps even as black. It cannot, however, on the basis of its own foundational ideology, view Cousin Two as white without thereby instituting a minimum limit, a sort of blood quantum, for multiracial identity, which would represent a most offensive development, to say the least. As will also be relevant in the final example, this inability (or unwillingness) to challenge whiteness can hardly be conceived of as a militant stance. On the other hand, if the movement avers that Cousin Two is multiracial, we would then have to revisit its decision in the case of Cousin One in order to see if the parallel designation was made there. If it was not, the movement would then be guilty of clear inconsistency, for how could Cousin Two be multiracial but Cousin One not be multiracial as well? But if the parallel designation was made, the previously examined hypocrisy of designating Cousin One as multiracial would have to be addressed, since Cousin One is indistinguishable from the average Afro-American. The only way to avoid any of these inconvenient outcomes would be to consider Cousin Two black, but this would be problematic as well since it would represent recourse to hypodescent. So it appears that, as in the case of Cousin One, Cousin Two complicates the notion of a postracial future.

Finally, what is the likely status of Cousin Three? In one respect this final case is the least problematic of the group, as the multiracial movement would surely claim Cousin Three as multiracial, an interpretation many Americans might agree with, although there remains the sticky problem that some vocal advocates with the multiracial identity movement have so championed the notion of excluding all but first-generation persons that it would result in the somewhat embarrassing situation of Cousin Three being denied membership in Generation Mix. However, leaving that particular ironic result out of account, we may note the interesting possibility that every black person in Cousin One's lineage could very well have lighter skin and straighter hair than every black/white person (first generation or not) in Cousin Three's lineage. Indeed, there is every reason for supposing that many if not all of the black persons in Cousin One's lineage would be interchangeable in terms of so-called obvious mixedness or obvious blackness (see Chapter 8) with many, if not all, of the black/white persons (first generation or not) in Cousin Three's lineage, since population mixture, both past and present, is what defines Afro-Americans in the most literal way.

To engage matters of a perhaps more practical nature, however, let us move to an issue considered rarely if, indeed, ever: What would it mean for multiraciality to be instantiated as a new racial category? Omitting for the sake of simplicity and focus the nevertheless important question of how black/white multiracials would relate *as* multiracials to other mixed-race combinations—in other words, how such an all-inclusive, super grouping of multiracials of differing ancestries would make classificatory sense—what is the implication of such a new (multi)racial category? How would it relate to and interact with the US racial paradigm and its associated hierarchy? Would this new (multi)racial category deconstruct the paradigm? Would it result in either an instant or a gradual lessening of Americans' embrace of the paradigm and its hierarchy? Or would it simply take its place within a generally unchanged system of hierarchical US race relations?

If *multiracial* were to become accepted as a racial category—especially on the federal level—it would stand alongside the current racial categories. It would be added to whatever systems, paradigms, or schematics contain the already existing categories. It would not, quite obviously, by its mere instantiation constitute the immediate deconstruction of its racial category stable mates. No one imagines that simply legitimizing multiracial identity on Monday will by Tuesday result in the death of race in the United States. But if multiraciality would not accomplish this deconstruction instantaneously, how then would it achieve the promised withering of the US racial order? By what long-term process would multiracial identity result in the termination of the race concept? Remember that the promise, the assurance—from the multiracial rank and file, from multiracial activists, from multiracial-supporting academics, and from the pages of glossy newsmagazines and the ostensibly serious press—is that multiracial identity will bring about the demise of race on these shores of ours that have been so tortured by race for so very long.

If we imagine that the United States does accept multiracial identity, both popularly and federally, how is this promised deconstruction of race supposed to take place? This is the critical question that is never, ever asked by anyone who has an interest in supporting the multiracial cause. The predictions of race's destruction at the hands of multiracial identity are legion, but in a circular fashion the multiracial camp has provided nothing in the way of a reasoned explanation of how this is to happen beyond the very assurances themselves, as if it is enough merely to make the promise. *Time* and *Newsweek* certainly are not interested in sticky details that serve only to get in the way of hip and melodramatic reporting. Nor are the political forces of conservatism and liberalism concerned as long as it means that they will themselves no longer have to be bothered with solving the race (i.e., black) problem. In an act of self-delusion America hears and accepts the multiracial promise and then sticks its head in the metaphorical sand.

Ronald Sundstrom expresses hope that racial and ethnic categories "are swept away by socially and politically cleansing waves of new immigrants who refuse those old categories and multiracial children for whom those categories do not fit and so they refuse them."[45] As we have seen, however, both in the historical past and in the present moment, immigrants and certain multiracial people are very much clinging to race via the mechanism of "honorary whiteness" and the subsequent transition to full whiteness. A more sober and useful assessment comes by way of Roediger, who, in noting that "often multiracial identities and immigration take center stage as examples of factors making race obsolete," points to the lack of explanation given for precisely how these or other factors will result in the coming death of race: "We are often told popularly that race and racism are on predictable tracks to extinction. But we are seldom told clear or consistent stories about why white supremacy will give way and how race will become a 'social virus' of the past."[46]

As an example of this very tendency, Sundstrom can do no better than assure us that his immigrants and multiracial children are "transforming the meaning of 'race' to such an extent that dominant conceptions of 'racial' equality, justice, and harmony will also inevitably shift toward a cosmopolitan direction."[47] Significantly, the precise nature of how this shift will "inevitably" take place is left out of account. Also recognizing this flaw, and while sympathetic in general to the multiracial movement, Williams responds to the movement's claim that "recognition of racial mixture" represents "the next logical step in civil rights," by averring: "Yet it is difficult to view this as a credible answer to a deeper set of questions about the future direction of civil rights advocacy. For one thing, the multiracial movement has emphasized the right to determine one's own identities (at the level of the individual), while its antiracism agenda (at a structural level) has been limited to vague declarations that multiracial recognition could somehow help to reduce racial strife."[48]

Despite the fact that the American Multiracial Identity Movement eschews its responsibility for providing an explanation of its grand promise of postraciality, we may ourselves do the work of investigating the claim that multiracial identity will lead to the deconstruction of race in the United States. To do this, let us place Cousin Three and those 10 of her direct ancestors who are black/white in the multiracial category along with anyone else who qualifies. (Those who insist strictly on an exclusionary first-generation membership may so place only her 6 first-generation black/white direct ancestors, and rule out her 4 non-first-generation black/white direct ancestors if they prefer.) We now have a US racial paradigm consisting of the following categories: white, Asian, Hispanic (if conceived of racially), Native American, multiracial, and black.[49] Life goes on. People check boxes (including a multiracial box) on forms requesting racial identification, statistics are tabulated, and multiracial schoolchildren presumably are no longer terrorized by bloody-fanged administrators entering their classrooms in order to "eyeball" them or ask the dreaded "What are you?" question (see Chapter 8).

Yes; life goes on. Americans grow to accept that *multiracial* is another legitimate biological racial identity; multiracial political interest groups and lobbyists arise; a Congressional Multiracial Caucus is formed; and despite continued occasional sniping between black/white multiracials and Afro-

Americans, multiracial identity enjoys a racial existence similar in general to the other categories. For purposes of clarity and focus we will leave out of account any consideration of potential conflict within the multiracial camp, such as Hapas (part-Asian persons) feeling that they have divergent political interests and concerns vis-à-vis black/white multiracials, for instance, and assume for the sake of our example that all the variety and diversity in the multiracial category subsumes itself to a common, *best of all worlds* will.

Given the normalized status of multiracial identity once it has been established and allowed to develop, at what point and due to what particular cause would the US racial order—of which the multiracial category would now represent a constituent part—begin to disintegrate? We might ask specifically if, now that multiracial identity is part of the accepted racial superstructure, multiracial people have any vested interest whatsoever in agitating for the abolition of the racial paradigm they are now a recognized element of. Why, after working so hard to become a legitimate and recognized component of it, would they then want to do away with it? The fact is that they would not want the US racial paradigm to then be dismantled. Nor need we be satisfied with this logical prediction, for it has already taken place. Reporting on the multiracial movement's myriad inconsistent actions during the mid-1990s debates over a federal multiracial category, Williams notes that "the advocates wanted it both ways: they wanted a piece of the pie (as a separate ethnoracial group), even as they sought to undermine the notion of separate ethnoracial groups."[50] Only the most naïve of commentators would refuse to acknowledge that advocates for and members of the multiracial category would fight to protect the idea of the paradigm as well as the inclusion of multiracial persons within its structuring.

We can see that nothing about the mere establishment of a multiracial category would lead to the immediate dissolution of race in the United States and, moreover, that in the long term the multiracial faction would itself have a compelling interest in conserving the US racial order and its own hard-won place within that order. Beyond all this there is an even more important reason why the racial order would survive the establishment of a new biological category. There is a consistent refusal by all concerned on the multiracial side of things to consider, interrogate, challenge, or otherwise acknowledge the status of whiteness in the schematic of race in the United States. Whiteness is what drives that US racial order; whiteness is at the top of the racial hierarchy in the United States, and nothing less than the complete deconstruction of whiteness has any hope of altering that order. Whiteness is in no sense bothered by the addition of yet another nonwhite category to the paradigm, for as long as such a category is both nonwhite and below whiteness on the racial scale (and multiraciality is both), it provides absolutely no threat to whiteness itself.

Regardless of persistent popular media accounts, multiracials do nothing to *blur the distinction between black and white*; rather, they reinforce that distinction by adding support to the notion that whiteness remains fixedly separate from blackness, for while blackness can migrate to multiracialness it can never—except by racial passing—migrate all the way to whiteness itself. There may be some reshuffling and reordering of the intermediate categories, but whiteness itself remains alone at the top. That multiraciality poses no threat to race itself is seen in King-O'Riain's observation that "mixed-race people neither bridge (mend) or blend race but become a site for the contestation and redefinition of race."[51] In her view, "mixed race does not mean the end of race as a concept or as a product of biological race thinking, where racial meaning is congealed and tied through its supposed association to the body to biology."[52] Consequently, "the mixed-race body then does not destroy race, but leads to a repoliticization and problematization of race."[53] But again, as long as such "repoliticization and problematization" does not encompass any threat to the status of whiteness, it is all essentially a surface phenomenon that is taken, wrongly and blindly, to be the end of race.

The black/white members of Generation Mix may imagine that they bridge the races, but the reality is that until the day that they—with their known sub-Saharan African ancestry—can actually be accepted fully as white, whiteness goes on unchallenged and unchanged. Multiracial ideology does not have the capacity to challenge the status of whiteness because multiracial identity, most especially black/white identity, is based on the veneration of white purity by way of the selective hypodescent that makes the very concept of black/white multiracials possible in the first place. To challenge whiteness would be, for multiracial ideology, to undo its own foundation. It would represent a suicidal self-negation in what would, as a consequence, become a quixotic pursuit of self-actualization. Indeed, to challenge whiteness would be, for the American Multiracial Identity Movement, a deployment of the most radical and militant weaponry it could possibly muster. We should not expect to see such a challenge any time soon.

Our consideration of three different and extended lines of mixed-race progeny reveals serious, indeed fatal, flaws in the promise that acceptance of multiracial identity will yield a postracial future. Recall that I designed this example in the interest of clarity, and that real-life contingencies (including and most especially the always already-mixed status of all blacks in the example) would serve to complicate even further the troubles for the dubious guarantee of race's demise. Not only is there no reason, no evidence, no compelling argument for the least expectation that multiraciality will lead to any deterioration of the race concept in the United States, but the very fact of instituting a multiracial category and the corresponding acceptance of multiracial identity would by itself result in the strong desire on the part of multiracial individuals and advocates to support the US racial order and to perpetuate multiracial people's newfound place within it. All of which is to state that the only thing multiracial identity can possibly accomplish in regard to the US racial schema is to further harden both the paradigm and the biological racial myths that underlie it, for Makalani is surely correct that "creating a new race that can exist outside the hierarchy is impossible."[54]

Without an accompanying deconstruction of whiteness, nothing about the establishment of a multiracial category would have the least impact on the general nature of the US racial order. It would, however, have the impact I discussed in Chapter 7 of abetting antiblackness by facilitating the transition from a white/black or white/nonwhite dynamic to one of several just as problematic variations. This will be the legacy of multiracial identity should it be accepted and established in this country. It will not be a legacy of "resistance," "revolution," and "change," nor will it be a legacy of transcending race, which is precisely why supporters of multiracial identity never venture to explain how a new biological racial category will actually bring about the end of race and usher the nation into its heralded, postracial future. If there is a US postracial future, it will not come by way of instantiating multiracial identity.

If one is to engage in true resistance, revolution, and change vis-à-vis the US racial paradigm, one must first undergo personal *racial death*, which simply means that one must allow one's belief in and accommodation to biological race to die. In other words, one must actively put one's own biological racial identity to death before one is qualified to be a racial revolutionary, before one can engage in militant multiraciality.[55] Indeed, it would be more proper to refer to this necessary first step as *racial suicide*. This requirement might seem shocking, perhaps preposterous or even profane to those who are invested heavily in their racial identities, but it is nonetheless critical to see that there can be absolutely no progress on deconstructing race in the United States without a significant departure from our hundreds of years of comfort with the status quo of accepting biological race. Nor will it do to follow the sociologists in reifying biological race via the subterfuge of race as a social construction or a social reality. Race is not a social reality in the United States; rather, fallacious belief in race is the US social reality. Destruction of that false consciousness must be pursued in an aggressive way, or else we may as well admit that we are in fact satisfied to remain under its sinister and dehumanizing influence. If we are not willing to pursue the annihilation of race in an active way, we ought to then cease all of our complaining about it.

But we nevertheless go on and on, complaining about race even as we continue to enable its perpetuation. Our creativity apparently knows no bounds when it comes to justifying different ways of validating biological race while pretending hypocritically to reject it. Such efforts are as counterfeit as the race concept itself. For instance, Frazier provides a seemingly forceful argument against the nonsense and unreality of race, warning us that we should take care to avoid being "ensnared in human-made constructs and others' definitions of who we are (or who they think we should be) that have little or nothing to do with reality."[56] This would appear to be a commendable foray against the social construction of race until only a few pages later she notifies us rather bluntly that "in this world no one is race-free."[57] Not content with rendering this general proviso, Frazier then goes on to state quite specifically that "we cannot escape people's need to classify racial differences or the social construct of race, even if we know its biological premise is faulty."[58] So much, one supposes, for the progressive conviction of refusing definition by others.

Sundstrom provides what might usefully be called the philosophical justification of sociological nonsense in his attempt to defend the idea of instituting multiracial identity through the philosophical notion of "metaphysical pluralism," a concept that "admits the reality of social kinds."[59] According to Sundstrom, "for a social category, such as race or mixed race, to be a real social kind at some site, given metaphysical pluralism, what has to be present are social forces—labels, institutions, individual intentions, laws, mores, values, traditions—combined in a dynamic with enough strength to give the category presence and impact at that site."[60] While not a "social kind" or "social category," one supposes that metaphysical pluralism would also find that the earth, at least in or from the perspective of Europe, actually was flat during medieval times—not merely that people thought it was, but that it actually was.

As is typical with futile defenses of race as a social reality, this particular attempt also involves a descent into absurdity. For instance, it is somewhat difficult to take Sundstrom seriously as he conjectures, not on the reality or unreality of race itself, but on the *relative reality* of one racial category vis-à-vis another: "I contend that mixed race has a degree of reality in the U.S. at this time too, but it is not as real at this time and site as Asian, Hispanic, black, Native American, and white are."[61] We might imagine ourselves, then, checking periodically some sort of *National Racial Realness Meter* to see whether metaphysical multiracial stock, and therefore the corresponding realness of multiracial people, has risen or fallen today: "This movement intends, in effect, to make mixed race a fully real human kind. It may be that in the future the social forces necessary to make mixed race real will be present, maybe not to the extent that they are for race, but enough to make the category more real than it is today."[62]

There is a deeper problem than even this in Sundstrom's analysis, though. Buried in his philosophical defense of one of sociology's most notorious and enduring fallacies is precisely what I have been describing in terms of supporters of multiracial identity pretending to reject race while in fact reifying it even further. Note carefully what Sundstrom claims—that declaring the offspring of two parents to be multiracial implies nothing whatsoever about the racial status of those parents: "The ontology of mixed race that I have presented depends on the complex dynamic of social forces. Nothing is implied about racial purity, nor does it necessarily reinforce the poles of racial duality. Mixed race identity results from the positioning of individuals in social spaces where they experience, as members of multiple racial groups, various combinations of the social forces that make race and the various racial groups real. The racial or experiential purity of parent groups, of blackness, whiteness, and so on does not follow from the claim that mixed race identity is possible."[63]

If we are to take Sundstrom seriously, he is actually stating that making the case for multiracial identity, for racial mixture, does not even require the concept of race itself. He is arguing in effect that the existence of a black/white multiracial child says nothing about the prior existence of racially black people or racially white people. It is the inherent sophism of these kinds of academic gymnastics deployed in defense of biological race and in support of multiracial identity that have aided in the perpetuation of the nonsense of race that still entangles us nearly three hundred years after its mistaken genesis. The world at the time of medieval Europe either was flat or it was not. The fact that many Europeans *thought* it was flat did not make it actually so; it only made those people mistaken, and continues to make them appear silly to us today. Likewise, race—including multirace—either is real or it is not. The fact that we have long since moved past medieval European flat-earth superstition but have not been able to move past the superstition of race demonstrates that stronger measures are needed. It is for this reason that racial suicide is necessary.

I can certainly anticipate a negative reaction to this serious call for racial suicide, especially from the very many Afro-Americans who are believers in race, whether overtly or at some deeper remove. This is because Afro-Americans, perhaps more than any other group in the United States, have been forced by others—indeed by their own government throughout the centuries—to accept the external imposition of a racialized identity and to cling to that identity as a means of self-protection against all manner of outside threats. This is to be seen most clearly in the acceptance and at times extraordinarily intense defense of hypodescent by Afro-Americans.[64] For many Afro-Americans, to suggest the obliteration of race is to suggest the obliteration of the very core of their own personal being. I take this feeling of personal—indeed communal—threat seriously, but I nonetheless insist on the necessity of exploding the race concept and racial blackness (as well as all other racial kinds) along with it.

What we have seen from the American Multiracial Identity Movement, though, is not racial revolution but racial sycophancy. True militant multiraciality would require a suicidal stance, not an attitude of accommodation. True militant multiraciality would require the vigorous assassination of race; it is certainly not represented or enabled by Daniel's *kumbaya* image of mixed-race racial parvenus holding hands and reciting Root's Bill of Rights around the metaphorical campfire. Actual militancy would involve a good bit more than the narcissistic celebration of one's mixedness and the recitation of a set of desired rights. It would involve active work against the notion of biological race, and it would be directed toward results that would actually be destructive of race. It would not, as are the efforts of Generation Mix, be directed at accommodating oneself to the US racial order by requesting the addition to that order of a single new category somewhere above the black category. True militancy would aim at effecting real change to race, and as such would demand the elimination of hypodescent in all its deployments—including the selective hypodescent that makes possible the black parents of supposed black/white multiracial children by recoding them as monoracial and thereby erasing those parents' always already-mixed status. True resistance, true revolution, and true change cannot be achieved by the proponents of Generation Mix celebrating themselves as a new biological race made possible by the imaginary and scientifically vacant racial differences of their parents. Real change can only be a consequence of real work undertaken by real militants.

The ironic reality in all of this is that the absolute best agents of militant multiraciality should be purported multiracial individuals themselves, most especially black/white persons. Imagine if such persons truly were interested in racial militancy. Instead of celebrating the fallacious nonsense of there being "races within them," they would reject race, they would refuse the conveniences of being complicit with the US racial order, and they would resist constructing yet another biological racial identity in the United States. Imagine if rather than strutting their alleged biological alterity, the members of Generation Mix instead offered themselves as physical examples of the fact that biological race does not exist, that they cannot be placed scientifically or logically in any biological racial group (including a multiracial one), that subjecting them to hypodescent is no more than the perpetuation of a corrupt social caste system, and that they have no interest whatsoever in either being nearer to whiteness or in distancing themselves from blackness—such proximity and distance being illusory accommodations to a fallacious biological racial schema.

Rather than claiming to be biologically multiracial, the members of Generation Mix would instead refuse racial identity altogether, taking the revolutionary step of preferring racial suicide to racial accommodation. Rather than dodging blackness by pleading hysterically for a multiracial category, white mothers of black/white children would instead argue that hypodescent in all forms is corrupt and that their children are neither black, white, nor multiracial—that those children are in fact living proof that race, and along with it hypodescent, is a false consciousness. Such uncomfortable positions would represent true radicalism in opposition to race in the United States. They would represent significant steps away from the hegemony and the hierarchy of race, a point to which I shall return in the closing pages of Part 3.

If the American Multiracial Identity Movement were actually concerned with real militancy in regard to race—if resistance, revolution, and change were truly sought, rather than accommodation to and complicity with the US racial order; if transcending that racial order were actually a goal—the movement could possibly represent an insurgent impulse. But as long as it involves itself in the logical contradiction of declaring on the one hand that race is a delusion whose spell ought to be broken, while on the other lobbying actively for the construction of biological multiracial identity, the American Multiracial Identity Movement will remain open to the charge of saying one thing and doing the hypocritical opposite. That kind of philosophical stance, that sort of ideological orientation, whatever else it might be called, surely cannot in any meaningful way be described as militant. The sad fact is that, at the level of the individual, multiracial identity has all the revolutionary political content of a personal fashion statement.

Notes

1. Kathleen O. Korgen, *From Black to Biracial: Transforming Identity Among Americans* (Westport, CT: Praeger, 1999), 7.
2. Lynette Clemetson, "Color My World: The Promise and Perils of Life in the New Multiracial Mainstream," *Newsweek*, May 8, 2000, 70.
3. Maria P. P. Root, "A Bill of Rights for Racially Mixed People," in *The Multiracial Experience: Racial Borders as the New Frontier*, ed. Maria P. P. Root, 3 (Thousand Oaks, CA: Sage, 1996).
4. Ibid., 6, 9, 12.
5. Ibid., 6.
6. Jill Olumide, *Raiding the Gene Pool: The Social Construction of Mixed Race* (London: Pluto Press, 2002), 63; Kimberly M. DaCosta, *Making Multiracials: State, Family, and Market in the Redrawing of the Color Line* (Stanford: Stanford University Press, 2007), 219n10.
7. G. Reginald Daniel, *More Than Black? Multiracial Identity and the New Racial Order* (Philadelphia: Temple University Press, 2002), 116.
8. Marion Kilson, *Claiming Place: Biracial Young Adults of the Post–Civil Rights Era* (Westport, CT: Bergin and Garvey, 2001), 172; Loretta I. Winters, "Epilogue: The Multiracial Movement: Harmony and Discord," in *New Faces in a Changing America: Multiracial Identity in the 21st Century*, ed. Loretta I. Winters and Herman DeBose, 373 (Thousand Oaks, CA: Sage, 2003).
9. Kim M. Williams, "Linking the Civil Rights and Multiracial Movements," in *The Politics of Multiracialism: Challenging Racial Thinking*, ed. Heather M. Dalmage, 88 (Albany: State University of New York Press, 2004).

10. Ursula Brown, *The Interracial Experience: Growing Up Black/White Racially Mixed in the United States* (Westport, CT: Praeger, 2001); Elliott Lewis, *Fade: My Journeys in Multiracial America* (New York: Carroll & Graf, 2006); Sundee T. Frazier, *Check All That Apply: Finding Wholeness as a Multiracial Person* (Downers Grove, IL: InterVarsity, 2000).

11. DaCosta, *Making Multiracials*, 34–35.

12. Root, "Bill of Rights," 7.

13. Ibid., 6.

14. Erica C. Childs, "Multirace.com: Multiracial Cyberspace," in *The Politics of Multiracialism: Challenging Racial Thinking*, ed. Heather M. Dalmage, 154 (Albany: State University of New York Press, 2004).

15. Eduardo Bonilla-Silva, "'New Racism,' Color-Blind Racism, and the Future of Whiteness in America," in *White Out: The Continuing Significance of Racism*, ed. Ashley W. Doane and Eduardo Bonilla-Silva, 272 (New York: Routledge, 2003).

16. See, for instance, Charles A. Gallagher, "Racial Redistricting: Expanding the Boundaries of Whiteness," in *The Politics of Multiracialism: Challenging Racial Thinking*, ed. Heather M. Dalmage (Albany: State University of New York Press, 2004); Jennifer Lee and Frank D. Bean, "America's Changing Color Lines: Immigration, Race/Ethnicity, and Multiracial Identification," *Annual Review of Sociology* 30 (2004): 221–242; and Bonilla-Silva, "'New Racism.'"

17. David R. Roediger, *How Race Survived U.S. History: From Settlement and Slavery to the Obama Phenomenon* (New York: Verso, 2008), 28–29.

18. I acknowledge having appropriated the words "revolutionary suicide" from Huey P. Newton, *Revolutionary Suicide* (New York: Harcourt, Brace, Jovanovich, 1973).

19. Gallagher, "Racial Redistricting," 72.

20. Ibid.

21. Rebecca C. King-O'Riain, *Pure Beauty: Judging Race in Japanese American Beauty Pageants* (Minneapolis: University of Minnesota Press, 2006), 27.

22. Lee and Bean, "America's Changing Color Lines," 237.

23. Bonilla-Silva, "'New Racism,'" 277–282.

24. Minkah Makalani, "Rejecting Blackness and Claiming Whiteness: Antiblack Whiteness in the Biracial Project," in *White Out: The Continuing Significance of Racism*, ed. Ashley W. Doane and Eduardo Bonilla-Silva, 81 (New York: Routledge, 2003).

25. Jared Sexton, "The Consequence of Race Mixture: Racialised Barriers and the Politics of Desire," *Social Identities* 9, no. 2 (2003): 265.

26. I acknowledge having borrowed the phrase "mixed and mixing" from Olumide.

27. Martha J. Cutter, "Sliding Significations: Passing as a Narrative and Textual Strategy in Nella Larsen's Fiction," in *Passing & the Fictions of Identity*, ed. Elaine K. Ginsberg, 90 (Durham: Duke University Press, 1997).

28. This would include, quite obviously, biological multiracial groups as well.

29. Minelle Mahtani, "What's in a Name? Exploring the Employment of 'Mixed Race' as an Identification," *Ethnicities* 2, no. 4 (2002): 471.

30. Stephen Small, "Colour, Culture and Class: Interrogating Interracial Marriage and People of Mixed Racial Descent in the USA," in *Rethinking "Mixed Race,"* ed. David Parker and Miri Song, 126–127 (London, Pluto Press, 2001).

31. Root, "Bill of Rights," 7.

32. Ibid.

33. Steve Garner, *Racisms: An Introduction* (Thousand Oaks, CA: Sage, 2010), 100.

34. King-O'Riain, *Pure Beauty*, 3.

35. DaCosta, *Making Multiracials*, 145.

36. Susan Gillman, *Blood Talk: American Race Melodrama and the Culture of the Occult* (Chicago: University of Chicago Press, 2003), 2–3.

37. DaCosta, *Making Multiracials*, 150.

38. Abby Ferber, *White Man Falling: Race, Gender, and White Supremacy* (Lanham, MD: Rowman & Littlefield, 1998), 23–24.

39. Childs, "Multirace.com," 143.

40. DaCosta, *Making Multiracials*, 183.

41. Ibid., 184.

42. Ibid.

43. Ellis Cose, *Color Blind: Seeing Beyond Race in a Race-Obsessed World* (New York: HarperPerennial, 1998), 9.

44. I list these 31 great-great-great-grandparents simply as black for the sake of illustration, leaving out the reality that none of them would truly be *monoracial* black.

45. Ronald R. Sundstrom, *The Browning of America and the Evasion of Social Justice* (Albany: State University of New York Press, 2008), 1.

46. Roediger, *How Race Survived U.S. History*, 214.

47. Sundstrom, *Browning of America*, 53.

48. Kim M. Williams, *Mark One or More: Civil Rights in Multiracial America* (Ann Arbor: University of Michigan Press, 2006), 111.

49. I realize that the former *Asian or Pacific Islander* category was split into two categories (*Asian*, and *Native Hawaiian or Other Pacific Islander*) as a result of the mid-1990s review of federal racial classification, but this change does not seem to have yet had a significant impact on mainland US conceptions of Asianness.

50. Williams, *Mark One or More*, 48.

51. King-O'Riain, *Pure Beauty*, 20.

52. Ibid., 21.

53. Ibid., 22.

54. Minkah Makalani, "A Biracial Identity or a New Race? The Historical Limitations and Political Implications of a Biracial Identity," *Souls* (Fall 2001): 77.

55. To eschew a biological racial identity does not imply the giving up of political consciousness or the giving up of commitments to antiracism efforts. Likewise, it does not imply any negation of one's ancestry or ethnic heritage.

56. Frazier, *Check All That Apply*, 71.

57. Ibid., 74.

58. Ibid., 75.

59. Ronald. R. Sundstrom, "Being and Being Mixed Race," *Social Theory and Practice* 27, no. 2 (April 2001): 294.

60. Ibid., 295.

61. Ibid., 296.

62. Ibid., 301.

63. Ibid., 300.

64. Despite being an attempt to place a positive connotation on this imposed racialization, the common saying that "black blood is so strong it only takes a single drop to make you black," is a common expression of this unfortunate acceptance. Moreover, nonsensical statements such as "the blacker the berry, the sweeter the

juice," only serve to mark darker skin as superior to lighter skin, and are, I might add, every bit as deviously offensive as Marcus Garvey's antimulatto platform or the pseudoscientific musings of Afrocentric melanin theory as holding that darker skin gives one more super powers than lighter skin. That Afro-American children of all shades are often exposed to such mindless effluvium as this without correction, and that they are enjoined to celebrate a Garvey who would likely have told them that they were inferior to unmixed blacks, are among the most odious of self-inflicted antiblack crimes. In this, they match the awful insidiousness of the brown paper-bag tests, tan-painted church doors, and blue-vein societies of the late nineteenth and early twentieth centuries. One form of colorism is equally as offensive as the other.

12

Conserving the
Racial Order

As opposed to the faux militancy of the American
Multiracial Identity Movement, arriving at an authentic position of racial
revolution first requires stepping back and interrogating the framework of
race and the way that framework has been superimposed wrongly—both
psychologically and sociologically—onto the human agent. Why, in the first
place, is a core component of raciality required in order for one to possess a
healthy self-conception? This question is never asked; instead, it is always
simply assumed that people need a primary racial identity in order to be
complete human beings either in themselves or within society. The blame
for this false consciousness can be laid squarely at the feet of both psychology and sociology. Psychologists tell us that we are not fully human without
a racial identity, and sociologists tell us that we cannot function in human
society without a racial identity. I contend that both claims are nonsense
that merely perpetuate the false consciousness of race. This false consciousness causes people, and, unfortunately, many quantitative researchers as
well, to run off madly in search of these unnecessary and counterfeit identities. But since we know that race is meaningless as a biological method of
dividing people into distinct and logically valid categories, and since we
know that race as a social construction is merely the same old biological
race categories reified euphemistically into a more socially acceptable form,
why do we nevertheless hang onto this massively—indeed, embarrassingly—
outdated concept?

It can be argued that Carolus Linneaus bequeathed our concept of race
to us by way of his 1735 book, *Systema Naturae*.[1] Yet how many other two-
and-three-quarter-century's-old ideas have we retained through to the present day, practically completely intact, the same way we have retained our
thralldom to biological race? I am not here going to engage the comprehensive argument for doing away with the notion of biological race, something
I have done in significant detail elsewhere.[2] That biological race is a false

consciousness that is both inconsistent logically and empty scientifically is not in question. I raise the issue instead to set the stage for a discussion of what true postraciality might look like, and to offer something substantively beyond the needed critique of multiracial identity. I have participated in the critique of race and undoubtedly will do so again in the future, but here I want to move past the critique itself and envision a postracial future that multiracial ideology only pretends to be able to see.

We may call once again on our three distant cousins from the previous chapter, this time to assist us in thinking about real multiracial militancy as opposed to the armchair militancy of the American Multiracial Identity Movement.[3] In this thought experiment we may consider these cousins as being of one opinion on the question of race and racial identity. Some readers, recalling these cousins' very different pedigrees (Cousin One having 1 first-generation black/white and 31 Afro-American great-great-great-grandparents, Cousin Two having 1 black/white and 31 white great-great-great-grandparents, and Cousin Three having 15 black, 15 white, and 2 first-generation black/white great-great-great-grandparents) might assume that these differing ancestries would affect their respective stances toward real racial revolution. The thought might be that Cousin One or perhaps Cousin Two would be somewhat more committed to race as a result of their ancestries. This would be a mistaken assumption, however, for since they are racial revolutionaries and therefore do not believe in biological race, no one of them feels at all the pull of the race fantasy.

Their attitudes are informed by their racial skepticism; anything else concerning their regard for race follows from that skepticism. In contradistinction to today's new millennium marginal man, our three cousins are not crushed emotionally by the fact that they might be taken by others as black, as white, and as multiracial or perhaps black, respectively. They are not moved to tears by the fact that other people may or may not have difficulty placing them in racial categories. That our three cousins are so placed occasionally does not make either themselves or those categories valid any more than if our cousins are not so placed occasionally makes either themselves or the categories invalid (the categories are invalid already).[4] They have transcended race; they do not allow the false consciousness of race to determine who they are or how they feel about themselves. They take to heart Sundee Frazier's advice that racial identity does not determine anything about a person, but unlike Frazier they do not then slip back hypocritically into advocating or adopting multiracial identity in order to fulfill their need for racial "wholeness."[5] Being authentic racial revolutionaries as opposed to the armchair revolutionaries of Generation Mix, they do not agree with Frazier that "being multiracial is a fundamental part of who you are."[6] Indeed, it is not that they simply refuse to allow race to determine their personal outlooks, but, rather, because they do not in the first place believe in race, it therefore cannot—a priori—determine anything about them. They understand that the only way to transcend race is to reject it, not to hold onto it whether biologically, socially, monoracially, or multiracially.

The authentic militancy of our three cousins would place them in direct opposition to the US racial order. They therefore cannot be accused of collaborative complicity by trying to modify that paradigm so as to fit into it more comfortably, for comfort is not the province of the true revolutionary. Maria Root's Bill of Rights for Racially Mixed People is not for them because, since they have rejected biological race in all its permutations, those rights based in racial identity have no relevance for them. So they refuse racial identification altogether. But should this not mean that they will cease to exist as a result? Will this not mean that our cousins will now be unable to function in US society? Will they not be affected in a negative way by the lack of understanding of others or by those others' resistance to our cousins' refusal to adopt racial identities for themselves?

No! Lo and behold! Despite the false warnings of the psychologists and the sociologists, not only do our three cousins continue to exist both as persons in themselves and as persons in US society, but they still function normally as well. It is true that they are irritated sometimes by the silliness of people who continue to believe in and hold onto race, but they can deal with that silliness without falling to pieces emotionally. One very real problem with the purported fundamental need for racial identity as put forth by psychology and sociology is that this alleged need for a *healthy* racial identity (and therefore a *healthy* self-concept) flies literally in the face of one very compelling and very relevant example. For centuries in North America, Africans and Afro-Americans were given the message by the whites who enslaved them, presumed to own them, abused them, restricted them, and sometimes murdered them, that they were inferior beings and therefore deserved their lower-caste status vis-à-vis whites. Faced with such massive negative messages, messages that were sponsored by their governments as well as by their individual oppressors, how did these Africans and Afro-Americans survive psychologically and socially?

While some doubtless did succumb to depression, madness, and even suicide, the great mass of Africans and Afro-Americans managed quite obviously to mentally reject the imposition of inferiority, regardless of the continuing fact of their enslavement. So even though their equality as human agents and their value as human beings were not being reflected back to them in terms of validation by society, they nonetheless refused to allow those false external messages (messages that could very well be called *silly* if not for the very serious physical subjugation behind them) to determine their own self-worth. I contend that the historical example of American slavery illustrates that it is not necessary for people to have their own preferred identities (in this case, a basic identity as an equal human being) validated by society at large in order for them to have *healthy* conceptions of themselves, in order to believe in their own positive self-worth.

But, it will doubtless be objected, even though whites sent those damaging messages, the slave community sent positive counter messages that did validate the slaves' self-worth. However, an overly romanticized portrait of the slave community as a personal sanctuary and cultural enclave is not particularly helpful here.[7] American slaves lived under an immense variety of conditions and situations ranging from one or two slaves owned by a yeoman farmer who worked by their sides to those relatively few but nonetheless largest of plantations containing hundreds of slaves. The slave community itself is a fascinating and complex subject that cannot be delved into here, but we must reject the temptation to exaggerate its possibilities and, as a consequence, replace "a mythical world in which slaves were objects of total control with an equally mythical world in which slaves were hardly slaves at all."[8] The continuing fact of physical enslavement enforced by colonial governments and then by state governments and the federal government had to have been an overwhelmingly negative message. And even if here and there a particular slave community might have been able to develop and deploy a countervailing message, it is not reasonable to suggest that such was the case for the vast majority of the four million slaves living at the time of the Civil War or their millions of ancestors going back through United States and British North American colonial history.

So I maintain my contention that the very survival of Afro-Americans and their ancestors from the beginning of American slavery through today—despite the constant invalidation of their human worth by the larger society throughout much of that time period—renders false the psychological and sociological warnings that one must adopt a positive and externally validated racial identity in order to be fully human and in order to function successfully in society. Even if one argues that African and Afro-American slaves did have racial identities that were reflected back to them by society, the fact remains that such identities were imbued with such tremendous negativity that on the sociological and psychological view these persons should not have been able to function properly. Indeed, on the sociopsychological account of the fundamental need for a positive personal racial identity, all four million slaves living at the time of the Civil War, and all their millions of ancestors, should have been quite insane and unable to function as members of society. And I also maintain my assertion that our three cousins can reject racial identity and nonetheless operate as normal members of US society, even if some people question their rejection of race. While they will of course face questions, criticism, and perhaps even mild opposition to their strong conviction in this matter, still they will not wilt emotionally as a result of that unreflective pressure or otherwise allow the idiocy of others to usurp their individual agency in so important and so personal a matter. Indeed, to succumb to such pressure would be to renounce their personal agency, which would be the truly pathological road to travel.

But, some readers may be anticipating, does their rejection of personal racial identity imply that the cousins will also refuse to check any boxes on forms requesting racial identity? Will they refuse to participate in such collection of racial data? No, they will not refuse to do so. In fact, Cousin One will check only the *Black* box, as Cousin Three may possibly do as well, while Cousin Two will check only the *White* box. It may appear to some readers that our cousins have now involved themselves in contradiction by only pretending to reject race, but this appearance is the result of a misunderstanding—a widespread national misunderstanding—concerning what the checkboxes are for and what they do. First, in order to unravel this misunderstanding, we must acquire a correct sense of why the checkboxes exist in the first place. This sense will be in the form of an overview only, as I have elsewhere set down the entirety of the comprehensive issues involved.[9]

In short, the vast majority of Americans are misinformed—completely—as to the purpose of the federal race categories and those categories' appearance via checkboxes on various forms. The federal race categories were approved decades ago by the Office of Management and Budget so that racial data could be shared between the various federal agencies in a useful way. Prior to the advent of the categories in the mid-1970s, each federal agency maintained its own set of racial criteria and its own statistics, which were, as a result, valid only within that particular agency and thus could not be shared with other units within the federal government. With the passage of major civil rights legislation such as the Civil Rights Act of 1964 and the Voting Rights Act of 1965, the necessity of ensuring compliance with those laws—which would entail the necessity of uncovering and eliminating the institutional discrimination that remained—began to take hold at the federal level, and it became clear that there needed to be a single set of racial data standards that could be used by all federal agencies in order to facilitate the sharing of information in pursuit of enforcing compliance with the new civil rights laws.

The standard categories that were adopted—*Black*, *Asian/Pacific Islander*, *American Indian/Alaskan Native*, and *Hispanic* (if conceived of racially)—reflected those groups that had been victimized specifically and significantly by the federal government, along with the dominant group that had not been so victimized, *White*. The purpose of the data collection was to track institutional discrimination (noncompliance with civil rights laws), a tracking that, unlike in cases of individual discrimination, cannot be accomplished without large data sets and statistics. Importantly, the federal race categories were not developed so as to match or otherwise facilitate people's personal identity choices, nor were they designed to be representative of every potential racial or ethnic group or combination of groups in the

United States.[10] However, this is precisely what Americans think, quite mistakenly, is the purpose of these categories.[11]

The tracking of racial discrimination I have described is known as civil rights compliance monitoring, and it remains the nation's best means of uncovering covert as well as unintentional institutional discrimination. Without the racial data—data that is recorded in the language of the racist—there is no way to determine accurately if racial discrimination is taking place in a variety of institutional contexts ranging from unjustified ability tracking in public schools to illegal real-estate redlining and loan disapprovals in the housing market to unfair promotion procedures at the Federal Bureau of Investigation. Without such data, we would not have anything other than the relative impotence of anecdotal claims to use in researching and investigating continuing racial discrimination. Given that a stand-alone federal multiracial category would disrupt this critical investigative ability, the motivation behind the far right's romance with the American Multiracial Identity Movement, as well as its championing of both a federal multiracial category and the complete elimination of collecting racial data becomes clear.[12] Lamenting its appropriation of the American Multiracial Identity Movement, Kim Williams criticizes "the Right's intent to undercut racial data collection as a way of dismantling race-conscious public policy. With these aims, the right wing, to repeat, has brazenly taken the lead in defining for Americans what 'multiracial' is."[13]

Understanding the true purpose of the federal categories and the checkboxes adjacent to them, Cousin One checks only the *Black* box because she is perceived as black by people who do not know her. In checking the *Black* box, she realizes that the checkboxes have no bearing on her personal identification, just as she realizes how silly it would be to think that checking one or another box could somehow be an insult to or a rejection of one of her parents or of others in her ancestral line. She checks only one box, even though the instructions inform her that she can check as many as apply, because the fact is that the only thing that really applies here is how she is perceived by others who might discriminate against her.[14]

Cousin Two checks only the *White* box because that is how she is perceived by people who do not know her. She is aware that she has sub-Saharan African ancestry, and she is also aware that both biological race and sociological race are fantasies, but she checks only the *White* box because she knows that it is important for the relevant databases to have her coded in the same way that she is perceived by people who might grant her white privilege, even if unconsciously, due to their perceptions of her as white. Like Cousin One, Cousin Two also realizes that checking a box on a form is not some grand psychological act of *being counted*, but is instead a rather mundane act of assuring that when some civil servant in the Small Business Administration is running various sets of statistics she will not skew the results by having checked a box that does not represent how people who do in fact believe in race perceive her.

What about Cousin Three, who has an equal number of black and white direct ancestors going back five generations (26 black, 26 white, 6 first-generation black/white, and 4 non-first-generation black/white)? Which box does she check? As with Cousin One and Cousin Two, the box she checks depends on how she is perceived by people who do not know her. This is something we cannot be certain of since, the nonsense of "multiracial radar" and the fantasy of "obviousness mixedness" (see Chapter 8) notwithstanding, she could just as readily be lighter or darker than either Cousin One or Cousin Two, with her other phenotypical features ranging just as widely as well. So if she is perceived generally as black she will check only the *Black* box; and if she is perceived generally as white, she will check only the *White* box. She does not consider checking both the *Black* box and the *White* box, even though the form allows it, because she realizes that in doing so she would be disrupting the important work of civil rights compliance monitoring, such a disruption in the long term amounting to a participation—however obliquely—in antiblackness efforts. Not being a racist, therefore, Cousin Three does not consider checking more than the one box that coincides with how she is perceived generally by others.

In an admittedly small and personal way our three cousins have demonstrated taking a truly militant stand against the US racial order by their rejection of biological race, a rejection expressed most clearly by their refusals to adopt personal racial identities. They have therefore declared themselves to be raceless—a far more revolutionary stance than that exemplified by the self-absorption of pleading mawkishly that a multiracial category be added to the US racial schema. Moreover, by supporting the federal government's efforts at civil rights compliance monitoring, they have also taken a stand against the racism that—a priori—cannot exist without the support of widespread belief in biological race. Finally, while each of our three cousins eschews a personal racial identity for herself, each nonetheless would react with disdain toward the suggestion that she is different from, or somehow more mixed than, or in possession of a more authentic mixture, than the average Afro-American. This is even true of Cousin Two, who (as also in the cases of her two cousins) by her very existence challenges us to draw a line that is valid both scientifically and logically between blackness, mixedness, and whiteness.

Some readers will raise the objection that, in presenting this argument via our three hypothetical cousins, I am engaging in precisely the same hypocrisy that I have excoriated the sociologists for, that I am defending the use of race as a social construction in my support of collecting federal racial statistics. I want to respond to this objection most straightforwardly. Let me state, and in no uncertain terms, that I reject such a claim in the strongest way possible. There is a fundamental difference between the argument for race as a social construction or a social reality on the one hand, and my reluctant agreement with the collection of racial statistics for civil rights compliance monitoring purposes on the other. I refer to it as a reluctant agreement because even though civil rights compliance monitoring is our best weapon against institutional discrimination it obviously still involves the fantasy of race at some level since the statistics must be rendered in the language of racism: *Black*, *White*, *Native American*, *Asian*, and *Hispanic*.

But the primary difference is clear. The social-construction apologist will assert that biological race does not exist, but that people laboring under a false consciousness act as though it does, so we therefore must *accept* this false consciousness and go so far as to declare normatively that all Americans must adopt a racial identity or face the undesirable consequence of being nonfunctioning members of society. I, on the other hand, assert that race does not exist either biologically or in its reified social construction version, but since racism based on the false consciousness of biological race *does* exist we must take action to stamp it out. One important variant of such action is to use statistical data to track the way people who are perceived to be of this or that racial group (regardless of how based in fantasy such perceptions might be) are treated. Unlike the social constructionist, however, I do not argue that people should themselves accept and adopt racial identities; indeed, I argue quite explicitly that they should not.

I have long argued that despite their use of racial language we must nonetheless continue using the federal race categories until such time as we come up with a better means of conducting civil rights compliance monitoring. Some may have misinterpreted this argument as sophistic insincerity on my part, but it has always been the most earnest of positions as I have been ever sensitive to the seeming paradox of arguing against race while supporting the use of racial statistics for monitoring institutional discrimination. As such, it therefore has never been a position that I have taken lightly. And while I have not found a better way of accomplishing the work of civil rights compliance monitoring, neither has anyone else produced any way of moving us beyond the dilemma of using racial statistics to track racial discrimination, the 1997 federal decision to allow persons to "mark all that apply" being a bland compromise that did nothing to solve the core problem. However, I am now going to endeavor to, so to speak, "go out on a limb" and "put my money where my mouth is."

I suggest a single step toward the day when race is deconstructed and racial statistics are no longer required. To be sure, it is a small step that, by itself, will not turn the system on its head, but it is a step that nevertheless endeavors to correct the fundamental misunderstanding that most Americans have about the racial checkboxes. That misunderstanding lies in thinking erroneously that the checkboxes are supposed to represent some innate racial essence that the individual is or that the individual has. As I have explained, though, the checkboxes are instead designed to track discrimination, a task that is best facilitated by recording how the individual is perceived by others. The purpose of the categories and of civil rights compliance monitoring is to track how people are treated due to the way they are perceived, not how they perceive themselves.

I therefore call on the Office of Management and Budget to require that all forms requesting racial statistics include the following preamble to the racial checkboxes: "I am generally perceived by others who do not know me as:" This requirement would profoundly change respondents' perceptions of what is being asked, for there is a fundamental difference between the question of how I perceive myself and the question of how others may perceive me. Perhaps in most cases the two perceptions will converge, but that is not the point. Rather, the point is that the way the question is posed currently requires the respondent to essentially accept a framework of biological race in order to answer it. Something along the lines of "Check as many races as apply to you" requires—if it is to be answered truthfully—the respondent to place herself in the framework of biological race and then select the racial category (or categories) that she feels best describes herself. The only people who escape this cooptation are the racial revolutionaries who in the first place realize the true function of the race categories and who are therefore already answering in terms of how they are perceived. The average American does not have this important realization, however, so it must be provided.

Science has for decades pointed out the truth that biological race is a myth; however, that empirical truth has had no effect on Americans' continuing belief in race. It has long been obvious to me that if the race construct is to be overturned eventually it will have to be a gradual effect of public education and improved public consciousness replacing the current false consciousness of race. Changing the formulation of the race-category question from "What race are you?" to "What race are you perceived to be?" must be the first step on that critical journey. At the very least it requires thinking people to think about the question, and, as they do, realize that what is being requested is not a self-perception but an external perception. This is again an admittedly small alteration, but I contend it would result in at least the beginnings of a fundamental realignment of how race is conceived in the United States. Nancy Leong, arguing for a broadly similar change to jurisprudence involving multiracial plaintiffs, brings up the absolutely essential point that the "key question is not whether someone is in fact of a particular race, but rather whether a discriminator perceives that person to be a member of that race."[15] In her view, "the discriminator's perspective is central to the act of discrimination."[16]

Leong's focus is on jurisprudence while mine here is on compliance monitoring, but the two have a strong connection and are related quite clearly, differing only in their place of residence along the antidiscrimination plane. According to Leong, "we should aspire to a more fluid understanding of race, one that acknowledges animus directed against a person's perceived race without an attendant need to define that person's 'objective' racial identity or to place that person in a category. A jurisprudence constructed around that understanding would focus entirely on whether the perception of someone's race—whatever that perceived race might be—motivated discriminatory treatment."[17] So complete is my agreement with Leong's analysis, that when she writes that "our race discrimination jurisprudence should focus on racism rather than on the social constructs we call races," and when she writes that "we should aspire to develop a jurisprudence that does not rely on categories per se, but rather targets animus directed at an individual due to a particular perception of his race," were one to substitute "compliance monitoring" for "jurisprudence" the resulting statements would be in precise concordance with the new formulation I am advancing.[18]

Consider as well that this new formulation of the race question should remove the checkbox-related angst of white mothers of black/white children, because no longer would answering the question be a statement of what those children are or are not, but it would instead quite obviously be a civil-rights-compliance-monitoring–based assessment of how the children are perceived by others. One hopes that such white mothers and their children, as well as all the members of Generation Mix, would have no problem answering the question honestly if phrased in the way I am suggesting. Indeed, G. Reginald Daniel's exaggerated warnings of "psychological oppression" (see Chapter 8) should simply evaporate in the face of the reformulated question. It might possibly be useful for the Bureau of the Census to ask both forms of the question, although in the interest of moving away from biological race I would opt for eliminating altogether the "What race are you?" version of the question from the federal lexicon. I also argue that, with this change, all variants of the race question should return to the "mark one only" format, since, with racism being a rather uncomplicated enterprise, racists do not make distinctions regarding a person's perceived pedigree. To the racist, black is black and Asian is Asian, regardless of mixture.

To those who will doubtless disparage my proposed reformulation of the federal race question with the criticism that such a small change would be inconsequential, I offer the rejoinder that I am at least attempting here to engage—honestly and seriously—the conundrum of moving away from race while not undermining the important work of civil-rights compliance monitoring. Here then is something practical that can be done to alter Americans' perception of race from something that is *in* them (as exemplified by

Maria Root's Bill of Rights in the previous chapter) to something that is perceived *about* them. It sets the stage for a potential national questioning of what race is and is not. A reformulated race question would also provide a practical benefit to civil-rights compliance monitoring by reflecting more accurately how people are perceived by others, which is precisely what needs to be tabulated in the interests of tracking racial discrimination. In light of all this, I would rather be criticized for proffering my admittedly small suggestion than be the party rendering that criticism with my hands in my pockets and my head in the sand.

Others may register concern that my proposed change to the race question would result in skewed statistics, since some people may refuse to answer the question truthfully. This is not a serious issue, however, since even now some respondents refuse to answer the question in a way that they would themselves consider truthful. Indeed, some persons are still thinking misguidedly that they are taking progressive action by either refusing to answer or by answering in a way that is purposely false—such as a black/white person marking *Native American* or marking *all* the categories as a form of protest—when all they are doing is hampering the government's ability to track racism effectively.

Others might argue that my reformulated question would result in undercounting—for example, the removal from black statistics of persons who previously marked *black* but who are perceived by others as white. It might do this, but if we really think about it in the interests of civil-rights compliance monitoring, we should actually want this outcome to obtain, for such a person already skews the statistics herself since she is being treated based on how she is perceived by others, not on how she perceives herself. Moreover, my proposed change would serve to correct the current statistics by reversing these sorts of instances. For example, while the person mentioned above would be removed from black statistical databases by virtue of her answer, in the opposite case the person who is perceived by others as black but who perceives herself as mixed-race or, in rare cases, as white would be added to black statistics by virtue of her answer, which would result in a more accurate representation of *who* is being treated *how* based on the perceptions of *others*. While I am not insensitive to valid concerns of overcounting and undercounting various subpopulations, the point remains that the purpose of the federal race categories is to track institutional discrimination, which is a matter of how people are perceived and treated by others as opposed to how they might perceive themselves. Ultimately, this goes back to the improper expectation that the federal race categories should serve a census-like function when they cannot do that and at the same time be most effective at tracking discrimination.[19]

A brief word or two is in order as well about a topic that raises its head from time to time in the continuing debate over a federal multiracial category. This is the question of racism directed against multiracial people specifically *as* multiracial people. There are two issues that need to be teased apart in order to address this concern. First, to provide one example, overt racism against someone who is black/white is always racism directed against one or the other component of the person's perceived ancestry. I have yet to encounter the white racist who will aver that he loves white people, barely tolerates black people, but fervently hates black/white people. Nor have I encountered the black racist whose distaste for black/white persons is not a function of his prior hatred of whites. The case of Revonda Bowen, often cited incorrectly by multiracial activists as an example of antimultiracial racism, is a perfect illustration. In March 1994, Bowen's high-school principal in Wedowee, Alabama, Hulond Humphries, called her a "mistake" because she was mixed race.[20] However, in studying Humphries's personal record it becomes clear very quickly that he is a garden-variety antiblack racist who objects to black/white mixture because of his prior racism against black people.[21] This is not some new type of racism that requires separate tracking; it is the same old antiblack racism that Afro-Americans have been facing for centuries.

Second, commentators who make the case that black/white people in particular face discrimination from Afro-Americans fail to distinguish between what we might call *actionable discrimination* and *nonactionable discrimination*. Despite the well-known fact that most Afro-Americans have been more than accommodating to black/white persons throughout this nation's history, it is undeniable that there are Afro-Americans who express racist attitudes against black/white people. Such instances range from merely not speaking to or not accepting such persons as friends to school-yard fighting to exclusion from black events or social clubs. There is no doubt that some Afro-Americans have engaged in such deplorable and immature practices, especially in the middle school through college years. However, one needs to distinguish this type of racist discrimination—which it no doubt is—from, say, an Afro-American employer refusing in an illegal way to promote black/white employees from the same racist impulse.[22] The latter case is an example of actionable illegal discrimination, while the former cases are not.

Yet when multiracial activists toss items into the kitchen sink of justifications for a multiracial category, they very wrongly and quite invalidly include *antimultiracial racism* in reference to the former type of situation. Unless such activists are suggesting seriously that certain Afro-American middle- or high-school students should be brought up on felony discrimination charges for making fun of or ostracizing their black/white peers, and unless such activists are suggesting seriously that some student presidents of campus black student organizations should face civil-rights trials on account of their organizations' expressing to black/white college students that they are not black enough, we should call into question the generalized multiracial complaint about black-sponsored antimultiracial racism. This critical distinction is rendered that much more obscure by multiracial advocates such as Ronald Sundstrom, who considers "equally as pressing" problems as far-flung from each other in seriousness as "affirmative action and the morality of same-race socializing in high school lunchrooms and college social clubs."[23]

Indeed, on this analysis, the very problem with such exaggerated complaints of discrimination is what can only, and with no small irony, be called their *undiscriminating* nature. I am certainly not attempting to make light of childhood teasing, for there are few of us who managed to escape being tormented about some aspect of our persons, but I nonetheless insist on refusing to allow these sorts of occurrences to be classed unreflectively as racial discrimination of a sort requiring tracking by the federal government, or of a sort justifying the establishment of a federal multiracial category. The fact is that the members of Generation Mix do not face any kind of racism that is not founded on a prior racism against some individual aspect of their perceived ancestry. It is that particular racism that is and must continue to be tracked by the current system, with the modification to the race question I have proposed.

I would be remiss here in failing to mention that Leong presents a powerful alternative viewpoint, arguing that there is discrimination enacted against multiracial persons that is distinct from the reductive formulation I claim here to be the case. Yet despite the fact that Leong and I disagree fundamentally on the specific question of whether antimultiracial discrimination reduces ultimately to discrimination against some perceived component of a person's ancestry (my view), or whether it is a stand-alone variety of discrimination in and of itself (her view), I nonetheless agree completely with her proposed solution, which, again, is to focus on the perception of the discriminator as opposed to constructing a new multiracial category for such purposes. For even while accepting the notion of antimultiracial discrimination, Leong nevertheless does "not advocate that we remedy the deficiency of racial categories by adding a new category—'multiracial' —thereby converting the ethno-racial pentagon into a hexagon. A multiracial category would itself reify prevailing racial classifications by implying that a multiracial person is the offspring of two members of such 'pure' races."[24]

Finally, there is yet another level of complexity that we must consider in regard to nonactionable discrimination and perhaps even to actionable discrimination as well. Owing to the overuse of intrinsically nondiverse snowball sampling by many pro-multiracial-identity researchers, many of the black/white persons who report having experienced alleged antimultiracial discrimination at the hands of blacks are themselves middle class, which opens up an entirely new arena of analysis on this question. As Minkah Makalani notes, "Black middle-class youths, typically have their 'blackness' called into question by working-class and poor Black youths. They are taunted for talking white or thinking they are better than their poorer kith," suggesting that the root issue in at least a portion of these cases is not even multiracial identity at all, but is instead a matter of conflicting social classes.[25]

Returning to our cousins, it might be supposed that Cousin Three exemplifies the movement claim that acceptance of multiracial identity will lead to a destabilizing über ambiguity and, therefore, the end of race. But let us once again take the time to investigate the case before accepting at face value such simplistic claims. First, we need to keep in mind that we are talking about very small numbers of people, with black/white persons representing both the smallest and slowest-growing of all multiracial groups. Second, despite unproven assertions that Generation Mix is blurring racial lines and deconstructing race, we have already seen that quite the opposite effect is actually taking place. While the smallest and slowest-growing multiracial group, black/white persons, can never become white as long as their sub-Saharan African ancestry is known, the much larger and much faster-growing Hispanic and part-Asian groups are in fact becoming white! The American Multiracial Identity Movement does not explain to us how it is that the phenomenon of Hispanics and part Asians moving to whiteness serves to deconstruct race. Indeed, the only line that is being blurred at all seems to be the line of whiteness, as it adapts to the times and alters just enough to allow certain Hispanics and part Asians into the formerly more exclusive club of whiteness.

I have with my own eyes and ears been witness to this willingness to bend the bars of whiteness just enough so that certain persons who are non-black—even while still nonwhite—may enter upon the hallowed ground of whiteness and thereupon replenish its numbers. As an observer attending the Multiracial Solidarity March of July 20, 1996, held on the Mall in Washington, DC, I heard that precise sentiment expressed by one of the sixteen featured speakers that day.[26] In what I can from my perspective only describe as a bizarre spectacle, Jeff Hitchcock, who identified himself as white and as director of the Center for the Study of White American Culture, concluded his remarks with the following statement: "We need to help the white community understand that replacing white skin with light skin is really no change at all."[27] While we may well be willing to dismiss Hitchcock from serious consideration, my point in bringing up his comments is to emphasize that he nonetheless was a featured speaker for the Multiracial Solidarity March, and his views, one presumes, were known by and palatable to the event's organizers. It is also of extreme interest to note that Hitchcock's plea for his fellow whites to allow into whiteness those nonwhites who have "light skin" received no boos, murmurs, or other dissent from the receptive audience of multiracial identity supporters.

In noting the phenomenon of whiteness seeking to slow the pace at which its boundaries are shrinking by absorbing certain phenotypically acceptable persons of Hispanic and Asian descent, we will recall Root's claim in the previous chapter that "the multiracial person's existence challenges the rigidity of racial lines." This very claim is what is at work in that absorption, as Root is interested in challenging the *rigidity* of the lines, but not in challenging the lines themselves, for to do so would be to undercut the racial foundation of multiracial identity. However, to challenge only the rigidity of the lines is something else altogether. Allowing the lines to open slightly, perhaps only temporarily, so that some people with the right backgrounds (nonblack) and the right looks (nonblack) can slip out of one category in order to reinforce another is hardly revolutionary. In fact, one would be correct to call it cooptation, accommodationism, and an example of a decidedly counterrevolutionary mindset. As Jenifer Bratter points out, "the likelihood of labeling a child as multiracial varies considerably by the type of racial interaction that characterizes the family. *Which* racial lines are crossed is strongly indicative of the degree of social distance that exists between these two groups, which ultimately results in the degree of flexibility their children experience in their identification."[28] In other words, some persons are able to move to multiraciality/honorary whiteness and then on to full whiteness and some persons are not.

As a result, the greatest significance of multiracial identity, its ultimate legacy, may be as an intermediary identity on some Hispanic or Asian family lines' transitional journey, first to honorary whiteness, and then, finally, to the safe harbor of achieving full whiteness a generation or two later. Multiraciality is a way station on the journey to terminal whiteness. Upon reaching the multiracial way station, select Asians and Hispanics are given transfer tickets for the connecting trains to honorary whiteness and the final destination, full whiteness, while black/white persons (unless they obscure their sub-Saharan African ancestry) are not. But even these latter will not long remain at the multiracial hub, for their descendants will likely blend into the Afro-American population or use racial passing to achieve whiteness. Commenting on the population projections of Barry Edmonston, Sharon Lee, and Jeffrey Passel (see Chapter 6), David Roediger also questions the stability of a multiracial grouping vis-à-vis the movements of certain multiracial persons to whiteness by pointing out "that no one knows what the racial identification of Latino mixed-race people, the largest single category projected, will be in 2100. It is entirely possible to imagine a white majority continuing for centuries based on choices that mixed-race people make."[29] The notion that a multiracial category will be a stable grouping with its members and their progeny remaining in and expanding it is completely unproven. To be sure, it has been assumed and asserted countless times, but no one has presented anything remotely representing an argument as to why this should be so.

There is no reason to suppose that multiracially identifying people and their offspring will remain so identified into ensuing generations, especially given the draw and the fascination of whiteness as a goal. Rather, this tiny category will continue to be populated primarily by the so-called first-generation offspring of so-called monoracial parents, and will not expand as a result of natural increase. The continual losses of some its members transitioning to honorary and then full whiteness will see to that, as will the departure of others back to one or another monoracial identity. Why should this happen? The real question is: Why should it not happen? I have presented an argument for expecting that a multiracial category will be a transitory phenomenon; it remains for advocates of such a category to demonstrate why it would not be so. Merely stating that I am wrong, with no further rationale or compelling argument, is not good enough. Lise Funderburg raises a similar point in noting that "in a certain respect, biracial people can never re-create their family of origin, that intersection of two separate groups. They are a one-time-only generation."[30] Unsurprisingly, arguments to the contrary, if they even exist, remain unarticulated.

Moreover, Bratter notes two very significant trends in connection with this question. First, "defying the norms of hypodescent that define 'white' as the absence of any racial mixture, families who have overlapping white racial backgrounds tend toward a white classification for their children."[31] We may see this quite clearly in the case of a couple consisting of a white father and an Asian/white mother. According to Bratter, these parents will likely categorize their children as white, providing a research-based encapsulation of the *multiraciality/honorary whiteness to full whiteness* trajectory model. Second, and most importantly, this pattern does not apply when one of the parents is (presumably monoracial) Asian or Afro-American, "as in both sets of analyses, racial overlap was negatively related to a multiracial identification for a child."[32] In these cases, we find movement toward either whiteness or toward the nonwhite monoracial identity, but, significantly, not toward multiracial identification. Moreover, the likelihood of multiracial identification for children drops even lower if the couple consists of one multiracial and one black parent, "whose families have the lowest rates of multiracial classification of all the multiracial parent families, and the presence of a multiracial parent [alongside a black parent] inspires the largest decline in odds of a multiracial classification compared to what is found in the other analyses."[33] Bratter's "analysis shows that Black/Non-black distinctions are still salient even when viewed through a multiracial lens."[34] Finally, I would be remiss in not mentioning that her findings do "show that multiracial identity does prevail in families where a multiracial parent and their partner do not have overlapping racial backgrounds, suggesting there is one such context in which multiracial identity does 'survive'—even though these cases are not highly common."[35] On the whole, however, the simple assumption that multiracial identity will perpetuate itself through the generations, and in the process deconstruct race in the United States, must be seen as damaged in quite a serious way.

Thinking beyond the present generation is yet another unanswered challenge that continues to go ignored by multiracial activists, multiracially supporting scholars and writers, and the so-called serious press as well as glossy media. But, in pressing the case, I ask: What happens in the multiracial future? Will multiracial persons act endogamously on the matter of procreation, or is it imagined that they will slowly branch out (one supposes that multiple centuries would be required) and consume monoracials through progressive intermixture, bringing to reality the white supremacist's worst nightmare? The widespread substitution of wishful thinking for critical thinking that is involved in accepting the premise that multiraciality will lead to the end of race is epitomized by John Cloud, writing in *Time* that "fortunately, all these questions of racial identity are becoming less important, as we inch ever closer to the day when the U.S. has no racial majority. One of these days, after all, we will all be celebrating our multiracial pride."[36] But power is unrelated to numerical strength or to whether one is talking about a situation of majority, minority, or plurality. Apparently making the faulty assumption that a white numerical majority is the primary problem, Cloud is unaware of the relatively tiny white minority in apartheid South Africa that wielded and abused its illegitimate power with extreme viciousness. White South Africans needed no racial majority to ensure that racial identity was extraordinarily important in that society. Cloud seems unaware as well of county after county and city after city in the pre–Voting Rights Act American South in which huge majorities of Afro-Americans were denied their supposedly constitutionally guaranteed right to vote, along with suffering all manner of other civil- and human-rights violations. They were denied their rights and suffered those abuses at the hands of white populations that were very much in the minority.

The point is not that multiracial identity will lead to a return of such overt abuses; rather, the point is that the overly heralded loss of white majority status is meaningless absent a corollary loss of white power—a loss that is neither here already nor visible on the horizon. The issue is not numbers; the issue is and always has been power, white power. As Eduardo Bonilla-Silva puts it, "*Whiteness, then, in all of its manifestations, is embodied racial power.*"[37] People are fond of saying that "knowledge is power," but in the case of race and society it is just as true to state that "power is knowledge." As Samira Kawash attests: "Power is multiple and multiplied, working simultaneously through the epistemological power to name and evaluate, through the subjectifying power that interpellates individuals into particular social locations as agents of power and knowledge, and through the regulative power to enforce the order so named. The production of racial knowledge is inseparable from the production of racially marked subjects and the racial ordering of society; each provides the conditions for the other."[38]

On this analysis, white support and especially far-right support for multiracial identity becomes much easier to situate and understand. Multiracial identity does not threaten whiteness or the racial order that whiteness has installed and that whiteness maintains through its power to name. This is why multiracial advocates must lobby as they do for recognition; this is why they need the blessing of the racial state in order to be what they think they already are; and this is why they seek to accommodate themselves to the racial order as opposed to subverting that order by asserting a truly militant identity that the racial state would not sanction. Official recognition for a new racial category (in both a federal as well as a more general, societal sense) can only be granted by whiteness, and whiteness will only allow the instantiation of a new racial category if that new category is not threatening to the established racial order. As we have seen, not only is multiracial identity unthreatening to whiteness, but it goes one better and provides dutiful aid to whiteness in at least two ways: (1) by furthering the existing division between blackness and whiteness, and (2) by serving as a way station that repopulates a numerically diminishing whiteness with phenotypically acceptable persons of Asian and Hispanic ancestry.[39] Those who are determined to see whiteness maintain its dominance and power are thrilled with simple-minded analyses such as Cloud's that equate a diminution of white numerical superiority with a corresponding diminution of white power. Such facile thinking provides a welcome cover behind which whiteness can continue its course unchallenged and unchecked as it manipulates and uses Generation Mix to its own advantage.

As we have noted, there has been one necessary, perhaps forced, concession on the part of whiteness, however. One significant change in regard to the US racial order is that whiteness appears to have given up its ultra purity. By this I mean that it is no longer true that whiteness is seen as being absolutely racially pure. Indeed, such purity has always been a fantasy, but that fantasy is no longer sustainable with the present incorporation of persons of Asian and Hispanic descent into the national white body. And while this is a significant change, to be sure, it nonetheless is still a relatively minor alteration of the paradigm overall. But how can that be if the very point of whiteness through the centuries has been its racial purity, its very Nordicness? I argue that the most critical consideration has never been a question of white purity per se, but rather that the condition that has been constitutive of whiteness has always and primarily been a question of freedom from a certain impurity. That impurity, of course, is blackness.

Certainly, racist whites of decades and centuries past have been opposed violently to mixture with Asians and Hispanics, but that aversion, on the grand scale of things, never reached the absurdly pathological and paranoid heights attained when it came to considering amalgamation with blacks. Regardless of the other categories, and with full consideration for the atrocities their members have suffered, it nonetheless remains the case that "the color line persists as the organizing principle of racial space, that is, the maintenance of an absolute boundary between black and white and, more especially, the exclusionary line demarcating and bounding whiteness and assuring the continued value of 'whiteness as property.'"[40] Whiteness depends on its absolute separation from blackness. The defenders of whiteness might prefer to not accept into the fold the part-Asian and part-Hispanic people it is now incorporating, but they will be accepted, at least for now, even if they or their descendants are purged at some later date. Persons of known sub-Saharan African ancestry will never be incorporated into whiteness, however. This is the reality of the absolute separation of blackness and whiteness, for that separation is how whiteness constitutes itself, and that separation must be enforced and maintained at all costs.

In Kawash's words: "Although whiteness certainly could be described in terms of its visual characteristics, whiteness could not be 'invisible'; whiteness then is the absence of both visible and invisible blackness. But if whiteness depends on the absence of something that cannot be perceived, then whiteness becomes increasingly precarious. The possibility that the body, which is meant to reflect transparently its inner truth, may in fact be a misrepresentation and that its meaning may be illegible threatens the collapse of the system of racial ordering and separation on which the hierarchical distribution of social, political, and economic opportunity is based. Thus the stability of discrete racial identities is based not only on visibility but on knowability."[41] But we must keep in mind that the most important of these discrete racial identities is black, for it is blackness that makes whiteness possible. It is also important to state that I am not suggesting that Asians and Hispanics are no longer part of the racial hierarchy. What I am arguing is that those particular part Asians and part Hispanics who qualify for whiteness do not disturb the racial paradigm or its attendant hierarchy when they transition to the white category. Instead, they are simply and quietly absorbed into whiteness. In the same way, multiracial identity does not trouble whiteness and it does not trouble the US racial order, for it is conservative of both. As Williams points out, the danger represented by the allure of whiteness on the one hand, and by its selective policy of admittance on the other, is clear: "If today's panethnics are tomorrow's whites, then racial fluidity could be leading to an exit from minority identification for a growing number of Latinos and Asians. This would leave blacks, among other things, with a diminishing pool of allies."[42]

Unless whiteness is deconstructed, indeed unless it is demolished, racial identity will remain crucial in US society. In fact, I argue that there can be no moral rest or relaxation in regard to race until whiteness ceases to be, existing as it is by first having created and then feeding perpetually upon blackness in order to maintain itself as a seemingly independent essence. Whiteness is the crux of the challenge to do away with race in the United States. Multiraciality is not the answer to this challenge, as it is not equipped for the mission; it cannot deconstruct whiteness precisely because it is a slave of whiteness. It is conservative of (and therefore cannot challenge) biological race. It is conservative of the US racial order and of whiteness in particular, since whiteness is the key to the racial order. Without whiteness and its concomitant creation and maintenance of blackness, there is no racial order. And, of course, without whiteness and blackness, there is no multiraciality—hence, the endless circularity and hypocrisy of the American Multiracial Identity Movement's empty claim to represent the vanguard of our postracial future. As Roediger, writing about the possibility of mixed-race identity and immigration doing away with race, points out, "history should make us wary of predictions that demographic changes will cause race to disappear, rather than simply to mutate. In any case, we are at this moment very far from such a reality, and are not on a road that leads in any sure direction."[43] Situated appropriately within the broad sweep of US history, Generation Mix, far from representing a progressive or transcendent impulse racially, instead reveals itself to be merely a recrudescence of a centuries-old distancing from blackness by yet another near-white group that desires such distancing and considers itself capable of achieving it.

Multiracial identity is not the means to the emancipatory postracialism that its adherents claim it to be; rather, it quite pointedly and quite unmistakably is simply an end in itself. The intended end is the creation of a new biological racial category that would take its place in the racial order amidst the already existing categories without in any sense acting or desiring to deconstruct that order or those categories. The invocation of multiracial identity represents a claim of essentiality, the defenses and justifications thereof designed to be proofs of a new racial essentialism. But even the potential instantiation of a new false consciousness to join the existing false consciousnesses is quite irrelevant to the greater questions of whiteness and power, for those who exist below whiteness in the paradigm's hierarchy may well do what they please as long as it does not disturb whiteness. The ever-present question is this: Who or what benefits from the potential legitimization of multiracial identity? The answer, as we have seen, is whiteness. This in turn inspires a further question: How does a multiracial identity that confers such distinct advantage to the perpetuation of whiteness represent anything approaching a militant attitude? The answer is that it does not and cannot.

Notes

1. Carolus Linneaus, *Systema Naturae, Sive Regna Tria Naturae Systematice Proposita Per Classes, Ordines, Genera, & Species* (Lugduni Batavorum [Netherlands]: Theodorum Haak, 1735).

2. For an extensive critique of biological race, see Rainier Spencer, *Spurious Issues: Race and Multiracial Identity Politics in the United States* (Boulder: Westview, 1999), chap. 1. For a recent and detailed scientific discussion of the falseness of biological race, see Barbara A. Koenig, Sandra Soo-Jin Lee, and Sarah S. Richardson, eds., *Revisiting Race in a Genomic Age* (New Brunswick: Rutgers University Press, 2008).

3. Although he is not the only person to have employed the concept of the "armchair militant" or "armchair revolutionary," I nonetheless again acknowledge my appropriation of the words of Huey P. Newton.

4. As Nancy Leong so correctly points out in a comment on multiracial identity that applies as well to all racial identities: "The fact that others identify various individuals as racially mixed does not necessarily impute any essence to the group itself." Nancy Leong, "Judicial Erasure of Mixed-Race Discrimination," *American University Law Review* 59, no. 3 (February 2010): 553.

5. The subtitle of Frazier's book (*Finding Wholeness as a Multiracial Person*) leaves no doubt of this, nor does the content of the text itself. Sundee T. Frazier, *Check All That Apply: Finding Wholeness as a Multiracial Person* (Downers Grove, IL: InterVarsity, 2000).

6. Ibid., 93.

7. See Peter Kolchin, *American Slavery, 1619–1877* (New York: Hill and Wang, 2003), chap. 5.

8. Ibid., 148–149.

9. See Spencer, *Spurious Issues*, chaps. 2 and 5; and Spencer, "Census 2000: Assessments in Significance," in *New Faces in a Changing America: Multiracial Identity in the 21st Century*, ed. Loretta Winters and Herman DeBose, 99–110 (Thousand Oaks, CA: Sage, 2003).

10. There is an argument to be made that the Bureau of the Census, which has a different data-collection mission, should be exempted from the constraints of the Office of Management and Budget's federal race categories—that census enumeration should be de-linked from compliance monitoring limitations—but that is a tangential issue. Spencer, *Spurious Issues*, 79–81.

11. That the issues surrounding civil rights compliance monitoring are often wildly mistaken may be seen in Ronald Sundstrom's advocating on behalf of Native Hawaiians by claiming that they are "without state or federal recognition" while at the same time (mis)placing them in the federally recognized *Native American* category. Native Hawaiians are, of course, recognized federally as members of the *Native Hawaiian or Other Pacific Islander* group, and, prior to 1997, as members of the *Asian or Pacific Islander* category. Ronald R. Sundstrom, *The Browning of America and the Evasion of Social Justice* (Albany: State University of New York Press, 2008), 60.

12. Although these two aims might seem contradictory, they have each been advanced by the far right from time to time.

13. Kim M. Williams, *Mark One or More: Civil Rights in Multiracial America* (Ann Arbor: University of Michigan Press, 2006), 122.

14. Or those who might discriminate against her due to perceiving her as white, although this seems a less likely proposition.

15. Leong, "Judicial Erasure of Mixed-Race Discrimination," 474.

16. Ibid., 549.

17. Ibid., 547.

18. Ibid., 554.

19. I appreciate the unfortunate fact that there is imperfection in my proposal, but the ultimate question is whether or not we want to actually steer a course away from our centuries-long dependence on biological race.

20. Alan Patreau, "Principal Called Mixed-Race Student a 'Mistake,'" *Atlanta Journal Constitution*, March 10, 1994, A3.

21. Spencer, *Spurious Issues*, 133.

22. It is important to understand that such a case would likely not be an instance of uncovering covert institutional discrimination so much as challenging direct discrimination, and as such would not rely on racial statistics except in a secondary sense of possibly establishing a pattern. The fact is that Afro-Americans are far, far away from holding enough positions of power such that they could actually be significant perpetuators of institutional discrimination.

23. Sundstrom, *Browning of America*, 100.

24. Leong, "Judicial Erasure of Mixed-Race Discrimination," 546–547.

25. Minkah Makalani, "A Biracial Identity or a New Race? The Historical Limitations and Political Implications of a Biracial Identity," *Souls* (Fall 2001): 92.

26. I refer to this event by the name given to it by its organizers; however, far from a "march" of any kind, my own eyewitness estimate of attendance was an audience of fewer than two hundred multiracial-identity supporters. For what is, as far as I know, the only comprehensive, firsthand account and scholarly analysis of this rally see Rainier Spencer, "Theorizing Multiracial Identity Politics in the United States," Ph.D. diss., Emory University, 1997, chap. 5.

27. Quoted in ibid., 184.

28. Jenifer L. Bratter, "Will 'Multiracial' Survive to the Next Generation?: The Racial Classification of Children of Multiracial Parents," *Social Forces* 86, no. 2 (December 2007): 827.

29. David R. Roediger, *How Race Survived U.S. History: From Settlement and Slavery to the Obama Phenomenon* (New York: Verso, 2008), 220.

30. Lise Funderburg, *Black, White, Other: Biracial Americans Talk About Race and Identity* (New York: William Morrow and Company, 1994), 197.

31. Bratter, "Will 'Multiracial' Survive to the Next Generation?" 842.

32. Ibid. According to Bratter, "household racial environments that include Asians may demonstrate a pattern of assimilation toward a white identity or maintain ethnic and racial distinctions of an Asian classification," 826. This coheres with the *multiraciality/honorary whiteness to full whiteness* trajectory model in that while some Asians may desire to maintain their Asian-ancestry links, those who are already part white may tend to move toward full whiteness.

33. Ibid., 843.

34. Ibid.

35. Jenifer Bratter, personal communication, November 4, 2009.

36. John Cloud, "Are Mixed-Race Children Better Adjusted?" *Time*, February 21, 2009, http://www.time.com/time/health/article/0,8599,1880467,00.html.

37. Eduardo Bonilla-Silva, "'New Racism,' Color-Blind Racism, and the Future of Whiteness in America," in *White Out: The Continuing Significance of Racism*, ed. Ashley W. Doane and Eduardo Bonilla-Silva, 271 (New York: Routledge, 2003).

38. Samira Kawash, *Dislocating the Color Line: Identity, Hybridity, and Singularity in African-American Literature* (Stanford: Stanford University Press, 1997), 129.

39. While it is true that population percentages alone do not determine white power, those who would preserve that power will do what they can to increase those numbers through the absorption of formerly excluded persons, as long as those persons are acceptable phenotypically and do not have sub-Saharan African ancestry. Both conditions must obtain.

40. Kawash, *Dislocating the Color Line*, 12.

41. Ibid., 132.

42. Williams, *Mark One or More*, 128.

43. Roediger, *How Race Survived U.S. History*, 219.

13

Mulatto (and White) Writers on Deconstructing Race

We have seen that contemporary multiracial identity in the persons of Generation Mix and in the ideology of the American Multiracial Identity Movement is accommodationist, protective of whiteness, and conservative of the US racial order. Where, then, is the path of true racial revolution, of true multiracial militancy? In the previous chapter, I suggested a change to the collection of racial statistics designed to move public consciousness forward in regard to the contingent nature of biological race, but clearly that will not be enough by itself. What would it take to challenge the notion of race such that it would eventually become as ridiculous a notion as a flat earth or a broom-riding witch? What would it take for everyone—including and most especially whites—to adopt raceless identities as our three cousins have, especially since the evidence of science has not yet proven persuasive enough? There are no easy answers to these questions, and given that whiteness is the sustainer and principle beneficiary of race in the United States, any potential solutions would seem to be necessarily neither close at hand nor easy to accomplish until some significant assault on the concept of whiteness itself can be launched. Perhaps all that can be done at this point is to continue the exhortation against race and whiteness, and also against the derivatives of race, such as multiracial identity, until such time as a more promising line of attack renders itself apparent.

Or could it be that a good portion of the necessary intellectual work, in addition to the input of science, has always been done for us? It may well be that the path to our postracial future might, somewhat ironically, be glimpsed via a look at the past. By this I mean that some of the most incisive writing against the false consciousness of race was authored decades and decades ago by persons whose qualifications to critique the concept of race were impeccable. I am referring of course to the American mulatto authors we reviewed in Chapter 4 in the contexts of racial passing and the question of innate mulatto marginality. Just as these authors towered intellectually over the sociological inventors of the marginal man hypothesis of their day, so too does their work still tower over the generally flimsy writing, both activist and academic, deployed in support of the American Multiracial Identity Movement and its goals today.

I want to examine a subset of three of those mulatto authors—Charles Chesnutt, James Weldon Johnson, and Nella Larsen—this time not for their work on racial passing, but for their work on deconstructing race itself, in order to see, with an eye on the future, what we might learn from them. I am convinced that what they have to tell us is considerable and still valid, and that even though we have failed to heed them thus far it is still not too late for us to do so now. Put simply, these individuals saw the null space that race did then and still represents today and strove to make that emptiness apparent to others through their writings. My goal is to demonstrate that in the context of Chesnutt, Johnson, and Larsen's critiques of race and racial identity, the simplistic analyses and pronouncements of the American Multiracial Identity Movement—from activist and scholar alike—pale into insignificance. As we have seen, not only do our mulatto authors prove that the marginal man theory was a lie, but, as we shall soon see, they also demonstrate that race and therefore multirace is a lie as well. We would do well to consider their critique, as in the intervening decades we have certainly done no better; indeed, we have done far worse. Following our mulatto authors, I shall also consider the work of several white authors of a similar mindset.

Clearly, simply acting the same way we always have in regard to race is not going to move us beyond false consciousness. Something that forces us to break with past practice is necessary for that kind of fundamental rupturing to take place. In terms of breaking with the past, it occurs to me that perhaps the concepts of heritage and inheritance might be a useful way to begin to think about this. One of the great crimes of American slavery and of the segregation era that followed it was (and still is) the disinheritance of millions of American mulattoes/Afro-Americans who would otherwise have been heirs or partial heirs to the estates of their white relations. Indeed, a fundamental reason for the persistence of Afro-American poverty and financial precariousness today is the fact that Afro-Americans have not had the advantage of being able to pass significant amounts of property—whether in terms of real estate, money, or, for that matter, whiteness—on to their progeny. So the question of inheritance, particularly lost inheritance, is a profound one for Afro-Americans especially.

Charles Chesnutt's remarkable novel of race, identity, inheritance, justice, and violence, *The Marrow of Tradition* (1901), provides a keen glimpse into the question of authentic racial identity and into the crime and injustice that racial identities allow.[1] The key characters in *The Marrow of Tradition* are two half sisters—Janet Miller, who is (part) black, and the slightly older Olivia Carteret, who is white. They are joined as sisters through their white father, Samuel Merkell. Janet and Olivia represent one of two sets of *virtual twins* (the other set being two men whom I will not consider here) Chesnutt presents us with in this novel in order to problematize our thinking about race and racial identity. That Chesnutt wants us to see these two women as twins is clear through several remarks repeated throughout the novel, such as the following one from Mammy Jane: "'Dis yer Janet, w'at's Mis' 'Livy's half-sister, is ez much like her ez ef dey wuz twins. Folks sometimes takes 'em fer one ernudder.'"[2] A similar example comes by way of the narrator during a particularly poignant episode at the climax of the narrative, as Chesnutt emphasizes the essentiality that there is no actual difference between Janet and Olivia, stressing both their twinned sisterhood as well as their nearly identical looks: "The two women stood confronting each other across the body of the dead child, mute witness of this first meeting between two children of the same father. Standing thus face to face, each under the stress of the deepest emotions, the resemblance between them was even more striking than it had seemed to [Janet's husband, Dr. William] Miller when he had admitted Mrs. Carteret to the house."[3]

As Samira Kawash describes, "Chesnutt's emphasis on the physical similarity between Janet and Olivia forces the reader to acknowledge the arbitrariness of the racial distinction that separates them."[4] Specifically, "through the twinned relationship between Olivia and Janet, the novel addresses the racial division codified in segregation law, asking, what sustains identity in relation to the color line? What counts as difference?"[5] The question of inheritance comes into play because through the white-supremacist chicanery of Olivia's aunt, Janet's black mother Julia was wrongly dispossessed of her inheritance of $10,000 and a modest portion of Merkell's property. And through her mother's dispossession, Janet is thereby disinherited as well, while her sister Olivia has received the entire estate. The latter would in any case have inherited the vast majority of it, but instead the entire estate has been stolen for her, as it were. It is important to note that after Olivia's mother dies and before Janet is born, Merkell marries Julia legally, making both Julia and Janet legitimate heirs in addition to his already legitimate daughter Olivia.

Thus, Chesnutt arrays for us two equivalent lines of descent extending in opposite directions from Samuel Merkell—a white line consisting of Olivia, her new-born son Dodie, and their future descendants, and a black line consisting of Janet, her young son (unnamed in the text), and their future descendants. These two lines have a mathematical, perhaps even an aesthetic, equivalence, but Chesnutt intends for us to see that they are in no sense equal—at least not under the reign of segregation and the color line. To be sure, they should be equal, not merely on some abstract moral basis, which would have been powerful enough, but on a strictly legal basis. In other words, even were Merkell and Julia not married, there would have been a strong moral basis for averring that their daughter should be considered equal to Merkell's slightly older white daughter. Such relationships represent, after all, the very history of American mulattoes/Afro-Americans in the United States under slavery. However, Chesnutt goes one step further and makes Janet a completely legal heir, leaving us to ponder both the nature of her supposed essential difference from her virtual twin Olivia, as well as the violence perpetrated by white power/white supremacy in the crime of Janet's disinheritance.

One is reminded of a similar critique in an earlier novel, Richard Hildreth's *The White Slave* (1836, 1852), in which the mulatto slave Archy Moore laments the fact of his forcible parting from his informal wife Cassy (who is also, although known to him but unknown to her, his half sister), by their mutual father and owner, Colonel Charles Moore, who desires his daughter Cassy for his own sexual pleasure. Commenting on the hypocritical attention paid to the "*decencies of life*," Archy asks how could that very hypocrisy "that refused to acknowledge our paternity, or to recognize any relationship between us, pretend at the same time, and on the sole ground of relationship, to forbid our union?"[6] Both Hildreth and Chesnutt, the former criticizing slavery and the latter criticizing Redemption, name and indict white supremacy for quite capriciously disrupting family, paternal acknowledgment, and inheritance, to the benefit of whites and the detriment of Afro-Americans.

We might accept an analogous motive using virtual twinning in George Washington Cable's *The Grandissimes* (1880), in which the acknowledged half siblings, the quadroon Honoré Grandissime, f. m. c. (free man of color), and his white half brother (also named) Honoré Grandissime (see Chapter 3), along with the unacknowledged half siblings, the quadroon Palmyre Philosphe and her white sibling Aurora De Grapion, are, as in the case of Chesnutt, utilized to illustrate the profound and divergent effect of race on the happiness, life chances, and social acceptance of the respective black and white siblings.[7]

Certainly Chesnutt provides a metaphor for the national crime committed by whiteness against Africans and Afro-Americans under slavery and segregation, but there is significantly more to it than merely that. What I am interested in is Chesnutt's deliberative positioning of these two sisters— their identical appearance, their each having married a man of substance, their each having given birth to a young son—and his challenge to readers to render a legitimate answer as to how these two sisters are not only different from each other, but how they are, as the color line would have it, binary opposites. In this, I think Chesnutt is demonstrating that just as it took illegitimate means to perpetrate the disinheritance of Julia and Janet, so too does it require illegitimate means to separate Janet and Olivia and place them on opposite sides of a presumed and enforced but actually nonexistent color line. The problem is not that Janet is really biracial and therefore not black; the problem is that race and racial identity are themselves fictions created and maintained by whites in order to provide the "ill-gotten gain" of whiteness as property to some people at the expense of others who can be marked by a null sign of difference that does not have a prior existence apart from the naming that first creates it as difference.[8]

While presenting something less of such an overt critique, there is a suggestion of virtual twinned sisterhood in Mayne Reid's *The Quadroon* (1856) as well, a suggestion that serves to raise similarly relevant questions of sameness/difference and racial equity. The characters I have in mind are the Louisiana plantation heiress, twenty-one-year-old Eugénie Besançon, and her nineteen-year-old quadroon maid, Aurore Besançon. The reader is not told whether Aurore was born on the Besançon plantation or purchased elsewhere and then brought there, although one is given to understand that she has been on the plantation for quite some time, as through the family's longtime black servant, Scipio Besançon, we are informed that Eugénie's father, "'Ole Mass'r Sançon, berry good to de coloured people—teach many ob um read de books—'specially 'Rore. 'Rore he 'struckt read, write, many, many tings.'"[9] Such favoritism on the part of Aurore's owner could very well be linked to issues of paternity. Moreover, Reid's white narrator-hero, Edouard, who also becomes Aurore's lover, muses over the latter's inordinately special status on the plantation: "For reasons I could not fathom, the treatment of the quadroon was, and had always been, different from the other slaves of the plantation. It was not the whiteness of her skin—her beauty neither—that had gained her this distinction. . . . There was some very different reason for the kindness shown her, though *I* could only *guess* at it."[10] Continuing his musings, Edouard notes that Aurore "had been tenderly reared alongside her young mistress, had received almost as good an education, and, in fact, was treated rather as a *sister* than a *slave*."[11]

Where I would in a very specific way link Eugénie and Aurore to Chesnutt's treatment of Olivia and Janet is in the divergent parallelism of both sister/twin sets' physical selves and social existences. Scipio points out as much when he first informs Edouard that Aurore is a quadroon: "'She be a gal ob colour—nebber mind—she white as young missa herseff. Missa larf and say so many, many time—but fr'all daat dar am great difference—one rich lady—t'other poor slave.'"[12] For all their similarities in terms of beauty, talent, intellect, perceived whiteness, the likelihood that they are sisters (and therefore virtual twins), and the noteworthy fact that they both fall in love with Edouard, there is indeed a great difference between Eugénie and Aurore—a legal, albeit arbitrary, difference that cannot be justified by any appeal to rationality.[13] As in the case of Chesnutt's *The Marrow of Tra-*

dition, Reid's *The Quadroon* likewise complicates and thereby interrogates the illogic of race, condemning its use in separating these two women by serving as the vehicle of an illegitimate prefiguring of their respective destinies in opposite directions as white and black.[14]

In the more than one hundred years since *The Marrow of Tradition* was published, the United States has failed, continuously and pitifully, to rise to Chesnutt's challenge. And we see that by failing to address that challenge, we have remained firmly in the grip of biological race and thereby subject to the path of destruction it brings in the form of continued white supremacy, ruined lives, and stolen opportunities. Chesnutt himself points out that "by modern research the unity of the human race has been proved (if it needed any proof to the careful or fair-minded observer), and the differentiation of races by selection and environment has been so stated as to prove itself. Greater emphasis has been placed upon environment as a factor in ethnic development, and what has been called 'the vulgar theory of race,' as accounting for progress and culture, has been relegated to the limbo of exploded dogmas."[15] But of course it has not been so relegated, as the "vulgar theory of race" lives on both in Americans' continuing belief in biological race as well as in sociology's euphemistic recoding and reification of that "vulgar" fallacy as a social reality. That it also lives on in the modern-day assertion of multiracial identity hardly requires pointing out.

Chesnutt made this statement concerning race as an "exploded dogma" in one of three brief essays published in the *Boston Evening Transcript* during the late summer of 1900, just prior to publication of *The Marrow of Tradition*. These three serialized essays constitute the complete piece, "The Future American."[16] Readers of those essays might be tempted to think that their very interesting contents countervail the portrait of Chesnutt's views that I have thus far presented, as in those essays Chesnutt seems to take a very different, indeed troubling, approach to resolving the race dilemma. As Kawash summarizes: "Chesnutt advocates a scheme of large-scale racial amalgamation as the solution to America's race problem."[17] In fact, Chesnutt offers this vision of racial reconciliation via a hypothetical story of governmentally enforced racial exogamy and progressive mixing so close in the basics to the Nation of Islam myth of Dr. Yacub and his creation of white people as to make one wonder whether Wallace Fard or Elijah Poole had perhaps somehow come across and read Chesnutt's "The Future American" during their respective early days in Detroit.[18] Indeed, interestingly, if not bizarrely, Ronald Sundstrom, in agreeing with Orlando Patterson, avers that the "solution" to distributive justice in the United States, "appears to be asserting that justice is found in the marital embrace of folks outside of one's race, and this message is especially aimed at darker peoples."[19]

Continuing with Kawash's summary: "This future amalgamated American race would be predominantly white (as was the population) but would be able to make no claims to racial purity because it would have absorbed and assimilated the blood of Indian and black. The result would be an end to racial struggle. . . . Chesnutt seems to imagine the possibility of eliminating the very division that is the basis for racial distinction, and thus racial prejudice. One is struck by Chesnutt's extremely mechanical understanding of race as presented in this essay; in his mathematical calculations of the effects of racial crossing only blood is at issue. Questions of culture and the complexities of racism do not arise. Moreover, Chesnutt does not balk at the idea that black and Indian *ought* to blend in and be absorbed; implicitly, it is *their* difference that stands in the way of national harmony."[20] Clearly, such a primacy of whiteness is a position that would accord, as I described in Chapter 7, with the desires of the racial state as well as with the ideology and goals of the American Multiracial Identity Movement, a troubling development to be sure, especially given that I have utilized Chesnutt as an exemplar of antiracialist philosophy in my argument thus far in this chapter.

Kawash is troubled as well and seeks to rehabilitate Chesnutt from a potentially damaging and otherwise very much out of character interpretation of him as essentially valorizing whiteness and devaluing blackness: "Chesnutt is more complicated, I think, than such a characterization would allow. While the 'Future Americans' of the eponymous essay seem based on a hopelessly myopic view of racial realities, the conclusion of *Marrow* also points toward a future American but this time in a manner finely attuned to the question of justice and the possibility of an end to violence."[21] Kawash's fine analysis does Chesnutt credit, but it is in a very real sense an unnecessary effort at rehabilitation. This is because, at least in my reading of "The Future American," I do not think Chesnutt is in the main at all serious in those essays. Let me be clear that I do not claim to be a Chesnutt expert any more than I claim to be an expert on any of the American mulatto authors whose writings I have reviewed and utilized throughout this book. I have merely read those authors honestly and have then attempted to apply my best understanding to their work. So at the risk of repeating someone else's conclusion possibly rendered decades ago or, alternatively, simply making a fool of myself, I submit the argument that Chesnutt's "The Future American" is largely "tongue-in-cheek," perhaps even anticipating one of Johnson's motivations in *The Autobiography of an Ex-Colored Man* through the use of a barely submerged threat to the very boundaries of whiteness.

I aver this not only because Chesnutt's thoughts in "The Future American" are so much at odds with his comprehensive argument concerning race, inheritance, and violence in *The Marrow of Tradition*, but also because so much of what he writes in "The Future American" is self-contradictory specifically within the narrow scope of the essay itself. Again, at the risk of demonstrating complete ignorance on my part, I am convinced that Chesnutt cannot have meant to be taken seriously in "The Future American." Consider that in the installment titled "A Stream of Dark Blood in the Veins of the Southern Whites," he writes of white-appearing persons who have a "strain of Negro blood," that such persons "are white to all intents and purposes" and that they are "in all conscience entitled to any advantage accompanying this status."[22] These are strange words coming from the author who had surely by this time already completed writing *The Marrow of Tradition*, with its strong and open indictment of white supremacy for the thefts that have allowed it to gain and maintain power.

That Chesnutt cannot possibly mean what he says in "The Future American" concerning the justified entitlements of whites is proven in the next week's installment, "A Complete Race-Amalgamation Likely to Occur," in which he writes that "the white people of the present generation did not make their civilization; they inherited it ready made, and much of the wealth which is so strong a factor in their power was created by the unpaid labor of the colored people."[23] How, then, can whites, whether fully so or not, be "in all conscience entitled to any advantage accompanying this status"? The answer is that they cannot, as Kawash points out in her analysis of *The Marrow of Tradition*, most particularly in the context of Olivia's advantage at the expense of her sister Janet. "In terms of both their father's property and Janet's desire for recognition, Chesnutt's position is clear: Olivia's status and privilege are the result of theft. Although Olivia is deeply troubled by her dawning conscience, the perpetuation of this crime is the necessary price of her whiteness. In his portrayal of Olivia's guilt and Janet's desire, Chesnutt suggests that the exclusive privilege of whiteness is the ill-gotten gain of a crime for which blackness must suffer the consequences."[24]

But this is not all, for via an unusual but significant choice of words throughout "The Future American" Chesnutt signals that he is indeed acting as an unreliable essayist. He does this, for instance, when he writes of "the *apparently intense* prejudice against color which prevails in the United States."[25] Nor is this a mistake, as in the very same paragraph he repeats his assertion that "this prejudice in the United States is *more apparent than real*."[26] One cannot conceive of Chesnutt feeling honestly that the race prejudice he describes so vividly in *The Marrow of Tradition*, a description based on actual events to which his own family members in North Carolina were subjected only two years earlier, is merely "apparent" and not so much "real." Moreover, Chesnutt offers that "the present anti-Negro legislation is but a *temporary* reaction," and that the vicious race massacre that took place in Wilmington, North Carolina, in 1898 (which forms the basis of the Wellington, North Carolina, massacre in the novel) was merely a "*temporary* success," contradicting the aura of bitterness and hopelessness that pervades the climaxing chapters of the novel.[27]

Despite Chesnutt's questionable references in "The Future American," to the "temporary" and merely "apparent" reactionary racism of Southern whites, it is clear when one is inside *The Marrow of Tradition* that the state of things is not envisioned as being temporary. There is no solution either provided or waiting on some shadowy horizon. One feels only bleakness and hopelessness. To be sure, there is Olivia's promise to patch things up with Janet after the latter has renounced her sister's belated recognition—a recognition extended only because Janet's physician husband is the sole person left in town who can save the life of Olivia's dying son—but it is a domineering and pretentious promise that disavows Janet's right and personal authority to renounce her sister as she had herself been renounced by that very sister for decades.

Replicating the naked white power that has been unleashed against the blacks of Wellington, it is as though Olivia is indicating that she will have her way in terms of becoming close to her sister regardless of Janet's wishes to the contrary. If, on the other hand, one focuses on Olivia's name, derived as it is from the word *olive*, and then invokes the image of the olive branch as a symbol of peace, perhaps Chesnutt intends for Olivia's change of heart toward her sister (and, presumably then, toward blacks in general) to be sincere, and that the white woman therefore represents the path toward racial reconciliation. Or perhaps Kawash is correct that it is possible to read Chesnutt as intending for racial reconciliation to come by way of the symbol of Olivia's son, Dodie, but, on either account, I still affirm that sycophantic concepts such as "temporary racism" and "apparent prejudice" are inappropriate descriptors of the world Chesnutt himself presents in *The Marrow of Tradition* and, as such, refute themselves in "The Future American" even as they are read.[28]

But this still leaves open the question of why Chesnutt would in the first place provide such false commentary. As I intimated previously, I think the answer lies in an anticipation of what Johnson would accomplish much more fully in *The Autobiography of an Ex-Colored Man* some dozen years later. First of all, it is important to see that "The Future American" is nothing less than the white supremacist's ultimate nightmare. Miscegenation and insistent, inexorable racial amalgamation represent deep threats to white racial identity itself, depending as it does on reliable knowledge that one's ancestry is free of blackness. In this connection, "The Future American" invokes precisely the sentiments contained in the infamous hoax pamphlet, *Miscegenation*, published nearly a year prior to the presidential election of 1864 in a failed attempt to link Abraham Lincoln and the Republican Party with the promotion of widespread racial amalgamation.[29] As does the *Miscegenation* pamphlet, Chesnutt's essay evokes—and indeed empathizes with via its calm, matter-of-fact tone—the specter of racial amalgamation being just around the corner, a sure threat to white identity.[30] Beyond this,

Chesnutt also pokes holes in white identity in a number of ways, including several examples of the uncomfortable fact that many whites have hidden blackness in their family trees of which they are unaware.

I think the ultimate purpose of Chesnutt's unreliable essay is found on the last pages of the final installment, "A Complete Race-Amalgamation Likely to Occur," of "The Future American." Commenting on the previously mentioned "temporary success in North Carolina" of vicious white supremacy, Chesnutt notes that "it is much easier . . . to knock the race down and rob it of its rights once and for all," and that such an effort, "makes it easy to maintain a superiority which it might in the course of a short time require some little effort to keep up."[31] Beyond the fact that this description belies the notion of a "temporary success," Chesnutt's purpose becomes clear as he discusses the implication of continuing antiblackness and white supremacy: "This very proscription, however, political and civil at the South, social all over the country, varying somewhat in degree, will, unless very soon relaxed, prove a powerful factor in the mixture of the races. If it is only by becoming white that colored people and their children are to enjoy the rights and dignities of citizenship, they will have every incentive to 'lighten the breed,' to use a current phrase, that they may claim the white man's privileges as soon as possible. That this motive is already at work may be seen in the enormous extent to which certain 'face bleachers' and 'hair straighteners' are advertised in the newspapers printed for circulation among the colored people."[32] So, continued white supremacy will cause blacks to try to make themselves white through the use of chemical products or by progressive lightening via the strategic selection of marriage partners until one's descendants can pass as white, the latter representing the same threat underlying much of *The Autobiography of an Ex-Colored Man*, and a strategy that novel's unnamed narrator chooses ultimately for himself.

Interestingly, in *The Marrow of Tradition*, Chesnutt includes as a minor plot device the use of face-bleaching and hair-straightening products by Jerry, a black character who serves as a symbol of racial accommodationism. Chesnutt clearly disapproves of such products, and causes Jerry's dark face, after he uses such a product, to be "splotched with brown and yellow patches," which Jerry then tries unsuccessfully to cover up "by the application of printer's ink."[33] Underneath the humor of this scene lie Chesnutt's dual critiques of white supremacy's unrecovered theft from black people and of the notion that black people should try to become white, as the narrator says of Jerry that "he had realized that it was a distinct advantage to be white—an advantage which white people had utilized to secure all the best things in the world; and he had entertained the vague hope that by changing his complexion he might share this prerogative."[34] So again, Chesnutt's true thoughts in *The Marrow of Tradition* contradict the unreliable thoughts he provides in "The Future American."

Finally, at the close of the penultimate paragraph of the last serialized essay in "The Future American," Chesnutt lays out the white supremacist's coming nightmare of full racial amalgamation should race prejudice continue unabated in the United States: "That it must come in the United States, sooner or later, seems to be a foregone conclusion, as the result of natural law—lex dura, sed tamen lex—a hard pill, but one which must be swallowed. There can manifestly be no such thing as a peaceful and progressive civilization in a nation divided by two warring races, and homogeneity of type, at least in externals, is a necessary condition of harmonious racial progress."[35] But of course Chesnutt cannot, does not, believe that physical "homogeneity" is "a necessary condition of racial progress," his positioning of Janet and Olivia as physically homogeneous virtual twins who nonetheless repudiate each other being a primary proof of this position. And even should Olivia's promise of reconciliation be sincere, such reconciliation will not come *because* she and Janet look the same. Rather, by using the example of the characters Janet and Olivia, Chesnutt shows throughout *The Marrow of Tradition* that biological race is an illogical fantasy that is unsustainable outside the bounds of the very race prejudice that creates and perpetuates it.

Chesnutt's primary point in "The Future American," therefore, is not to advocate for racial amalgamation or to argue that such amalgamation is inevitable; rather, his purpose is to deliver to white supremacists an ultimatum to give up their race prejudice or face the fact of human nature that those blacks who can do so will indeed pass as white. In other words, some racial amalgamation will indeed be inevitable if blacks are continually faced with a bleak world in which whiteness retains its supremacy by feeding on blackness. Surely, Chesnutt wants to see an end to race prejudice and to biological race as well, but the purpose of "The Future American" is to attack what is perhaps the easier of the two problems, race prejudice, by an appeal to the vanity and insecurity of white racial identity.

As I have mentioned several times, this is precisely the strategy of James Weldon Johnson in *The Autobiography of an Ex-Colored Man* (1912), which can be seen in the "publisher's preface to the first edition . . . in which the writer notes that 'these pages . . . reveal the unsuspected fact that prejudice against the Negro is exerting a pressure which . . . is actually and constantly forcing an unascertainable number of fair-complexioned coloured people over into the white race.'"[36] As Kawash asks: "Is this the nervous voice of a white writer or the warning voice of a black writer? It is not known who wrote this preface; perhaps it was Johnson himself. But whichever tone we hear, the message is clear: the white race is not the white race that it seems; it has in fact been infiltrated by an unknowable black presence. This is an 'unsuspected fact;' 'they,' those fair-complexioned colored people, might be anywhere, might be anyone. Apparent whiteness is no guarantee of true whiteness. There is no longer any way to tell the true whites from the imposters. This uncertainty, which might be seen on one side as paranoia and on the other as opportunity, is exactly the point of passing."[37]

If we keep this preface in mind along with the important fact that the novel was published initially as an anonymous work, the following first paragraph of the first chapter reiterates this potentially threatening sense of revelation, danger, and excitement: "I know that in writing the following pages I am divulging the great secret of my life, the secret which for some years I have guarded far more carefully than any of my earthly possessions; and it is a curious study to me to analyse the motives which prompt me to do it. I feel that I am led by the same impulse which forces the un-found-out criminal to take somebody into his confidence, although he knows that the act is likely, even almost certain, to lead to his undoing. I know that I am playing with fire, and I feel the thrill which accompanies that most fascinating pastime; and, back of it all, I think I find a sort of savage and diabolical desire to gather up all the little tragedies of my life, and turn them into a joke on society."[38]

These are some very seductive promises being made by Johnson here. Note in particular the language: "great secret," "playing with fire," and "savage and diabolical desire." One of the first things we ought to consider is the audience to whom Johnson is writing. To whom is he going to be divulging this great secret? Who would be more surprised or interested by Johnson's thrilling confession—the white or the black reader? It would seem safe to assume that he is writing primarily to white readers. Black readers, after all, would be familiar with stories such as Johnson's, and they would find it to be no great revelation to them. This is not to say that Afro-American readers did not find passing narratives to be of interest. They did, to be sure, but the *inside peek* that Johnson seems to promise would, on the surface view, simply be the intimate details of the very black life that Afro-Americans would already know. But from a white perspective, however, the ever-present white paranoia over invisible blackness taken together with Johnson's cryptic comment about turning the tragedies of his life "into a practical joke on society," threaten a cataclysmic eruption of the formerly stable white universe.

There is some difficulty in interpreting Johnson insofar as his unnamed narrator also appears to be an unreliable one. The most obvious clue in this regard is when the narrator suggests that Harriet Beecher Stowe's 1852 novel, *Uncle Tom's Cabin*, provides a realistic portrayal of slavery in the South: "I do not think it is claiming too much to say that *Uncle Tom's Cabin* was a fair and truthful panorama of slavery."[39] Some readers might contend that the narrator is indeed meant to be reliable in making this statement, based on his explanation that Stowe presents good and bad white characters as well as good and bad black characters. However, as Johnson was surely aware, such diversity of characterizations does not in itself make the narrative an accurate representation of slavery, which is a different question entirely. Moreover, there is an additional clue in the parallel structuring of the paragraph, for at the end of the same paragraph in which the narrator claims that *Uncle Tom's Cabin* is a "fair and truthful panorama of slavery," he muses on the relationship between his always absent white father and his late Afro-American mother, saying of his mother that "she died firmly believing that he loved her more than any other woman in the world. Perhaps she was right. Who knows?"[40] Her pathetic belief in the love of the white man who moved her away when he married a white woman and who would not answer her dying letter is clearly meant to be seen as having been as false as the narrator's assertions regarding the "fairness and truthfulness" of *Uncle Tom's Cabin.*[41]

To this we might add the narrator's bizarre and highly feminine description of himself, a description that nearly matches the description of Eliza and George's son Harry in *Uncle Tom's Cabin*. First, consider Stowe's description of Harry: "Here the door opened, and a small quadroon boy, between four and five years of age, entered the room. There was something in his appearance remarkably beautiful and engaging. His black hair, fine as floss silk, hung in glossy curls about his round, dimpled face, while a pair of large dark eyes, full of fire and softness, looked out from beneath the rich, long lashes, as he peered curiously into the apartment. A gay robe of scarlet and yellow plaid, carefully made and neatly fitted, set off to advantage the dark and rich style of his beauty; and a certain comic air of assurance, blended with bashfulness, showed that he had been not unused to being petted and noticed by his master."[42]

Then, compare the foregoing to the narrator's self-description, as he studies himself in a mirror for the first time since *learning* that he is actually black: "I had often heard people say to my mother: 'What a pretty boy you have!' I was accustomed to hear remarks about my beauty; but now, for the first time, I became conscious of it and recognized it. I noticed the ivory whiteness of my skin, the beauty of my mouth, the size and liquid darkness of my eyes, and how the long, black lashes that fringed and shaded them produced an effect that was strangely fascinating even to me. I noticed the softness and glossiness of my dark hair that fell in waves over my temples, making my forehead appear whiter than it really was."[43] The description is nearly identical to Stowe's, and considering that Johnson also mentions Stowe's novel specifically, it cannot be mere coincidence. Yet given that Harry is a fictional character, what should we make of the narrator painting his own appearance in precisely the same strokes? It may be that Johnson is indicating, via his narrator's feminized and fictional appearance, that what we see when we look at that narrator is not reality but is instead illusory.

As mentioned in my earlier discussion of Johnson's novel (see Chapter 4), the narrator spends much of it moving from place to place. While in

Florida, our narrator announces that he "had formulated a theory of what it was to be coloured; and was now getting the practice."[44] So, the question to ask here is just what type of passing, if any, is going on at this point in the narrative? Can we say with any plausibility that the unnamed narrator is actually passing for black at this point? In other words, is he a black man who formerly passed as white (albeit unknowingly) and who is now trying to return to his roots? Is he really a white man passing as black or is he, in fact, neither passing for either?

Kawash questions whether the narrator is properly any race at all. She points out that his whiteness as a child is inauthentic because he did not know his mother was black, rather like a similar doubled situation in an interesting work by Mark Twain that I shall address later in this chapter. Further, she argues that the narrator's "blackness is also a copy, a specular image of the blackness he observes in others," which returns us to the question of whether the narrator was really black in Florida or was merely performing blackness.[45] We might note as well the instructive choice of words he uses after describing his life in Jacksonville: "In this way I *passed* three years."[46] The narrator tries consciously to become black, but we must decide if he ever accomplishes his goal. Is he black in Florida, is he black in New York, is he black in Europe, and finally, is he black on his return to the Deep South? And if the answers to any of these questions is "no," is he then white in those instances in which he is not black?

Kawash argues that "the preface has positioned the reader as a spectator who will, through the eyes of the narrator, 'glimpse behind the scenes of this race drama which is here being enacted.' But, in fact, the narrator is just as much a spectator as the reader."[47] The surface reading merely follows the story along, accepting everything the narrator says as fact, while the more complex reading refuses to trust the narrator and questions his observations as to their truthfulness. Thus, Kawash informs us, "Once we suspend the commonsense reading of *The Autobiography* as being about a black man who passes for white, we are constantly faced with the difficulty of determining what is passing and what is not."[48] In other words, we cannot accept that the narrator is passing if we do not know what his true identity really is, and I do not mean his lack of a true name. The fact is that one can argue that the narrator is not clearly either white or black, and that therefore it is possible that he is either *never* passing or is *always* passing.

Rather than being seen as a black man passing for white, or even as a white man passing for black, Kawash avers that Johnson's narrator defies the possibility of true racial identity. It is not that he really is black but looks white, but that in the novel he clearly is really neither one nor the other. Johnson's message is that there really is no racial identity, that everything we claim as identity is really just a copy and an imitation of something that was already copied previously. To be sure, not all passing novels or passing films can be read or viewed in this way. Johnson's novel, because of the particular way he wrote it—the lack of names, the inauthenticity of any racial identity the narrator tries on for size—is a unique articulation of passing that clearly is in a class of its own.

For those who would hold that Johnson's narrator really is a black man passing for white, we must ask what this blackness consists in. He looks white and once thought he was white; but, even so, how is he then suddenly black? The reality is that there is not any true, authentic, essential, inner racial identity that we either correspond to correctly or fail to correspond to correctly. If one transcends the standard reading of *The Autobiography of an Ex-Colored Man* by problematizing the narrator's assertions and by refusing to take his word at face value, one begins to see that while he tells us he is a black man, he in fact only *wants* to be a black man. And indeed, when he thinks he is a white boy, he is wrong as well. The narrator's thoughts and experiences, on a close and careful reading, belie the possibility of a stable, discrete racial identity—and not just for him, but for anyone. In this regard, we can note the narrator's lament that "sometimes it seems to me that I have never really been a Negro, that I have been only a privileged spectator of their inner life."[49] To attempt to argue for one racial identity over the other is to be duped by the narrative; on the other hand, to realize that such arguments are irrelevant because there is in the first place no racial identity is to grasp and understand the narrative.

Significantly, Johnson's novel begins and ends with the notions of heritage and inheritance—specifically, what he does not receive from his father (the rights and property that would pass normally from father to son), as well as what he does not receive from his mother (information, at least initially, about his true ancestry) on the one hand, and what he decides he will pass on to his children (nothing of their black heritage) on the other. He also questions the legitimacy of presumed white heritage via the novel's constant insinuation throughout that some American mulattoes who can escape racism through passing will do so (even unknowingly, as in the case of his children), throwing into question the heritage of every white person, and throwing into question as well the inheritances they may think they are passing forward but that may well be tainted with invisible blackness against which there can be no defense.

William Faukner, in *Absalom, Absalom!* (1936), suggests a similar threat when the only remaining descendant, male or female, of the erstwhile estate builder Thomas Sutpen is his part-Negro great-grandson, Jim Bond, grandson of his disowned son Charles Bon (see Chapter 2) and his octoroon wife, and son of Charles Etienne Saint-Valery Bon and a Negro woman. Commenting on this situation at the novel's finale, Faulkner has the white character Shreve McCannon say: "I think that in time the Jim Bonds are going to conquer the western hemisphere. Of course it won't quite be in our time and of course as they spread toward the poles they will bleach out again like the rabbits and the birds so, so they won't show up so sharp against the snow. But it will still be Jim Bond; and so in a few thousand years, I who regard you will also have sprung from the loins of African kings."[50]

Likewise, Pauline Hopkins, in *Hagar's Daughter* (1901–1902), invokes the provocative specter of an invisible blackness that has already infiltrated American whiteness, and that menaces white heritage and inheritance, by having a white newspaper editor remark on the recent discovery that one of Washington, DC's most upstanding citizens, wife of the late Senator Zenas Bowen, has Negro ancestry: "'This story, showing, as it does, the ease with which beautiful half-breeds may enter our best society without detection, is a source of anxiety to the white citizens of our country. At this rate the effects of slavery can never be eradicated, and our most distinguished families are not immune from contact with this mongrel race. Mrs. Bowen has our sympathy, but we cannot, even for such a leader as she has been, unlock the gates of caste and bid her enter. *Posterity forbids it.*'"[51] These examples by Faulkner and Hopkins mesh perfectly with the threat of invisible blackness to white heritage and inheritance posed by Chesnutt and Johnson.

In Nella Larsen's *Quicksand* (1928), one might say that the mulatto main character has something of a fixation on clothing, the narrator informing us that "Helga Crane loved clothes, elaborate ones."[52] It is a fixation, however, that is perhaps appropriate given that her clothes adorn what amounts to physical perfection. Helga Crane is beautiful, stunningly so, a testament to Larsen's powers of description and mood. It would do well to get a sense of Larsen's writing via her initial description of Helga: "A slight girl of twenty-two years, with narrow, sloping shoulders and delicate, but well-turned, arms and legs, she had, none the less, an air of radiant, careless health. In vivid green and gold negligee and glistening brocaded mules, deep sunk in the big high-backed chair, against whose dark tapestry her sharply cut face, with skin like yellow satin, was distinctly outlined, she was—to use a hackneyed word—attractive. Black, very broad brows over soft, yet penetrating eyes, and a pretty mouth, whose sensitive and sensuous lips had a slight questioning petulance and a tiny dissatisfied droop, were the features on which the observer's attention would fasten; though her nose was good, her ears delicately chiseled, and her curly blue-black hair plentiful and always straying in a little wayward, delightful way. Just then it was tumbled, falling unrestrained about her face and on her shoulders."[53]

I do not mean to imply that Helga's clothing represents in any way a main storyline of *Quicksand*, for there are a number of arguably far more important avenues from which to analyze the novel. I have chosen to begin by concentrating on Helga's clothes, though, because they are such a potent symbol of something else Larsen undertakes in both *Quicksand* and *Passing*, and that is her sustained critique of authentic identities. In Martha Cutter's words, "the assumption of only one guise or form of passing causes Larsen's characters to become stable, static, fixed in their meaning, entrapped within social definitions. To assume a single identity in a world in which identity itself is often a performance—a mask, a public persona—is to endure psychological suicide. Larsen's novel *Quicksand* demonstrates the fallacy of belief in a 'true self' most clearly through the character Helga Crane: Helga attempts repeatedly to find a true identity, only to learn that no such thing exists, only a variety of social roles."[54] Likewise, at various critical points in the novel Larsen uses Helga's clothing as symbols or representations of uncertainty, error, and the impossibility of true authenticity in terms of identity. Larsen's message is that everything is performance, performance that requires clothing and masks to make it complete but that nonetheless can provide only the mirage and not the substance of authenticity.[55]

Upon making the decision to soon embark on a sailing voyage to Denmark in order to visit with relatives, Helga considers clothing for a party she is to attend that evening. She decides on a "cobwebby black net touched with orange, which she had bought last spring in a fit of extravagance and never worn, because on getting it home both she and [her friend] Anne had considered it too *décolleté*, and too *outré*."[56] In Helga's words—which are also the words of an unreliable speaker—this skimpy outfit "would be a symbol" that "she was about to fly."[57] Yet, in Denmark, Helga's aunt declares the orange and black net with the low neckline to be "too high."[58] While acknowledging that different people and different societies of course have different standards for what is taken to be appropriate clothing, I believe Larsen is pointing to something far more significant here in her metaphorical use of this dress. The dress represents Helga herself in the sense that in and of itself it is cut neither too low nor too high. There is no singular essentiality that simply *is* the appropriateness of the dress, just as there is no singular essentiality that *is* Helga Crane.

It is Helga's unsuccessful search for such a singular, essential identity that serves as the driving force of the novel as she moves from one unsatisfying identity to another. "As soon as she lets go of a particular social identity, however, as soon as she stops passing for something, she feels a terrifying sense of 'apprehension' and even vertigo. . . . Throughout the novel, such moments of vertigo mark Helga's abandonment of a specific social identity—her sensation before she has located a new social role. Cut free from social restrictions, Helga experiences not liberation but fear and a sensation of falling. Indeed, she may be falling into a void of nothingness— the nothingness of identity stripped from all its social moorings. In these moments, Helga is confronting the possibility that perhaps she has no 'essential self' to discover; she is glimpsing the idea that perhaps identity itself is a mask, a social and public role, rather than a reflection of some core of being."[59]

Moreover, Helga's assessment of the dress's symbolism is unreliable, for in Denmark Helga does not fly but instead becomes a "new and strange species of pet dog being proudly exhibited," "A decoration. A curio. A peacock."[60] Helga enjoys the new attention initially, but eventually comes to resent it and her aunt's insistence on Helga's dressing up in so spectacular and ultimately degrading a fashion. Helga's Aunt Katrina is attempting to use Helga in order to raise her own social standing in Copenhagen and does not seem to appreciate Helga apart from that personal desire. Thus, there are multiple performances being enacted here. Helga is performing a degrading role that she does not care for in return for clothing that, while exotic and certainly expensive, is not what she would choose to wear on her own. Aunt Katrina is pretending to be doing this for Helga's own good while she is in fact looking out primarily for herself. Far from "flying," Helga is once again falling due to an inability to find her authentic self.

Helga's departure from Denmark is hastened by her irremediable contretemps with the aristocratic painter Axel Olsen, whom Katrina wants Helga to marry. At one point Olsen says to Helga: "'I didn't want to love you, but I had to. That is the truth. I make of myself a present to you. For love.'"[61] Yet what is the truth? It cannot be Olsen's declaration—a declaration he makes only after having suggested that he and Helga engage in a "more informal arrangement"—for in the very next sentence the narrator informs us of Olsen that, in making this vow of love, "his voice held a theatrical note."[62] When Olsen unveils the portrait of Helga that he has been painting, calling it the "true Helga Crane," she is revolted because "it wasn't, she contended, herself at all, but some disgusting sensual creature with her features."[63] Helga ends the chapter by remarking that, "'Yes, anyone with half an eye could see that it wasn't she,'" a statement that the reader, via Helga's unreliable speech, understands to possess a meaning exactly opposite to that which is expressed.[64] That these false observations and expressions of Helga's often occur at the ends of chapters serves to emphasize even more the unreliability that suffuses the novel, as well as Helga's blindness to the reality that the singular, authentic identity she is seeking does not exist. She will not find it because it is not there to be found.

As the novel begins the downward arc toward its dismal conclusion, Helga finds herself angry, depressed, and exhausted emotionally, walking the streets of New York wearing inappropriate clothing and lacking an umbrella or rubbers in a veritable downpour of rain. Indeed, it can be argued that everything that follows is the result of her having chosen the wrong clothes on this fateful evening, as Larsen depicts Helga uncharacteristically not paying appropriate attention to her choice: "Distracted, agitated, incapable of containing herself, she tore open drawers and closets trying desperately to take some interest in the selection of her apparel."[65] Losing strength, and having been tossed by the wind into a water-filled gutter,

Helga stumbles into a storefront Negro church where the dripping-wet and clinging red dress she is wearing causes the worshippers to mistake her for a prostitute in search of repentance. But even apart from the parishioners' incorrect interpretation of Helga's clothing, this scene is full of inauthenticity and lies. After "wriggling" out of her rain-soaked coat, Helga is eyed by the "swaying man at her right," who, "at the sight of the bare arms and neck growing out of the clinging red dress," is shaken by a "shudder."[66] Larsen then presents a vision of religious redemption in terms that cannot be described as even *veiled* eroticism. Beginning with the music, which is a "frankly irreverent melody," Larsen lets us see "writhings and weepings of the feminine portion," "Bacchic vehemence," "mixture of breaths," "contact of bodies," "contorted convulsions," and Helga's being "penetrated" by a "curious influence" during this "weird orgy."[67]

There are certainly many points to be made here in terms of female sexuality and its repression by the social mores that were ascendant in the late 1920s. Indeed, Deborah McDowell offers a foundational analysis of this particular perspective.[68] However, I am focusing on this scene for a different purpose. I am focusing on it as yet another, and indeed quite powerful, example in *Quicksand* of the presented scene not matching the actual reality, of yet more performance of identity as opposed to actual or authentic identity. Have we just been witness to a religious conversion or a sexual orgy? The surface text seems to be clear, and I am aware that certain Afro-American churches of a more Pentecostal bent are often frenetic and emotional. Yet, it must be said that Larsen seems to go beyond even that particular archetype in her description of Helga's ultimately inauthentic conversion: "Arms were stretched toward her with savage fury. The women dragged themselves upon their knees or crawled over the floor like reptiles, sobbing and pulling their hair and tearing off their clothing. Those who succeeded in getting near to her leaned forward to encourage the unfortunate sister, dropping hot tears and beads of sweat upon her bare arms and neck."[69] And, one might add with significance, these were the very same "bare arms and neck" that first inspired the swaying parishioner next to Helga to "shudder," thus bringing to full circle an orgy scene beginning with male desire and ending with female consummation of that desire.

Again, my interest is not in the strong critique of religion's role in the repression of female sexuality deployed here; rather, my interest is specifically in this scene as a narrative forgery, a visual lie, down to the red dress that is mistaken for the garb of a prostitute, as well as the mistaken but obviously welcome (albeit for dubious reasons) impression of the woman wearing it. What we see is not what is, which therefore brings into question all manner of identity. It is important to understand that *Quicksand* is not a novel of outright or obvious duplicity; rather, the inauthentic performances are all presented as sincere, and so the reader must work, sometimes fairly hard, to find them even while they seem to be the very stuff of which the novel is composed. Masked faces, clothing as costumes standing for authentic identity—these are all part of Larsen's vision of true authenticity's impossibility.

The novel's finale is a reiteration of Larsen's consistent theme that authentic identity is fictive. In a last and ultimately unsuccessful attempt to acquire a stable identity and also to enable the expression of her sexuality in a way that would be acceptable socially, Helga seduces and then marries the "fattish yellow man who had sat beside her," the same man who had shuddered at the sight of her "bare arms and neck," returning with him to Alabama where he is a preacher.[70] As usual, Helga's initial enthusiasm soon gives way to vertigo as she realizes that being a *rural, black community-uplifting preacher's wife* is merely another social role and not the authentic identity she is searching for. This time, however, she becomes burdened by children—four of them—three living and one having died not long after birth. Weakened and often delirious as she recuperates from her most recent and nearly unendurable pregnancy, Helga plans to leave this husband and take her children with her. But we know that she will never be able to accomplish this for she uses the same phrase that the women of her community use to console themselves in the face of their unending misery—"by and by." Helga says "by and by" four times in the brief space of two pages, letting the reader understand as she declares that she will leave her husband when she gets stronger—"by and by"—that it will never happen. Or, to put it another way, the reader is meant to understand that "tomorrow ain't comin'; tomorrow will always be where it was."[71] *Quicksand*'s final sentence is the perfect, if always disturbing, denouement: "AND HARDLY had she left her bed and become able to walk again without pain, hardly had the children returned from the homes of the neighbors, when she began to have her fifth child."[72]

Not only does Helga never find the authentic identity she has been searching the entire novel for, but that very search results essentially in her death sentence. While acknowledging McDowell's groundbreaking work in interpreting *Quicksand* in terms of female sexuality and its repression by society and religion, and particularly her analysis of the novel's conclusion as likening "marriage to death for women," my interest is in the way both the novel and its finale emphasize Helga's fruitless search for a singular, authentic identity that does not exist.[73] And it is important to see that Larsen's point is not merely that Helga is somehow wrong or misguided to search for such an identity; it is more complicated than that. Nor is Larsen suggesting that the novel's characters who accept their social identities and the social roles they play are correct. It seems to me that even though Helga fails to find her true identity, Larsen nevertheless paints all those other people—the ones who accept society's normative proscriptions, the successful role-players—as utterly contemptible.

Such people are always shown as empty inside. They may have position or money or the assurance of righteousness, but they lack—for want of a better word—real authenticity. Whether it is the sycophantic administrators at the Southern Negro college Helga flees from at the novel's outset; or the hypocritical upper-class Negroes she runs to who claim to hate whites but who "aped their clothes, their manners, and their gracious ways of living"; to her wealthy but decadent family in Denmark whose entire existence seems to revolve around masking their true selves in order to move up the social ladder; to the pathetic rural blacks who ever so impotently invoke the hope "by and by" for a better day that never arrives—all these characters are intended to evoke the reader's contempt in virtue of their mindless role playing in lieu of actual, authentic identity.[74] Helga's children as well are doomed to live such inauthentic lives since she quite obviously will be unable to teach them otherwise, thus giving them by default an inheritance of mindless obeisance to the masks and the performances of identity that she has been fleeing from all of her brief life.

Helga may be on a fool's errand, but she is at least sincere in her pursuit of that errand. While she is perhaps foolish to search for what she can never have, the real lesson of *Quicksand* is that Helga is trapped in a world of blind fools who are oblivious to their own ignorance and who in a sense force her to try to fit in by adopting one supposedly authentic identity after another. What Helga should have realized is that there is no singular, authentic identity that is the true essence of the self. What she should have realized is that simply being herself and refusing to accommodate society's demand that she perform this or that socially prescribed identity would have represented the path to peace and security. There can be no better metaphor for the situation facing the racial skeptic today, seeking to educate the masses as to the profound emptiness of both race and multirace as those masses either accept blindly the racial identities prescribed for them or, like Helga, try to don different or new racial identities in a pathetic attempt to fit themselves into the corrupt edifice that is the US racial order.

In Larsen's next novel, *Passing* (1929)—which, as with Johnson's *The Autobiography of an Ex-Colored Man*, we reviewed in Chapter 4 during our discussion of passing novels vis-à-vis the marginal man thesis—she reverses the direction, not of her critique of identity, but of her angle of attack. In other words, she moves from a demonstration of the impossibility of a fixed, stable, authentic identity to a disruption of all identity through the racially mixed main character Clare Kendry, who refuses to accept the prescriptions and proscriptions society would impose on her. According to Cutter, "*Quicksand* and *Passing* are inverse images of each other, as even their titles hint."[75] "Whereas Helga Crane vacillates between black and white identities, Clare chooses to have both a black and white identity. Or rather, Clare chooses not to be constrained by either a black or white identity; she chooses to slide back and forth between these identities. . . . To have all she wants, Clare must maintain multiple identities—multiple subject positions—and pass back and forth between them."[76] As in *Quicksand*, the secondary characters remain stuck in their prescribed social identities; but, unlike in *Quicksand*, whose secondary characters are oblivious to the main character and her turmoil over identity, in *Passing* they cannot avoid the tornado-like disruption that Clare Kendry carries along in her wake. In George Hutchinson's view: "If *Quicksand*, as its epigraph implies, is about a woman 'neither white not black,' *Passing* . . . is about the disturbance generated by a woman *both* white *and* black. With her combination of skin color, social positioning, and racial background, Clare Kendry is, literally, both a black white woman and a white black woman."[77]

In Kawash's analysis, "the truth of race is not the apparent, natural race identities that form the foundation of social order; rather, it is the possibility that any apparent truth is *not* true, that because race is a *nothing*, it can never in fact be what it appears to be."[78] This disruption of naturally accepted truth is precisely what Clare represents. Clare is "the figure of passing" who "tears open the surface of orderly relations, threatening to expose what must, from the perspective of presumed certainty and order, be a terrifying emptiness at the center of race, at the center of desire, at the center of knowledge."[79] There are those who would see the foregoing as being supportive of the notion of multiraciality's deconstructive power over race, but in fact the reverse is true. Multiracial identity does not and cannot deconstruct race in this way because the disruption that Clare represents is *prior* to race, and indeed forecloses the possibility of race. Clare's disruption of our stable and ordered existence reveals the emptiness of race as "a nothing," and serves to destroy the notion that race exists and has meaning apart from that which is given to it ever so illegitimately in the misbegotten falseness of its construction and maintenance.

In other words, it is not that Clare as a biracial woman throws exclusively monoracial knowledge into chaos and opens a space for multiracial epistemology to assert and announce itself. No; Clare throws *all* racial epistemology into the chaotic abyss, monoracial as well as multiracial. "Clare throws into question racial divisions, as well as the idea of firm and irrevocable differences between the races. Larsen's descriptions of Clare's appearance also continually remind the reader that Clare refuses easy racial categorization and that race itself is unknowable, mysterious, and even unstable."[80] It is important to understand this latter point in relation to not only supposed monoracial identity but also to the nonsense of "obvious and visible mixedness" trumpeted by Generation Mix (see Chapter 8). Seen in this light, the emptiness of that simplistic notion and its unchallengeable dependence on biological race are both made plain. Hutchinson informs us that, for Larsen, racial and class divisions "bred an attitude of sardonic skepticism toward all collective notions of identity, with their attendant idealizations of the 'group'; a strongly developed sense of irony; and a private unwillingness or inability to fully identify with either the class from which she came or that to which her own future was ineluctably tied"; and that "at the heart of her fiction was one of the most incisive protests against the inhumanity of the color line and its psychic cost ever penned in American literature."[81]

The issue of heritage/inheritance is presented in *Passing* as well, in the form of Clare's young daughter Margery, who is mentioned only briefly, is never present physically, and whose only purpose seems to be to raise the question of how the child is going to be identified racially in the future once her mother has died. This is a problem because Clare's racist white husband, Jack Bellew, discovers only at the novel's climax that Clare has black ancestry, leaving the reader to ponder just what he is going to do with his suddenly motherless daughter. Larsen sets up a real dilemma, since, as we are given no evidence to suggest that Bellew does not love his daughter, and as we know that Bellew is a monumental racist, we wonder whether he will reject or embrace his daughter and her tainted blood. Given Clare's death, there is no one aside from her few black friends in Harlem—with whom Bellew will surely never cross paths again—to reveal his daughter's invisible blackness. Which will win out—love or racist ideology?

Larsen has Bellew declare his racism quite openly during a scene in which he jokes in front of Clare's two black friends, who are passing for the moment as white, about Clare's skin seeming to grow darker with age, which is the reason he has nicknamed her "Nig": "'But I declare she's gettin' darker and darker. I tell her if she don't look out, she'll wake up one of these days and find she's turned into a nigger.'"[82] Clare responds by having a bit of ironic fun with her unseeing husband for the benefit of her black friends: "Speaking with confidence as well as with amusement, she said: 'My goodness, Jack! What difference would it make if, after all these years, you were to find out that I was one or two per cent coloured?'"[83] This gives Bellew the opportunity to lay his race ideology out in the open for all to see: "Bellew put out his hand in a repudiating fling, definite and final. 'Oh, no, Nig,' he declared, 'nothing like that with me. I know you're no nigger, so it's all right. You can get as black as you please as far as I'm concerned, since I know you're no nigger. I draw the line at that. No niggers in my family. Never have been and never will be.'"[84]

We may substantiate the sincerity of Bellew's conviction here when, at the end of the novel, he tracks Clare to Harlem in order to confirm a suspicion that his wife might not be white after all. Facing his "Nig," Bellew explodes: "'So you're a nigger, a damned dirty nigger!' His voice was a snarl and a moan, an expression of rage and pain."[85] Bellew, the racist white man, has been duped by the passing Clare, and realizes to his utter chagrin that his previous proud declaration of there being "no niggers in my family," that there "never have been and never will be" is a ridiculous prevarication laying in shattered ruins about his feet. He is helpless, for the abominable act—the unknowing miscegenation—has already occurred; he has been a blind party to it in the production of his part-black daughter, and there is no way for it to be undone. His family's whiteness is now a lie.

But what of Margery, the always absent and previously white daughter? Bellew may well repudiate her also, but let us remember what he said about Clare, that she "can get as black as you please as far as I'm concerned," because he thought he knew she was white. This statement nonetheless leaves open the possibility that for the sake of his daughter, who played no part at all in his deception, he might make an exception, that he might, for the sake of love for a child that would have to be different from love for a wife, facilitate her unknowing passing, just as did Johnson's unnamed narrator for his children. Margery is, after all, his innocent daughter, and she did not deceive him; indeed, she has no idea that she has black ancestry. So the reader is left to ponder what Bellew's future course will be in this matter. Will he desert his beloved daughter for the sake of his racist ideology or will he continue to love her and as a result effect her unknowing passing as white? Moreover, if he takes the latter course, which seems even for the racist to be the only human course to take—Faulker's Thomas Sutpen notwithstanding (see Chapter 2)—how, except for intention, does his beloved daughter's blackness differ from that of his "damned dirty nigger" wife? This is a key question, since absent Clare's intention to deceive, her ostensible blackness is no different from her daughter's. And of course, the question before Bellew also stands before every white person who reads *Passing*—a nagging, uncomfortable question, asking: "What would you do?"

One of the most valuable things we can glean from Larsen's novels *Quicksand* and *Passing* is that racial identity, including by extension multiracial identity, is nothing less than unreliable narration. Just as the exotic pieces of clothing adorning Helga Crane's body in the literary world of *Quicksand* are metaphors for interchangeable, synthetic identities that are in fact neither essential nor authentic, racial identity too is merely something draped over, laid upon, ornamental in nature. Such a claim will no doubt inspire howls of disagreement from people who are invested heavily in their personal identities, most especially their racial identities. But just as Johnson's unnamed narrator of *The Autobiography of an Ex-Colored Man* demonstrates the emptiness of the notion of essentialized racial identity, so too must we acknowledge that the racial identities we so desperately want to have (and that we so desperately want others to have as well) are at base decorative garnishes covering an essentiality that whatever else it might be is certainly not racial.

As with Johnson's narrator, and as we see with Margery, we learn to be black or to be white or to be multiracial. Some learn passively through everyday interactions with our racialized society and some are indoctrinated by parents motivated by specific agendas, but for everyone it is the superimposition of a racial structure over our lives and within which we are expected to find our prescribed, acceptable, and socially validated racial identities.[86] Or, to be more precise, we, as with Johnson's narrator or Larsen's Helga, only *think* we are learning when in fact we are each merely performing a role that neither uncovers any essentiality within us innately nor essentializes us in a retroactive fashion. This is precisely the challenge of Chesnutt's virtual twins in *The Marrow of Tradition* (and also of another author's set of virtual twins to which I shall turn shortly). What is true racial essentiality? Is there any racial essentiality apart from and anterior to—temporally and ontologically—the performance of race?

What is learned, what is uncovered, what is revealed, when one accepts the purported knowledge—whether passively or via indoctrination—that one is multiracial? Is there a sense in which a dormant essentiality is disinterred and brought to light, or in which a heretofore absent essentiality is thereby instilled? This is a question that goes directly to the heart of psychology and sociology's *identity fascism.* If I were to learn today that I was actually adopted at birth upon my true parents' accidental deaths, and that both my birth parents were something other than what my newfound adoptive parents are, being in other words of neither European nor sub-Saharan African ancestry, something else, say, Asian or some combination of Asian that would account reasonably for my phenotype—would that new knowledge change who I am in some essential way? Should I, as a result, adopt an Asian mindset (whatever that might mean)? Would continuing to live my life as I have lived it thus far be an exercise in inauthenticity on my part? Should I begin marking *Asian* on forms requesting racial identification even though no one takes me for Asian and even though when I am discriminated against it is as a black male? Would I be disrespecting and rejecting my birth parents if I did not do so? And suppose I readjusted my identity toward that Asian mindset, but then after a year's time learned that it was all a mistake and that I was actually born in Brooklyn to the same parents just as I have always thought. How, in all of this, would any internal essentiality on my part have been changed during my year of Asianness?

As I have already described to some extent, Chesnutt engages precisely these sorts of questions via the virtual twins Janet and Olivia in *The Marrow of Tradition*; however, I do not want to leave the impression that it is only mulatto authors who deal with these issues of authenticity in regard to race and racial identity. Lydia Maria Child, in her 1867 novel, *A Romance of the Republic*—an expansion of her short story, "The Quadroons" (1842 and 1846)—provides via both the impossibility of confirming race visually as well as the device of baby switching a narrative that challenges the conventions of authentic racial identity.[87] In this highly sentimental work, Child attacks the possibility of secure and accurate racial knowledge: "Along with showing readers 'blacks' who look 'white,' she insists that 'whites' can in fact look 'black.' Thus she underscores the perceptual invalidity of racial judgment and prejudice: ultimately, white and black logic points to nothing real. Rather than being a difference based in nature, Child suggests that the motivation of racial prejudice is often about protecting (ill-gotten) economic gains."[88] As one of Child's characters puts it when commenting on antimiscegenation law in the case of a white man and the octoroon slave woman with whom that white man had a child, "the only effect of the law was to deprive her of a legal right to his support and protection, and to prevent her son from receiving any share of his father's property."[89] The resonance with Chesnutt's critique in *The Marrow of Tradition* requires no elaboration.

In pursuit of demonstrating the illogic of race, Child gives us quadroon and octoroon females whose racial ancestry it is not possible to determine visually, as well as the children those quadroon females have with white men—children who are equally impervious to racial typing as having black ancestry. To be sure, the well-bred and white-appearing female of sub-Saharan African ancestry was not a new device—most especially not for Child—and indeed, presents in itself troubling problems for moving away from racialized and prejudicial thinking; but to her credit, Child also provides racially mixed male characters who work to complicate the illusion of a simplistic racial schema. She gives us as well the reality of racially mixed slaves whose ancestries have "become so mixed up that they advertise runaway negroes with sandy hair, blue eyes, and ruddy complexion."[90] Significantly, Child goes a step further than even this in driving the point home by having a white abolitionist character respond to such an advertisement with the facetious but telling declaration that it was a description of him, and that he had not theretofore known that he was a mulatto.[91]

In her analysis of *A Romance of the Republic*, Cassandra Jackson sees Child representing "cross-racial hereditary intersections as a trade of both physiognomy and character traits that will eventually reduce bodily evidence of race into a series of signless parts, liquefying and reformulating the signs of identity. Ultimately, her mulatto figures represent the transmission of bodily signs that throw the system of racial categorization into flux."[92] I would disagree with Jackson, though, and suggest that rather than Child signifying the reduction of "bodily evidence of race," she is instead demonstrating that any such racial "evidence" is always already unreliable, hence the ability of mulattoes to confound visual recognition of race as they do.

In addition to the outright unreliability of vision in confirming racial identity, Child raises the question of knowable ancestry and its impact on racial knowledge by having a desperate and temporarily deranged slave mother who has learned of her recently transacted sale switch her own infant with his white half brother by the same father: "'Unfortunately Chloe had come to the cottage that day, with Mrs. Fitzgerald's babe, and he was lying asleep by the side of mine. I had wild thoughts of killing both the babies, and then killing myself. . . . Thank God, I was saved from committing such horrible deeds. But I was still half frantic with misery and fear. A wild, dark storm was raging in my soul. I looked at the two babes, and thought how one was born to be indulged and honored, while the other was born a slave, liable to be sold by his unfeeling father or by his father's creditors. Mine was only a week the oldest, and was not larger than his brother. They were so exactly alike that I could distinguish them only by their dress. I exchanged the dresses, Alfred; and while I did it, I laughed to think that, if Mr. Fitzgerald should capture me and the little one, and make us over to Mr. Bruteman, he would sell the child of his Lily Bell.'"[93] Some two decades later we meet the half brothers again—the white one having lived the hard life of a black slave and his part-black sibling having grown up as a Negro-hating white man amidst surroundings of wealth and finery, thereby providing an interesting conundrum for proponents of racial authenticity. Child here challenges the reader to distinguish properly and logically between these two young men who are nearly identical in appearance and who are distinct only in terms of their respective upbringings and the resources they can muster toward their development.

In the words of Eve Raimon, Child's novel works to "dramatize the inextricability of the races one to another," suggesting that "paradoxically, the 'tragic mulatta' represents at once both America's changeling and its maternal figure; the orphan whose identity is forever contested and, in some sense, potentially anyone's mother. This conception of the mutability of racial identity and the idea that such mutability is itself an indelible fact of American history and identity—ideas so antithetical to preeminent modes of thinking in the nineteenth century—constitute Child's most radical contributions to antislavery literature."[94] Thus, although beset by problems involving the equating of visible blackness with backwardness and visible whiteness with character of a more noble bent (though not nearly on the order of a Harriet Beecher Stowe, however), Child nonetheless does make the compelling case that one cannot with logic and accuracy categorize either of these half brothers as black or white, for through their characters themselves we come to understand that race is "a nothing."

The same might be said to have been accomplished, albeit in considerably less depth, in Kate Chopin's 1893 short story, "The Father of Désirée's Baby," in which the racist husband Armand rejects his wife Désirée and their seemingly mixed-race infant (causing the crushed and heartbroken Désirée to commit apparent suicide and infanticide) on account of the wife's purported hidden blackness, when at the end of the story we learn instead, through his own dead mother's testimony via a discovered letter to his also-dead father, that it is Armand himself who is black.[95] According to Susan Gubar, "the end of the tale effectively divides physiology from race, complexion from origin, making the visual unreliable."[96] As Werner Sollors puts it, in noting that "Chopin's story plays hide-and-seek with its readers about her characters' race," "what the birth of the child makes necessary is to resolve the problem of ascertaining who is black and who is white."[97] In a brief story a mere six pages long, Chopin weaves in ambiguity upon ambiguity, since "though we presumably know that Armand is the black father of the mixed child, we remain unsure about Désirée's racial background. In this regard, the story resists racial categories altogether."[98]

Mark Twain, in his 1894 novel, *Pudd'nhead Wilson*, covers similar ground but in a more direct way than Child's novel, and of course far more extensively than Chopin's short story.[99] The narrative drama in Twain's novel revolves around the cradle switching of two nearly identical baby boys, one (part) black (Chambers) and one white (Tom), by their respective mother and caretaker, Roxana (Roxy), who, as we shall see directly, herself disrupts the notion of stable racial identity. Roxy is the slave of Percy Driscoll, and "on the 1st of February, 1830, two boy babes were born in his house; one to him, the other to one of his slave girls, Roxana by name. Roxana was twenty years old. She was up and around the same day, with her hands full, for she was tending both babies. Mrs. Percy Driscoll died within the week. Roxy remained in charge of the children. She had her own way, for Mr. Driscoll soon absorbed himself in his speculations and left her to her own devices."[100]

In Roxy, Twain creates something of a dilemma for the reader, as "from Roxy's manner of speech, a stranger would have expected her to be black, but she was not. Only one-sixteenth of her was black, and that sixteenth did not show. She was of majestic form and stature, her attitudes were imposing and statuesque, and her gestures and movements distinguished by a noble and stately grace. Her complexion was very fair, with the rosy glow of vigorous health in the cheeks, her face was full of character and expression, her eyes were brown and liquid, and she had a heavy suit of fine soft hair which was also brown, but the fact was not apparent because her head was bound about with a checkered handkerchief and the hair was concealed under it. Her face was shapely, intelligent and comely—even beautiful. She had an easy, independent carriage—when she was among her own caste—and a high and 'sassy' way, withal; but of course she was meek and humble enough where white people were."[101]

Note that in this description, there are exactly three things that paint Roxy as black: her speech, her clothing, and public knowledge of her ancestry. Of these three, only the handkerchief is a visible marker, but it can be removed or changed as can any other items of clothing that might mark her as nonwhite. Of the remaining two markers, her speech has of course been learned and is thereby contingent, while her ancestry actually has no manifestation whatsoever apart from what people impute to it. Her appearance is that of a beautiful white woman, and Twain paints a fascinating image for us as we imagine this white-appearing woman speaking in black Southern dialect as Twain has her do throughout the novel. This by itself presents an unnerving sort of disruption as the reader is left to ponder why a white-looking woman would speak this way. In fact, it would be an interesting exercise to ask readers if, as they advance through the text, they maintain this white image of Roxy or begin to imagine her in darker and darker tones based purely on her speech.

Through Roxy, and even more so through her child, Twain challenges us to accept the operation of hypodescent at a seemingly absurd extreme: "To all intents and purposes Roxy was as white as anybody, but the one-sixteenth of her which was black out-voted the other fifteen parts and made her a negro. She was a slave, and saleable as such. Her child was thirty-one parts white, and he, too, was a slave, and by a fiction of law and custom a negro. He had blue eyes and flaxen curls like his white comrade, but even the father of the white child was able to tell the children apart—little as he had commerce with them—by their clothes; for the white babe wore ruffled soft muslin and a coral necklace, while the other wore merely a course tow-linen shirt which barely reached to its knees, and no jewelry."[102] Again, we see how weak the concept of race is via the effect that clothing has seemingly to determine it. When Pudd'nhead Wilson asks Roxy how she can tell her two charges apart when they are naked, she replies: "Oh, *I* kin tell 'em 'part, Misto Wilson, but I bet Marse Percy couldn't, not to save his life."[103]

After nearly being sold down river for an offense she did not commit, Roxy becomes obsessed to the point of terror with the idea that her child faces the same danger as long as he is a slave. But then Roxy has a stunning idea: "She stepped over and glanced at the other infant; she flung a glance back at her own; then one more at the heir of the house. Now a strange light dawned in her eyes, and in a moment she was lost in thought. She seemed in a trance; when she came out of it she muttered, 'When I 'uz a-washin' 'em in de tub, yistiddy, his own pappy asked me which of 'em was his'n.' She began to move about like one in a dream. She undressed Thomas à Becket, stripping him of everything, and put the tow-linen shirt on him. She put his coral necklace on her own child's neck. Then she placed the children side by side, and after earnest inspection she muttered: 'Now who would b'lieve clo'es could do de like o' dat? Dog my cats if it ain't all *I* kin do to tell t'other fum which, let alone his pappy.'"[104]

I would point out most especially the statement that by undressing the white child Roxy is thereby "stripping him of everything." On the surface reading, the word "everything" of course refers simply to the white child's clothing, but on a deeper reading Twain is letting us know that each child's clothing represents the only ascertainable racial markers, and as such are false and unreliable markers. The two children cannot yet speak and so one cannot even make a racial judgment based on the unreliable marker of dialect, and by switching their clothing Roxy is quite literally switching the two boys' ancestry as well. Indeed, what Twain seems to be implying is that race is not even merely skin deep; it is in fact only clothing deep. Here, again, we see the use of virtual twins in the effective deconstruction of race as a stable concept.

The contingent nature of racial identity is emphasized by Roxy, who has little difficulty in getting used to the racial switch she has performed: "As she progressed with her practice, she was surprised to see how steadily and surely the awe which had kept her tongue reverent and her manner humble toward her young master was transferring itself to her speech and manner toward the usurper, and how similarly handy she was becoming in transferring her motherly curtness of speech and peremptoriness of manner to the unlucky heir of the ancient house of Driscoll."[105] The reader as well is assisted in making the switch, as Twain's narrator refers to the former black child Chambers as *Tom*, and former white child Tom as *Chambers*. Interestingly, and most disruptively, about one-third of the way into the novel Roxy reveals to Tom his true ancestry and she begins referring to the false Tom as *Chambers*, while the narrator nevertheless continues to refer to him as *Tom*. Is this perhaps because he really *is* Tom in the sense that he is what he has become and is not, cannot really be, what he was and what Chambers has become? Until the novel's final pages, only Roxy and Tom are aware of the switched identities of Tom/Chambers and Chambers/Tom.

Needless to say, growing up under the influence of slavery, the young Tom (the former black, slave child) becomes a worthless, immoral profligate who learns to hate Negroes, including his own (albeit unknown) mother, Roxy, who at one point laments: "'He struck me, en I warn't no way to blame—struck me in de face, right before folks. En he's al'ays callin' me nigger-wench, en hussy, en all dem mean names, when I's doin' de very bes' I kin. Oh Lord, I done so much for him—I lift' him away up to what he is— en dis is what I git for it.'"[106] The idea of a boy beating his mother stands as an essential disruption, and forces us to consider the absurdity of race that causes that disruption to take place. Whereas Chesnutt, in *The Marrow of Tradition*, challenges race by questioning how one blood sister can usurp the whole of her virtual twin's inheritance, Twain, in *Pudd'nhead Wilson*, challenges race by inverting completely the notion of inheritance—taking everything away from the ostensibly deserving white child and granting it to the ostensibly undeserving black one, all the while bringing into question the ideas of race, racial identity, and the supposedly logical and legitimate organization of society around these dubious concepts, including the metaphorical critique that it is the black who has lifted the white "away up to what he is."

This absurdity is captured when the false Chambers, whom Roxy has just insulted as a "mis'able imitation nigger," replies to her sarcastically, indeed, perhaps ironically.[107] Keep in mind that in making his reply Chambers thinks Roxy is his mother and that he does not know that he is *really* white: "'Yah-yah-yah! jes listen to dat! If I's imitation, what is you? Bofe of us is imitation *white*—dat's what we is—en pow'ful good imitation, too—yah-yah-yah!'"[108] The spectacle of the unknowing son of the respected white man Percy Driscoll believing he is black and speaking in black dialect to the woman he thinks is his one-sixteenth-black mother while commenting sarcastically on his own white appearance represents the complete breakdown of the racial order's logic, although not of its continuing power. Twain's language again is key: "Bofe of us is imitation *white*," as it is obvious that Chambers is neither *imitation* white nor *really* white, for the fiction of whiteness has, as has the fiction of blackness, been revealed to reside far more in the clothing and in the speech than in any physical reality. Tom is neither white nor black, Chambers neither black nor white, and Roxy neither black nor white (nor for that matter, multiracial)—as every one of these categorizations represents a farcical absurdity.

Even though it may appear that the racial order has been reestablished at the novel's end, with the usurping false Tom having been exposed and sold down river into slavery, there remains a very clear and disturbing dissonance in the figure of the former Chambers, who has been restored to his rightful place as the heir of Percy Driscoll: "The real heir suddenly found himself rich and free, but in a most embarrassing situation. He could neither read nor write, and his speech was the basest dialect of the negro quarter. His gait, his attitudes, his gestures, his bearing, his laugh—all were vulgar and uncouth; his manners were the manners of a slave. Money and fine clothes could not mend these defects or cover them up; they only made them the more glaring and the more pathetic. The poor fellow could not endure the terrors of the white man's parlor, and felt at home and at peace nowhere but in the kitchen. The family pew was a misery to him, yet he could nevermore enter into the solacing refuge of the 'nigger gallery'—that was closed to him for good and all."[109]

If we are moved by the situation of the former Chambers to grant that we might as well concede that he is really black and that the former Tom is really white, then we would in effect be conceding that there is actually no difference between white and black—that it really is a question of clothing, upbringing, and language that determine race, not ancestry. We would be conceding that the essence of racial identity is no more than ontological emptiness adorned by a kind of clothing that is for all practical purposes interchangeable. But if, on the other hand, we want to hold that race is real and that the racial order has been restored appropriately, we must somehow, and with a straight face, answer and account for the seemingly endless absurdities that Twain has deployed throughout nearly the whole of the novel.

A bit of clarification should be offered here, as I begin to close this discussion of *Pudd'nhead Wilson*. Fairly early on in the novel, Percy Driscoll dies penniless as a result of unsuccessful land speculations, but his brother, Judge York Leiscester Driscoll, takes the false Tom in and continues raising him; and it is the judge's estate that the real Tom inherits ultimately, the judge having been murdered by the false Tom, who, having been found guilty of the murder is then—since he is a slave—pardoned so that he may be claimed by the creditors against Percy Driscoll's estate who thereupon sell him down river. If that summary seems confusing, it merely replicates the confusion underlying the fictively stable status of race and its inheritance as illustrated throughout the novel itself.

Crucial as well is the fact that the hero of the novel, Puddn'head Wilson, discovers the fact of the long-ago switching of the two infants through his use of fingerprinting. Note the language Wilson uses in explaining to the jury in the Judge Driscoll murder trial the importance of the fingerprint to a person's true identity: "'These marks are his signature, his physiological autograph, so to speak, and this autograph cannot be counterfeited, nor can he disguise it or hide it away, nor can it become illegible by the wear and mutations of time.'"[110] If we take Wilson's description of the fingerprint's immutability and of its surety in identifying a person, and then compare that description to the demonstrated emptiness of race (which fails miserably in every aspect at which the fingerprint excels) as being of any use whatsoever in identifying someone—an emptiness demonstrated so vividly and in so many ways in the novel—we see the full impact of Twain's message in *Pudd'nhead Wilson*. It is a message that can also be seen in the subplot involving a pair of Italian twins who, based on circumstantial evidence, are charged wrongly with Judge Driscoll's murder.[111] In showing why it is not reasonable to believe that the twins had anything to do with the murder, Wilson goes through an exercise of commonsense thinking, which he ends with the declaration: "'Let us not slander our intelligence to that degree'"—a declaration that is as much a statement about the reasonableness of racial identity as it is of the Italian twins' erroneous implication in the judge's murder.[112] We would do well to apply Wilson's commonsense analysis to our own contemporary situation regarding race and racial identity, and then heed his still timely advice.

Chesnutt, Johnson, Larsen, Child, Chopin, and Twain all present us with compelling challenges to—indeed, outright derision of—race as a reasonable concept and of racial identities as containing any true meaning. The first three in particular, each of them very light-skinned American mulattoes, are most especially compelling since they are precisely the sort of people whom one might expect to advance racial mixedness as an essential identity. But they do not. Just as in Chapter 4 we saw these three authors, along with Walter White and Jessie Fauset, debunk the marginal man thesis by rejecting the sociologists' racist and self-projected assurance that mulattoes want desperately to be white, in this chapter we have seen how they go even further in rejecting race itself as any sort of meaningful categorization. In doing this, they of necessity reject the idea of multiracial identity as well, for if race stands exposed as an illogical fantasy so too does mixed race.

What, then, is the mulatto future, and how is it tied to the US future? As I pointed out in Chapter 2, the racist novelist Thomas Dixon asked in 1902 what he surely considered to be a question both inflammatory and rhetorical: "Shall the future American be an Anglo-Saxon or a Mulatto?"[113] My answer to Dixon is that the future American shall in fact be a mulatto, but not in the crudely and racially amalgamated sense abhorred by him then and valorized by Generation Mix today. I am speaking instead of the mulatto in the abstract sense as a figure that transcends race and leads us to our postracial future by deconstructing race in one of two ways.[114]

The first is by representing the physical embodiment of the reality that distinct and exclusive race does not, indeed cannot, exist. By her or his very existence the mulatto challenges anyone to place her or him into a racial category without resorting to some arbitrary and bankrupt calculus such as hypodescent, whether general or selective. It simply cannot be done; and because it cannot be done, race itself is thereby deconstructed since it is unable to account for the fact that there are people who cannot be categorized racially. As Naomi Zack puts it, writing about the "American who identifies herself as mixed black and white race," it is "such a person's very newness racially that gives her the option of racelessness. To be raceless in contemporary racial and racist society is in effect, to be *anti-race*."[115] I agree with Zack that racelessness is to be commended and enacted even while I reject the imputation of "newness" (see Chapter 6), but I must caution, however, that Zack's proposition holds *only* if the person then commits racial suicide and gives up her identification as "mixed black and white race." If she does not give it up and instead retains that racial identity of "mixed black and white race," she then situates herself squarely as a racial being and therefore not as raceless.

I would also extend the same sort of limited agreement to Tavia Nyong'o, who avers that "the product of amalgamation, when she is not scorned as a mongrel bastard, is held to somehow contain a secret *agalma* that holds some mysterious power to redeem a fallen province of racism and racial awareness. Just as Socrates disavowed the treasures Alcibiades claimed were hidden within him, without disavowing Alcibiades' quest for truth and redemption, so must the hybrid child disavow the faulty expectation that she, in herself, holds some kind of passport to a future transcendence of race."[116] The point that Zack and Nyong'o both come close to but both preclude ultimately, is that the hybrid child does possess the power, at the level of abstract conception, to disrupt the racial schema if—and only if—the hybrid child then disavows race and racial hybridity, the dissolution of the racial self following immediately and necessarily upon the dissolution of race. The mulatto can lead us to the transcendence of race, but only by a complete rejection of race and race thinking—only by committing racial suicide.

This is the very conclusion Kawash draws when she points out that "the mulatto body transgresses the boundedness of whiteness and blackness, illustrating the arbitrariness of the boundary."[117] Kawash is certainly correct in this, and it is vital to see—despite the misleading information with which we are bombarded constantly—that Kawash's theoretical point is not at all the same thing as the self-serving political position of Generation Mix. The American Multiracial Identity Movement does not want the theoretical concept of multiraciality to be seen as falsifying the racial boundary; its adherents want multiraciality to be seen as both verifying and being verified by that boundary. They do not want the multiracial idea to vanquish biological race; rather, they desire a corporeal multiracialism that makes them special, and they desire the conservation of biological race that makes that specialness possible. They desire the perpetuation of race, not its death. The crucial difference between the race-conserving Generation Mix future and the race-transcending mulatto future could not be more stark.

The second way the mulatto deconstructs race is by demonstrating that even if one insists on deploying a more flexible concept of race, one must still account for racial mixtures. In other words, if we are to take racial mixture seriously in this way, then such mixture must represent something special and unique in and of itself. Therefore, a serious accounting of racial mixture cannot be by way of constructing a singular (multi)racial category containing all and only persons who do not fit into the standard monoracial categories, for in addition to being a negative definition (indeed, representing no more than a euphemistic recoding of the despised label, *other*) it ignores the logical reality that different mixes would of necessity have to produce radically different people. One might even say that having a single multiracial category for all racial mixtures disrespects the very importance and individuality of such mixture by lumping it all together indistinguishably and unceremoniously. For instance, why should a black/white mix reside in the same biological racial category as a Native American/Asian mix, and why then should that category as a result not simply be labeled *other*?

Rather, a serious accounting for racial mixtures would have to be by way of creating a new and singular category for each and every new mixture, as each one would of necessity be different from any other. In other words, going back to the example of our hypothetical cousins of Chapters 11 and 12, the three children of our cousins' great-great-great-grandfather (each, for ease of illustration, having a mother who is black, white, and black/white respectively) would each require their own separate racial category, and any children they each have would be different from them, thus requiring a new and separate category, and on and on, ad infinitum. The ultimate result would be that each individual human being would represent a different racial category in and of herself or himself. In other words, there would be as many races as there are people, which would, in effect, represent a sort of partial deconstruction of race. I call such a potentiality a partial deconstruction because we would still have the problem of whiteness and the property value given to it, since people taken to be white would have the least interest in relinquishing that valued property. Additionally, it bears noting that such a deconstructive outcome—as many racial categories as there are human beings—is precisely not what the American Multiracial Identity Movement wants, as it desires one single and unique category for its members to fit into.

Naomi Riley reports that the members of Generation Mix are themselves demonstrating that multiraciality is prone to an internal disunity and fracturing that is merely a logical extension of its current project of achieving ever and ever more exclusiveness of identity. Even multiracial campus groups at US colleges are discovering that their constituent members often prefer their own individual subgroupings to the general multiracial umbrella. According to Riley, "the level of specificity that seems to be required for many young men and women to feel comfortable today is bordering on the absurd. Ultimately, it's sad. . . . Students do not seem to be learning to be more tolerant of people unlike them. They are demanding to be surrounded and sheltered by people who are *exactly* like them."[118]

Riley laments quite rightly that "we are exacerbating an already problematic tendency with faddish ideology. When a 'multicultural' sensibility doesn't seek to overcome race but makes it central to one's identity, and when one can be truly at home only with people who share that identity, the result is a ludicrous situation in which people can empathize only with a smaller and smaller group of the their peers."[119] This is the Generation Mix (as opposed to the mulatto) future—separate coalitions of black/whites, black/Hispanics, white/Hispanics, and various assortments of Hapa subgroupings, all complaining that the overly broad multiracial label does not describe their individual mixtures and specific identifications, and each instead demanding a more exclusive label so as to distinguish itself from the others. Indeed, the respective members of these subgroupings would likely complain that the multiracial label is an insulting, externally imposed designation that does not give due respect to their own unique individuality as persons or to their parents' very existence.

316 The Mulatto Future

I do not believe, though, that the process Riley describes as taking place currently on US college campuses will deliver the abstract result I described above in terms of each human being representing a unique racial category unto herself or himself, even ignoring for the moment the continuing problem of whiteness. If it would have that particular result, it might well be worth allowing the process to play itself out to that deconstructive end. Instead, though, we will be far more likely to see people stuck at some certain level of Balkanized, (multi)racial tribalness without devolving further. And, once established, that Balkanized Generation Mix future is one that would be difficult to correct or to backtrack away from, as our nation's history and human nature itself have shown us that people find exclusion and splintering to be far preferable to true coalition. This Generation Mix future must be avoided. We have the tools with which to forge a different path; all that is lacking is the vision and the will.

Between on the one hand what science laid down decades ago regarding the falseness of race and racial categories, and on the other the devastating critiques of race delivered by authors who were themselves seen as being black/white, such as Chesnutt, Johnson, and Larsen (and also others such as Twain, Chopin, and Child), but who deconstructed the notion of race in their writings, there is no need for any new breakthrough in the matter of racial skepticism. We have sufficient raw materials and adequate tools presently, whether employed via the lenses of science, history, philosophy, or literature, to debunk and deconstruct the false consciousness of race. All that remains is to accept the reality that race is a fantasy and then walk away from it. All that remains is to step out of the flawed understanding of our racial childhood and into the enlightenment of our raceless maturity.

In the end, the question we must ask and answer is this: What kind of US future do we desire? If we desire a future in which race continues to exist, in which whiteness is not challenged, and in which the US racial order is allowed to continue as a primary organizing principle of our society, then we should support the American Multiracial Identity Movement and Generation Mix in their quest to instantiate multiracial identity as a new biological racial identity. If we desire a future in which Afro-Americans are marginalized further and are seen by other nonwhites as the one group to distance oneself from by migrating to a multiracial category on the way toward honorary and, if possible, full whiteness, then we should advance the cause of antiblackness by supporting the call for recognizing multiracial identity. If we desire a future in which postraciality is seen as consisting in postblackness but not in postwhiteness, then we should work for the acceptance of multiracial identity.

But if we desire a US future in which whiteness is deconstructed, and in which the false consciousness of race is understood as an unfortunate historical artifact that is no longer heeded, then we should take up the cause of real racial radicalism and militancy by first committing personal racial suicide, and then by continuing the attack against race in general, most especially by attacking whiteness and the white supremacy it makes possible. If we are not willing to engage in this kind of militancy, if we do not desire to make this kind of commitment, if we are not prepared to bequeath to future generations something other than the same reliance on biological race that we have inherited, then we should simply stop complaining and accept the status quo.

Notes

1. Charles W. Chesnutt, *The Marrow of Tradition* (New York: Houghton Mifflin & Co., 1901; repr. New York: Penguin, 1993).
2. Ibid., 8.
3. Ibid., 325–326.
4. Samira Kawash, *Dislocating the Color Line: Identity, Hybridity, and Singularity in African-American Literature* (Stanford: Stanford University Press, 1997), 90.
5. Ibid., 91.
6. Richard Hildreth, *The White Slave. Another Picture of Slave Life in America* (London: George Routledge, 1852; repr. Rye Brook, NY: Adamant Media, 2006), 21.
7. George W. Cable, *The Grandissimes* (1880; repr. New York: Hill and Wang, 1957).
8. Kawash, *Dislocating the Color Line*, 111. See also and especially, Cheryl I. Harris, "Whiteness as Property," *Harvard Law Review* 106, no. 8 (June 1993): 1707–1791.
9. Mayne Reid, *The Quadroon; or, Adventures in the Far West* (London: J. & C. Brown and Company, 1856; repr. Rye Brook, NY: Adamant Media, 2006), 93.
10. Ibid., 138.
11. Ibid.
12. Ibid., 95.
13. Significantly, Edouard consistently throughout the novel finds Aurore more attractive physically than the also beautiful Eugénie.
14. I am not insensitive to the fact that Aurore lives an extremely pampered existence for a slave, but the fact remains that at the end of the day she still is just that, a slave.
15. Charles W. Chesnutt, "The Future American," 1900, in *Charles W. Chesnutt: Stories, Novels, & Essays* (New York: Library of America, 2002), 846.
16. I learned this from reading Kawash, *Dislocating the Color Line*, 119.
17. Ibid., 119–120.
18. Wallace Fard is considered to be the founder of the Nation of Islam, and Elijah Pool, later Elijah Muhammad, was his protégé and eventual successor as leader of that organization.
19. Ronald R. Sundstrom, *The Browning of America and the Evasion of Social Justice* (Albany: State University of New York Press, 2008), 104.
20. Kawash, *Dislocating the Color Line*, 120.
21. Ibid.

22. Chesnutt, "Future American," 853, 854.

23. Ibid., 859.

24. Kawash, *Dislocating the Color Line*, 111.

25. Chesnutt, "Future American," 858. Italics added.

26. Ibid. Italics added.

27. Ibid., 860, 861. Italics added.

28. Kawash, *Dislocating the Color Line*, 122.

29. David G. Croly, *Miscegenation: The Theory of the Blending of the Races Applied to the American White Man and Negro* (New York: H. Dexter, Hamilton & Co., 1864; repr. Upper Saddle River, NJ: Literature House, 1970); Sidney Kaplan, "The Miscegenation Issue in the Election of 1864," *Journal of Negro History* 34, no. 3 (July 1949): 274–343.

30. It is tempting to link Chesnutt's usage of *Miscegenation*-like thoughts to a possible resurgence of interest in the pamphlet at the turn of the century when the wife of the pamphlet's co-author wrote about her late husband's involvement in the hoax (David Croly died in 1889). From what I can determine, however, it appears that Mrs. Croly's ruminations came in December 1900, some three months after Chesnutt's essays were published; and her death in 1901, which also might have served to revive interest in her husband's hoax, was of course even later still. So despite coming frustratingly close to a definitive link between Chesnutt's "The Future American" and the analogous thoughts contained in the *Miscegenation* pamphlet, their very close similarity must be attributed either to Chesnutt's perhaps likely familiarity with the pamphlet or simply to coincidence. Kaplan, "Miscegenation Issue in the Election of 1864," 336–338.

31. Chesnutt, "Future American," 861.

32. Ibid.

33. Chesnutt, *Marrow of Tradition*, 243–245.

34. Ibid., 245.

35. Chesnutt, "Future American," 862.

36. Kawash, *Dislocating the Color Line*, 135.

37. Ibid.

38. James W. Johnson, *The Autobiography of an Ex-Colored Man*, 1912, reprinted in *Three Negro Classics* (New York: Avon, 1976), 393.

39. Ibid., 415.

40. Ibid.

41. Kawash also challenges the idea that the narrator is meant to be taken seriously in his assessment of *Uncle Tom's Cabin*, pointing out that such assessment is instead a clue of the narrator's spectatorship regarding what are nothing more than Afro-American stereotypes. Kawash, *Dislocating the Color Line*, 142–143.

42. Harriet B. Stowe, *Uncle Tom's Cabin* (1852; repr. New York: Pocket Books, 2004), 7.

43. Johnson, *Autobiography of an Ex-Colored Man*, 401.

44. Ibid., 433.

45. Kawash, *Dislocating the Color Line*, 140.

46. Johnson, *Autobiography of an Ex-Colored Man*, 438. Italics added.

47. Kawash, *Dislocating the Color Line*, 143.

48. Ibid., 144.

49. Johnson, *Autobiography of an Ex-Colored Man*, 510.

50. William Faulkner, *Absalom, Absalom!* (1936; repr. New York: Viking International, 1990), 302.

51. Pauline E. Hopkins, *Hagar's Daughter: A Story of Southern Caste Prejudice*, *Colored American Magazine*, 1901–1902, reprinted in *The Magazine Novels of Pauline Hopkins* (Oxford: Oxford University Press, 1988), 266–267. Italics added.

52. Nella Larsen, *Quicksand*, 1928, in *Quicksand* and *Passing* (New Brunswick: Rutgers University Press, 1995), 18. Larsen's biographer notes that when Larsen was a child her mother worked out of their home as a dressmaker; that in Larsen's fiction, "a woman's ability to dress herself in garments of her own choosing would always signify . . . her freedom and personal agency"; and that "Larsen had a dress designer's eye for color and texture, and a feminist resentment of social restrictions on women's clothing." George Hutchinson, *In Search of Nella Larsen: A Biography of the Color Line* (Cambridge: Belknap Press of Harvard University Press, 2006), 18, 40, 41, 102.

53. Larsen, *Quicksand*, 2.

54. Martha J. Cutter, "Sliding Significations: Passing as a Narrative and Textual Strategy in Nella Larsen's Fiction," in *Passing & the Fictions of Identity*, ed. Elaine K. Ginsberg, 76 (Durham: Duke University Press, 1997).

55. Larsen uses the specific motif of masked faces at several points in the narrative, emphasizing that one must be wary of superficial identities.

56. Larsen, *Quicksand*, 56.

57. Ibid.

58. Ibid., 69.

59. Cutter, "Sliding Significations," 78.

60. Larsen, *Quicksand*, 70, 73.

61. Ibid., 87.

62. Ibid., 87, 88.

63. Ibid., 88, 89.

64. Ibid.

65. Ibid., 110.

66. Ibid., 112.

67. Ibid., 112, 113.

68. Deborah E. McDowell, "Introduction," in *Quicksand* and *Passing* by Nella Larsen (New Brunswick: Rutgers University Press, 1995).

69. Larsen, *Quicksand*, 114.

70. Ibid., 115.

71. Gil Scott-Heron, "The Other Side, Part I," on *Spirits* by Gil Scott-Heron, TVT Records (TVT 4310), 1994.

72. Larsen, *Quicksand*, 135.

73. McDowell, "Introduction," xxi.

74. Larsen, *Quicksand*, 48.

75. Cutter, "Sliding Significations," 97.

76. Ibid.," 92. Although Helga Crane never actually passes for white in *Quicksand*, I think Cutter's remark here can nonetheless be sustained given Helga's rejection of blackness at various points in the novel. One might, therefore, say that in *Quicksand* Helga vacillates between accepting and rejecting various black identities.

77. Hutchinson, *In Search of Nella Larsen*, 294.

78. Kawash, *Dislocating the Color Line*, 164.

79. Ibid., 165.

80. Cutter, "Sliding Significations," 93.

81. Hutchinson, *In Search of Nella Larsen*, 50, 186.

82. Larsen, *Passing*, 1929, in *Quicksand* and *Passing* (New Brunswick: Rutgers University Press, 1995), 171.

83. Ibid.

84. Ibid.

85. Ibid., 238.

86. Even multiracial identity can be validated socially, as such validation is of course one of the missions of the American Multiracial Identity Movement.

87. Lydia M. Child, *A Romance of the Republic* (Boston: Ticknor and Fields, 1867; repr. Lexington: University Press of Kentucky, 1997).

88. Dana D. Nelson, "Introduction," in *A Romance of the Republic*, by Lydia M. Child (Boston: Ticknor and Fields, 1867; repr. Lexington: University Press of Kentucky, 1997), xi.

89. Child, *Romance of the Republic*, 390.

90. Ibid., 323.

91. Ibid., 322.

92. Cassandra Jackson, *Barriers Between Us: Interracial Sex in Nineteenth-Century American Literature* (Bloomington: Indiana University Press, 2004), 57.

93. Child, *Romance of the Republic*, 352.

94. Eve A. Raimon, *The "Tragic Mulatta" Revisited: Race and Nationalism in Nineteenth-Century Antislavery Fiction* (New Brunswick: Rutgers University Press, 2004), 60.

95. Kate Chopin, "The Father of Désirée's Baby," 1893, in *The Awakening and Other Stories* (New York: Oxford University Press, 2000), 198.

96. Susan Gubar, *Racechanges: White Skin, Black Face in American Culture* (New York: Oxford University Press, 1997), 209.

97. Werner Sollors, *Neither Black Nor White Yet Both: Thematic Explorations of Interracial Literature* (New York: Oxford University Press, 1997), 71, 70.

98. Gubar, *Racechanges*, 214.

99. Mark Twain, *Pudd'nhead Wilson* (1894; repr. Mineola, NY: Dover, 1999).

100. Ibid., 3.

101. Ibid., 7.

102. Ibid.

103. Ibid., 8.

104. Ibid., 12–13.

105. Ibid., 14.

106. Ibid., 20.

107. Ibid., 35.

108. Ibid.

109. Ibid., 122.

110. Ibid., 115.

111. Interestingly, and again poking holes in the notion of race vis-à-vis Chambers and Tom, Twain describes these white twins thusly: "One was a little fairer than the other, but otherwise they were exact duplicates." Ibid., 25.

112. Ibid., 114.

113. Thomas Dixon Jr., *The Leopard's Spots* (1902; repr. Gretna, LA: Firebird Press, 2001), 159, 198, 333, 383, 433, 438; also see note 19, Chapter 2.

114. A more comprehensive explication of the two ways I assert that the multiracial idea in its abstract sense deconstructs race may be found in Rainer Spencer, "Beyond Pathology and Cheerleading: Insurgency, Dissolution, and Complicity in the Multiracial Idea," in *The Politics of Multiracialism: Challenging Racial Thinking*, ed. Heather M. Dalmage, 108–116 (Albany: State University of New York Press, 2004).

115. Naomi Zack, *Race and Mixed Race* (Philadelphia: Temple University Press, 1993), 164.

116. Tavia Nyong'o, *The Amalgamation Waltz: Race, Performance, and the Ruses of Memory* (Minneapolis: University of Minnesota Press, 2009), 178.

117. Kawash, *Dislocating the Color Line*, 131.

118. Naomi S. Riley, "The Risks of Multiracial Identification," *The Chronicle of Higher Education*, November 10, 2006, B5.

119. Ibid.

14

Beyond
Generation Mix

In her dreamlike novel, *A Mercy* (2008), Toni Morrison presents us with what we might call a pre-America, an incipient America.[1] Set in late seventeenth-century North America, the novel suggests that the nation's history could have been different had people made different choices long ago. Although the future is, of course, already known to the reader, many things in the novel are nonetheless in flux, with Morrison giving us characters who represent that flux. There are black slaves and a respected free black, there are free white women and indentured white women, free white men and indentured white men, and a Native American character that is prominent and interacts with all these others. We also have an America that is simultaneously a land of immense beauty and also of grave danger.

Existing in a time before slavery hardened and solidified into the highly regulated system it would become eventually, Morrison's America is a land where more than blacks alone are threatened with bondage of one kind or another, and where more than blacks alone may be purchased in one way or another. Women, men, whites, blacks, slaves, Native Americans, indentured servants, all populate this world and are each threatened by it. Morrison also places heavy emphasis on religious intolerance and the unthinking belief that one's religious identity means that anyone who believes differently is not only wrong, but subject to some sort of punitive action.

Morrison depicts an America whose future is not yet fixed, an America that could turn this way or that, an America that could rise to the height of its beautiful wilderness or fall to the depths of its many dangers. It is a question of potential. Throughout the narrative's development, the small group of women who, despite their superficial differences, had banded together in a time of crisis has, by the novel's end, gone their separate ways, their collective effort ultimately for naught. It is a huge missed opportunity, a metaphorical stepping onto the wrong path that will have disastrous consequences through the centuries. Jakob Vaark's unfinished house represents the dream of America, its possibility. Yet by the end of the novel the house lies unoccupied and at the mercy of the ravages of weather, with the young slave woman Florens sneaking in at night to write her personal history on its walls and floors. This is the house we occupy today.

Speaking from the past, as it were, Florens's mother provides the narrative-ending advice that "to be given dominion over another is a hard thing; to wrest dominion over another is a wrong thing; to give dominion of yourself to another is a wicked thing."[2] In the context of the novel's illustration of how the nation need not have taken the path it did, I would submit that we have given dominion of ourselves to the fiction of race, a consequence of poorly made and still uncorrected steps in our national past. At an earlier point in the novel, the free black carpenter with whom Florens is infatuated gives her important advice as well, suggesting that her mental slavery is more onerous than her physical slavery by admonishing her to: "'Own yourself, woman.'"[3] Bringing the carpenter's advice into accord with my thesis throughout this book, I would argue that adopting multiracial identity is *not* owning oneself; it is merely trading monoracial bondage for multiracial bondage. Race is still race, whether the shackles are monoracial or multiracial.

As we attempt to imagine *our* American future, an eventual postracial future in which racelessness is the norm and anyone advocating the assignation of racial identities is considered as strange and as beyond the fringe as someone today would be in asserting that some people are broom-riding witches and that others are animals who have been turned into people and given the power of speech, we must accept responsibility for bringing that dream to fruition. If we say that we desire a nonracial future, then we should be willing to do the work needed to bring it about, rather than pretend that incorporation of a new biological (multi)racial category will destroy the present system of racial categorization. We must become racial assassins, beginning with our own racial suicides, in order to bring a true postracial future into reality, a future in which "'racial' identities—hegemonic or oppositional—are no longer thought useful or appealing, even to those who have historically been most disadvantaged by racism."[4] Part of being a racial revolutionary is refusing to accept a biological racial identity; that part of the revolution is internal and quite simple once one makes the mental commitment.

Another just as critical part, though, is working actively to deconstruct race in ways external to ourselves. That task can be more difficult since many people do not know where to begin given that race is embedded all around us. One obvious way to begin is to eschew descriptions of persons in racial language. Imagine if news reports referred to people in terms of their estimated height, weight, and age; in terms of the relative tone of their skin and texture/style of their hair; in terms of their clothing—without reference to someone being black, white, or Hispanic, etc., whether overtly or through coded language. This would be a small step to be sure, but it is a step that could potentially garner significant results merely by forcing people to think about the description given rather than placing the subject into an arbitrary and meaningless category. Just as the individual adopts a raceless identity, then, so too would she or he refer to others without reliance on the outdated and inaccurate categories of race. This is just one means, admittedly minor, of beginning to chip away at race.

It seems to me, however, that the most important target is whiteness, that attacking whiteness must be the top priority if we are concerned to have truly successful results. This is because the future will be postracial only and precisely to the extent that it is postwhite. It is at best a mistake, and at worst a devious subterfuge, to suggest or otherwise imply that postraciality simply means postblackness, as if it is the lingering nature of blackness that is the problem. Rather, the lingering nature of blackness is merely a symptom of the deeper and originary problem, which is the ferocious tenaciousness of whiteness. To ask that Afro-Americans give up their hold on blackness in a unilateral way, especially in regard to the more practical form of political blackness, would be to ask them to give up their only method of defense while their oppressor (whiteness and the white supremacy it enables) remains armed. In fact, Afro-Americans cannot deconstruct blackness unilaterally, because as long as whiteness exists they will continue to be seen and treated as black, regardless of whether they see themselves that way or not.

Certainly some Afro-Americans are prepared to give up their biological racial identities and I encourage them to do so. For those Afro-Americans who are not yet ready, however, I would point back to the discussion in Chapter 12 of my suggested change to the way the federal race question is asked, and encourage those who are reluctant to relinquish their biological racial identities to think of themselves not in terms of "what I am racially," but rather in terms of "what I am perceived as racially." This, along with a strong version of Afro-American political solidarity, could be for Afro-Americans the beginning of a movement away from the nonsense of biological race (although not away from the crucial recognition that antiblack racism will nonetheless endure for some time), but without giving in to the trap of color blindness and its attendant dangers before whiteness itself is deconstructed as well.

Putting forth an argument for what he terms a "thin" conception of blackness and for "pragmatic black nationalism," Tommie Shelby acknowledges that "what holds blacks together as a unified people with shared political interests is the fact of their racial subordination and their collective resolve to triumph over it. The 'racial' blackness of blacks, then, while in one sense only skin-deep—constituted as it is by relatively superficial phenotypic traits—has tremendous social importance, as these somatic traits carry the stigma of subordinate social standing. Yet blacks need not cherish or valorize this peculiar ascribed identity in order to see that it makes them all vulnerable to various forms of mistreatment."[5] Shelby has described the way that whiteness maintains blackness and thereby stigmatizes those so designated via the imposition of a "subordinate social standing," but, importantly, he also reinforces the truth that race itself is a fiction: "Pragmatic black nationalism openly rejects racial and ethnic 'essences' and has no need to deploy them, strategically or otherwise, in order to carry out its emancipatory aims. It does not require idealizing fictions about race, nationality, or primordial origins, but simply recognition that antiblack racism unjustly circumscribes the freedom and opportunities of millions in the United States and around the globe. . . . Pragmatic black solidarity does not require those who are racialized as black to embrace blackness, or any ethnoracial genre, as a valued or necessary component of the 'self' at all."[6]

Biological racial blackness should be given up immediately by those who are capable of doing so, but in order for political blackness to be given up safely, it is whiteness that must first be targeted for elimination and then eliminated successfully—not people who think they are white, of course, but rather the idea, the concept of whiteness, the property interest in it and the valorization it expects and receives in US society. According to David Roediger, "a sharp questioning of whiteness within American culture opens the opportunity to win people to far more effective opposition to both race and class oppression. To take advantage of such possibilities requires that we not only continue to talk about race but that we pay attention to the most neglected aspects of race in America, the questions of why people think they are white and of whether they might quit thinking so."[7] Unmasking the falseness of whiteness's claim to purity (even apart from the recent acceptance of Hispanic- and Asian-ancestried persons into that whiteness) is necessary to this cause. And while I would disagree with Roediger in that I do think we must continue to demystify all race generally, I am certainly committed to the idea that a very specific critique of whiteness must be a significant part of that general attack on race.

We should then heed Eduardo Bonilla-Silva in his suggestion that "the task for progressive social scientists and activists fighting contemporary white supremacy and color-blind racism is to unmask the racial character of many of these practices [i.e., 'covert, subtle, institutional, and apparently nonracial, white privilege'] and accompanying beliefs; and to make visible what remains invisible. To this effect, we can follow the lead of the department of Housing and Urban Development, which has developed the audit strategy of sending out testers evenly matched on all characteristics except race to investigate claims of housing discrimination. . . . Another strategy that may prove useful is to do undercover work on racial affairs.

Investigative news shows such as *Prime Time*, *20/20*, and others have used this technique quite successfully to document discrimination. . . . We can use this technique in an even more effective manner if white progressives do the undercover work."[8] These sorts of activities, while essential, are not enough, however, as Bonilla-Silva advises: "Yet uncovering these new racism practices and documenting the whiteness of color blindness, as important as this is, will not lead to a major change unless we can organize a new Civil Rights movement."[9]

These are merely a few of the tactics that must be deployed as part of the overall strategic goal of eliminating whiteness. Whiteness must be revealed as not only empty but as impure as well, as impure as any other racial category. To accomplish this will require concerted action, not complacency, as Roediger is correct in warning us of "the misplaced faith (or fear) that broad, legal, demographic, and/or economic trends will make white supremacy a thing of the past, without the need to take deep and conscious anti-racist action."[10] Such "misplaced faith" is embodied in the simplistic, seductive, and ahistorical lure of Generation Mix. What we absolutely must not do is allow ourselves to succumb to the dangerous course prescribed by Ronald Sundstrom, who in making his argument for multiracial identity avers that "'white supremacy' is too broad and vague a category to be helpful, and that focusing on such a flawed category of power can be positively harmful."[11]

I would offer instead that continued and certain harm will come from ignoring white supremacy, as opposed to engaging and challenging it—the latter being a crucible that Generation Mix has failed rather spectacularly to meet. As Heather Dalmage points out so correctly, "without an antiracism agenda, multiracial organizations seem to be distancing themselves socially and politically from blacks, creating one more layer in the racial hierarchy in which whites remain privileged, blacks disadvantaged, and multiracials somewhere in the middle."[12] Steve Garner calls into question the possibility of Generation Mix deconstructing race and thereby working against racism when he asks: "By saying 'mixed race' is challenging the idea of 'race,' do we not call into play the very thing that is supposed to be effaced: the relevance of the natural world (which presents bodies in particular ways), and again subject these bodies to the same visual regime of racialisation? Might this actually bolster the hierarchies integral to racism rather than stripping it of its power to wound?"[13]

As I mentioned in Chapter 1 and reiterate here, the solution to our national racial madness does not lie in altering the racial order so that it is somehow more equal or so that it includes more groups; the solution lies in rejecting both the idea of biological race and the hypodescent that flows from that idea. A revived and reconstructed marginal man in the form of Generation Mix serving as a junior partner in the conservation of the US racial order via the perpetuation of contemporary antiblackness and white supremacy is not the answer. What popular wisdom tells us is the supposed twilight of how we have thought about race is merely a minor tweaking of the same old racial order that has kept Afro-Americans at the bottom of our vicious paradigm since its very inception. Multiracial ideology simply represents the latest means of facilitating and upholding that racial order—while claiming quite disingenuously to be doing the opposite. We can and must do better than that.

Notes

1. Toni Morrison, *A Mercy* (New York: Alfred A. Knopf, 2008).
2. Ibid., 167.
3. Ibid., 141.
4. Tommie Shelby, *We Who Are Dark: The Philosophical Foundations of Black Solidarity* (Cambridge, MA: Belknap Press of Harvard University Press, 2005), 56–57.
5. Ibid., 56–57, 58.
6. Ibid., 59. Some may protest that acknowledging the racialization of some people as black is analogous to the position of Ronald Sundstrom that I criticized in Chapter 10, but such an analogy would be faulty. Whereas Shelby (and me, as well, in agreeing with him) says that people are racialized as black and are thereby stigmatized by white supremacy, Sundstrom avers that one can posit multiracial people without also positing racialized parents of those children. In the former case, the racialization as black is imposed and criticized quite emphatically as fallacious, whereas in the latter case, Sundstrom intends for the racialization as multiracial to represent "a fully real humankind," as he himself puts it. Ronald. R. Sundstrom, "Being and Being Mixed Race," *Social Theory and Practice* 27, no. 2 (April 2001): 301.
7. David R. Roediger, *Towards the Abolition of Whiteness* (New York: Verso, 1994), 12.
8. Eduardo Bonilla-Silva, "'New Racism,' Color-Blind Racism, and the Future of Whiteness in America," in *White Out: The Continuing Significance of Racism*, ed. Ashley W. Doane and Eduardo Bonilla-Silva, 283 (New York: Routledge, 2003).
9. Ibid.
10. David R. Roediger, *How Race Survived U.S. History: From Settlement and Slavery to the Obama Phenomenon* (New York: Verso, 2008), xiv.
11. Ronald R. Sundstrom, *The Browning of America and the Evasion of Social Justice* (Albany: State University of New York Press, 2008), 4.
12. Heather M. Dalmage, *Tripping on the Color Line: Black-White Multiracial Families in a Racially Divided World* (New Brunswick: Rutgers University Press, 2000), 139.
13. Steve Garner, *Racisms: An Introduction* (Thousand Oaks, CA: Sage, 2010), 99.

Bibliography

Anderson Cooper CNN Blog. "I Am Neither Black Nor White. I'm Both." July 25, 2008, http://ac360.blogs.cnn.com/2008/07/25/i-am-neither-black-nor-white-im -both/.

Andrews, William L. "Foreword." In *The House Behind the Cedars*, by Charles W. Chesnutt, vii–xxi. New York: Houghton Mifflin & Co., 1900. Reprint, Athens: University of Georgia Press, 2000.

Baldwin, James. *The Fire Next Time*. New York: Vintage International, 1993.

Band of Angels. Produced by Warner Brothers. Directed by Raoul Walsh. 128 min. Warner Brothers, 1957. DVD.

Bean, Frank D., and Jennifer Lee. "Plus ça Change . . . ? Multiraciality and the Dynamics of Race Relations in the United States." *Journal of Social Issues* 65, no. 1 (2009): 205–219.

Beaumont, Gustave de. *Marie; or, Slavery in the United States: A Novel of Jacksonian America*. 1835. Translated by Barbara Chapman. Baltimore: Johns Hopkins University Press, 1999.

Bell, Derrick. *Faces at the Bottom of the Well: The Permanence of Racism*. New York: Basic Books, 1992.

Binning, Kevin R., Miguel M. Unzueta, Yuen J. Huo, and Ludwin E. Molina. "The Interpretation of Multiracial Status and Its Relation to Social Engagement and Psychological Well-Being." *Journal of Social Issues* 65, no. 1 (2009): 35–49.

Bird, Stephanie R. *Light, Bright, and Damned Near White: Biracial and Triracial Culture in America*. Westport, CT: Praeger, 2009.

Blow, Charles M. "Black in the Age of Obama." *New York Times*, December 5, 2009, A19.

Bonam, Courtney M., and Margaret Shih. "Exploring Multiracial Individuals' Comfort with Intimate Interracial Relationships." *Journal of Social Issues* 65, no. 1 (2009): 87–103.

Bonilla-Silva, Eduardo. "'New Racism,' Color-Blind Racism, and the Future of Whiteness in America." In *White Out: The Continuing Significance of Racism*, edited by Ashley W. Doane and Eduardo Bonilla-Silva, 271–284. New York: Routledge, 2003.

Bonilla-Silva, Eduardo, and David G. Embrick. "Black, Honorary White, White: The Future of Race in the United States?" In *Mixed Messages: Multiracial*

Identities in the "Color-Blind" Era, edited by David L. Brunsma, 33–48. Boulder: Lynne Rienner, 2006.

Boucicault, Dion. *The Octoroon; or, Life in Louisiana*. 1859. Reprinted in *Plays by Dion Boucicault*, edited by Peter Thomson, 133–169. London: Cambridge University Press, 1984.

Bratter, Jenifer L. "Will 'Multiracial' Survive to the Next Generation?: The Racial Classification of Children of Multiracial Parents." *Social Forces* 86, no. 2 (December 2007): 821–849.

Bratter, Jenifer L., and Karl Eschbach. "'What About the Couple?' Interracial Marriage and Psychological Distress." *Social Science Research* 35 (2006): 1025–1047.

Bratter, Jenifer L., and Rosalind B. King. "'But Will It Last?': Marital Instability Among Interracial and Same-Race Couples." *Family Relations* 57 (April 2008): 160–171.

Brown, Nancy G., and Ramona E. Douglass. "Making the Invisible Visible: The Growth of Community Network Organizations." In *The Multiracial Experience: Racial Borders as the New Frontier*, edited by Maria P. P. Root, 323–340. Thousand Oaks, CA: Sage, 1996.

Brown, Sterling A. "Negro Character as Seen by White Authors." *The Journal of Negro Education* 2, no. 2 (April 1933): 179–203.

———. "Imitation of Life: Once a Pancake." *Opportunity: Journal of Negro Life* 13 (March 1935): 87–88.

Brown, Ursula. *The Interracial Experience: Growing Up Black/White Racially Mixed in the United States*. Westport, CT: Praeger, 2001.

Brunsma, David L., ed. *Mixed Messages: Multiracial Identities in the "Color-Blind" Era*. Boulder: Lynne Rienner, 2006.

Cable, George W. *The Grandissimes*. 1880. Reprint, New York: Hill and Wang, 1957.

Carmichael, Stokely, and Charles V. Hamilton. *Black Power: The Politics of Liberation in America*. New York: Vintage Books, 1967.

Cheng, Simon, and Kathryn J. Lively. "Multiracial Self-Identification and Adolescent Outcomes: A Social Psychological Approach to the Marginal Man Theory." *Social Forces* 88, no. 1 (September 2009): 61–98.

Chesnutt, Charles W. *The House Behind the Cedars*. New York: Houghton Mifflin & Co., 1900. Reprint, Athens, GA: University of Georgia Press, 2000.

———. *The Marrow of Tradition*. New York: Houghton Mifflin & Co., 1901. Reprint, New York: Penguin, 1993.

———. "What Is a White Man?" 1889. Reprinted in *Charles W. Chesnutt: Stories, Novels, & Essays*. New York: Library of America, 2002.

———. "The Future American." 1900. Reprinted in *Charles W. Chesnutt: Stories, Novels, & Essays*. New York: Library of America, 2002.

Child, Lydia M. "The Quadroons." In *Fact and Fiction: A Collection of Stories*, 61–76. New York: C. S. Francis, 1846.

———. "A Letter from L. Maria Child: Emancipation and Amalgamation." 1862. Reprinted in *A Lydia Maria Child Reader*, edited by Carolyn L. Karcher, 262–266. Durham: Duke University Press, 1997.

———. *A Romance of the Republic*. Boston: Ticknor and Fields, 1867. Reprint, Lexington: University Press of Kentucky, 1997.

Childs, Erica C. "Multirace.com: Multiracial Cyberspace." In *The Politics of Multiracialism: Challenging Racial Thinking*, edited by Heather M. Dalmage, 143–159. Albany: State University of New York Press, 2004.

Chiong, Jane A. *Racial Categorization of Multiracial Children in Schools.* Westport, CT: Bergin & Garvey, 1998.

Chopin, Kate. "The Father of Désirée's Baby." 1893. In *The Awakening and Other Stories*, 193–198. New York: Oxford University Press, 2000.

Cleaver, Eldridge. *Soul on Ice.* New York: Delta, 1968.

Clemetson, Lynette. "Color My World: The Promise and Perils of Life in the New Multiracial Mainstream." *Newsweek*, May 8, 2000, 70–74.

Cloud, John. "Are Mixed-Race Children Better Adjusted?" *Time*, February 21, 2009, http://www.time.com/time/health/article/0,8599,1880467,00.html.

Cose, Ellis. *Color Blind: Seeing Beyond Race in a Race-Obsessed World.* New York: HarperPerennial, 1998.

Croly, David G. *Miscegenation: The Theory of the Blending of the Races Applied to the American White Man and Negro.* New York: H. Dexter, Hamilton, 1864. Reprint, Upper Saddle River, NJ: Literature House, 1970.

Cutter, Martha J. "Sliding Significations: Passing as a Narrative and Textual Strategy in Nella Larsen's Fiction." In *Passing & the Fictions of Identity*, edited by Elaine K. Ginsberg, 75–100. Durham: Duke University Press, 1997.

DaCosta, Kimberly M. "Mixing It Up." *Contexts* (Fall 2005): 15–16.

——. *Making Multiracials: State, Family, and Market in the Redrawing of the Color Line.* Stanford: Stanford University Press, 2007.

Dalmage, Heather M. *Tripping on the Color Line: Black-White Multiracial Families in a Racially Divided World.* New Brunswick: Rutgers University Press, 2000.

Daniel, G. Reginald. *More Than Black? Multiracial Identity and the New Racial Order.* Philadelphia: Temple University Press, 2002.

——. *Race and Multiraciality in Brazil and the United States: Converging Paths?* University Park: Pennsylvania State University Press, 2006.

Das, Sushi. "They've Got the Look." *The Age*, April 20, 2004, http://www.theage.com.au/articles/2004/04/19/1082357106748.html.

Davis, Angelique M. "Multiracialism and Reparations: The Intersection of the Multiracial Category and Reparations Movements." *Thomas Jefferson Law Review* 29, no. 2 (Spring 2007): 161–188.

Dixon, Thomas Jr. *The Leopard's Spots.* 1902. Reprint, Gretna, LA: Firebird Press, 2001.

Douglass, Frederick. *Narrative of the Life of Frederick Douglass, an American Slave.* 1845. Reprinted in *The Classic Slave Narratives*, 391–511. New York: Signet Classics, 2002.

DuBois, William E. B. *The Souls of Black Folk.* 1903. Reprinted in *Three Negro Classics*, 207–389. New York: Avon, 1976.

Edmonston, Barry, Sharon M. Lee, and Jeffrey S. Passel. "Recent Trends in Intermarriage and Immigration and Their Effects on the Future Racial Composition of the U.S. Population." In *The New Race Question: How the Census Counts Multiracial Individuals*, edited by Joel Perlmann and Mary C. Waters, 227–255. New York: Russell Sage Foundation, 2002.

Elam, Michele. "The Mis-education of Mixed Race." In *Identity in Education*, edited by Susan Sánchez-Casal and Amie A. Macdonald, 131–150. New York: Palmgrave Macmillan, 2009.

El Nasser, Haya. "Multiracial No Longer Boxed In by the Census." *USAToday*, March 2, 2010, http://www.usatoday.com/news/nation/census/2010-03-02-census-multi-race_N.htm?csp=hf.

Faulkner, William. *Absalom, Absalom!* 1936. Reprint, New York: Viking International, 1990.

Fauset, Jessie R. *Plum Bun: A Novel Without a Moral*. New York: Frederick A. Stokes Company, 1929. Reprint, Boston: Beacon Press, 1990.

Ferber, Abby. *White Man Falling: Race, Gender, and White Supremacy*. Lanham, MD: Rowman & Littlefield, 1998.

Fernández, Carlos A. "Government Classification of Multiracial/Multiethnic People." In *The Multiracial Experience: Racial Borders as the New Frontier*, edited by Maria P. P. Root, 15–36. Thousand Oaks, CA: Sage, 1996.

Forbes, Jack D. *Africans and Native Americans: The Language of Race and the Evolution of Red-Black Peoples*. Urbana and Chicago: University of Illinois Press, 1993.

Frazier, Sundee T. *Check All That Apply: Finding Wholeness as a Multiracial Person*. Downers Grove, IL: InterVarsity, 2000.

Funderburg, Lise. *Black, White, Other: Biracial Americans Talk About Race and Identity*. New York: William Morrow and Company, 1994.

Gallagher, Charles A. "Racial Redistricting: Expanding the Boundaries of Whiteness." In *The Politics of Multiracialism: Challenging Racial Thinking*, edited by Heather M. Dalmage, 59–76. Albany: State University of New York Press, 2004.

Garner, Steve. *Racisms: An Introduction*. Thousand Oaks, CA: Sage, 2010.

Genovese, Eugene D. *Roll, Jordan, Roll: The World the Slaves Made*. New York: Vintage, 1976.

Gillman, Susan. *Blood Talk: American Race Melodrama and the Culture of the Occult*. Chicago: University of Chicago Press, 2003.

Gould, Stephen J. *The Mismeasure of Man*. New York: W. W. Norton, 1981.

Graham, Susan R. "The Real World." In *The Multiracial Experience: Racial Borders as the New Frontier*, edited by Maria P. P. Root, 37–48. Thousand Oaks, CA: Sage, 1996.

Griffin, John H. *Black Like Me*. New York: Signet, 1996.

Gubar, Susan. *Racechanges: White Skin, Black Face in American Culture*. New York: Oxford University Press, 1997.

Harper, Frances E. W. *Iola Leroy, or Shadows Uplifted*. 2d ed. Philadelphia: Garrigues, 1893. Reprint, Oxford: Oxford University Press, 1988.

Harris, Cheryl I. "Whiteness as Property." *Harvard Law Review* 106, no. 8 (June 1993): 1707–1791.

Herbert, Bob. "The Scourge Persists." *New York Times*, September 19, 2009, A17.

Hilden, Patricia P. *When Nickels Were Indians: An Urban, Mixed-Blood Story*. Washington, DC: Smithsonian Institution Press, 1995.

Hildreth, Richard. *The White Slave. Another Picture of Slave Life in America*. London: George Routledge, 1852. Reprint, Rye Brook, NY: Adamant Media, 2006.

Hopkins, Pauline E. *Contending Forces: A Romance Illustrative of Negro Life North and South*. Boston: The Colored Co-operative Publishing Co., 1900. Reprint, New York: Oxford University Press, 1988.

———. *Hagar's Daughter: A Story of Southern Caste Prejudice*. Colored American Magazine, 1901–1902. Reprinted in *The Magazine Novels of Pauline Hopkins*. Oxford: Oxford University Press, 1988.

———. *Of One Blood; Or, The Hidden Self*. 1902–1903. Reprint, New York: Washington Square Press, 2004.

Hurst, Fannie. *Imitation of Life*. New York: Harper, 1933. Reprint, Durham, NC: Duke University Press, 2004.

Hutchinson, George. *In Search of Nella Larsen: A Biography of the Color Line*. Cambridge: Belknap Press of Harvard University Press, 2006.

Imitation of Life. Produced by Carl Laemmle. Directed by John M. Stahl. 111 min. Universal Studios, 1934. DVD.

Imitation of Life. Produced by Ross Hunter. Directed by Douglas Sirk. 125 min. Universal Studios, 1959. DVD.

Itzkovitz, Daniel. "Introduction." In *Imitation of Life*, by Fannie Hurst, vii–xlv. New York: Harper, 1933. Reprint, Durham, NC: Duke University Press, 2004.

Jackson, Cassandra. *Barriers Between Us: Interracial Sex in Nineteenth-Century American Literature*. Bloomington: Indiana University Press, 2004.

Jacobs, Harriet A. *Incidents in the Life of a Slave Girl, Written by Herself.* 1861. Reprint, Cambridge: Harvard University Press, 1987.

Jensen, Elizabeth. "Indecency Penalty Against CBS Is Rejected." *New York Times*, July 22, 2008, C1, C6.

Jet. "Jamie Lee Curtis Expresses Shock About Uproar over Magazine Cover with Gault." March 4, 1991, 35.

Johnson, James W. *The Autobiography of an Ex-Colored Man.* 1912. Reprinted in *Three Negro Classics*, 393–511. New York: Avon, 1976.

Jones, Lisa. *Bulletproof Diva: Tales of Race, Sex, and Hair.* New York: Doubleday, 1994.

Jordan, Winthrop D. *White over Black: American Attitudes Toward the Negro, 1550–1812.* New York: W. W. Norton, 1977.

Kaplan, Sidney. "The Miscegenation Issue in the Election of 1864." *Journal of Negro History* 34, no. 3 (July 1949): 274–343.

Kawash, Samira. *Dislocating the Color Line: Identity, Hybridity, and Singularity in African-American Literature.* Stanford: Stanford University Press, 1997.

Khanna, Nikki. "Country Clubs and Hip-Hop Thugs: Examining the Role of Social Class and Culture in Shaping Racial Identity." In *Multiracial Americans and Social Class: The Influence of Social Class on Racial Identity*, edited by Kathleen O. Korgen, 53–71. New York: Routledge, 2010.

———. "If You're Half Black, You're Just Black: Reflected Appraisals and the Persistence of the One-Drop Rule." *The Sociological Quarterly* 51 (2010): 96–121.

Kilson, Marion. *Claiming Place: Biracial Young Adults of the Post–Civil Rights Era.* Westport, CT: Bergin and Garvey, 2001.

King-O'Riain, Rebecca C. "Model Majority? The Struggle for Identity Among Multiracial Japanese Americans." In *The Politics of Multiracialism: Challenging Racial Thinking*, edited by Heather M. Dalmage, 177–191. Albany: State University of New York Press, 2004.

———. *Pure Beauty: Judging Race in Japanese American Beauty Pageants.* Minneapolis: University of Minnesota Press, 2006.

Koenig, Barbara A., Sandra Soo-Jin Lee, and Sarah S. Richardson. "Introduction: Race and Genetics in a Genomic Age." In *Revisiting Race in a Genomic Age*, edited by Barbara A. Koenig, Sandra Soo-Jin Lee, and Sarah S. Richardson, 1–17. New Brunswick: Rutgers University Press, 2008.

———, eds. *Revisiting Race in a Genomic Age.* New Brunswick: Rutgers University Press, 2008.

Kolchin, Peter. *American Slavery, 1619–1877.* New York: Hill and Wang, 2003.

Korgen, Kathleen O. *From Black to Biracial: Transforming Racial Identity Among Americans.* Westport, CT: Praeger, 1999.

———. "Black/White Biracial Identity: The Influence of Colorblindness and the Racialization of Poor Black Americans." *Theory in Action* 2, no. 1 (January 2009): 23–39.

La Ferla, Ruth. "Generation E. A.: Ethnically Ambiguous." *New York Times*, December 28, 2003, ST1, ST9.

Larsen, Nella. *Quicksand* and *Passing*. 1928 and 1929. Reprinted, New Brunswick: Rutgers University Press, 1995.

Lee, Jennifer, and Frank D. Bean. "America's Changing Color Lines: Immigration, Race/Ethnicity, and Multiracial Identification." *Annual Review of Sociology* 30 (2004): 221–242.

Leong, Nancy. "Judicial Erasure of Mixed-Race Discrimination." *American University Law Review* 59, no. 3 (February 2010): 469–555.

Lewis, Elliott. *Fade: My Journeys in Multiracial America.* New York: Carroll & Graf, 2006.

Linneaus Carolus. *Systema Naturae, Sive Regna Tria Naturae Systematice Proposita Per Classes, Ordines, Genera, & Species.* Lugduni Batavorum [Netherlands]: Theodorum Haak, 1735.

Long, Edward. *History of Jamaica, Volume II: Reflections on Its Situation, Settlements, Inhabitants, Climate, Products, Commerce, Laws and Government.* London: T. Lowndes, 1774. Reprint, Montreal: McGill-Queen's University Press, 2003.

Macdonald, Andrew. *The Turner Diaries.* New York: Barricade Books, 1996.

Mahtani, Minelle. "What's in a Name? Exploring the Employment of 'Mixed Race' as an Identification." *Ethnicities* 2, no. 4 (2002): 469–490.

Makalani, Minkah. "A Biracial Identity or a New Race? The Historical Limitations and Political Implications of a Biracial Identity." *Souls* (Fall 2001): 73–102.

————. Blackness and Claiming Whiteness: Antiblack Whiteness in the Biracial Project." In *White Out: The Continuing Significance of Racism*, edited by Ashley W. Doane and Eduardo Bonilla-Silva, 81–94. New York: Routledge, 2003.

Matthews, Julie. "Eurasian Persuasions: Mixed Race, Performativity and Cosmopolitanism." *Journal of Intercultural Studies* 28, no. 1 (February 2007): 41–54.

McDowell, Deborah E. "Introduction: Regulating Midwives." In *Plum Bun: A Novel Without a Moral*, by Jessie Redmon Fauset, ix–xxxiii. New York: Frederick A. Stokes Company, 1929. Reprint, Boston: Beacon Press, 1990.

————. "Introduction." In *Quicksand* and *Passing*, by Nella Larsen, ix–xxxv. New Brunswick: Rutgers University Press, 1995.

————. "Introduction." In *Of One Blood; Or, The Hidden Self*, by Pauline E. Hopkins, v–xxi. New York: Washington Square Press, 2004.

McNeil, Daniel. *Sex and Race in the Black Atlantic: Mulatto Devils and Multiracial Messiahs.* New York: Routledge, 2010.

Mencke, John G. *Mulattoes and Race Mixture: American Attitudes and Images, 1865–1918.* Ann Arbor: UMI Research Press, 1979.

Miville, Marie L., Madonna G. Constantine, Matthew F. Baysden, and Gloria So-Lloyd. "Chameleon Changes: An Exploration of Racial Identity Themes of Multiracial People." *Journal of Counseling Psychology* 52, no. 4 (2005): 507–516.

Montagu, Ashley. *Man's Most Dangerous Myth: The Fallacy of Race.* 6th ed. Walnut Creek, CA: AltaMira, 1997.

Moran, Rachel F. *Interracial Intimacy: The Regulation of Race and Romance.* Chicago: University of Chicago Press, 2001.

————. "*Loving* and the Legacy of Unintended Consequences." *Wisconsin Law Review*, no. 2 (2007): 239–281.

Morrison, Toni. *A Mercy.* New York: Alfred A. Knopf, 2008.

Myrdal, Gunnar. *An American Dilemma: The Negro Problem and Modern Democracy.* New York: Harper & Brothers, 1944.

Nelson, Dana D. "Introduction." In *A Romance of the Republic*, by Lydia M. Child, v–xxii. Boston: Ticknor and Fields, 1867. Reprint, Lexington: University Press of Kentucky, 1997.

Newton, Huey P. *Revolutionary Suicide*. New York: Harcourt, Brace, Jovanovich, 1973.

Northup, Solomon. *Twelve Years a Slave*. 1853. Edited by Sue Eakin and Joseph Logsdon. Reprint, Baton Rouge: Louisiana State University Press, 1968.

Nyong'o, Tavia. *The Amalgamation Waltz: Race, Performance, and the Ruses of Memory*. Minneapolis: University of Minnesota Press, 2009.

Olmsted, Frederick L. *The Cotton Kingdom: A Traveller's Observations on Cotton and Slavery in the American Slave States*. 1861. Reprint, New York: Modern Library, 1984.

Olumide, Jill. *Raiding the Gene Pool: The Social Construction of Mixed Race*. London: Pluto Press, 2002.

Park, Robert E. "Human Migration and the Marginal Man." *American Journal of Sociology* 33, no. 6 (May 1928): 881–893.

———. "Mentality of Racial Hybrids." *American Journal of Sociology* 36 (1930–1931): 534–551.

Pascoe, Peggy. *What Comes Naturally: Miscegenation Law and the Making of Race in America*. New York: Oxford University Press, 2009.

Patreau, Alan. "Principal Called Mixed-Race Student a 'Mistake.'" *Atlanta Journal-Constitution*, March 10, 1994, A3.

Pauker, Kristin, and Nalini Ambady. "Multiracial Faces: How Categorization Affects Memory at the Boundaries of Race." *Journal of Social Issues* 65, no. 1 (2009): 69–86.

Raimon, Eve A. *The "Tragic Mulatta" Revisited: Race and Nationalism in Nineteenth-Century Antislavery Fiction*. New Brunswick: Rutgers University Press, 2004.

Reid, Mayne. *The Quadroon; or, Adventures in the Far West*. London: J. & C. Brown and Company, 1856. Reprint, Rye Brook, NY: Adamant Media, 2006.

Reuter, Edward B. "The Superiority of the Mulatto." *American Journal of Sociology* 23, no. 1 (July 1917): 83–106.

———. *The Mulatto in the United States: Including a Study of the Rôle of Mixed-Blood Races Throughout the World*. Boston: Richard G. Badger, 1918. Reprint, New York: Negro Universities Press, 1969.

Riley, Naomi S. "The Risks of Multiracial Identification." *The Chronicle of Higher Education*, November 10, 2006, B5.

Roberts, Sam, and Peter Baker. "Asked to Declare His Race for Census, Obama Checks 'Black.'" *New York Times*, April 3, 2010, A9.

Rockquemore, Kerry Ann, David L. Brunsma, and Daniel J. Delgado. "Racing to Theory or Retheorizing Race? Understanding the Struggle to Build a Multiracial Identity Theory." *Journal of Social Issues* 65, no. 1 (2009): 13–34.

Roediger, David R. *Towards the Abolition of Whiteness*. New York: Verso, 1994.

———. *How Race Survived U.S. History: From Settlement and Slavery to the Obama Phenomenon*. New York: Verso, 2008.

Romano, Renee C. *Race Mixing: Black-White Marriage in Postwar America*. Cambridge: Harvard University Press, 2003.

Root, Maria P. P. "A Bill of Rights for Racially Mixed People." In *The Multiracial Experience: Racial Borders as the New Frontier*, edited by Maria P. P. Root, 3–14. Thousand Oaks, CA: Sage, 1996.

Rosenblatt, Paul C., Terri A. Karis, and Richard Powell. *Multiracial Couples: Black & White Voices*. Thousand Oaks, CA: Sage Publications, 1995.

Roth, Philip. *The Human Stain: A Novel.* New York: Vintage, 2001.

Scott-Heron, Gil. "The Other Side, Part I." On *Spirits.* Gil Scott-Heron. TVT Records. (TVT 4310), 1994.

Senna, Danzy. *Caucasia: A Novel.* New York: Riverhead, 1999.

Sexton, Jared. "The Consequence of Race Mixture: Racialised Barriers and the Politics of Desire." *Social Identities* 9, no. 2 (2003): 241–275.

———. *Amalgamation Schemes: Antiblackness and the Critique of Multiracialism.* Minneapolis: University of Minnesota Press, 2008.

Shelby, Tommie. *We Who Are Dark: The Philosophical Foundations of Black Solidarity.* Cambridge: Belknap Press of Harvard University Press, 2005.

Shih, Margaret, and Diana T. Sanchez. "When Race Becomes Even More Complex: Toward Understanding the Landscape of Multiracial Identity and Experiences." *Journal of Social Issues* 65, no. 1 (2009): 1–11.

Small, Stephen. "Colour, Culture and Class: Interrogating Interracial Marriage and People of Mixed Racial Descent in the USA." In *Rethinking "Mixed Race,"* edited by David Parker and Miri Song, 117–133. London, Pluto Press, 2001.

Smedley, Audrey. *Race in North America: Origin and Evolution of a Worldview.* 2nd ed. Boulder: Westview, 1999.

[Smucker, Samuel M.]. *The Planter's Victim; or, Incidents of American Slavery.* Philadelphia: Wm. White Smith, 1855.

Sollors, Werner. *Neither Black Nor White Yet Both: Thematic Explorations of Interracial Literature.* New York: Oxford University Press, 1997.

Spencer, Rainier. "Theorizing Multiracial Identity Politics in the United States." Ph.D. diss., Emory University, 1997.

———. *Spurious Issues: Race and Multiracial Identity Politics in the United States.* Boulder: Westview, 1999.

———. "Census 2000: Assessments in Significance." In *New Faces in a Changing America: Multiracial Identity in the 21st Century,* edited by Loretta Winters and Herman DeBose, 99–110. Thousand Oaks, CA: Sage, 2003.

———. "Beyond Pathology and Cheerleading: Insurgency, Dissolution, and Complicity in the Multiracial Idea." In *The Politics of Multiracialism: Challenging Racial Thinking,* edited by Heather M. Dalmage, 101–124. Albany: State University of New York Press, 2004.

———. *Challenging Multiracial Identity.* Boulder: Lynne Rienner, 2006.

———. "New Racial Identities, Old Arguments: Continuing Biological Reification." In *Mixed Messages: Multiracial Identities in the "Color-Blind" Era,* edited by David L. Brunsma, 83–102. Boulder: Lynne Rienner, 2006.

Spickard, Paul. "Does Multiraciality Lighten? Me-Too Ethnicity and the Whiteness Trap." In *New Faces in a Changing America: Multiracial Identity in the 21st Century,* edited by Loretta I. Winters and Herman DeBose, 289–300. Thousand Oaks, CA: Sage, 2003.

Squires, Catherine R. *Dispatches from the Color Line: The Press and Multiracial America.* Albany: State University of New York Press, 2007.

Stocking, George W. Jr. *Race, Culture, and Evolution: Essays in the History of Anthropology.* Chicago: University of Chicago Press, 1982.

Stonequist, Everett V. "The Problem of the Marginal Man." *American Journal of Sociology* 41, no. 1 (July 1935): 1–12.

———. *The Marginal Man: A Study in Personality and Culture Conflict.* New York: Charles Scribner's Sons, 1937. Reprint, New York: Russell & Russell, 1961.

Stowe, Harriet B. *Uncle Tom's Cabin.* 1852. Reprint, New York: Pocket Books, 2004.

Streeter, Caroline A. "The Hazards of Visibility: 'Biracial' Women, Media Images, and Narratives of Identity." In *New Faces in a Changing America: Multiracial Identity in the 21st Century*, edited by Loretta I. Winters and Herman DeBose, 301–322. Thousand Oaks, CA: Sage, 2003.

Stuckey, Mike. "Multiracial Americans Surge in Number, Voice." MSNBC.com, May 28, 2008, http://www.msnbc.msn.com/id/24542138/.

Sundquist, Eric. J. "Introduction." In *The Marrow of Tradition*, by Charles W. Chesnutt, vii–xliv. New York: Houghton Mifflin & Co., 1901. Reprint, New York: Penguin, 1993

Sundstrom, Ronald R. "Being and Being Mixed Race." *Social Theory and Practice* 27, no. 2 (April 2001): 285–307.

———. *The Browning of America and the Evasion of Social Justice*. Albany: State University of New York Press, 2008.

———. "Mixed-Race Looks." *Contemporary Aesthetics* Special 2 (2009), http://www.contempaesthetics.org/newvolume/pages/article.php?articleID=540.

Swarns, Rachel L., and Jodi Kantor. "First Lady's Roots Reveal Twisty Path from Slavery." *New York Times*, October 8, 2009, A1, A20.

Thornton, Michael C. "The Quiet Immigration: Foreign Spouses of U.S. Citizens, 1945–1985." In *Racially Mixed People in America*, edited by Maria P. P. Root, 64–76. Newbury Park, CA: Sage, 1992.

———. "Policing the Borderlands: White- and Black-American Newspaper Perceptions of Multiracial Heritage and the Idea of Race, 1996–2006." *Journal of Social Issues* 65, no. 1 (2009): 105–127.

Toner, Robin. "In Tight Senate Race, Attack Ad on Black Candidate Stirs Furor." *New York Times*, October 26, 2006, A1, A22.

Twain, Mark. *Pudd'nhead Wilson*. 1894. Reprint, Mineola, NY: Dover, 1999.

US House Subcommittee on Census, Statistics, and Postal Personnel. Committee on Post Office and Civil Service. *Hearings on the Review of Federal Measurements of Race and Ethnicity*. Testimony by Marvin. C. Arnold on June 30, 1993. 103d Cong., 1st sess., April 14, June 30, July 29, and November 3, 1993, 159–171.

———. Testimony by Carlos Fernández on June 30, 1993. 103d Cong., 1st sess., April 14, June 30, July 29, and November 3, 1993, 125–157.

———. Testimony by Susan Graham on June 30, 1993. 103d Cong., 1st sess., April 14, June 30, July 29, and November 3, 1993, 105–125.

US House Subcommittee on Government, Management, Information, and Technology. Committee on Government Reform and Oversight. *Hearings on Federal Measures of Race and Ethnicity and the Implications for the 2000 Census*. Testimony by Susan Graham on May 22, 1997. 105th Cong., 1st sess., April 23, May 22, and July 25, 1997, 327–382.

Van Vechten, Carl. *Nigger Heaven*. New York: Alfred A. Knopf, 1926. Reprint, New York: Harper Colophon, 1971.

Warren, Robert P. *Band of Angels*. Baton Rouge: Louisiana State University Press, 1994.

Weatherly, Ulysses G. "Race and Marriage." *American Journal of Sociology* 15, no. 4 (January 1910): 433–453.

White, Walter. *Flight*. New York: Alfred A. Knopf, 1926. Reprint, Baton Rouge: Louisiana State University Press, 1998.

Whitehead, Colson. *The Intuitionist: A Novel*. New York: Anchor, 2000.

Williams, Kim M. "Linking the Civil Rights and Multiracial Movements." In *The Politics of Multiracialism: Challenging Racial Thinking*, edited by Heather M. Dalmage, 77–97. Albany: State University of New York Press, 2004.

———. *Mark One or More: Civil Rights in Multiracial America.* Ann Arbor: University of Michigan Press, 2006.

Williams, Teresa Kay. "Race as Process: Reassessing the 'What Are You' Encounters of Biracial Individuals." In *The Multiracial Experience: Racial Borders as the New Frontier*, edited by Maria P. P. Root, 191–210. Thousand Oaks, CA: Sage, 1996.

Williamson, Joel. *New People: Miscegenation and Mulattoes in the United States.* New York: Free Press, 1980.

Winfrey, Yayoi L. "In the Mix: Issue of Mixed Race Stirs Controversy for Census." *International Examiner*, January 21, 2010, http://www.iexaminer.org /category/issue/volume-37-no-02/.

Winters, Loretta I. "Epilogue: The Multiracial Movement: Harmony and Discord." In *New Faces in a Changing America: Multiracial Identity in the 21st Century*, edited by Loretta I. Winters and Herman DeBose, 373–379. Thousand Oaks, CA: Sage, 2003.

Yancey, George. *Who Is White? Latinos, Asians, and the New Black/Nonblack Divide.* Boulder: Lynne Rienner, 2003.

Zack, Naomi. *Race and Mixed Race.* Philadelphia: Temple University Press, 1993.

Zeleny, Jeff. "Obama, in His New Role as President-Elect, Calls for Stimulus Package." *New York Times*, November 8, 2008, A10.

Ziv, Alon. *Breeding Between the Lines: Why Interracial People Are Healthier and More Attractive.* Fort Lee, NJ: Barricade, 2006.

Index

Abolitionist literature, 21, 25, 37, 90

Absalom, Absalom! (Faulkner), 19–20

Activism. *See* American Multiracial Identity Movement; Ideology of multiracial identity activists; Multiracial identity, consequences of activism; White activist mothers of black/white children

Adopted children, 200–203, 214–215

Advertising, 22, 33(n33), 157–160

Afro-American writers: multiracial activists' cooptation of historical black figures, 103–104; whites' beliefs about ability to detect black ancestry lampooned, 27–28. *See also* Mulatto writers

Afro-Americans: defense of hypodescent, 251; discrimination against multiracial people, 267–268; discrimination due to social class difference confused with racism, 269–270; distinction between denial of blackness and antiblackness, 141; fallacy of accepting stereotypes about black vs. white culture, 192–195, 210(n30); fallacy of assuming population is monoracial, 105, 112, 115–119, 122–127; further isolation resulting from racial bridging narrative, 186–188; hate crime statistics, 144; individual successes of prominent figures, 143; and multiracial activists' "us vs. them" mentality, 231; and multiracial

identification on 2000 census, 114; multiracial identity stance as continued privileging of whiteness/devaluing of blackness, 121–124, 134(n50), 139–150, 210(n30), 239, 242; and need for cessation of belief in race, 251–253; negative views of dissenters from multiraciality, 142, 147; and "obviously mixed-looking" fallacy, 169–172; and "people of color" language, 147; status of descendents of first-generation multiracial people, 148, 239–244, 258, 273. *See also* Biological race; Blackness, distancing from; Hypodescent; Monoracial people; Mulatto writers; Mulattoes; Racial order in the United States; *headings beginning with* Multiracial

Agassiz, Louis, 28

Ambady, Nalini, 171

American Multiracial Identity Movement, 2; as antiblackness project, 139–150, 186–187; contradiction between objections to "eyeballing" and pride in identifying other "visibly mixed-race people," 172–175, 178; contradictory stance on biological race, 102, 154; endorsement of "problem approach" to multiracial identity, 213–214; as nonmilitant enterprise, in spite of rhetoric, 227–253; and political right,

About the Book

Is postraciality just around the corner? How realistic are the often-heard pronouncements that mixed-race identity is leading the United States to its postracial future? In his provocative analysis, Rainier Spencer illuminates the assumptions that multiracial ideology in fact shares with concepts of both white supremacy and antiblackness.

Spencer links the mulatto past with the mulatto present in order to plumb the contours of the nation's mulatto future. He argues cogently, and forcefully, that the deconstruction of race promised by the American Multiracial Identity Movement will remain an illusion of wishful thinking unless we truly address the racist baggage that serves tenaciously to conserve the present racial order.

Rainier Spencer is professor of Afro-American studies in the Department of Anthropology at the University of Nevada, Las Vegas.